Hands-On Artificial Intelligence on Amazon Web Services

Decrease the time to market for AI and ML applications with the power of AWS

Subhashini Tripuraneni
Charles Song

Packt

BIRMINGHAM - MUMBAI

Hands-On Artificial Intelligence on Amazon Web Services

Commissioning Editor: Pravin Dhandre
Acquisition Editor: Aditi Gour
Content Development Editor: Nazia Shaikh
Senior Editor: Ayaan Hoda
Technical Editor: Dinesh Chaudhary
Copy Editor: Safis Editing
Project Coordinator: Kirti Pisat
Proofreader: Safis Editing
Indexer: Priyanka Dhadke
Production Designer: Aparna Bhagat

First published: October 2019

Production reference: 1041019

Published by Packt Publishing Ltd.
Livery Place
35 Livery Street
Birmingham
B3 2PB, UK.

ISBN 978-1-78953-414-6

www.packt.com

Contributors

About the authors

Subhashini Tripuraneni has several years of experience leading AI initiatives in financial services and convenience retail. She has automated multiple business processes and helped to create a proactive competitive advantage for businesses via AI. She is also a seasoned data scientist, with hands-on experience building machine learning and deep learning models in a public cloud. She holds an MBA from Wharton Business School, with a specialization in business analytics, marketing and operations, and entrepreneurial management. In her spare time, she enjoys going to theme parks and spending time with her children. She currently lives in Dallas, TX, with her husband and children.

Charles Song is a solutions architect with a background in applied software engineering research. He is skilled in software development, architecture design, and machine learning, with a proven ability to utilize emerging technologies to devise innovative solutions. He has applied machine learning to many research and industry projects, and published peer-reviewed papers on the subject. He holds a PhD in computer science from the University of Maryland. He has taught several software engineering courses at the University of Maryland for close to a decade. In his spare time, he likes to relax in front of his planted aquariums, but also enjoys martial arts, cycling, and snowboarding. He currently resides in Bethesda, MD, with his wife.

About the reviewer

Doug Ortiz is an experienced enterprise cloud, big data, data analytics, and solutions architect who has architected, designed, developed, re-engineered, and integrated enterprise solutions. His other areas of expertise include Amazon Web Services, Azure, Google Cloud, business intelligence, Hadoop, Spark, NoSQL databases, and SharePoint, to name but a few. He is also the founder of Illustris, LLC.

> *Huge thanks to my wonderful wife, Milla, Maria, Nikolay, and our children, for all their support.*

Packt is searching for authors like you

If you're interested in becoming an author for Packt, please visit `authors.packtpub.com` and apply today. We have worked with thousands of developers and tech professionals, just like you, to help them share their insight with the global tech community. You can make a general application, apply for a specific hot topic that we are recruiting an author for, or submit your own idea.

Table of Contents

Section 2: Building Applications with AWS AI Services

Section 3: Training Machine Learning Models with Amazon SageMaker

Section 4: Machine Learning Model Monitoring and Governance

Preface

Hands-On Artificial Intelligence on Amazon Web Services teaches you about the various artificial intelligence and machine learning services available on AWS. Through practical hands-on exercises, you'll learn how to use these services to generate impressive results. You will be able to design, develop, monitor, and maintain machine learning and deep learning models on AWS effectively.

The book starts with an introduction to AI and its applications in different industries along with an overview of AWS on AI/machine learning services and platforms. It will teach you all about detecting and translating text with Amazon Rekognition and Amazon Translate. You will learn how to perform speech-to-text with the help of Amazon Transcribe and Amazon Polly.

It covers the use of Amazon Comprehend for extracting information from text and Amazon Lex for building voice chatbots. You will gain an understanding of the key capabilities of Amazon SageMaker – wrangling big data, discovering topics in text collections, and classifying images. Lastly, the book explores sales forecasting with deep learning and auto regression and model accuracy degradation.

By the end of this book, you will have all the knowledge required to work with and implement AI in AWS through immersive hands-on exercises covering all the aspects of the model life cycle.

Who this book is for

This book is ideal for data scientists, machine learning developers, deep learning researchers, and AI enthusiasts who want to use the power of AWS services to implement powerful AI solutions. A basic understanding of machine learning concepts is expected.

What this book covers

`Chapter 1`, *Introduction to Artificial Intelligence on Amazon Web Services*, introduces the umbrella term "AI," which includes machine learning and deep learning. We will cover some of the hottest topics in AI, including image recognition, natural language processing, and speech recognition. We will provide a high-level overview of AWS' AI and machine learning services and platforms. AWS offers both managed services for ready-to-use AI/machine learning capabilities and managed infrastructures to train your own custom machine learning models. We will provide guidance on when to leverage managed services and when to train custom machine learning models. You will learn how to install and configure your development environment. We will guide you through the process of setting up for Python, the AWS SDK, and web development tools you will need for the hands-on projects in later chapters. We will also help you to verify your environment setup with working code that interacts with AWS platforms programmatically.

`Chapter 2`, *Anatomy of a Modern AI Application*, dives into the architecture and components of a modern AI application. We start to introduce patterns and concepts of a well-architected application; these will help you to design production-grade intelligent solutions. Not only will these concepts help you to rapidly experiment with and prototype solutions, but they will also help you to develop solutions that are flexible, extensible, and maintainable throughout the application life cycle. You will build the skeleton of a target architecture, which you will fill out in later chapters.

`Chapter 3`, *Detecting and Translating Text with Amazon Rekognition and Translate*, demonstrates how to build your first AI application that can translate foreign texts appearing in pictures into their native language. You will get hands-on experience with Amazon Rekognition and Amazon Translate. You will first build a reusable framework with AI and machine learning capabilities from AWS, and then build the application on top of that framework. We will demonstrate how separation between the capabilities and application logic can lead to flexibility and reusability; a concept that will become increasingly clear as the hands-on projects continue in later chapters.

`Chapter 4`, *Performing Speech-to-Text and Vice Versa with Amazon Transcribe and Polly*, shows you how to build an application that can translate voice conversations to and from different languages. You will get hands-on experience with Amazon Transcribe and Amazon Polly. Not only will you continue to build out the reusable framework of AI capabilities, but you will also reuse the translation capability of the framework that you built in the previous chapter. This will reinforce the concepts and benefits of well-architected production-ready AI solutions to increase experimentation and speed to market.

`Chapter 5`, *Extracting Information from Text with Amazon Comprehend,* demonstrates how you can build an application that can extract and organize information from photos of business cards. You will gain hands-on experience of Amazon Comprehend and reuse the text detection capability from previous chapters. In addition to this, we will introduce the concept of *human-in-the-loop*. You will build a human-in-the-loop graphical user interface that can allow users to verify and even correct information extracted by Amazon Comprehend.

`Chapter 6`, *Building a Voice Chatbot with AWS Lex,* enables you to continue the hands-on project by building a voice chatbot to look up business card contact information that was extracted and stored in the previous project. You will get hands-on experience of building a chatbot with Amazon Lex and integrating the chatbot interface into the application as a digital assistant.

`Chapter 7`, *Working with Amazon SageMaker,* explores the key capabilities of Amazon SageMaker – from wrangling big data to training and deploying a built-in model (Object2Vec), to identifying the best performing model to bring your own model and container to the SageMaker ecosystem. We illustrate each of the components through the book ratings dataset. First, we predict the rating of a book for a given user; that is, a book that the user has never rated. Second, we automate hyperparameter optimization with SageMaker's HPO capability, while also discovering the best performing model and its corresponding train and test sets through SageMaker search. Third, we illustrate how seamless it is to bring your model and container to SageMaker, avoiding the effort required to rebuild the same model in SageMaker. By the end of this chapter, you will know how to leverage all the key features of Amazon SageMaker.

`Chapter 8`, *Creating Machine Learning Inference Pipelines,* walks you through how SageMaker and other AWS services can be employed to create machine learning pipelines that can process big data, train algorithms, deploy trained models, and run inferences—all while using the same logic for data processing during model training and inference.

`Chapter 9`, *Discovering Topics in Text Collection,* introduces a new topic. In all the preceding NLP chapters, you learned how to use several NLP services offered by Amazon. In order to have fine-grained control over the model training and deployment, and to build models for scale, we'll use algorithms in Amazon SageMaker.

`Chapter 10`, *Classifying Images Using Amazon SageMaker*, follows on from what you have learned about Amazon Rekognition. Here, you'll learn how to classify your own images beyond the predetermined images classified by the Rekognition API. In particular, we will focus on labeling our own image dataset and using SageMaker's image classification algorithm to detect custom images. We will learn how to conduct transfer learning from ResNet50, a pretrained deep residual learning model trained on ImageNet (an image database organized by nouns and supported by Stanford University and Princeton University).

`Chapter 11`, *Sales Forecasting with Deep Learning and Autoregression*, explains how **deep learning and autoregression** (**DeepAR**) can be used for sales forecasting. In particular, a thorough understanding will be gained of **Long Short Term Memory** (**LSTM**), a form of **Recurrent Neural Networks** (**RNNs**). RNNs are networks with loops, allowing information to persist, connecting previous information to the present task. Autoregression uses observations from previous time steps as input to the regression equation to predict the value at the next time step. By the end of this chapter, you will have built a robust sales forecasting model with Amazon SageMaker.

`Chapter 12`, *Model Accuracy Degradation and Feedback Loops*, explains why models degrade in production. To illustrate this, we discuss how to predict ad-click conversion for mobile apps. As new data becomes available, it is important to retrain models to achieve optimal production performance.

`Chapter 13`, *What Is Next?*, summarizes the concepts that we have learned so far. Additionally, we will briefly discuss the AI frameworks and infrastructures that AWS offers.

To get the most out of this book

A basic understanding of machine learning and AWS concepts is expected.

Download the example code files

You can download the example code files for this book from your account at `www.packt.com`. If you purchased this book elsewhere, you can visit `www.packtpub.com/support` and register to have the files emailed directly to you.

You can download the code files by following these steps:

1. Log in or register at `www.packt.com`.
2. Select the **Support** tab.
3. Click on **Code Downloads**.
4. Enter the name of the book in the **Search** box and follow the onscreen instructions.

Once the file is downloaded, please make sure that you unzip or extract the folder using the latest version of:

- WinRAR/7-Zip for Windows
- Zipeg/iZip/UnRarX for Mac
- 7-Zip/PeaZip for Linux

The code bundle for the book is also hosted on GitHub at `https://github.com/PacktPublishing/Hands-On-Artificial-Intelligence-on-Amazon-Web-Services`. In case there's an update to the code, it will be updated on the existing GitHub repository.

We also have other code bundles from our rich catalog of books and videos available at `https://github.com/PacktPublishing/`. Check them out!

Download the color images

We also provide a PDF file that has color images of the screenshots/diagrams used in this book. You can download it here: `https://static.packt-cdn.com/downloads/9781789534146_ColorImages.pdf`.

Conventions used

There are a number of text conventions used throughout this book.

`CodeInText`: Indicates code words in text, database table names, folder names, filenames, file extensions, pathnames, dummy URLs, user input, and Twitter handles. Here is an example: "Let's create a directory for the project and name it `ObjectDetectionDemo`."

A block of code is set as follows:

```
{
   "Image": {
     "Bytes": "..."
    }
}
```

Any command-line input or output is written as follows:

```
$ brew install python3
$ brew install pip3
```

Bold: Indicates a new term, an important word, or words that you see on screen. For example, words in menus or dialog boxes appear in the text like this. Here is an example: "The capability is built using deep learning techniques such as **automatic speech recognition** (**ASR**) and **natural language understanding** (**NLU**) in order to convert speech into text and to recognize intents within text."

Warnings or important notes appear like this.

Tips and tricks appear like this.

Get in touch

Feedback from our readers is always welcome.

General feedback: If you have questions about any aspect of this book, mention the book title in the subject of your message and email us at `customercare@packtpub.com`.

Errata: Although we have taken every care to ensure the accuracy of our content, mistakes do happen. If you have found a mistake in this book, we would be grateful if you would report this to us. Please visit `www.packtpub.com/support/errata`, selecting your book, clicking on the Errata Submission Form link, and entering the details.

Piracy: If you come across any illegal copies of our works in any form on the internet, we would be grateful if you would provide us with the location address or website name. Please contact us at `copyright@packt.com` with a link to the material.

If you are interested in becoming an author: If there is a topic that you have expertise in and you are interested in either writing or contributing to a book, please visit `authors.packtpub.com`.

Reviews

Please leave a review. Once you have read and used this book, why not leave a review on the site that you purchased it from? Potential readers can then see and use your unbiased opinion to make purchase decisions, we at Packt can understand what you think about our products, and our authors can see your feedback on their book. Thank you!

For more information about Packt, please visit `packt.com`.

1
Section 1: Introduction and Anatomy of a Modern AI Application

This section aims to introduce **artificial intelligence** (**AI**) and provide an overview of AI capabilities offered by **Amazon Web Services** (**AWS**). It will provide a step-by-step setup for AI development on AWS, including the AWS **Software Development Kit** (**SDK**) and Python development toolset. Additionally, it will give an introduction to the components and architecture of a modern AI application.

This section comprises the following chapters:

- `Chapter 1`, *Introduction to Artificial Intelligence on Amazon Web Services*
- `Chapter 2`, *Anatomy of a Modern AI Application*

1
Introduction to Artificial Intelligence on Amazon Web Services

In this chapter, we will start with a high-level overview of **artificial intelligence** (**AI**), including its history and the broad set of methods that it uses. Then, we will take a look at a few applications of AI that have the potential to profoundly change our world. With growing interests in AI, many companies, including Amazon, are offering a plethora of tools and services to help developers create intelligent-enabled applications. We will provide a high-level overview of AI offerings from Amazon Web Services, and we will also provide our guidance on how to best leverage them. Being a hands-on book, we will quickly dive into intelligent-enabled application development with Amazon Web Services.

We will cover the following topics:

- Overview of AI and its applications.
- Understanding the different types of Amazon Web Services offerings for AI.
- How to set up an Amazon Web Services account and the environment for intelligent-enabled application development.
- Get hands-on experience with Amazon Rekognition and other supporting services.
- Develop our first intelligent-enabled application.

Technical requirements

This book's GitHub repository, which contains the source code for this chapter, can be found at `https://github.com/PacktPublishing/Hands-On-Artificial-Intelligence-on-Amazon-Web-Services`.

What is AI?

AI is an umbrella term that describes a branch of computer science that aims to create intelligent agents. The field of AI is highly technical and specialized; there is a broad set of theories, methods, and technologies in AI that allow computers to see (computer vision), to hear (speech recognition), to understand (natural language processing), to speak (text-to-speech), and to think (knowledge reasoning and planning).

It may seem that AI is a buzzword of our current times, but it has existed since the 1950s, when early work on artificial neural networks that mimic led the human brain stirred up excitement for thinking machines. With all the fanfare it receives in the media today, it is hard to believe that this field had to endure two AI winters, where interest in AI research and development dwindled. Today, AI has become popular again, thanks to the increased volume of data, cheaper storage, advancements in algorithms, and an increase in computing power.

One of the most important subfields of AI is **machine learning** (**ML**). ML is such a prominent part of AI that these two terms are often used interchangeably today. ML is the most promising set of techniques to achieve AI. These techniques gave us a new way to program computers through self-learning algorithms that can derive knowledge from data. We can train ML models that can look for patterns and draw conclusions like humans would. With these self-learning algorithms, the data itself has become the most valuable asset. Data has become the competitive advantage in industries; it is the new intellectual property. Between similar ML techniques (even inferior ML techniques), the best data will win.

What's old is new again. Artificial neural networks, once again, became the focus for ML research and development. More data, more compute, and new algorithms such as backpropagation, are enabling neural networks to have many hidden layers, also known as deep neural networks or deep learning. The increase in the accuracy of deep neural network models was almost impossible just a few years ago. Today, deep learning is the major breakthrough that is driving the modern-day AI boom. This combination of data, software, and hardware is creating a new breed of intelligent agents that can often see, hear, understand, speak, and even think like humans when provided with abundant information that is related to the world.

AI has become a vital part of the technology landscape. Businesses, big and small, are solving problems by leveraging AI. AI capabilities are seeping into every aspect of our lives, giving us better memory, better vision, better cognitive abilities, and much more. In most cases, AI will not be sold as the product by itself. Rather, products you already use will be improved with AI, and will become intelligent-enabled solutions. What is most exciting to us is the democratization of AI and ML technologies and services. The abundance of such technologies and services means practitioners can easily leverage AI to add intelligence to products that affects the way we live, work, and play.

This book will help you become an AI practitioner. We will teach you, through hands-on projects, the tools and techniques that are needed to embed AI capabilities into software solutions. Successful intelligent-enabled solutions require a combination of architecture design, software engineering, and data science. You will learn how to design, develop, deploy, and maintain production-grade software solutions with AI capabilities. As an AI practitioner, it is important to see AI through the lens of business capabilities, rather than just technologies. This book aims to bring together various skills to help you develop an intuition for well-designed intelligent-enabled solutions that solve real-world problems.

Applications of AI

Our lives have already been greatly impacted by applications of AI, including the way we search for information, shop for products, communicate with each other, and much more. However, we are only in the nascency of this intelligent software renaissance. So many amazing AI applications already exist, so let's look at a few examples.

Autonomous vehicles

One AI application that's getting much media attention is autonomous vehicles, also known as self-driving cars. These vehicles are capable of perceiving the world around them, and drive with little or no human intervention.

These autonomous vehicles are the perfect fusion of sensors and AI technologies that have been combined to create the self-driving capability. To develop the self-driving capability, these vehicles have logged millions of miles on highways and local roads, and billions more in simulations. Gobs of data coming from arrays of sensors, including cameras, radar, lidar, sonar, GPS, and many more, are used to train numerous ML models to perform the various perception and actuation tasks that are required to move vehicles safely in real-world conditions. The resulting AI capabilities, such as computer vision, object detection, predictive modeling, and obstacle avoidance algorithms, can create complex models of the environment that onboard computers can understand in order to control, to plot paths, and to navigate.

Self-driving technology is less error-prone than human drivers, and can potentially save hundreds of thousands of lives from crashes and accidents. This technology can also be a mobility provider for individuals who are unable to drive themselves, such as the elderly or disabled. At the time of writing, there are no true fully autonomous vehicles in large deployment in the world. We can't even imagine how this technology will reshape and mold our world in the decades to come.

AI in medical care

AI and ML is starting to transform the healthcare industry. These technologies are being used to improve diagnostic capabilities and clinical decision-making to speed up the detection and treatment of many diseases. These AI programs do not just follow preprogrammed guidelines for how to diagnose a disease. Instead, the AI is *taught* to recognize the symptoms of particular medical conditions, such as heart arrhythmias, diabetes-related vision loss, and even cancer.

A medical image is a rich source of data about a patient's health. With high-resolution images from X-rays, MRIs, and CAT scans, ML models can be trained with millions of example images labeled with particular medical conditions. With sufficient examples, the resulting ML models can diagnose diseases with accuracies that rival, if not surpass, human doctors. With AI programs tirelessly analyzing for valuable medical insights, they can aid doctors with faster and more accurate diagnoses, and the patients can receive treatment sooner.

More profoundly, the resulting AI capabilities incorporate the knowledge and experience of the best doctors and clinicians that helped to develop these capabilities. Once developed, the capabilities can be massively replicated and distributed to primary care offices and walk-in clinics, where this level of medical expertise was previously inaccessible. This can save thousands of lives through the early detection and treatment of diseases. It will have a profound impact on people's lives, especially in locations of the world where specialized doctors are scarce.

Personalized predictive keyboards

While there is a lot of excitement in ground-breaking, revolutionary, and even moon-shot AI applications that will no doubt change our world, you don't always have to chase after these fundamentally difficult problems to bring value to our world with AI.

One good example of an apt intelligent-enabled solution for a recent real-world problem is predictive keyboards on mobile devices. When touchscreen mobile devices became popular, we had to learn to type on small virtual keyboards, often on the go, with fewer fingers and with more distractions. These predictive keyboards facilitated faster typing by suggesting words and punctuation that we may wish to type, thus reducing friction in mobile communication.

The predictive capabilities of these keyboards are often built with ML and **natural language processing** (**NLP**) technologies that combine language models, custom dictionaries, and learned preferences in their prediction engines. The best prediction engines are likely built using a form of **recurrent neural network** (**RNN**) called **long short-term memory** (**LSTM**). These are neural networks that try to predict the next word given a window of previously typed words. The key to a successful prediction is in its speed and personalization. Each key press results in a prediction, and so the prediction engines must run fast on mobile hardware. These prediction engines are designed to get more intelligent as we use them; they are good examples of human-in-the-loop online learning systems.

Even though they are not saving lives by the thousands, the users of these predictive keyboards have saved trillions of keystrokes. We just love the elegance of these intelligent-enabled software solutions that have applied the right AI technologies to the right problems. We hope that, with the skills and insights you will have gained from this book, you will be able to find elegant AI applications to make our lives better, as well.

Why use Amazon Web Services for AI?

Amazon Web Services or **AWS** is by far the largest, most comprehensive cloud computing platform. AWS offers a broad set of on-demand cloud-based services, including compute, storage, databases, networking, analytics, and much more. For many years, developers have leveraged these services to build enterprise-grade software solutions at scale and speed that cannot be matched by any other cloud computing platform.

What's exciting is that AWS also offers a plethora of AI services that provide pre-trained AI capabilities, including image recognition, NLP, speech recognition and generation, and conversation agents. AWS also has ML services that simplify the building, training, and deployment of custom AI capabilities via ML and deep learning models. Companies and developers can leverage these AI and ML services to add intelligence to their software solutions just as easily as with AWS' other cloud computing services.

However, the true power of developing intelligent-enabled solutions on AWS is unlocked when developers combine the AWS AI and ML services with the rest of the AWS cloud computing ecosystem. By combining various AWS services, you instantly get access to an enterprise-grade cloud computing platform with a highly reliable, scalable, and secure infrastructure. This enables you, the AI practitioner, to easily collect and process large datasets so that you can integrate various AI capabilities, rapidly prototype ideas, and continuously experiment and iterate solutions.

As the title of this book suggests, this is a hands-on guide. We aim to bring together the various skills that are needed to design and build end-to-end AI solutions on the AWS platform. The keyword here is *skills*. We not only cover the important concepts of AI, but we also help you put these concepts into practice with numerous hands-on projects. It is only through these practical hands-on experiences that you will develop an intuition for well-designed, intelligent-enabled solutions. The projects in this book can be deployed to the AWS cloud platform; you can learn from them, you can enhance them, and you can even showcase them to others.

Working within the enormous AWS ecosystem will require a steep learning curve. New users can easily be overwhelmed by the AWS offerings. In this book, we will teach you about the patterns and practices that are needed to develop intelligent-enabled solutions, along with many of the services offered by the AWS platform. You will become intimately familiar with many of the AWS services and their **application programming interfaces** (**APIs**). Not only will you build working applications, but you will also understand the choices of the services and patterns that are being used. Along the way, we will also show you tips and tricks for working on the AWS platform.

AWS is composed of a huge number of services, and it is still growing. There are countless books and online resources that dive deeper into various subsets of these services. In this book, we will be focusing on some of the AWS services that work well together to help you build intelligent-enabled applications. We will cover most of the ML services, as well as various services for compute, storage, networking, and databases. Keep in mind that it is beyond the scope of this book to cover all the aspects of these services, let alone every AWS service.

Overview of AWS AI offerings

To better understand AWS AI offerings, we can group the services into two main groups.

The following diagram shows the subsets of AWS AI capabilities and AWS ML platforms that we will be covering in this book, organized by the two groups:

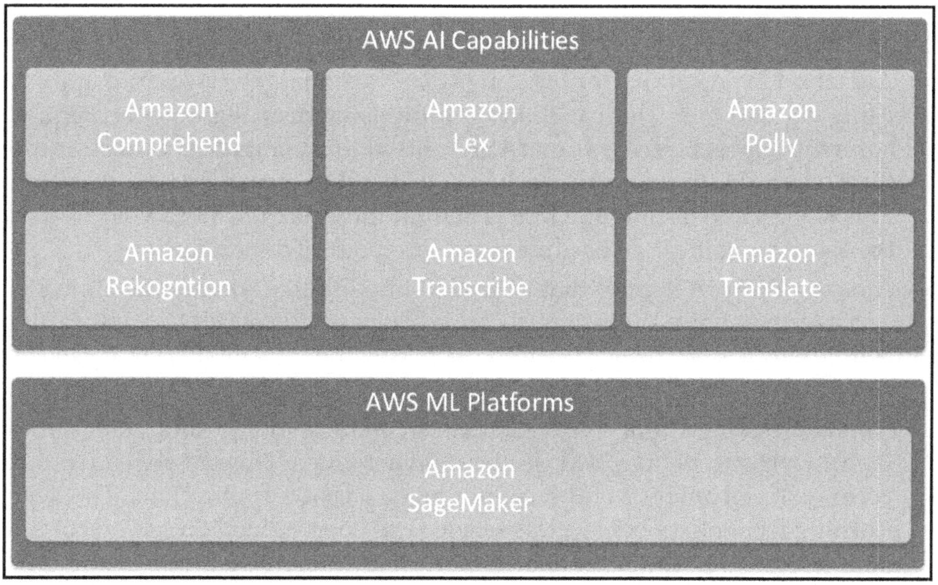

The list of AWS ML services is growing every year. For example, Amazon Personalize, Forecast, Textract, and DeepRacer were announced at the *AWS re:Invent 2018* conference, and were in limited preview. These services became available for general use around mid 2019.

The first group in the preceding diagram are the AWS AI capabilities. These services are built on top of AWS pre-trained AI technologies. They work right *out of the box* to provide ready-made intelligence for your applications. You do not need to understand the AI techniques that make them tick, and you do not need to maintain the infrastructure to host them. AWS has done all the hard work for you, and has made these AI capabilities available via APIs. As AWS continuously improve these capabilities, your application will automatically get more intelligent without any effort on your part. These managed services can provide quick lifts to your applications, thus allowing intelligent solutions to be built quickly and economically.

These AWS AI capabilities are as follows:

- **Amazon Comprehend:** A NLP service that uses ML to find insights and relationships in text. This technology allows your applications to sift through mountains of unstructured text and dig up golden nuggets of information. This service can perform various tasks, including automatic classification of documents; identification of entities such as company names, people, and addresses; and extraction of topics, key phrases, and sentiments within the text.
- **Amazon Lex:** A service for building conversational interfaces into applications using voice or text. This capability is built using deep learning techniques such as **automatic speech recognition** (**ASR**) and **natural language understanding** (**NLU**) in order to convert speech into text and to recognize intents within text. This is the same technology that is behind the Amazon Alexa voice assistant, and the same capability can be embedded into your own applications.
- **Amazon Polly:** A service that turns text into life-like speech that allows you to add a human voice to your application. The text-to-speech technology that is behind this service uses advanced deep learning technologies that can synthesize a voice with different languages, genders, and accents.
- **Amazon Rekognition:** A service that can analyze images and videos in order to identify objects, people, text, scenes, and activities. This service can also provide accurate facial analysis and recognition for various applications. The deep learning technology behind this service has been trained on billions of images and videos for a high level of accuracy on a variety of analysis tasks.
- **Amazon Transcribe:** An ASR service that provides speech-to-text capabilities to your applications. This technology allows your applications to analyze stored audio files or live audio streams, and get transcription text in real time.

- **AWS Translate:** A neural machine translation service that delivers natural and fluent language translation. This service is backed by deep learning models that can provide accurate and natural sounding translations for many languages. You can even configure this service with custom language models that can include brand names, product names, and other custom terms.

The second group in the preceding diagram are the AWS ML platforms. These services are fully managed infrastructures and toolsets that help developers build and run their custom AI capabilities via ML. AWS provides the development constructs and handles the ML training compute resources in order to make developing custom AI capabilities easier. The AI practitioners are responsible for designing the inner workings of these AI capabilities. This might include: the collection and cleaning of training data; selection of ML libraries and algorithms; tuning and optimization of ML models; and designing and the development of interfaces to access the AI capabilities. Leveraging the AWS ML platforms to build custom AI capabilities is definitely more involved than using the managed AI services, but this group of services gives you the most flexibility to create innovative solutions.

The AWS ML platform we will be covering in this book is: **Amazon SageMaker**—A fully managed service that covers the entire ML workflow. With SageMaker, you can collect and process your training data; you can choose your ML algorithms and ML libraries, including TensorFlow, PyTorch, MXNet, Scikit-learn, and so on; you can train the ML models on ML-optimized compute resources; and you can tune and deploy the resulting models to provide AI capabilities that are specifically created for your applications.

TIP

We highly recommend that you leverage the AWS-managed AI services as much as you can first. Only when there is a need for custom AI capabilities should you then build them with the AWS AI ML platform.

Hands-on with AWS services

Without further ado, let's get our hands dirty with a few AWS services. The services that we will use and the tasks that we will perform in this section will set you up for intelligent-enabled application development on AWS.

Creating your AWS account

If you don't already have an account with AWS, you can sign up for one at `https://aws.amazon.com/` and then click on the **Sign Up** button. You will see the following screen:

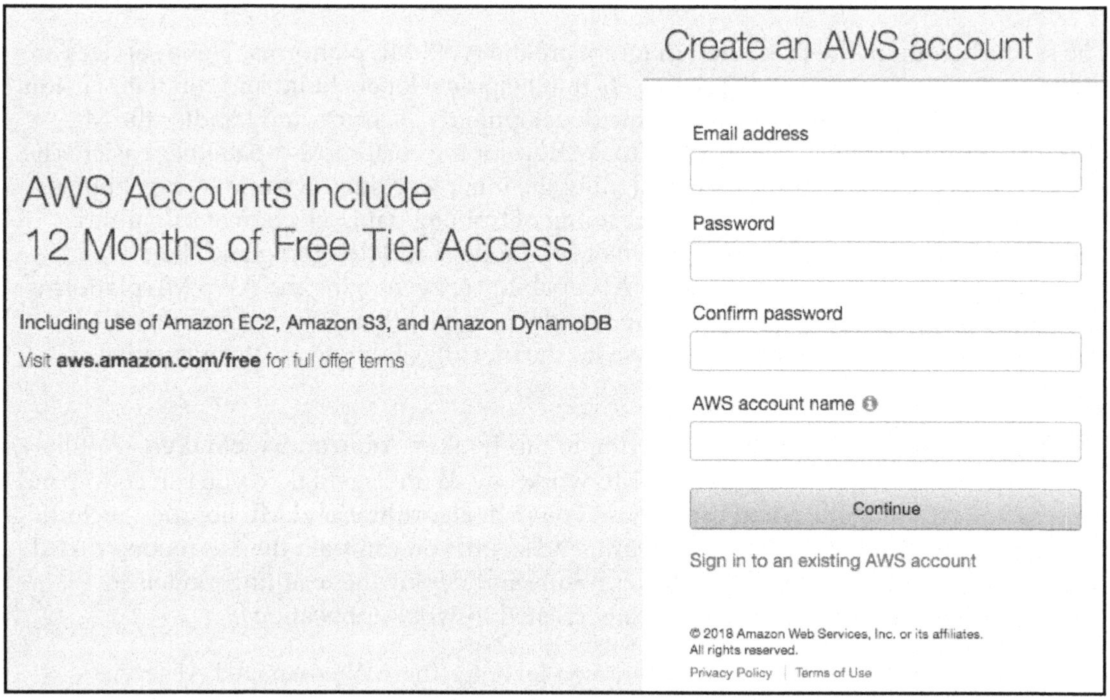

Your AWS account gives you access to all services in AWS on demand. But don't worry – with AWS' pay-as-you-go pricing model, you only pay for the services that you actually use, at industry-leading affordable prices. If this is the first time you are signing up for an AWS account, your account automatically includes 12 months of free tier access. The free tier offers a certain amount of AWS services for free, including compute, storage, database, and API calls. There are even non-expiring free resources after the 12 month free tier period. Visit `https://aws.amazon.com/free` for more details.

Navigating through the AWS Management Console

Now, let's get familiar with the AWS Management Console. The first time you log in to your AWS account, you will see the AWS Management Console. It might look something like the following screenshot:

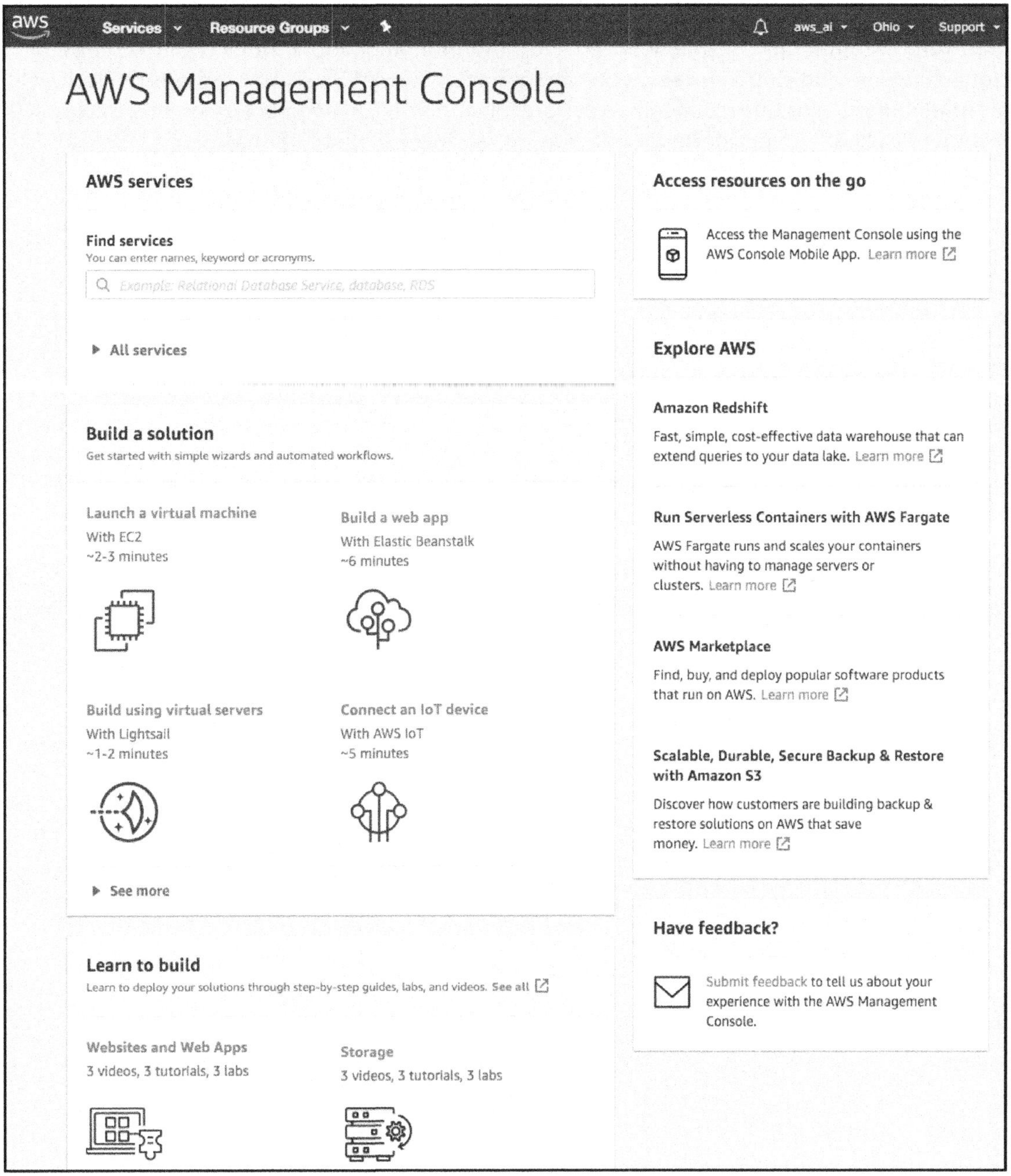
aws
Services
Resource Groups
aws_ai
Ohio
Support
AWS Management Console
AWS services
Find services
You can enter names, keyword or acronyms.
Example: Relational Database Service, database, RDS
All services
Build a solution
Get started with simple wizards and automated workflows.
Launch a virtual machine
With EC2
~2-3 minutes
Build a web app
With Elastic Beanstalk
~6 minutes
Build using virtual servers
With Lightsail
~1-2 minutes
Connect an IoT device
With AWS IoT
~5 minutes
See more
Learn to build
Learn to deploy your solutions through step-by-step guides, labs, and videos. See all
Websites and Web Apps
3 videos, 3 tutorials, 3 labs
Storage
3 videos, 3 tutorials, 3 labs
Access resources on the go
Access the Management Console using the AWS Console Mobile App. Learn more
Explore AWS
Amazon Redshift
Fast, simple, cost-effective data warehouse that can extend queries to your data lake. Learn more
Run Serverless Containers with AWS Fargate
AWS Fargate runs and scales your containers without having to manage servers or clusters. Learn more
AWS Marketplace
Find, buy, and deploy popular software products that run on AWS. Learn more
Scalable, Durable, Secure Backup & Restore with Amazon S3
Discover how customers are building backup & restore solutions on AWS that save money. Learn more
Have feedback?
Submit feedback to tell us about your experience with the AWS Management Console.

The AWS Management Console is a web interface where you manage the AWS cloud platform. Through this console, you can start, monitor, and stop various resources such as cloud compute and cloud storage; you can manage your AWS account settings, including monthly billing, and fine-grained access control; and you can even get access to educational resources to help you get started on the various services that are offered.

The AWS Management Console is one of three ways you can interact with the AWS cloud platform. The other two methods are the AWS **Command-line Interface** or **CLI** and the AWS **Software Development Kit** or **SDK**. We will cover these other methods later in this chapter.

Finding AWS services

On the AWS Management Console, you can click on the **Services** tab at the top-left corner of the console. Here, you will see the plethora of AWS services organized into groups. You can also search for services by name; searching is usually the faster way to navigate to a particular service that you are looking for.

Your **Services** tab should look similar to this:

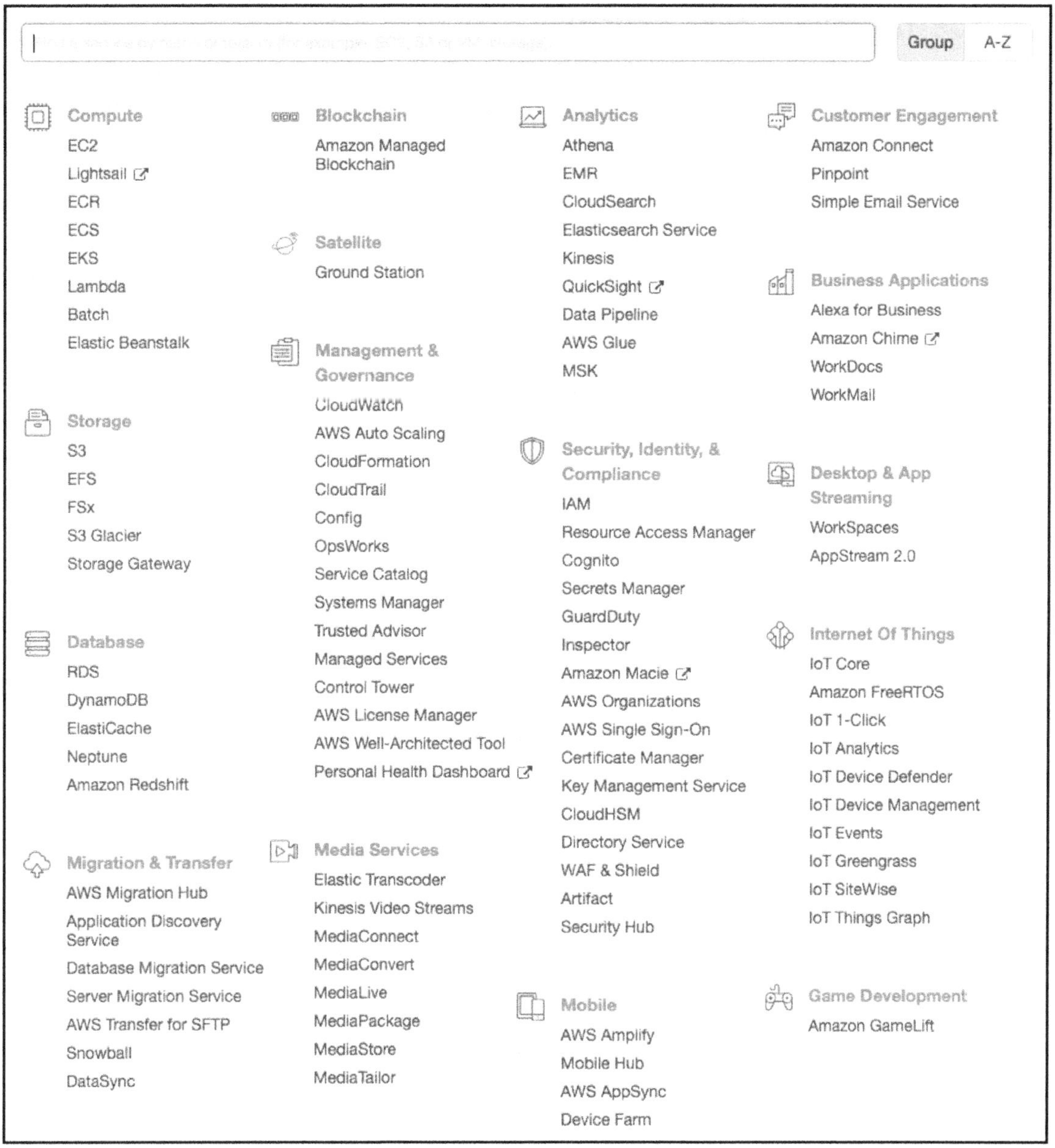
Group
A-Z
Compute
EC2
Lightsail
ECR
ECS
EKS
Lambda
Batch
Elastic Beanstalk
Storage
S3
EFS
FSx
S3 Glacier
Storage Gateway
Database
RDS
DynamoDB
ElastiCache
Neptune
Amazon Redshift
Migration & Transfer
AWS Migration Hub
Application Discovery Service
Database Migration Service
Server Migration Service
AWS Transfer for SFTP
Snowball
DataSync
Blockchain
Amazon Managed Blockchain
Satellite
Ground Station
Management & Governance
CloudWatch
AWS Auto Scaling
CloudFormation
CloudTrail
Config
OpsWorks
Service Catalog
Systems Manager
Trusted Advisor
Managed Services
Control Tower
AWS License Manager
AWS Well-Architected Tool
Personal Health Dashboard
Media Services
Elastic Transcoder
Kinesis Video Streams
MediaConnect
MediaConvert
MediaLive
MediaPackage
MediaStore
MediaTailor
Analytics
Athena
EMR
CloudSearch
Elasticsearch Service
Kinesis
QuickSight
Data Pipeline
AWS Glue
MSK
Security, Identity, & Compliance
IAM
Resource Access Manager
Cognito
Secrets Manager
GuardDuty
Inspector
Amazon Macie
AWS Organizations
AWS Single Sign-On
Certificate Manager
Key Management Service
CloudHSM
Directory Service
WAF & Shield
Artifact
Security Hub
Mobile
AWS Amplify
Mobile Hub
AWS AppSync
Device Farm
Customer Engagement
Amazon Connect
Pinpoint
Simple Email Service
Business Applications
Alexa for Business
Amazon Chime
WorkDocs
WorkMail
Desktop & App Streaming
WorkSpaces
AppStream 2.0
Internet Of Things
IoT Core
Amazon FreeRTOS
IoT 1-Click
IoT Analytics
IoT Device Defender
IoT Device Management
IoT Events
IoT Greengrass
IoT SiteWise
IoT Things Graph
Game Development
Amazon GameLift

Choosing the AWS region

Not every AWS service that you see in the list is available in every AWS region. AWS is a global cloud infrastructure that is built around the concept of AWS regions. An AWS region is a physical location in the world where you can operate your cloud applications. Depending on the region in which you choose to operate, some services might not be available. For example, when we created our account, the region defaulted to US East (Ohio). At the time of writing, the Ohio region does not have the Amazon Lex service.

If a service is not available in a region, you will see a **Region Unsupported** message, similar to this:

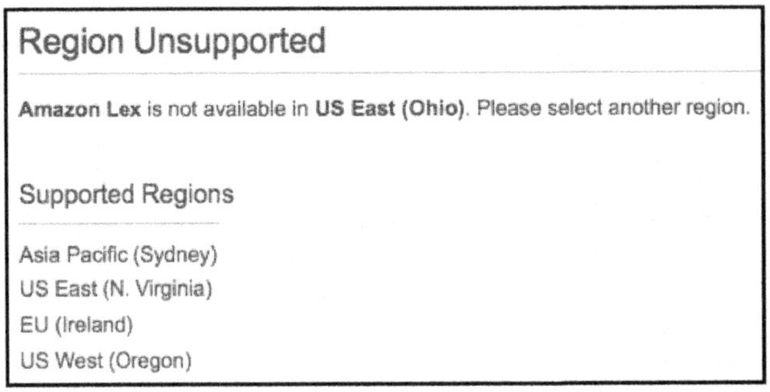

Region Unsupported
Amazon Lex is not available in US East (Ohio). Please select another region.
Supported Regions
Asia Pacific (Sydney)
US East (N. Virginia)
EU (Ireland)
US West (Oregon)

For this book, we recommend that you change the region to **US East (N. Virginia)**, also known as region **us-east-1**. This Northern Virginia region has all of the AWS services available, and it is also the region that gets the newest AWS services first.

Select the Northern Virginia region by clicking on the region name next to your AWS account name. It is important for you to do this to ensure that the examples and projects in this book are consistent. The **US East (N. Virginia)** region is the first choice in the following screenshot:

Test driving the Amazon Rekognition service

Let's try out one of the AWS-managed AI services, Amazon Rekognition, to get a feel for the power of AWS's AI offerings:

1. Click on **Rekognition** from the list of services under **Machine Learning** to navigate to its home page.
2. Rekognition provides a collection of visual analyses for images and videos. With Rekognition, you can quickly add powerful capabilities to detect objects, faces, and text in images and videos. You do not need to understand the deep learning technologies behind these capabilities in order to add them to your applications. We will create several such applications in the hands-on projects throughout this book, but for now, let's see Rekognition's capabilities in action with one of the provided demos.

3. From the Amazon Rekognition home page's left-hand pane, click on **Object and scene detection** under the **Demos** section.
4. AWS has already provided a couple of sample images to show off the power of Rekognition. In one of the images, you and I can easily see that a skateboarder is performing a trick on a road with two rows of parked cars on either side. This is actually a pretty busy image for computers to perform analysis on.
5. So, how did Rekognition do? Rekognition has drawn boxes around the objects that it has detected, and you can mouse over the boxes in order to see what Rekognition thinks each object is.

Here is the Rekognition demo page with the skateboarder image detection results:

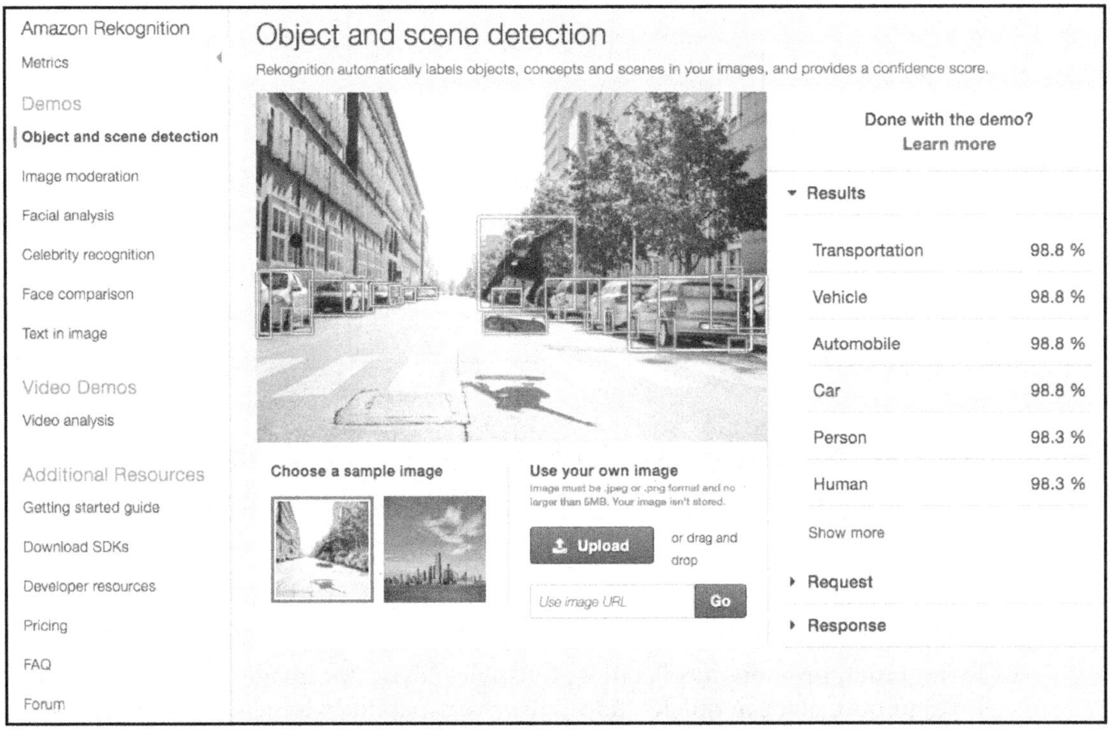

6. On the right-hand side of the image, under **Results**, Rekognition also provides the confidence levels for all the objects that it has detected.

There are also **Request** and **Response** underneath the confidence levels. In fact, this demo page is actually making API calls to Rekognition's object and scene detection API on your behalf. If you expand the request, it reveals some details about the API call:

```
{
 "Image": {
   "S3Object": {
        "Bucket": "console-sample-images",
        "Name": "skateboard.jpg"
    }
   }
}
```

The request is in the **JavaScript Object Notation** or **JSON** format. The request specifies an image that is to be analyzed by the Rekognition API. More specifically, this is an image that's stored as an object in the Amazon **Simple Storage Service** or **S3**. From the request, we can tell that the image is stored in the `console-sample-images` bucket, with the name of `skateboard.jpg`.

This demo application is using the Amazon S3 service to store the sample images, and Rekognition can directly analyze images that are stored in S3. We will be leveraging this pattern in many of the projects in later chapters as well. As we mentioned earlier, the power of the AWS ecosystem is the interoperability of many of its services.

The response is also in JSON format. The response contains a lot of information about the objects that were detected in the sample image. This information includes the name of the object, the confidence of the detection, and even the coordinates for the bounding box where each object is located within the image. In our projects, we will learn how to process such JSON responses in order to use the results in our intelligent-enabled applications.

In this demo, you can also upload your own images to test out Rekognition. Find an image and give it a try. When you upload your image to the demo page, you will notice that the request that is sent to the API is slightly different. In the request, you will see the following:

```
{
   "Image": {
     "Bytes": "..."
    }
}
```

This time, instead of specifying an image in S3, the raw bytes of the image that was uploaded were sent directly to the Rekognition API. This Rekognition API has multiple variations: one that takes reference to an S3 object and another that takes the raw bytes of an image. Which variation you choose depends on the nature of your application.

Working with S3

The Amazon S3 service is one of the first services that was offered by AWS. S3 provides secure, durable, and scalable object storage at a very low cost. Object storage just means that the things you store in S3 are accessible at the file level, instead of at the block or byte level. S3 is a very flexible service, with many usage patterns. You can read more about Amazon S3 at `https://aws.amazon.com/s3`.

Let's start working with Amazon S3 by creating a bucket. You can think of a bucket as a folder that can hold an unlimited number of files (objects).

Navigate to the Amazon S3 home page from the Amazon Management Console by clicking on the **Services** tab in the top-left corner, and then click or search for **S3** under **Storage**. If this is your first time using S3, you will see a screen similar to this:

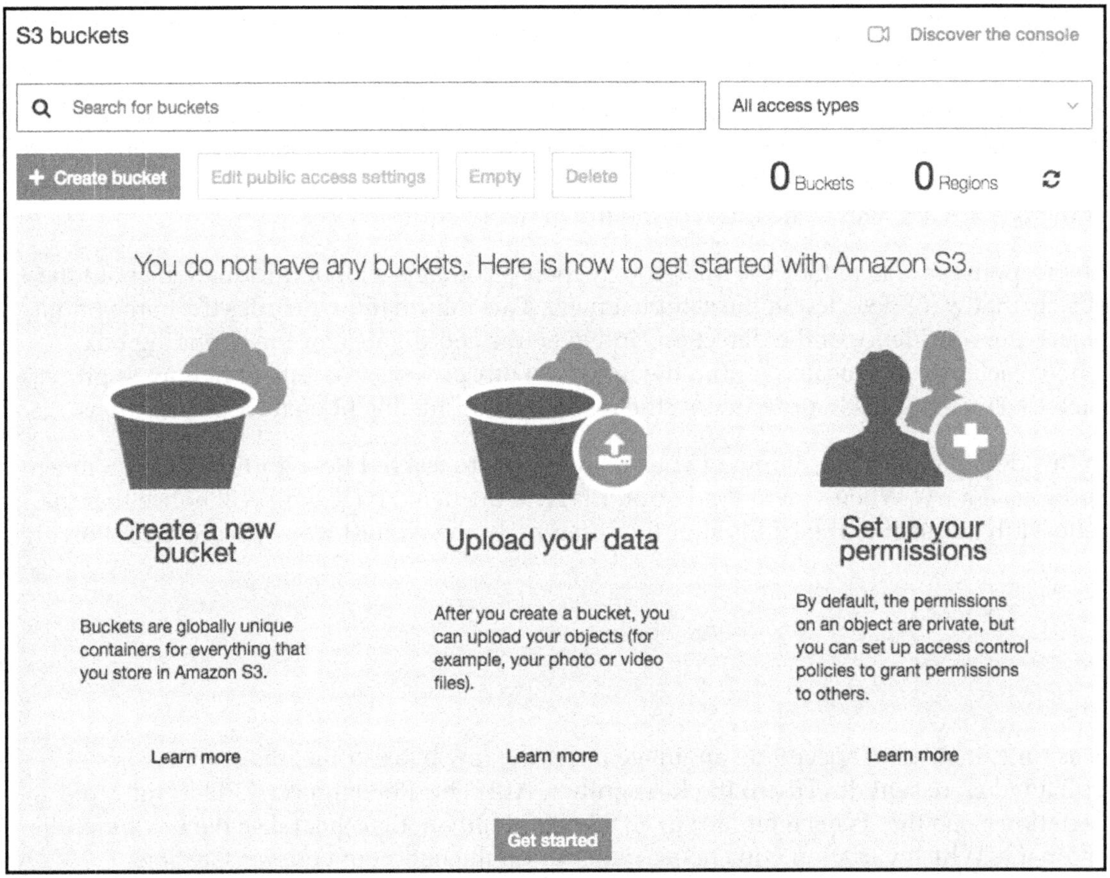

In this book, we will be leveraging S3 a lot in our hands-on projects. We will be using S3 for three main purposes. The first purpose is storing media files and other contents for other AWS services to access. Many of the AWS AI services are tightly integrated with S3; for example, this is the pattern that we have seen in the Rekognition demo. The second purpose is hosting entire static websites with S3, including HTML files, images, videos, and client-side JavaScript. This gives us the ability to host interactive web applications without the need for traditional web servers. The third purpose is using S3 as a data store for data collection, processing, and analytics tasks when we train our custom ML models.

There is a range of S3 storage classes that have been redesigned for different use cases and cost levels. For your enterprise-grade application, you might need to take advantage of the different storage classes in order to balance performance and cost. In this book, we will be using the Amazon S3 standard class for general-purpose storage. This is the default class and it will be sufficient for the projects in this book.

Click on the **Create bucket** button to create a new bucket:

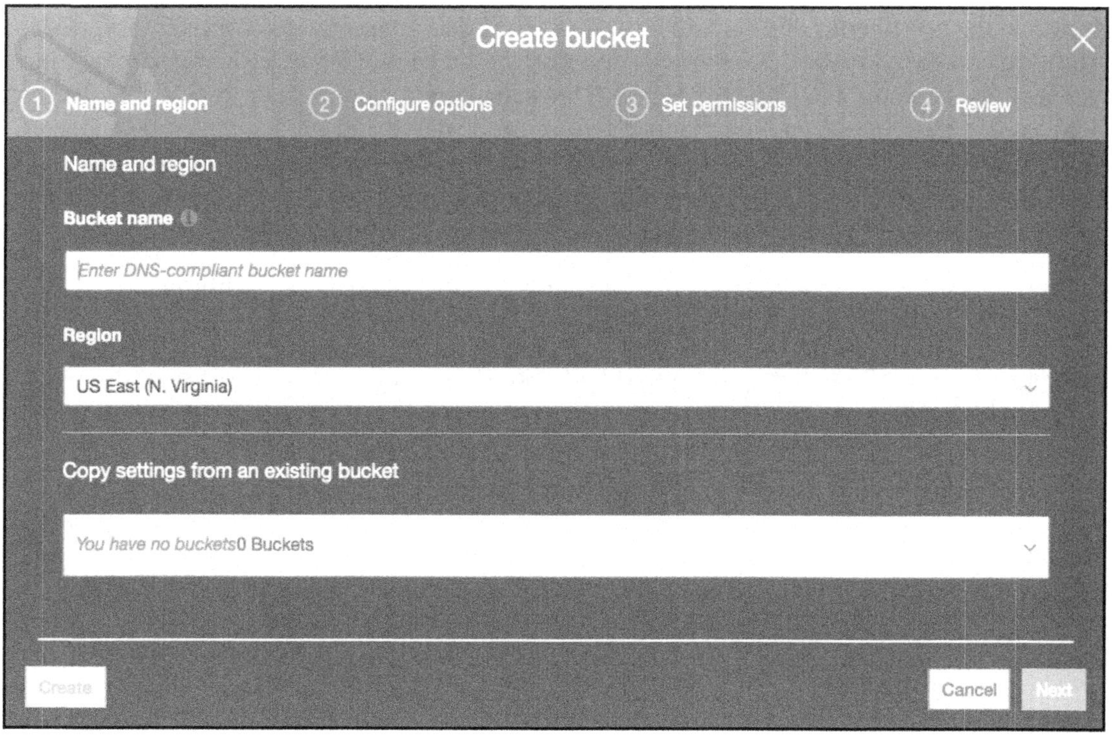

The first screen in the model asks for three pieces of information: the **Bucket name**, the **Region**, and **Copy settings from an existing bucket**. Since this is your first bucket, we can ignore the third piece of information.

The S3 bucket name must be globally unique. This means that every bucket that's ever created by you and others must have a unique name. Coming up with a globally unique bucket name can be challenging; you cannot expect bucket names such as `contents`, `website`, or `data` to still be available. The S3 bucket names must be DNS-compliant so that you can follow similar patterns for the domain names. For example, if we choose `aws.ai` as our root domain, we can create buckets such as `contents.aws.ai`, `website.aws.ai`, and `data.aws.ai` to avoid conflicts. Think about which root domain you would like to use.

> You don't have to own the domain to name the buckets with a given root domain name; however, if you do own a domain, it would be a good idea to use that as your root domain.

You must also specify the region of your bucket. This will determine in which physical region in the world your objects will be stored. The AWS regions are completely isolated from each other by design. Objects stored in one region cannot be accessed by services and applications running in a different region. This can be important if your line of business has high-performance requirements that need your applications and data to be located closer to your customers. This can also be important if your line of business must comply with industry and government regulations that require your applications and data to be located within a certain geographic location.

For the projects in this book, we do not have either of these concerns. Therefore, for consistency, let's pick the **US East (N. Virginia)** region again.

Here's what your **S3 buckets** page might look like after creation, but of course, with different bucket names:

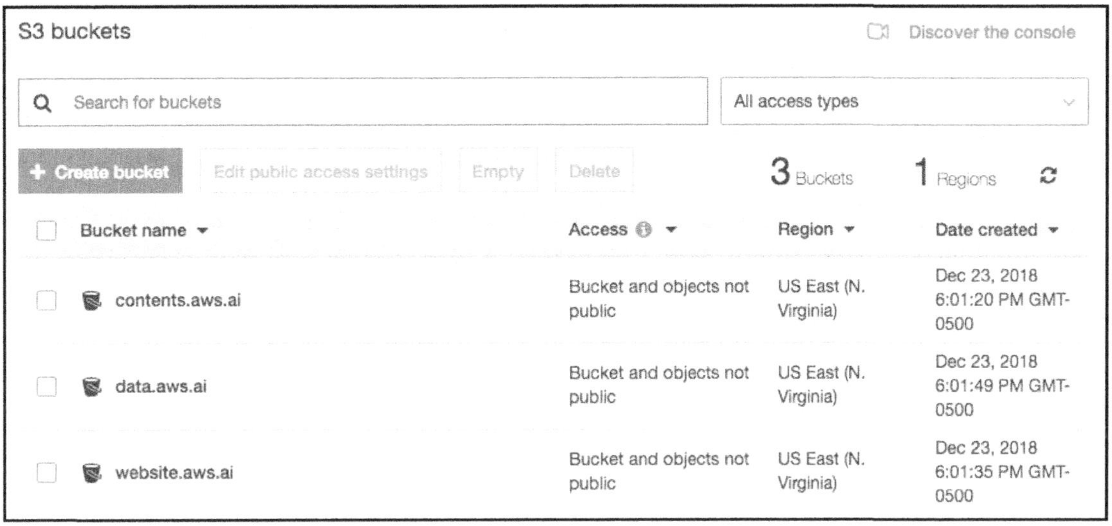

Once you have created the S3 buckets, go ahead and click on the **contents.aws.ai** bucket. You will see a screen similar to this:

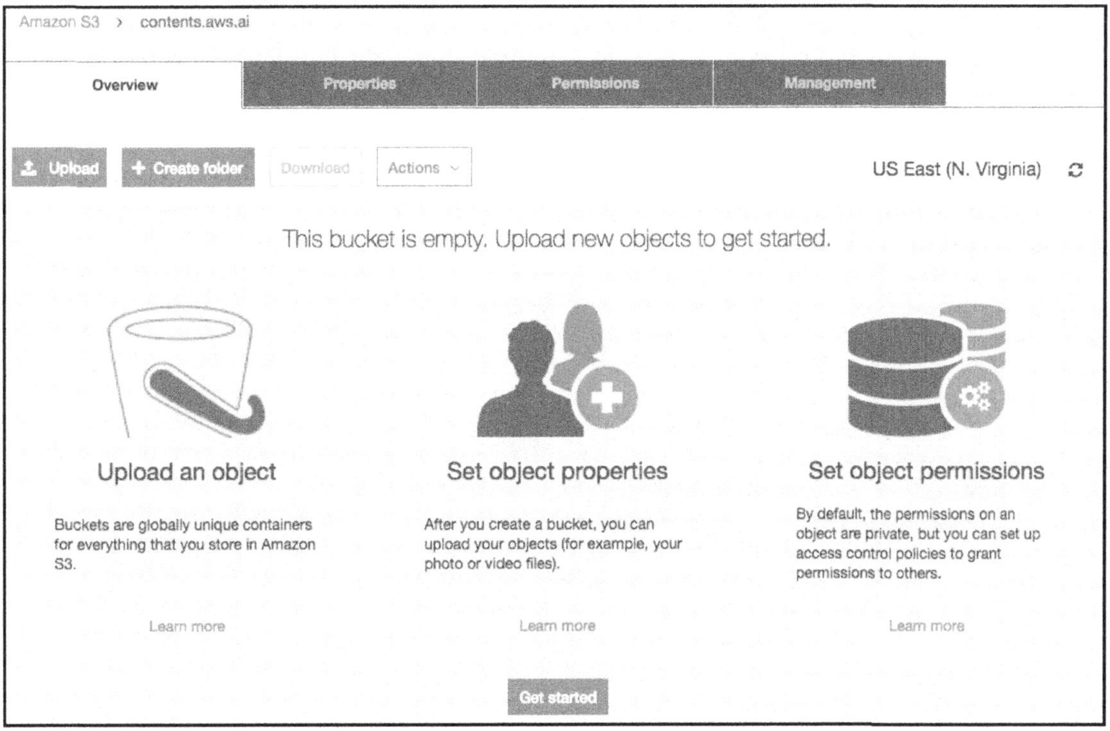

On this screen, you will be able to upload files to the bucket, configure bucket properties, set access permissions, and perform advanced settings such as life cycle rules and cross-region replication. We will come back to some of these settings later on, but for now, upload one or more photos that you want to analyze with the Rekognition service. You can click on the **Upload** button or simply drag and drop the photos to this page to upload them. We can leave all the file settings as default for now.

Congratulations, you just stored some files in the AWS cloud platform with 99.999999999% durability and 99.99% availability! In other words, if you store 10,000 files in S3, statistically, you would lose one file every 10 million years, and all of the files are available for your application to access 525,547.4 minutes out of 525,600 minutes every year.

Identity and Access Management

The next AWS service we will be looking at is the **Identity and Access Management** or **IAM**. IAM allows you to manage access to other AWS services and resources securely. AWS offers enterprise-grade security and access control, which is great for building production-ready applications in the cloud. However, if you are new to AWS, working around IAM can be challenging at first. If the necessary access was not granted, the services will simply refuse to perform the desired actions. We will be working with IAM quite a lot to build the projects in this book. You will get familiar with concepts such as users, groups, and roles so that you can provide your applications with the necessary access to the required services.

Let's go to the IAM home page by clicking on **IAM** from the list of services under **Security, Identity, and Compliance** in order to navigate to its home page. The IAM home page should look similar to this:

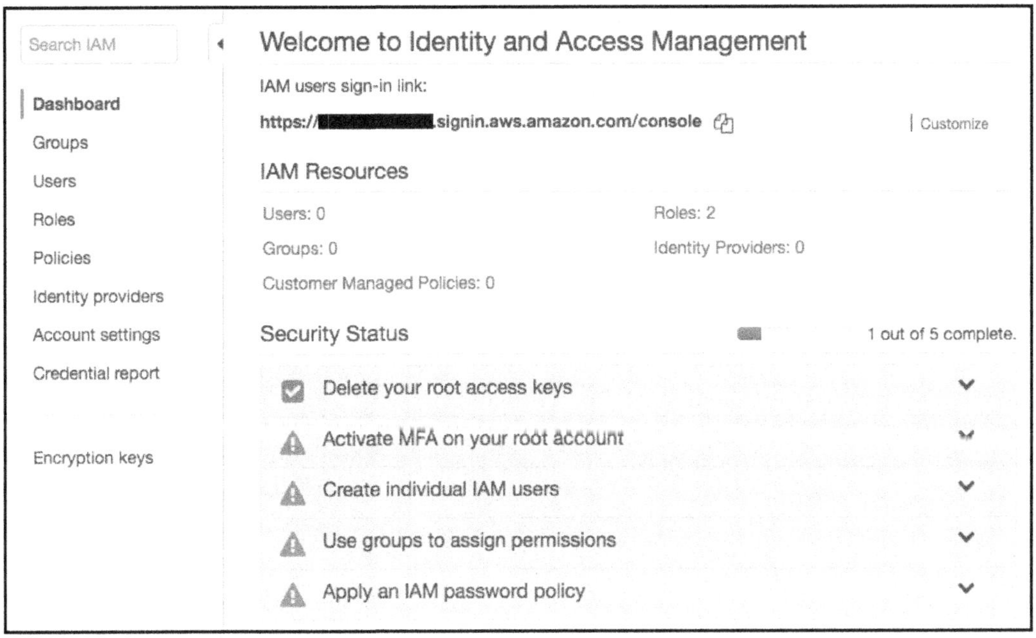

The IAM dashboard gives you an overview of the IAM resources and their security status. So far, we don't have any users or groups, but AWS has created two roles by default.

We have been accessing the AWS Management Console using our root account. This account, by default, can only access the AWS Management Console; it will not be able to interact with AWS services programmatically. Let's create a new user with programmatic access for the hands-on projects.

Click on **Users** on the left-hand pane, and then click on the **Add user** button:

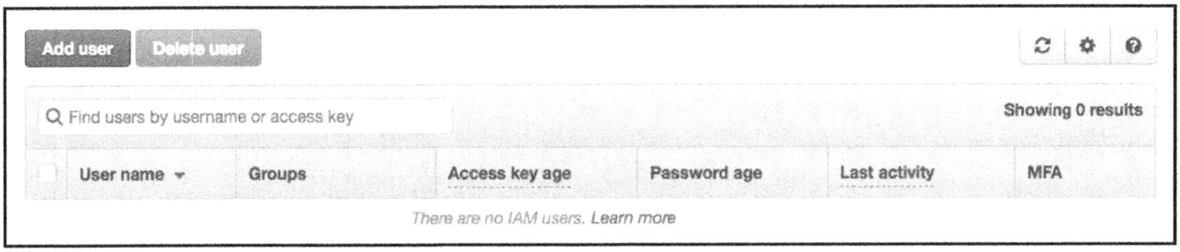

After entering the desired username, be sure to select only **Programmatic access**. Programmatic access will enable an access key ID and a secret access key pair. This key pair can be used by AWS APIs, the CLI, and the SDK. It is good practice to limit each user to either programmatic access or AWS Management Console access.

Here, we created an `aws_ai` user with only programmatic access:

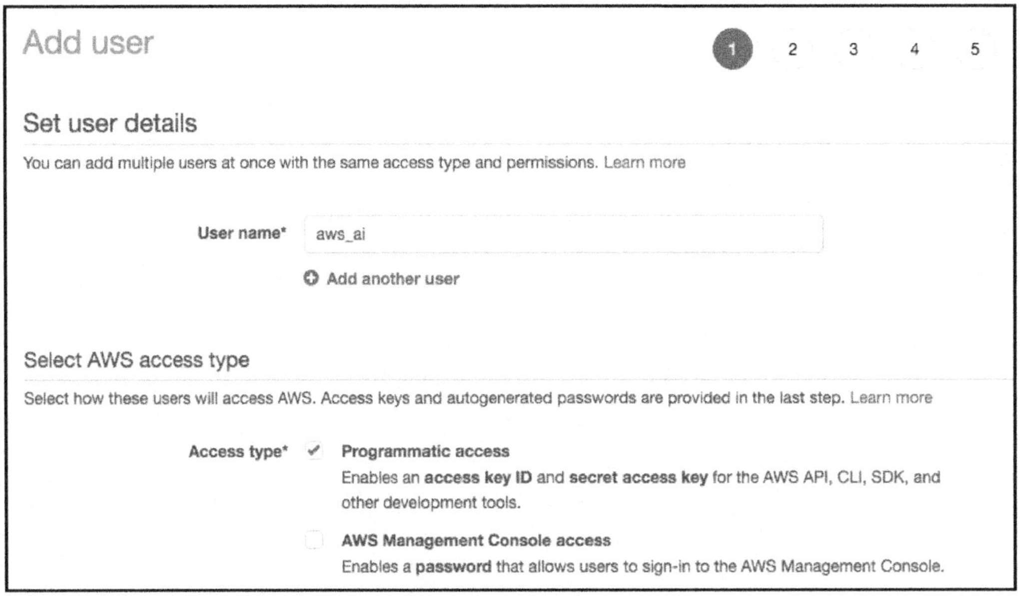

On the next screen, let's also create a group to manage the permissions. We recommend adding users to one or more groups with the necessary permissions, rather than attaching the individual permissions and policies to the users directly. This way, it's much easier to manage the permissions when there are numerous users that require different permissions in your organization.

Click on the **Create group** button under **Add user to group**, as follows:

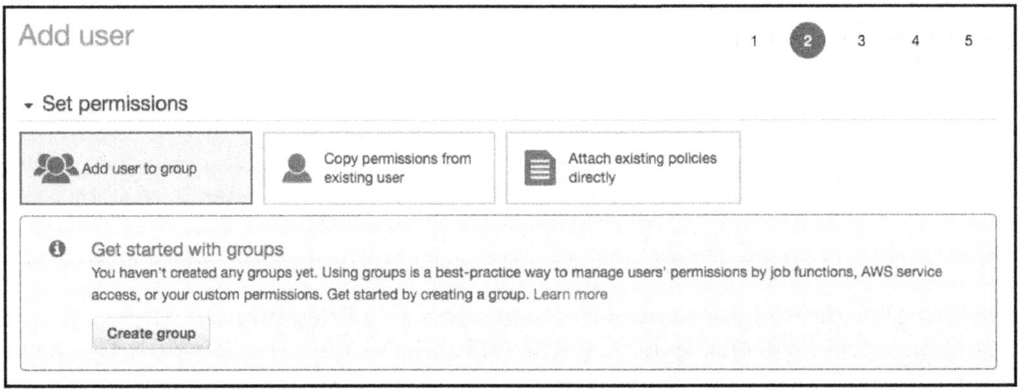

For our group, let's name it `Developer`, and then attach the **AdministratorAccess** policy to this group:

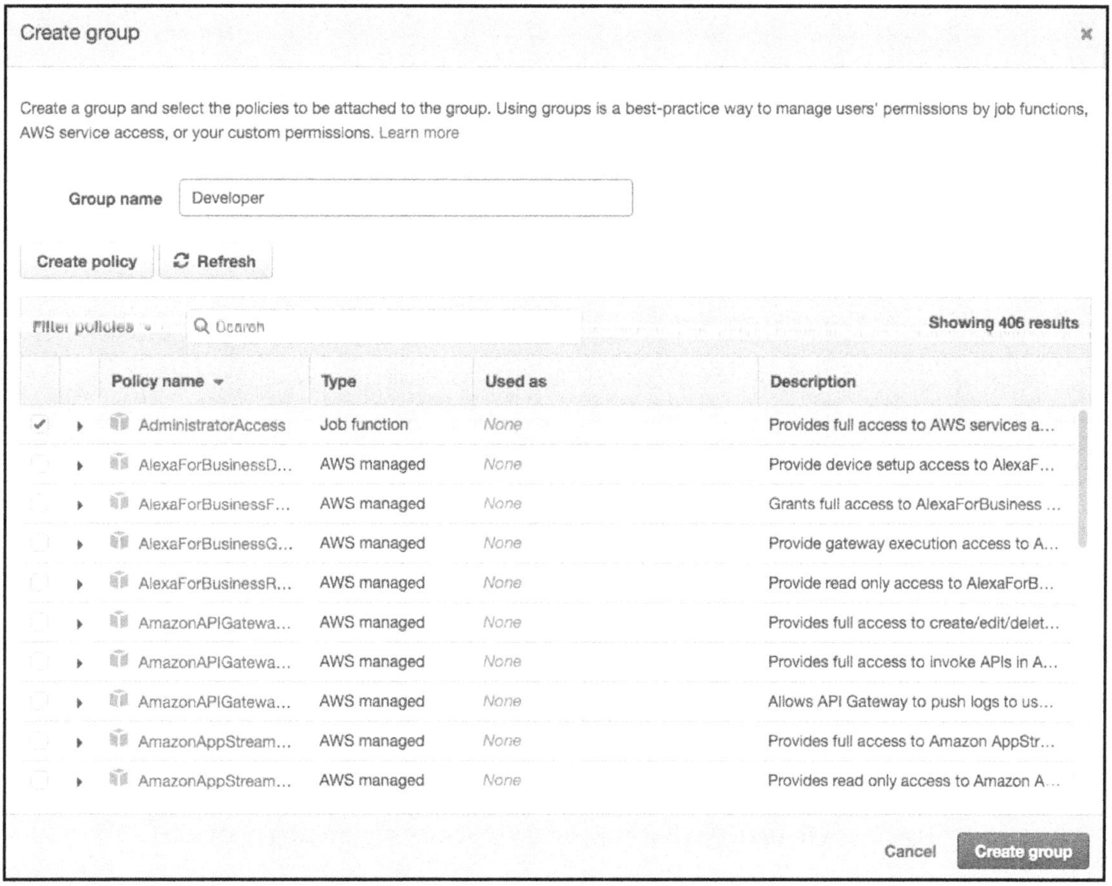

We do not need to create any tags, so just review and create the user.

For simplicity, we are attaching a very powerful policy with full access to AWS services. For your production environment, you will want to be more fine-grained with your permissions and policies. You always want to follow the principle of least privilege when it comes to system security.

Once the user has been created, you will see the **Success** screen:

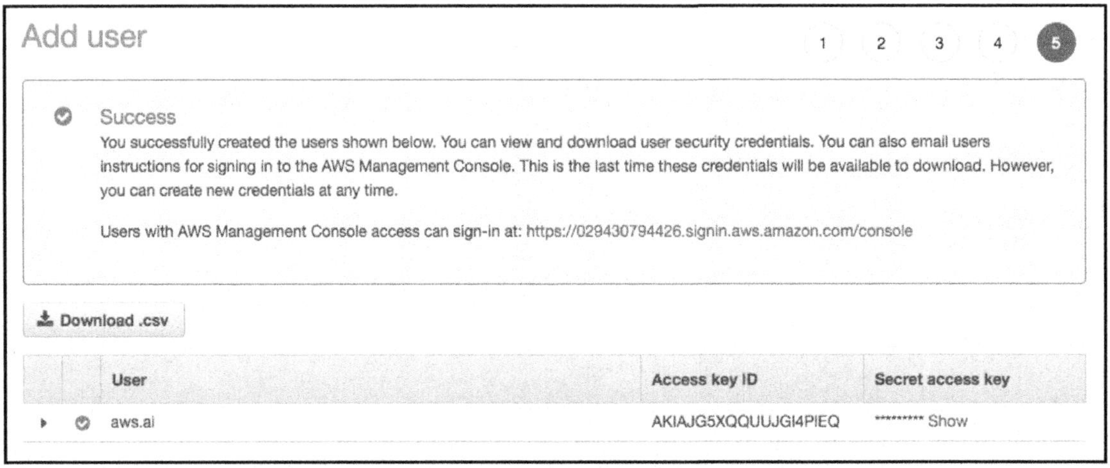

On this screen, you have the option to view or download the access key pair that we mentioned earlier. This is the only time that the secret access key can be displayed or downloaded, so go ahead and download the CSV file onto your computer. We will need this key pair when we use the AWS CLI and the AWS SDK later in this chapter.

> The access key pair is equivalent to your username and password combination. It is vital that you do not share your key pairs with others, as it will give other access to your AWS resources, but leaving you to foot the bill. Also, never hardcode the key pairs in the source code and then check them into a public source code repository. There are automated bots out there that scan the code repositories for AWS key pairs in order to steal resources to perform hacking or cryptocurrency mining activities.

Congratulations, you just used the IAM service to create a user and added it to a group with administrative permissions! If you go back to the dashboard, you will see that we have added it to the IAM resources and made progress regarding the security status:

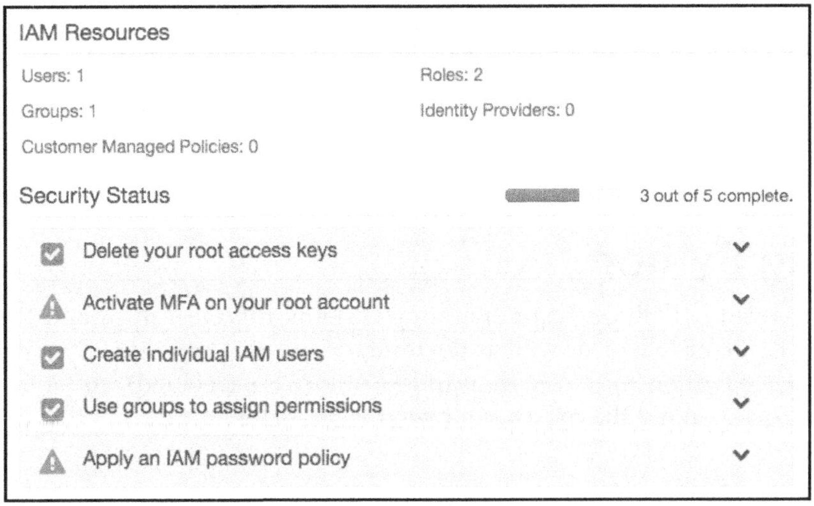

We highly recommend that you complete the remaining two steps in the security status section. The first remaining step is to activate **multi-factor authentication** (**MFA**) on your root account. Activating MFA will add extra security on your root account by requiring anyone to log in with both the root account password (something you know) and a one-time token from an authentication device (something you have), for example, your smartphone. The second remaining step is to set up a IAM password policy to ensure that secure password practices are followed. You can define the password's length, complexity, expiration period, and more.

Getting familiar with the AWS CLI

The AWS CLI is a tool that allows you to interact with AWS services by issuing commands from your Terminal shell. Earlier in this chapter, we interacted with a few AWS services through the web-based AWS Management Console. While the web console is the easiest interface for new users to get familiar with AWS, it can be cumbersome to use during the software development process. With the AWS CLI tool, you get all of the same functionalities as the web console but at your fingertips in the Terminal shell, where most of your development tools reside. This way, your development process is more fluid without the context switching to and from the browser.

The AWS CLI is primarily distributed via the Python package manager; therefore, you need to install Python on your development machine first. Note that we will be using Python for the development of the projects as well. It is important that you install Python by following the instructions in order to ensure the compatibility of your development environment later.

Installing Python

Python is available for all three major operating systems; macOS, Linux, and Microsoft Windows. There are installers, as well as documentation, at `https://www.python.org`. This book is written for Python 3.7.x or higher (unless otherwise specified), and it is recommended that you use the most recent version available.

Installing Python on macOS

While Python is pre-installed on macOS, that version of Python is 2.7. To install a newer version of Python, we recommend using a package manager for macOS called Homebrew. Homebrew is touted as the missing package manager for macOS; it simplifies the installation of many macOS software packages, including Python. To install Homebrew, follow the instructions on its website: `https://brew.sh`. At the time of writing, the command to install Homebrew in the Terminal is as follows:

```
$ /usr/bin/ruby -e "$(curl -fsSL
https://raw.githubusercontent.com/Homebrew/install/master/install)"
```

Once Homebrew has been installed, we can install the latest Python and pip, the Python package management system, with the following commands in the Terminal prompt:

```
$ brew install python3
$ brew install pip3
```

Check whether the latest Python and pip version have been correctly linked on your system with the commands in the Terminal prompt:

```
$ python --version
$ pip --version
```

The outputs of these commands should state versions similar to 3.7+ and 18.0+, respectively.

Installing Python on Linux

There are many different distributions of Linux available. The instructions to install Python might be different, depending on your specific Linux distribution. In general, you should first check to see if Python is already installed on your system in the Terminal:

```
$ python --version
$ pip --version
```

If Python or pip is not installed, or a different version is installed, install them with your Linux distribution's package manager:

- For Debian derivatives such as Ubuntu, use `apt`:

  ```
  $ sudo apt-get install python3 python3-pip
  ```

- For Red Hat derivatives such as Fedora, use `yum`:

  ```
  $ sudo yum install python python-pip
  ```

- For SUSE derivatives, use `zypper`:

  ```
  $ sudo zypper install python3 python3-pip
  ```

Installing Python on Microsoft Windows

There are different options for setting up the Python environment, depending on whether you are running Microsoft Windows 10 or an earlier version of Windows.

Windows 10

If you are running Windows 10, we highly recommend that you install the **Windows Subsystem for Linux** or **WSL**. WSL allows you to run a Linux distribution of your choice on the Windows operating system.

First, you need to enable the WSL, which is an optional feature within Windows 10. To do this, open PowerShell as the administrator and run the following command:

```
> Enable-WindowsOptionalFeature -Online -FeatureName Microsoft-Windows-
Subsystem-Linux
```

Restart your computer if prompted.

Next, you can download and install your preferred Linux distribution from the Windows Store. At the time of writing, there are five Linux distributions available for the WSL: Ubuntu, OpenSUSE, SUSE Linux Enterprise Server, Debian GNU/Linux, and Kali Linux.

Once your preferred Linux distribution has been installed, you can then follow the Python installation instructions for that particular Linux distribution.

Earlier Windows versions

If you are running an earlier version of Windows, we recommend using the Anaconda Python distribution and package manager. The Anaconda installer, as well as its documentation, can be found at `https://www.anaconda.com/download`.

Installing the AWS CLI

Once Python has been successfully installed on your development machine, we can move on to installing the AWS CLI. The AWS CLI is primarily distributed via the Python package manager, `pip`, which we just installed. You can install and verify the AWS CLI with the following commands:

```
$ pip install awscli
$ aws --version
```

Note that the AWS CLI command is `aws`, even though the package we installed is `awscli`.

Configuring the AWS CLI

Before we can use the AWS CLI, we need to perform a few configuration steps. The fastest way to configure your AWS CLI is with the following command:

```
$ aws configure
AWS Access Key ID [None]: <your access key>
AWS Secret Access Key [None]: <your secret key>
Default region name [None]: us-east-1
Default output format [None]: json
```

The explanation of the preceding code is as follows:

- The first two items that we need to enter are the security credentials so that the CLI has the permissions to perform actions on your behalf. This is the key pair that is contained within the CSV file that we downloaded during the creation of a new user with the IAM service. Open the CSV file and copy and paste the access key ID and the secret access key into the configuration command prompt.
- Next, for the default region name, we will again use `us-east-1` for consistency throughout this book.
- Finally, for the default output format, enter `json`. This will set the output for the AWS CLI to be JSON format.

The AWS configure command creates a hidden directory, `.aws`, in your user home directory, for example, `~/.aws` on macOS and Linux. In this directory, two files are created. One is `.aws/credentials`, with the following code:

```
[default]
aws_access_key_id = YOUR_ACCESS_KEY
aws_secret_access_key = YOUR_SECRET_KEY
```

The other is `.aws/config`, with the following code:

```
[default]
region = us-east-1
output = json
```

Locate these files on your system and verify their contents.

In case you did not copy down or download the access key pair, you can obtain a new key pair in the AWS Management Console:

1. Navigate to the **IAM** service under the **Security, Identity, & Compliance** heading.
2. In the **IAM Management Console**, click on **Users** on the right-hand pane and click on your username.
3. On the user summary page, click on the **Security credentials** tab.
4. Under the **Access keys** section, click on the **Create access key** button and a new access key will be created for you.
5. Remember to delete the old key pair after the new one has been created.

This is how your screen will look:

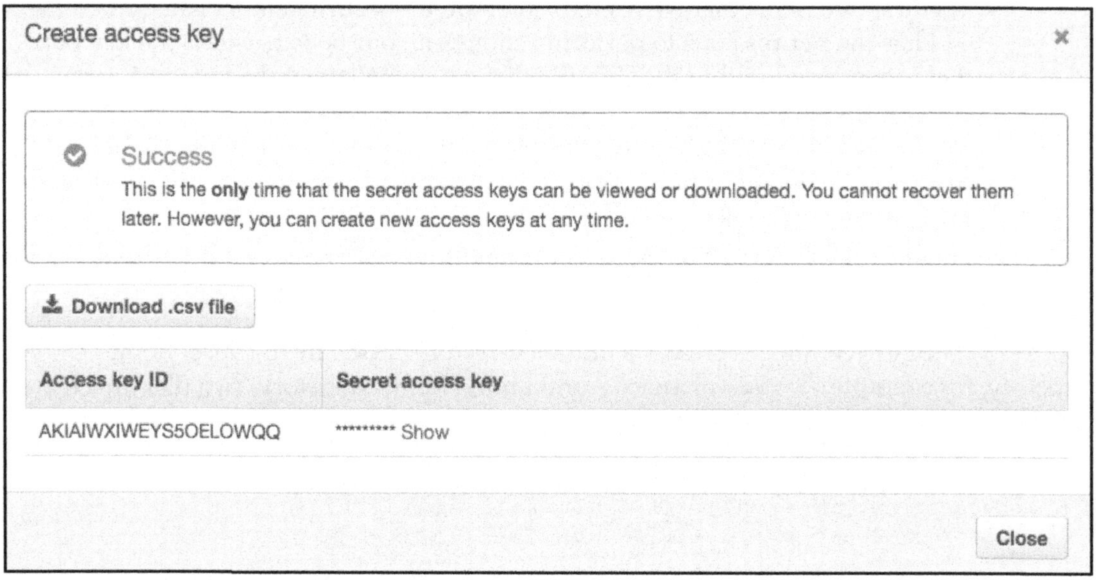

Remember to configure your AWS CLI with the following command, each time you change your access key:

```
$ aws configure
```

Enter your security credentials, default region, and default output format as we explained in the initial AWS CLI configuration.

To test whether the AWS CLI is configured properly, issue the following command:

```
$ aws s3 ls
2018-12-01 18:01:20 contents.aws.ai
2018-12-01 18:01:49 data.aws.ai
2018-12-01 18:01:35 website.aws.ai
```

This command will print all of the S3 buckets in your AWS account. More specifically, this command lists the S3 buckets that the user who is associated with the access key has permissions to see. Remember the key pair we configured the CLI with, which belongs to the user to whom we granted the administrative policy? One of the permissions within the administrative policy gives the user access to S3. In any case, you should see the S3 bucket that we created in the previous section of this chapter via the AWS Management Console.

Invoking the Rekognition service using the AWS CLI

Now, let's invoke the object detection capability of Amazon Rekognition via the AWS CLI. This time, let's perform the object detection on an image that's stored in one of our S3 buckets. We will be using a sample image from Pexels, a website with thousands of royalty-free images. Download the image at `https://www.pexels.com/photo/animal-beagle-canine-close-up-460823/` and upload it to the `contents` S3 bucket.

Here, we can see an adorable beagle puppy laying on what appears to be a bed of gravel:

You should see the following output when you list the objects in your `contents` bucket:

```
$ aws s3 ls s3://<YOUR BUCKET>
2018-12-02 13:31:32     362844 animal-beagle-canine-460823.jpg
```

Now that we have an image, we can invoke the object detection capability of Rekognition via the following CLI command. Note that we must escape the `{` and `}` characters with a `\`, and we must not include any spaces when specifying the S3 object on the command line:

```
$ aws rekognition detect-labels --image S3Object=\{Bucket=<YOUR
BUCKET>,Name=animal-beagle-canine-460823.jpg\}
```

The results come back almost instantly:

```
{
 "Labels": [
 {
 "Name": "Mammal",
 "Confidence": 98.9777603149414
 },
 {
 "Name": "Pet",
 "Confidence": 98.9777603149414
 },
 {
 "Name": "Hound",
 "Confidence": 98.9777603149414
 },
 {
 "Name": "Dog",
 "Confidence": 98.9777603149414
 },
 {
 "Name": "Canine",
 "Confidence": 98.9777603149414
 },
 {
 "Name": "Animal",
 "Confidence": 98.9777603149414
 },
 {
 "Name": "Beagle",
 "Confidence": 98.0347900390625
 },
 {
 "Name": "Road",
 "Confidence": 82.47952270507812
 },
 {
 "Name": "Gravel",
 "Confidence": 74.52912902832031
 },
 {
 "Name": "Dirt Road",
 "Confidence": 74.52912902832031
 }
 ]
}
```

The output is in JSON format, just like we configured the CLI to the output. From the output, the Rekognition service detected several objects or labels. Rekognition is very sure that it detected a dog; it even identified the breed of the dog as a beagle! Rekognition also detected the gravel in the image, which could be a part of a dirt road. The AWS CLI can be very useful when trying out an AWS service, and to see how the output is structured when we are developing our applications.

Using Python for AI applications

Python is one of the most popular programming languages. Thanks to its popularity with the data science and ML community, Python is also one of the fastest-growing programming languages. There is a large number of add-on libraries from its developers and the open source community. These libraries enable Python developers to do almost anything, from data analytics to deep neural networks, from simple scripting to web application development.

For AI and ML, Python is the de facto language. There's the popular scikit-learn library that gives developers access to many useful ML algorithms. There are also many libraries for deep neural networks, such as MXNet and TensorFlow.

We will be using Python for every hands-on projects throughout this book:

- In the first half of this book, we will create intelligent-enabled solutions using AWS AI services. For these projects, we will use Python to create the backend components, APIs, and web applications that will bring our intelligent creations to life. AWS offers a Python SDK called Boto. With Boto, we can interact with all of the AWS services from our applications, including the managed AI capabilities.
- In the second half of this book, we will be training custom ML models using AWS ML services. For these projects, we will use Python to process data, train ML models, and deploy intelligent capabilities. In addition to the Boto SDK, we will also use AWS libraries for SageMaker, **Elastic MapReduce** (**EMR**), and many more.

Setting up a Python development environment

Let's start by setting up our local development environment. Since we are building end-to-end solutions in the projects, there are numerous packages and dependencies that we will need. The packages we will need don't always come as part of the standard library. Our projects will sometimes need specific versions of the libraries to get all of the moving pieces working together. Therefore, it is very important that you follow these instructions to install the packages, as described in this chapter.

Setting up a Python virtual environment with Pipenv

We will use a Python virtual environment to manage the packages for the projects in this book. A virtual environment is a Pythonic way to create a self-contained project directory tree that includes a particular combination of a Python version and packages that are specific to a project.

There are many benefits of using Python virtual environments:

- Since all of the packages and dependencies of a project are specified in a configuration file, the project's development environment can be easily duplicated by other developers; this is very useful when you are working within a development team.
- Even if you are working by yourself, having a virtual environment will help you with creating (and recreating) the environment on one or more computers for development, testing, and deployment.
- A virtual environment also allows you to create separate Python environments, where parallel copies of Python dependencies can be installed. This way, we can keep conflicting Python versions and packages for different projects on the same computer.

Pipenv is the new kid on the block when it comes to Python virtual environments, but it has already been promoted as the officially recommended Python packaging tool from `python.org`. To install `pipenv`, we will use Pip, the Python package management tool:

```
$ pip install pipenv
$ pipenv --version
```

This command will help you install and verify `pipenv`.

Creating your first Python virtual environment

Now that we have installed the Python toolset, let's take it for a test drive by creating a Python project that can interact with the AWS cloud platform. First, let's create a directory for the project and name it `ObjectDetectionDemo`. Within this directory, we initialize a Python 3 virtual environment with `pipenv`, as follows:

```
$ mkdir ObjectDetectionDemo
$ cd ObjectDetectionDemo
$ pipenv --three
```

After these commands, the `ObjectDetectionDemo` directory will contain a `Pipfile`. The `Pipfile` is a `pipenv` configuration file that specifies this project's Python packages and their dependencies.

Next, we specify and install the AWS Python SDK, Boto, for the `ObjectDetectionDemo` project:

```
$ pipenv install boto3
```

It might take a few minutes for Pipenv to synchronize with the Python package index and to install the `boto3` package, along with its dependencies. After the installation, your Pipefile should have the following contents:

```
[[source]]
url = "https://pypi.org/simple"
verify_ssl = true
name = "pypi"

[packages]
"boto3" = "*"

[requires]
python_version = "3.7"
```

As you can see here, `boto3` has an entry under the packages section. Currently, the version number is listed as `*`, which means, use the latest version. You can replace `*` with a specific version for any of the packages for your project if necessary.

First project with the AWS SDK

Now, let's write our first Python application that will detect the objects in the images that are stored in an S3 bucket. To do this, we will leverage `boto3` to interact with both the Amazon S3 service and the Amazon Rekognition service:

> TIP: You can use any text editor, or your favorite Python **Integrated Development Environment** (**IDE**), to create the Python source files. If you don't have a preference, we recommend that you check out JetBrains PyCharm, `https://www.jetbrains.com/pycharm/`, a cross-platform Python IDE that provides code editing, code analysis, a graphical debugger, an integrated unit tester, and integration with a version control system.

1. The first source file that we will create is `storage_service.py`. Create this source file in the `ObjectDetectionDemo` directory. The following is the Python code for `storage_service.py`:

```
import boto3

class StorageService:
    def __init__(self):
        self.s3 = boto3.resource('s3')

    def get_all_files(self, storage_location):
        return self.s3.Bucket(storage_location).objects.all()
```

In this code, please note the following information:

- `storage_service.py` contains a Python class, `StorageService`, that encapsulates the business logic of interacting with Amazon S3.
- This class implements just one method, `get_all_files()`, which returns all of the objects stored within a bucket specified by the `storage_location` parameter.
- Other functionalities related to Amazon S3 can also be implemented in this file, such as listing the buckets, uploading files to buckets, and so on.

2. The next source file that we will create is `recognition_service.py`. Create this source file in the `ObjectDetectionDemo` directory as well. The following is the Python code for `recognition_service.py`:

```
import boto3

class RecognitionService:
    def __init__(self):
        self.client = boto3.client('rekognition')

    def detect_objects(self, storage_location, image_file):
        response = self.client.detect_labels(
            Image = {
                'S3Object': {
                    'Bucket': storage_location,
                    'Name': image_file
                }
            }
        )

        return response['Labels']
```

In this code, please note the following information:

- `recognition_service.py` contains a Python class, `RecognitionService`, that encapsulates the business logic of interacting with the Amazon Rekognition service.
- This class implements just one method, `detect_objects()`, that calls Rekognition's detect label API, and then returns the labels from the response.
- Callers of this method can specify the S3 bucket and the filename with the `storage_location` and `image_file` parameters, respectively.
- Other functionalities related to Amazon Rekognition can also be implemented in this file, such as detecting text, analyzing face, and so on.

3. The final file that we will create is `object_detection_demo.py`. Create this source file in the `ObjectDetectionDemo` directory. The following is the Python code for `object_detection_demo.py`:

```
from storage_service import StorageService
from recognition_service import RecognitionService
```

```
storage_service = StorageService()
recognition_service = RecognitionService()

bucket_name = 'contents.aws.ai'

for file in storage_service.get_all_files(bucket_name):
    if file.key.endswith('.jpg'):
        print('Objects detected in image ' + file.key + ':')
        labels =
recognition_service.detect_objects(file.bucket_name, file.key)

        for label in labels:
            print('-- ' + label['Name'] + ': ' +
str(label['Confidence']))
```

In this code, `object_detection_demo.py` is a Python script that brings together our two service implementations in order to perform object detection on the images that are stored in our S3 bucket.

Here is the interaction diagram that depicts the flow of the demo application:

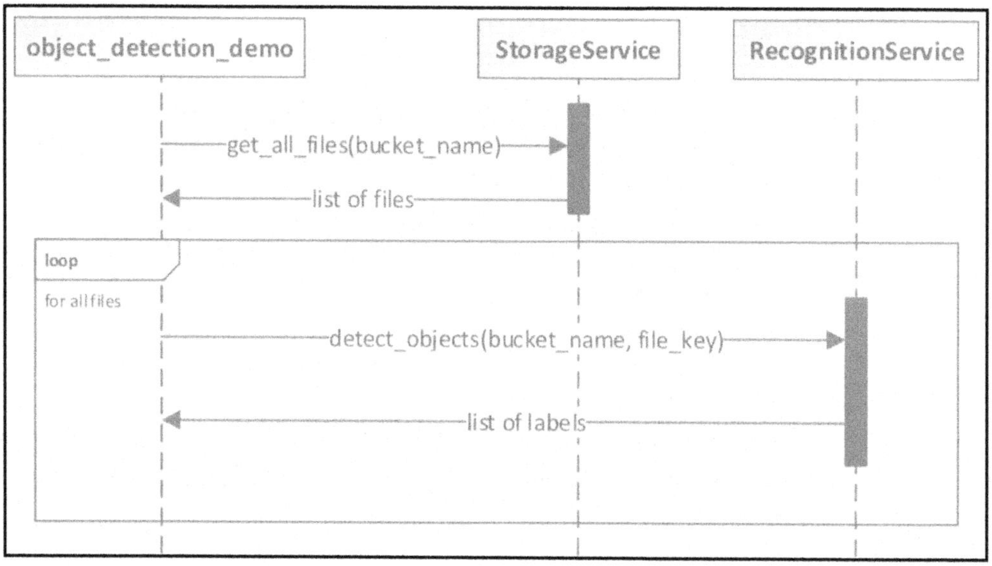

Please note the following information, all of which is shown in the preceding diagram:

- This script calls the **StorageService** to get all of the JPG image files that are stored in the `contents.aws.ai` bucket (you should replace this with your own bucket).
- Here, we are hardcoding the bucket name for simplicity, but you can take in the bucket name as a parameter in order to make the script more generic.
- Then, for each image in the specified bucket, the script calls our **RecognitionService** to perform object detection and returns the labels that are found.
- The script also formats and prints out the labels, along with their confidence scores for the objects that were detected.

Note that we are using `boto3` in both **StorageService** and **RecognitionService**. The `boto3` objects manage the sessions between our project code and the AWS services. These sessions are created using the available credentials in the runtime environment. If you are running the script on your local development machine, then the AWS access key pair is taken from the `~/.aws/credentials` file. We will cover how the credentials are used in other runtime environments in later chapters.

> For simplicity, we kept the project code relatively short and simple. We will enhance these Python classes in later hands-on projects.
> Even though this is only a demo project, it is still good practice to organize the code into different components with separation of concerns. In this project, all of the business logic that will interact with the Amazon S3 service are encapsulated within the `StorageService` class; the same is done for all the logic that will interact with the Amazon Rekognition service in the `RecogntionService` class. We will see more benefits of this design practice as our projects get larger and more complex.

4. Now, let's run the following script in the Python virtual environment by entering the virtual environment shell:

```
$ pipenv shell
```

In this command, please note the following information:

- This command starts a shell with the Python virtual environment within your normal Terminal shell.
- Within the virtual environment shell, the Python version and the packages that we specified and installed with `pipenv` are available to our script.

5. Within the virtual environment, invoke the `object_detection_demo.py` script via the following command:

```
$ python object_detection_demo.py
```

The output of this command should display the objects that are detected in the images that are stored in the specified S3 bucket:

```
Objects detected in image animal-beagle-canine-460823.jpg:
-- Pet: 98.9777603149414
-- Hound: 98.9777603149414
-- Canine: 98.9777603149414
-- Animal: 98.9777603149414
-- Dog: 98.9777603149414
-- Mammal: 98.9777603149414
-- Beagle: 98.0347900390625
-- Road: 82.47952270507812
-- Dirt Road: 74.52912902832031
-- Gravel: 74.52912902832031
```

6. Remember to exit the virtual environment and to return to your normal Terminal shell with the `exit` command:

```
$ exit
```

Congratulations, you just created your first intelligent-enabled application that leverages the power of AI to perform image analysis on the AWS platform! Sit back and think about it; with just a few lines of code, you were able to create a piece of software that can detect and identify countless numbers of objects in our world. This is the quick lift you can get when leveraging AWS AI services.

Summary

In this chapter, we learned that AI has existed for a long time, but it is becoming popular again due to the renewed interested in ML, more specifically, with artificial neural networks. We looked at a few real-world applications of AI and ML. We got an overview of the two groups of AI offerings from AWS; the AWS AI services that give you a quick lift when developing intelligent-enabled applications, and the AWS ML platforms that allow you to build custom AI capabilities that are tailored to your application. We recommended that you try to leverage the provided AWS AI services first, and only develop custom AI capabilities if you have a specialized need and you have a data-competitive advantage.

We got familiar with several services on AWS through hands-on experience, including the AI services and the other complimentary cloud services. We also set up our local development environment for AI applications, including Python, the AWS CLI, and Python virtual environments. We then created our first intelligent-enabled application using the Amazon S3 and Amazon Rekognition services.

In the next chapter, we will dive into the components and the architecture of AI applications. We will set up an architecture template for many of the upcoming hands-on projects, and more importantly, we will cover the design principles and decisions that this architecture template is based on.

References

You can access the following links for more information on AI on AWS:

- `https://www.sciencenews.org/article/future-ai-may-diagnose-eye-problems`
- `https://www.sas.com/en_us/insights/analytics/what-is-artificial-intelligence.html`
- `https://adage.com/article/cmo-strategy/google-backed-video-puts-viewers-a-driving-cars/312542/`
- `https://blog.swiftkey.com/whats-difference-predictive-keyboards-predictive-text/`
- `http://www.futurile.net/2013/10/03/virtualenv-and-virtualenvwrapper-for-python-development/`

2
Anatomy of a Modern AI Application

In this chapter, we will discuss the importance of good architecture design for **artificial intelligence** (**AI**) applications. First, we will cover the architecture design principles and then create a reference architecture for our hands-on projects. In this chapter, we will recreate the Amazon Rekognition demo with our reference architecture and the components that make it up. We will learn how to use several AWS tools and services to build our hands-on project in the serverless style and then deploy it to the AWS cloud.

We will cover the following topics in this chapter:

- Understanding the success factors of artificial intelligence applications
- Understanding the architecture design principles for AI applications
- Understanding the architecture of modern AI applications
- Creating custom AI capabilities
- Developing an AI application locally using AWS Chalice
- Developing a demo application web user interface

Technical requirements

This book's GitHub repository, which contains the source code for this chapter, can be found at `https://github.com/PacktPublishing/Hands-On-Artificial-Intelligence-on-Amazon-Web-Services`.

Understanding the success factors of artificial intelligence applications

Let's talk about what makes an AI application successful, and really, what makes any software application successful. There are two main factors that determine application success:

- The first factor is whether the application is a solution that actually solves a particular problem.
- The second factor is how well the application is implemented to deliver the solution to the problem.

Basically, we are talking about *what to build* and *how to build it*. Both of these factors are difficult to get right and for the majority of cases, both of them are required to make an application successful.

The fact is, deciding on precisely *what to build* is the more important factor of the two. If we get this factor wrong, we will have a flawed product that will not deliver a viable solution to the problem. It will not matter how elegant the architecture is or how clean the code base is—a flawed product will be unsuccessful. Deciding on precisely what to build is rarely a one-shot deal, though. It is a fallacy to believe that the perfect solution can be designed in advance. In many cases, your target customers don't even know what they want or need. Successful solutions require extensive iterations of product development, customer feedback, and a tremendous amount of effort to refine the product requirements.

This need to iterate and experiment with the solution makes *how to build it* an important factor for finding out *what to build*. It doesn't take a tremendous amount of skill to get an application to work. You can always get the first iteration, the first version, or the first pivot, to work with sheer determination and brute force. It might not be elegant, but the application works. However, when the first iteration is not the right solution to the problem, then a more elegant architecture and a cleaner code base will enable faster iterations and pivots, thus giving you more opportunities to figure out *what to build*.

Understanding the architecture design principles for AI applications

Building elegant applications is not trivial, but building elegant AI applications can be even harder. As AI practitioners in a rapidly changing technology landscape, it's important to understand good architecture design principles and to have a passion for software craftsmanship since it takes relentless discipline to build and maintain applications that can adapt to the fast-evolving AI technologies. Good architecture design can easily adapt to changes. However, it is impossible to predict all future changes. Therefore, we need to rely on a set of well-accepted design principles to guide us on good application architecture. Let's go over them now:

- A well-architected application should be built on top of small services with focused business capabilities. By small, we don't necessarily mean a small amount of code. Instead, small services should follow the single responsibility principle; that is, to do one or very few things well.
- These small services are much easier to implement, test, and deploy. They are also easier to reuse and to compose more business capabilities.
- A good application architecture should have well-defined boundaries to enforce separation of concerns.
- The services and components of the application should maintain this separation by hiding internal implementation details from the others.
- This separation allows services and components to be replaceable with minimal impact on the rest of the application, thus supporting easier evolution and improvement of the solution.

If you are new to software architecture design, the differences between good and bad designs might appear subtle. It will take you a lot of experience to acquire the knowledge and skills you need to truly appreciate good design. In this book, we will provide you with examples of elegant designs that are good starting points for AI applications.

Understanding the architecture of modern AI applications

Defining a clean architecture design is a necessary step for developing successful AI applications, and we recommend four basic components that make it up.

These four components are as follows:

- **User interfaces**: These are the user-facing components that deliver the business capabilities of your application to the end users:
    - They are also known as frontends. Examples of user interfaces include websites, mobile apps, wearables, and voice assistant interfaces.
    - The same application can deliver different tailored user experiences by choosing different device form factors, interaction modalities, and user interfaces.
    - How you deliver intelligent capabilities on a web page is going to be very different than how you would do so on wearable devices.

  As an AI practitioner, an important skill is designing the user experience to deliver your intelligent capabilities to the users. Getting this part right is one of the most important factors for the success of your AI applications.

- **Orchestration layer**: These are the public APIs that will be called by your user interfaces to deliver the business capabilities:
    - Usually, these APIs are the entry points to the backend.
    - The public APIs should be tailored to the specific interfaces and modalities in order to deliver the best experiences to the users.
    - The public APIs will call upon one or more small services (through private APIs) to deliver business capabilities.

  They play an orchestration role to combine several lower-level capabilities to compose higher-level capabilities that are needed by the user interfaces. There are other names for these public APIs that you might be familiar with; that is, **Backends for Frontends** (or **BFFs**) and experience APIs.

- **Private APIs**: The private APIs define the interaction contracts that are used by the public APIs to access lower-level services:
    - The private APIs wrap the service implementations, which provide certain capabilities, in order to hide their details.
    - These APIs play a key role in the composability and the replaceability qualities of software systems.
    - The private APIs are the interfaces for the common capabilities that can be composed and reused by multiple applications.
    - These private APIs follow the service-oriented design pattern. You might be familiar with this pattern from similar architectures, such as microservices architecture and **service-oriented architecture** (or **SOA**).
    - They should be designed with the single responsibility principle in mind.

A set of well-designed private APIs is a valuable asset and competitive advantage for any organization. The organization will be able to rapidly innovate, improve, and deploy solutions to the market.

- **Vendor/custom services:** These are the implementations of the business capabilities, whether they are AI or otherwise:
    - These implementations can be provided by vendors as web services or hosted within your infrastructure. They can also be custom solutions that have been built by your organization.
    - These services have their own APIs, such as RESTful endpoints or SDKs that the private APIs will call upon to wrap the implementations.

In this book, we will be leveraging Amazon as the vendor to provide many of the web services via the *boto3* SDK. Later in this book, we will also teach you how to build custom AI capabilities using AWS' Machine Learning services and deploy them as ML models with RESTful endpoints.

The following diagram illustrates the organization of these basic architecture components and layers:

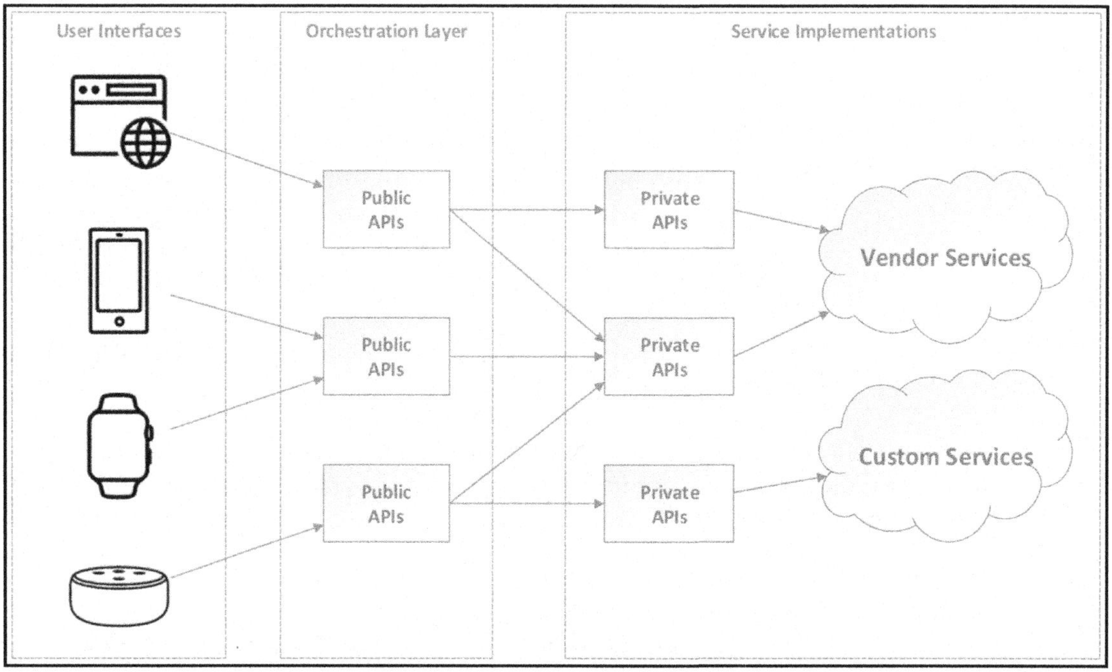

The key to a clean architecture is to keep these components separated through well-defined interaction contracts between each layer:

- The user interfaces should only know about the public APIs in the orchestration layer.
- The public APIs should only know about the private APIs that they depend on.
- The private APIs should only know about the service implementations they wrap around.
- This is the principle of information hiding, which is applied at the architecture level.

There are many benefits to enforcing these logical boundaries at the architecture level, for example, if we would like to switch to a better vendor service. All we need to do is create a new set of private APIs to wrap around the new vendor service while keeping the same private API contracts to the public APIs (and then retire the old private APIs). This way, the public APIs, as well as the user interfaces, won't be affected by this change. This limits the impact of the change to a specific part of the application.

> Most of the applications we use today are composed of a frontend and a backend. The frontend usually runs in a browser or on a mobile device, while the backend runs on server infrastructure in the cloud or in a private data center. The architecture that's recommended here is a good starting point for these types of applications. There are more specialized applications, such as embedded systems, that might require a different architecture design. We will not dive into the architecture needs of these more specialized applications in this book.

Creation of custom AI capabilities

As AI practitioners, there are two distinct development life cycles we can be involved in:

- The AI application development life cycle
- The AI capability development life cycle

Usually, especially in larger organizations where roles are more specialized, an AI practitioner only participates in one of these life cycles. Even if you do not participate in one of these life cycles, getting a good understanding of both is useful for all AI practitioners.

The AI application development life cycle involves iterating the solution, designing the user experience, defining the application architecture, and integrating the various business capabilities. This is similar to the traditional software development life cycle, but with the intent of embedding intelligence into the solutions.

The AI capability development life cycle deals with developing intelligent capabilities using data and machine learning techniques. The data products that are created during the AI capability's development life cycle can then be integrated into the applications as AI capabilities or AI services. In other words, the AI capability development life cycle produces custom AI capabilities that the AI application development life cycle consumes.

Different sets of technical and problem-solving skills are needed by these two life cycles. The following diagram provides an overview of the steps that are required to create AI capabilities:

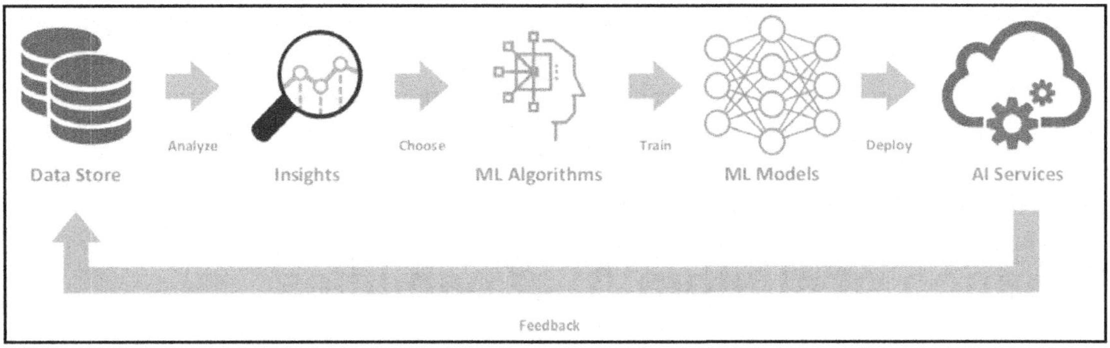

AI capabilities are at the heart of AI applications. As we mentioned in `Chapter 1`, *Introduction to Artificial Intelligence and Amazon Web Services*, data is the new intellectual property. Any successful organization should have a well-defined data strategy to collect, store, process, and disseminate data. Raw and processed datasets should be safely placed and made available in data storage systems such as databases, data lakes, and data warehouses. From these data stores, data scientists can access data to support the analysis that's specific to a business problem or question they are working on. Some of the analysis results will generate useful business insights with the potential to perform predictive analysis. With these insights, data scientists can then choose from various machine learning algorithms to train machine learning models to perform automated predictions and decision-making, including classifications and regression analysis.

Once trained and tuned, machine learning models can then be deployed as AI services with interfaces for applications to access their intelligence. For example, Amazon SageMaker lets us train machine learning models and then deploy them as web services with RESTful endpoints. Finally, as a part of your data strategy, the feedback data from deployed AI services should be collected to improve future iterations of the AI services.

> As we mentioned in the previous chapter, we highly recommend that you first leverage existing AI services from vendors such as AWS as much as possible for your intelligent-enabled applications. Each one of the AWS AI capabilities has gone through numerous iterations of the AI capability development life cycle with a massive amount of data that most organizations do not have access to. It only makes sense to build your own AI capabilities if you have a true data intellectual property or a need that's not addressed by the vendor solutions. It takes a tremendous amount of effort, skill, and time to train production-ready machine learning models.

The second part of this book will focus on the AI application development life cycle, while the third part of this book will focus on the AI capability development life cycle.

Working with a hands-on AI application architecture

In the previous section, we recommended an architecture design for modern AI applications. In this section, we will define the specific technologies and tech stacks we will use in this book to implement the recommended architecture design. We evaluated several factors when deciding on the best choices for this book, including simplicity, learning curve, industry trends, and others. Keep in mind that there can be many valid technology choices and implementations for the recommended architecture design.

For the hands-on AI application development projects, we will use the following architecture and technology stack:

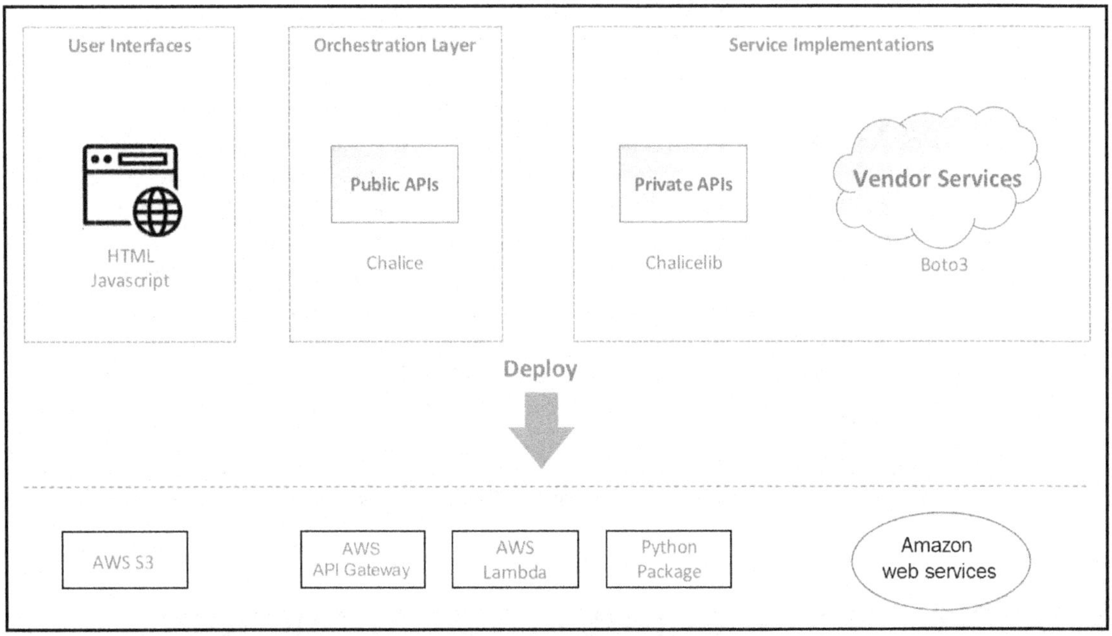

As the preceding diagram illustrates, the AI application projects will be made up of the four basic architectural components we discussed earlier:

- **User interfaces**: We will be using web pages as user interfaces. We will develop relatively simple user interfaces using HTML, CSS, and JavaScript. HTML and CSS will display the UI components and handle user inputs. JavaScript will communicate with the server backend via the public APIs in the orchestration layer. The project web pages will be deployed on AWS S3 as a static website without the need for traditional web servers. This is known as serverless because we don't need to manage and maintain any server infrastructure.

> **TIP**
>
> We are using plain HTML and JavaScript to limit the scope of this book. You should consider single-page web application frameworks such as Angular, React, or Vue for your web user interfaces after finishing the hands-on projects in this book.
>
> Also, you are not limited to web applications as the only choice for AI applications. Other user interfaces and modalities, such as mobile or voice assistant devices, can sometimes provide a better user experience. We recommend that you think about how the application design should be changed in order to support these other user interfaces and modalities. These thought experiments will help you build the design muscles for AI practitioners.

- **Orchestration layer**: We will be using AWS Chalice, a Python serverless microframework for AWS. Chalice allows us to quickly develop and test Python applications in its local development environment, and then easily deploy the Python applications to Amazon API Gateway and AWS Lambda as highly available and scalable serverless backends. Amazon API Gateway is a fully managed service that will host our public APIs as RESTful endpoints. The API Gateway will forward the RESTful requests that were issued to our public APIs to AWS Lambda functions where our orchestration logic will be deployed to. AWS Lambda is a serverless technology that lets us run code without provisioning or manage servers. When a Lambda function is invoked, for instance, from the API Gateway, the code is automatically triggered and run on the AWS infrastructure. You only pay for the computing resources that are consumed.
- **Private APIs**: We will be packaging the private APIs as Python libraries within the Chalice framework. Chalice allows us to write code in a modular way by structuring some services as libraries in the `Chalicelib` directory. In our hands-on projects, the private APIs are plain old Python classes with well-defined method signatures to provide access to the service implementations. In our projects, the boundary between the public and private APIs is logical rather than physical; therefore, attention must be paid to ensure the cleanliness of the architecture layers.

We will be reusing some of the private APIs in multiple projects. Our mechanism of reuse is similar to shared libraries. In larger organizations, the private APIs are usually deployed as RESTful endpoints so that different applications can easily share them.

- **Vendor services**: We will be leveraging AWS for various capabilities. For example, we need to develop these intelligent-enabled applications, including AI capabilities and more. The private APIs will access the AWS services in the cloud via the *boto3* SDK. Clean design requires *boto3* and AWS implementation details to be completely wrapped and hidden by the private APIs; the public APIs should not know which vendor services or custom solutions are used by the private APIs to provide these capabilities.

Object detector architecture

We will be recreating the *Amazon Rekognition* demo with our own web frontend and Python backend. First, let's understand the architecture of the Object Detector application we are about to develop.

Using the reference architecture design and the technology stack we discussed previously, here is the architecture for the Object Detector application:

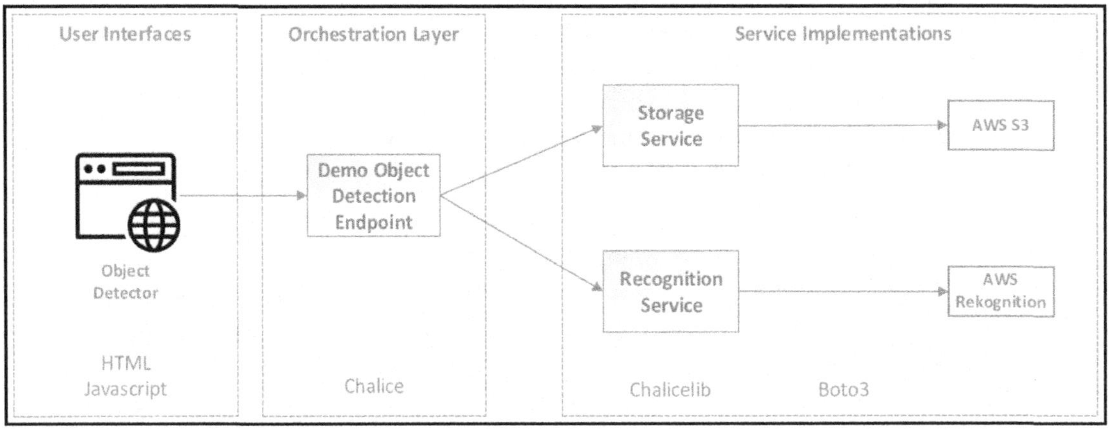

The user will interact with the Object Detector through a web user interface:

- We will provide a web user interface for users so that they can see the Object Detection demo.
- The web user interface will interact with the orchestration layer containing just one RESTful endpoint: the Demo Object Detection endpoint.
- The endpoint interacts with both the Storage Service and the Recognition Service to perform the Object Detection demo.
- The Storage Service and the Recognition Service calls the Amazon S3 and Amazon Rekognition services using the *Boto3* SDK, respectively.

Component Interactions of the Object Detector

Let's understand the interactions between the various components of the Object Detector application:

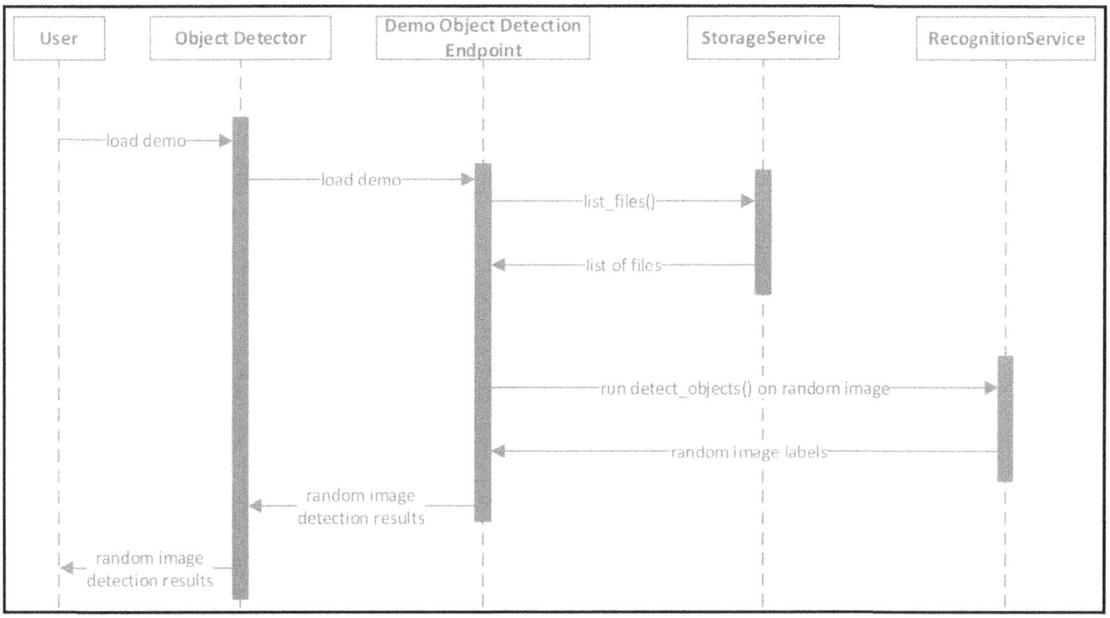

From the user's perspective, the application loads a random image and displays the objects (or labels) that have been detected within that image. The demo workflow is as follows:

1. The object detector application's web interface calls the Demo Object Detection endpoint to start the demo.
2. The endpoint calls the Storage Service to get a list of files that are stored in a specified S3 bucket.
3. After receiving the list of files, the endpoint randomly selects an image file for the demo.
4. The endpoint then calls the Recognition Service to perform object detection on the selected image file.
5. After receiving the object labels, the endpoint packages the results in JSON format.
6. Finally, the web interface displays the randomly selected image and its detection results.

Creating the base project structure

Next, let's create the hands-on project structure. Follow these steps to create the architecture and technology stack:

1. In Terminal, we will create the root project directory and enter it with the following commands:

```
$ mkdir ObjectDetector
$ cd ObjectDetector
```

2. We will create placeholders for the web frontend by creating a directory named `Website`. Within this directory, we will have two files, `index.html` and `scripts.js`, as follows:

```
$ mkdir Website
$ touch Website/index.html
$ touch Website/scripts.js
```

3. We will create a Python 3 virtual environment with `pipenv` in the project's root directory. Our Python portion of the project needs two packages, `boto3` and `chalice`. We can install them with the following commands:

```
$ pipenv --three
$ pipenv install boto3
$ pipenv install chalice
```

4. Remember that the Python packages that were installed via `pipenv` are only available if we activate the virtual environment. One way to do this is with the following command:

```
$ pipenv shell
```

5. Next, while still in the virtual environment, we will create the orchestration layer as an AWS Chalice project named `Capabilities` with the following commands:

```
$ chalice new-project Capabilities
```

This command will create a Chalice project structure within the `ObjectDetector` directory. The Chalice project structure should look similar to the following:

```
├── ObjectDetector/
    ├── Capabilities/
        ├── .chalice/
            ├── config.json
    ├── app.py
    ├── requirements.txt
...
```

In this project structure, we have the following:

- The `config.json` file contains configuration options for deploying our Chalice application to AWS.
- The `app.py` file is the main Python file where our public orchestration APIs are defined and implemented.
- The `requirements.txt` file specifies the Python packages that are needed by the application when it is deployed to AWS. These packages are different from the packages we installed using Pipenv. The Pipenv installed packages are the ones we need during development in the local environment; the packages in the `requirements.txt` file are the ones the application needs to run in the AWS cloud. For example, AWS Chalice is required during the development of the application but it is not needed once the application has been deployed to AWS.

> `boto3` is required when we're running our projects in the AWS cloud; however, it is already provided in the AWS Lambda runtime environment, and so we do not need to explicitly specify it in the `requirements.txt` file. Do remember to include any other Python packages that the applications need in that file, though.

6. Now, we need to create a `chalicelib` Python package within the Chalice project structure in the `Capabilities` directory. Chalice will automatically include any of the Python files in `chalicelib` in the deployment package. We will use `chalicelib` to hold the Python classes that implement our private APIs.

To create the `chalicelib` package, issue the following commands:

```
cd Capabilities
mkdir chalicelib
touch chalicelib/__init__.py
cd ..
```

Note that `__init__.py` makes `chalicelib` a proper Python package.

We should have the following project directory structure:

```
Project Structure
------------
├── ObjectDetector/
    ├── Capabilities/
        ├── .chalice/
            ├── config.json
        ├── chalicelib/
            ├── __init__.py
        ├── app.py
        ├── requirements.txt
    ├── Website/
        ├── index.html
        ├── script.js
    ├── Pipfile
    ├── Pipfile.lock
```

This is the project structure for the `ObjectDetector` application. It contains all the layers of the AI application architecture we defined earlier. This project structure is also the base structure for all the hands-on projects in part 2 of this book.

Developing an AI application locally using AWS Chalice

First, let's implement the private APIs and services that provide common capabilities. We will have two services; both of them should be created in the `chalicelib` directory:

1. `StorageService`: The `StorageService` class that's implemented in the `storage_service.py` file connects to AWS S3 via `boto3` to perform tasks on files we need for the applications.

   Let's implement `StorageService`, as follows:

```
import boto3

class StorageService:
    def __init__(self, storage_location):
        self.client = boto3.client('s3')
        self.bucket_name = storage_location

    def get_storage_location(self):
        return self.bucket_name

    def list_files(self):
        response = self.client.list_objects_v2(Bucket =
self.bucket_name)

        files = []
        for content in response['Contents']:
            files.append({
                'location': self.bucket_name,
                'file_name': content['Key'],
                'url': "http://" + self.bucket_name +
".s3.amazonaws.com/" + content['Key']
            })
        return files
```

   In the class, there is currently a constructor and two methods:

   - The `__init__()` constructor takes a parameter, `storage_location`. In this implementation of `StorageService`, `storage_location` represents the S3 bucket where files will be stored. However, we purposely gave this parameter a generic name so that different implementations of `StorageService` can use other storage services besides AWS S3.

- The first method, `get_storage_location()`, just returns the S3 bucket name as `storage_location`. Other service implementations will use this method to get the generic storage location.
- The second method, `list_files()`, retrieves a list of files from an S3 bucket specified by `storage_location`. The files in this bucket are then returned as a list of Python objects. Each object describes a file, including its location, filename, and URL.

Note that we are also describing the files using more generic terms, such as location, filename, and URL, rather than bucket, key, and s3 URL. In addition, we are returning a new Python list with our own JSON format, rather than returning the available response from *boto3*. This prevents AWS implementation details from leaking out of this private API's implementation.

The design decisions in `StorageService` are made to hide the implementation details from its clients. Because we are hiding the `boto3` and S3 details, we are free to change `StorageService` so that we can use other SDKs or services to implement the file storage capabilities.

2. `RecognitionService`: The `RecognitionService` class that's implemented in the `recognition_service.py` file calls the Amazon Rekognition service via `boto3` to perform image and video analysis tasks.

   Let's implement `RecognitionService`, as follows:

```
import boto3

class RecognitionService:
    def __init__(self, storage_service):
        self.client = boto3.client('rekognition')
        self.bucket_name = storage_service.get_storage_location()

    def detect_objects(self, file_name):
        response = self.client.detect_labels(
            Image = {
                'S3Object': {
                    'Bucket': self.bucket_name,
                    'Name': file_name
                }
            }
        )

        objects = []
```

```
        for label in response["Labels"]:
            objects.append({
                'label': label['Name'],
                'confidence': label['Confidence']
            })
        return objects
```

In this class, it currently has a constructor and one method:

- The `__init__()` constructor takes in `StorageService` as a dependency to get the necessary files. This allows new implementations of `StorageService` to be injected and used by `RecognitionService`; that is, as long as the new implementations of `StorageService` implement the same API contract. This is known as the dependency injection design pattern, which makes software components more modular, reusable, and readable.
- The `detect_objects()` method takes in an image filename, including both the path and name portions, and then performs object detection on the specified image. This method implementation assumes that the image file is stored in an S3 bucket and calls Rekognition's `detect_labels()` function from the `boto3` SDK. When the labels are returned by *boto3*, this method constructs a new Python list, with each item in the list describing an object that was detected and the confidence level of the detection.

Note that, from the method's signatures (the parameters and return value), it does not expose the fact that the S3 and Rekognition services are used. This is the same information-hiding practice we used in `StorageService`.

In `RecognitionService`, we could use the `StorageService` that was passed in through the constructor to get the actual image files and perform detection on the image files. Instead, we are directly passing the image files' buckets and names through the `detect_labels()` function. This latter implementation choice takes advantage of the fact that AWS S3 and Amazon Rekognition are nicely integrated. The important point is that the private API's contract allows both implementations, and our design decision picked the latter implementation.

3. `app.py`: Next, let's implement the public APIs that are tailored for our image recognition web application. We only need one public API for the demo application. It should be implemented in the `app.py` file in the Chalice project structure.

   Replace the existing contents of `app.py` with the following code block. Let's understand the components of the class:

   - The `demo_object_detection()` function uses `StorageService` and `RecognitionService` to perform its tasks; therefore, we need to import these from `chalicelib` and create new instances of these services.
   - `storage_location` is initialized to `contents.aws.ai`, which contains the image files we uploaded in the previous chapter. You should replace `contents.aws.ai` with your own S3 bucket.
   - This function is annotated with `@app.route('/demo-object-detection', cors = True)`. This is a special construct used by Chalice to define a RESTful endpoint with a URL path called `/demo-object-detection`:
     - Chalice maps this endpoint to the `demo_object_detection()` Python function.
     - The annotation also sets `cors` to true, which enables **Cross-Origin Resource Sharing** (**CORS**) by adding certain HTTP headers to the response of this endpoint. These extra HTTP headers tell a browser to let a web application running at one origin (domain) so that it has permission to access resources from a different origin (domain, protocol, or port number) other than its own. Let's have a look at the implementations in the following class:

> The Chalice annotation syntax might look familiar to Flask developers. AWS Chalice borrows a lot of its design and syntax from the Flask framework.

```
from chalice import Chalice
from chalicelib import storage_service
from chalicelib import recognition_service

import random
```

```
#####
# chalice app configuration
#####
app = Chalice(app_name='Capabilities')
app.debug = True


#####
# services initialization
#####
storage_location = 'contents.aws.ai'
storage_service = storage_service.StorageService(storage_location)
recognition_service =
recognition_service.RecognitionService(storage_service)


@app.route('/demo-object-detection', cors = True)
def demo_object_detection():
    """randomly selects one image to demo object detection"""
    files = storage_service.list_files()
    images = [file for file in files if
file['file_name'].endswith(".jpg")]
    image = random.choice(images)

    objects =
recognition_service.detect_objects(image['file_name'])

    return {
        'imageName': image['file_name'],
        'imageUrl': image['url'],
        'objects': objects
    }
```

Let's talk about the preceding code in detail:

- The `demo_object_detection()` function gets a list of image files (files that have a `.jpg` extension) from `StorageService` and then randomly selects one of them to perform the object detection demo.
- Random selection is implemented here to simplify our demo application so that it only displays one image and its detection results.
- Once the image has been randomly selected, the function calls `detect_objects()` from `RecognitionService` and then generates an HTTP response in the **JavaScript Object Notation (JSON)** format.

- Chalice automatically wraps the response object in the proper HTTP headers, response code, and the JSON payload. The JSON format is part of the contract between our frontend and this public API.

We are ready to run and test the application's backend locally. Chalice provides a local mode, which includes a local HTTP server that you can use to test the endpoints.

4. Start the `chalice local` mode within the `pipenv` virtual environment with the following commands:

```
$ cd Capabilities
$ chalice local
Restarting local dev server.
Found credentials in shared credentials file: ~/.aws/credentials
Serving on http://127.0.0.1:8000
```

Now, the local HTTP server is running at the address and port number in the Terminal output; that is, `http://127.0.0.1:8000`. Keep in mind that even though we are running the endpoint locally, the services that the endpoint calls are making requests to AWS via the `boto3` SDK.

Chalice's local mode automatically detected the AWS credentials in the `~/.aws/credentials` file. Our service implementations, which are using `boto3`, will use the key pairs that are found there and will issue requests with the corresponding user's permissions. If this user does not have permissions for S3 or Rekognition, the request to the endpoint will fail.

5. We can now issue HTTP requests to the local server to test the `/demo-object-detection` endpoint. For example, you can use the Unix `curl` command as follows:

```
$ curl http://127.0.0.1:8000/demo-object-detection
{"imageName":"beagle_on_gravel.jpg","imageUrl":"https://contents.aw
s.ai.s3.amazonaws.com/beagle_on_gravel.jpg","objects":[{"label":"Pe
t","confidence":98.9777603149414},{"label":"Hound","confidence":98.
9777603149414},{"label":"Canine","confidence":98.9777603149414},{"l
abel":"Animal","confidence":98.9777603149414},{"label":"Dog","confi
dence":98.9777603149414},{"label":"Mammal","confidence":98.97776031
49414},{"label":"Beagle","confidence":98.0347900390625},{"label":"R
oad","confidence":82.47952270507812},{"label":"Dirt
Road","confidence":74.52912902832031},{"label":"Gravel","confidence
":74.52912902832031}]}
```

Note that, in this code, we just append the endpoint URL path to the base address and port number where the local HTTP server is running. The request should return JSON output back from the local endpoint.

This is the JSON that our web user interface will receive and use to display the detection results to the user.

Developing a demo application web user interface

Next, let's create a simple web user interface with HTML and JavaScript in the `index.html` and `script.js` files in the website directory.

Refer to the code in the `index.html` file, as follows:

```
<!doctype html>
<html lang="en"/>

<head>
    <meta charset="utf-8"/>
    <meta name="viewport" content="width=device-width, initial-scale=1.0"/>

    <title>Object Detector</title>

    <link rel="stylesheet" href="https://www.w3schools.com/w3css/4/w3.css">
    <link rel="stylesheet"
href="https://www.w3schools.com/lib/w3-theme-blue-grey.css">
</head>

<body class="w3-theme-14" onload="runDemo()">
    <div style="min-width:400px">
        <div class="w3-bar w3-large w3-theme-d4">
            <span class="w3-bar-item">Object Detector</span>
        </div>

        <div class="w3-container w3-content">
            <p class="w3-opacity"><b>Randomly Selected Demo Image</b></p>
            <div class="w3-panel w3-white w3-card w3-display-container"
                style="overflow: hidden">
                <div style="float: left;">
                    <img id="image" width="600"/>
                </div>
                <div id="objects" style="float: right;">
                    <h5>Objects Detected:</h5>
```

```
                </div>
            </div>
        </div>
    </div>

    <script src="scripts.js"></script>
</body>

</html>
```

We are using standard HTML tags here, so the code of the web page should be easy to follow for anyone familiar with HTML. A few things worth pointing out are as follows:

- We are including a couple of **Cascading Style Sheets** (**CSS**) from `www.w3schools.com` to make our web interface a bit prettier than plain HTML. Most of the classes in the HTML tags are defined in these style sheets.
- The `<img>` tag with the `image` ID will be used to display the randomly selected demo image. This ID will be used by JavaScript to add the image dynamically.
- The `<div>` tag with the `objects` ID will be used to display the objects that were detected in the demo image. This ID will also be used by JavaScript to add the object labels and confidence levels dynamically.
- The `scripts.js` file is included toward the bottom of the HTML file. This adds the dynamic behaviors that were implemented in JavaScript to this HTML page.
- The `runDemo()` function from `scripts.js` is run when the HTML page is loaded in a browser. This is accomplished in the `index.html` page's `<body>` tag with the `onload` attribute.

Please refer to the code of the `scripts.js` file, as follows:

```
"use strict";

const serverUrl = "http://127.0.0.1:8000";

function runDemo() {
    fetch(serverUrl + "/demo-object-detection", {
        method: "GET"
    }).then(response => {
        if (!response.ok) {
            throw response;
        }
        return response.json();
    }).then(data => {
        let imageElem = document.getElementById("image");
        imageElem.src = data.imageUrl;
        imageElem.alt = data.imageName;
```

```
            let objectsElem = document.getElementById("objects");
            let objects = data.objects;
            for (let i = 0; i < objects.length; i++) {
                let labelElem = document.createElement("h6");
                labelElem.appendChild(document.createTextNode(
                    objects[i].label + ": " + objects[i].confidence + "%")
                );
                objectsElem.appendChild(document.createElement("hr"));
                objectsElem.appendChild(labelElem);
            }
        }).catch(error => {
            alert("Error: " + error);
        });
    }
```

Let's talk about the preceding code in detail:

- The script has only one function, `runDemo()`. This function makes an HTTP `GET` request to the `/demo-object-detection` endpoint running on the local HTTP server via the Fetch API that's available in JavaScript.
- If the response from the local endpoint is `ok`, then it converts the payload into a JSON object and passes it down to the next processing block.
- The `runDemo()` function then looks for an HTML element with the `image` ID, which is the `<img>` tag in HTML, and specifies the `src` attribute as the `imageUrl` returned by the endpoint. Remember, this `imageUrl` is set to the URL of the image file stored in S3. The `<img>` tag's `alt` attribute is set to `imageName`. `imageName` will be displayed to the user if the image cannot be loaded for some reason.
- Note that the image in S3 must be set to public readable in order for the website to display it. If you only see the `alt` text, double-check that the image is readable by the public.
- The `runDemo()` function then looks for an HTML element with the `objects` ID, which is a `<div>` tag, and appends a `<h6>` heading element for each object returned by the local endpoint, including each object's label and detection confidence level.

Now, we are ready to see this website in action. To run the website locally, simply open the `index.html` file in your browser. You should see a web page similar to the following screenshot:

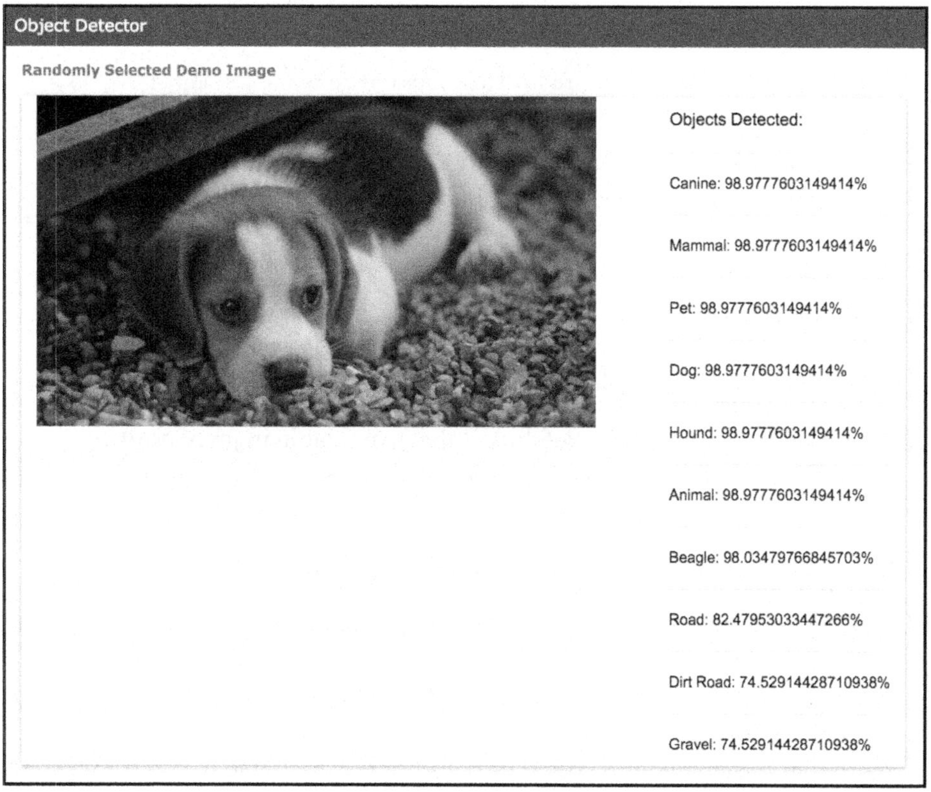

Upload a few JPEG image files and refresh the page a few times to see the object detection demo run; the demo will select a different image that's stored in your S3 bucket each time it runs. The `ObjectDetector` application is not as fancy as the Amazon Rekognition demo, but pat yourself on the back for creating a well-architected AI application!

The local HTTP server will run continuously unless you explicitly stop it. To stop the local HTTP server, go to the Terminal window that's running `chalice local` and press *Ctrl* + *C*.

The final project structure for the `ObjectDetector` application should look as follows:

```
Project Organization
------------
├── ObjectDetector/
```

```
├── Capabilities/
    ├── .chalice/
        ├── config.json
    ├── chalicelib/
        ├── __init__.py
        ├── recognition_service.py
        ├── storage_service.py
    ├── app.py
    ├── requirements.txt
├── Website/
    ├── index.html
    ├── script.js
├── Pipfile
├── Pipfile.lock
```

It's now time to make our AI application public and deploy it to the AWS cloud.

Deploying AI application backends to AWS via Chalice

Deployment to AWS with Chalice is amazingly simple yet powerful. Chalice automatically translates the endpoint annotations in `app.py` into HTTP endpoints and deploys them onto the Amazon API Gateway as public APIs. Chalice also deploys the Python code in `app.py` and `chalicelib` as AWS Lambda functions and then connects the API gateway endpoints as triggers to these Lambda functions. This simplicity is the reason why we chose a serverless framework such as AWS Chalice to develop our hands-on projects.

When we ran the backend locally, Chalice automatically detected the AWS credentials in our development environment and made them available to the application. Which credentials will the application use when it is running in AWS? Chalice automatically creates an AWS IAM role for the application during the deployment process. Then, the application will run with the permissions that have been granted to this role. Chalice can automatically detect the necessary permissions, but this feature is considered experimental at the time of writing and does not work well with our projects' structures. For our projects, we need to tell Chalice to *not* perform this analysis for us by setting `autogen_policy` to `false` in the `config.json` file in the `.chalice` directory of the project structure. The following is the `config.json` file:

```
{
    "version": "2.0",
    "app_name": "Capabilities",
    "stages": {
        "dev": {
```

```
                "autogen_policy": false,
                "api_gateway_stage": "api"
            }
        }
    }
```

> Note that, in this configuration, there is a `dev` stage in `config.json`. Chalice provides us with the ability to deploy our application in multiple environments. Different environments are used by mature software organizations to perform various software life cycle tasks, such as testing and maintenance in an isolated manner. For example, we have the development (`dev`) environment for rapid experimentation, quality assurance (`qa`) for integration testing, user acceptance testing (`uat`) for business requirement validation, performance (`prof`) for stress testing, and product (`prod`) for live traffic from end users.

Next, we need to create a new file, `policy-dev.json`, in the `.chalice` directory to manually specify the AWS services the project needs:

```
    {
        "Version": "2012-10-17",
            "Statement": [
            {
                "Effect": "Allow",
                "Action": [
                    "logs:CreateLogGroup",
                    "logs:CreateLogStream",
                    "logs:PutLogEvents",
                    "s3:*",
                    "rekognition:*"
                ],
                "Resource": "*"
            }
        ]
    }
```

Here, we are specifying S3 and Rekognition, in addition to some permissions to allow the project to push logs to CloudWatch.

Now, we are ready to deploy the backend on the AWS Chalice framework:

1. Run the following command within the `Capabilities` directory:

```
$ chalice deploy
Creating deployment package.
Creating IAM role: Capabilities-dev
```

```
Creating lambda function: Capabilities-dev
Creating Rest API
Resources deployed:
  - Lambda ARN: arn:aws:lambda:us-
east-1:<UID>:function:Capabilities-dev
  - Rest API URL:
https://<UID>.execute-api.us-east-1.amazonaws.com/api/
```

When the deployment is complete, in the output, Chalice will show a RESTful API URL that looks similar to `https://<UID>.execute-api.us-east-1.amazonaws.com/api/`, where `<UID>` is a unique identifier string. This is the server URL your frontend app should hit to access the application backend running on AWS.

> You can now verify the results of the Chalice deployment in the AWS Management Console under three services:
>
> - Amazon API Gateway
> - AWS Lambda
> - Identity and Access Management
>
> Take a look at the console pages of these services and see what AWS Chalice has set up for our application.

2. Use the `curl` command to test the remote endpoint, as follows. You should get similar output to when we were testing with the local endpoint:

```
$ curl
https://<UID>.execute-api.us-east-1.amazonaws.com/api/demo-object-d
etection
{"imageName":"beagle_on_gravel.jpg","imageUrl":"https://contents.aw
s.ai.s3.amazonaws.com/beagle_on_gravel.jpg","objects":[{"label":"Pe
t","confidence":98.9777603149414},{"label":"Hound","confidence":98.
9777603149414},{"label":"Canine","confidence":98.9777603149414},{"l
abel":"Animal","confidence":98.9777603149414},{"label":"Dog","confi
dence":98.9777603149414},{"label":"Mammal","confidence":98.97776031
49414},{"label":"Beagle","confidence":98.0347900390625},{"label":"R
oad","confidence":82.47952270507812},{"label":"Dirt
Road","confidence":74.52912902832031},{"label":"Gravel","confidence
":74.52912902832031}]}
```

Congratulations! You've just deployed a serverless backend for an AI application that is highly available and scalable, running in the cloud.

Deploying a static website via AWS S3

Next, let's deploy the frontend web user interface to AWS S3.

One of the buckets we created in the previous chapter was for the purpose of website hosting. Let's configure it via the AWS Management Console for static website hosting:

1. Navigate to the **Amazon S3** service in the management console and click on your bucket.
2. In the **Properties** tab, as shown in the following screenshot, click on the **Static website hosting** card:

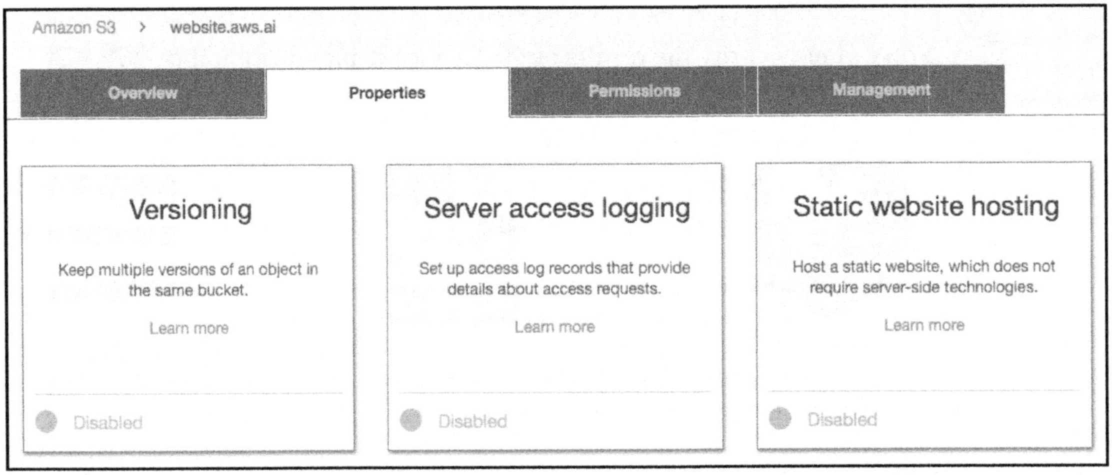

3. When you click on the **Static website hosting** card, a configuration card will pop up.
4. Select **Use this bucket to host a website** and enter `index.html` and `error.html` for the **Index document** and **Error document** fields, respectively.

5. Copy the **Endpoint** URL on your configuration page and then click **Save**. This endpoint URL will be the public address of your static website:

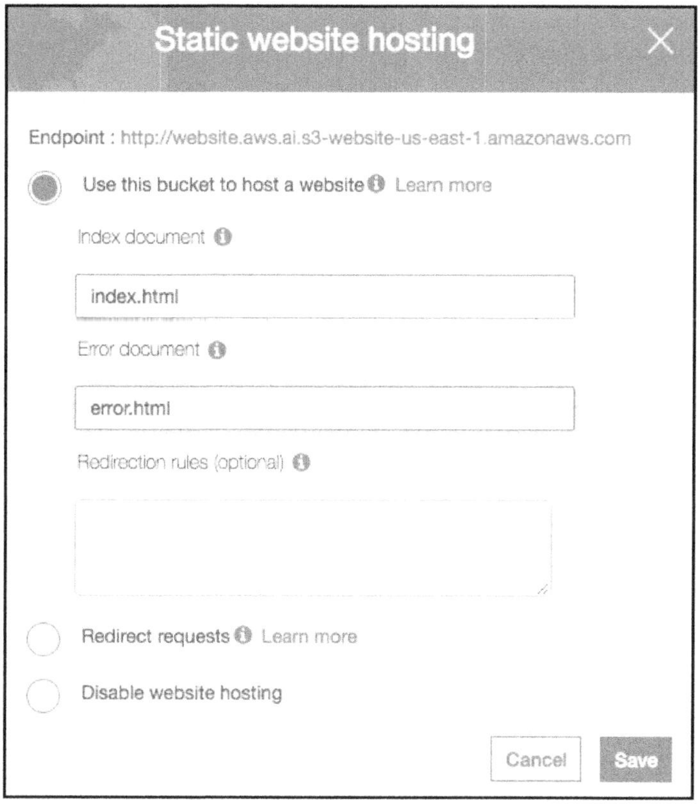

6. Next, we can upload the `index.html` and `scripts.js` files to this S3 bucket. Before we do that, we need to make a change in `scripts.js`. Remember, the website will be running in the cloud now, and won't have access to our local HTTP server.

7. Replace the local server URL in the `scripts.js` file with the one from our backend deployment, as follows:

```
"use strict";

const serverUrl =
"https://<UID>.execute-api.us-east-1.amazonaws.com/api";
...
```

8. Finally, set the permissions of the `index.html` and `scripts.js` files to publicly readable. To do that, we need to modify the S3 bucket permissions under the **Permissions** tab.
9. Click on the **Public access settings** button, uncheck all four checkboxes, and then type `confirm` to confirm these changes. This will allow the contents of this S3 bucket to be made publicly accessible, as follows:

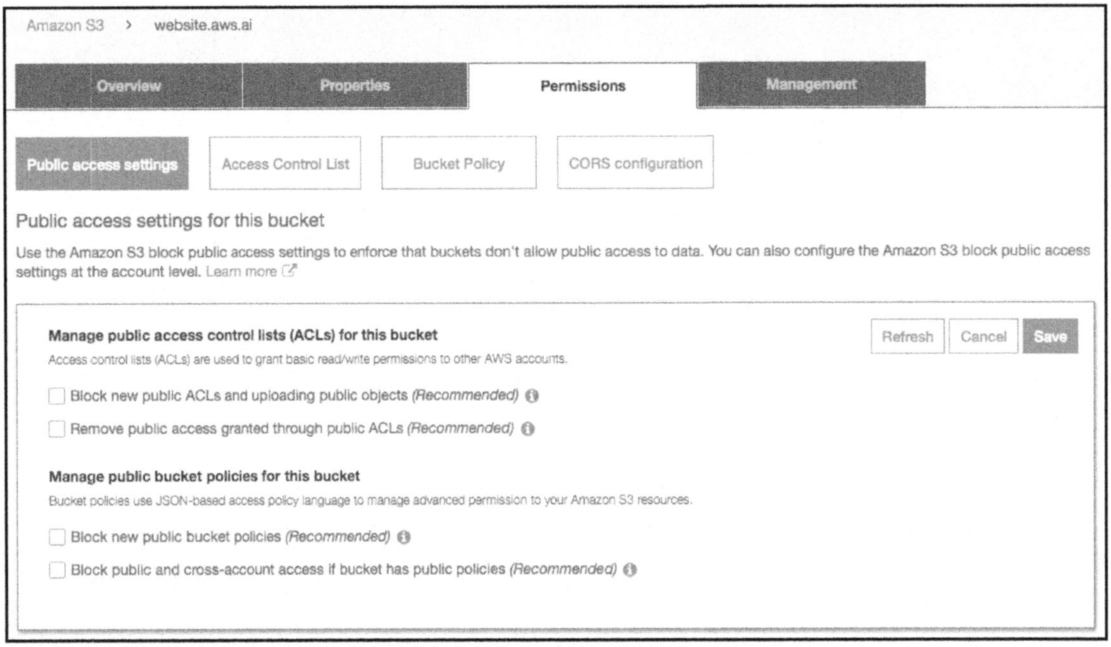

10. Now, we are able to make the files public by selecting both files, clicking on **Actions**, and clicking on **Make public**, as shown in the following screenshot:

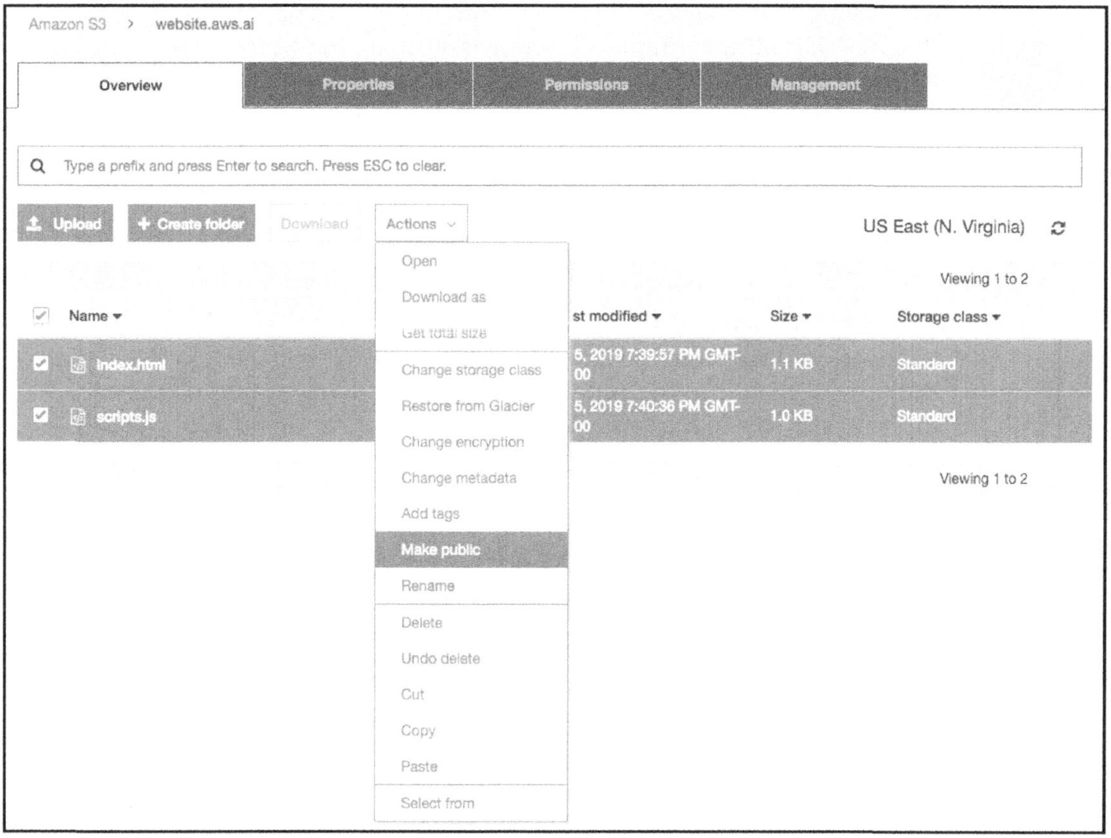

Open the S3 endpoint URL in your browser. The URL should look something like http://<BUCKET>.s3-website-us-east-1.amazonaws.com/.

Your ObjectDetector website is now running in your browser and it's communicating with the backend running on AWS to demo your intelligent-enabled application's capability. Both the frontend and the backend are serverless and both are running on the AWS cloud infrastructure, which scales automatically with demand.

Congratulations! You've just developed an end-to-end AI application to AWS! You can now share this AI application with anyone in the world with a browser.

Even though your new AWS account might have free-tier services, you should still limit the number of people you share the website URL and API endpoints with. You will be charged if the AWS resources that are consumed exceed the amount that's covered under the free-tier plan.

Summary

In this chapter, we discussed the importance of good architecture design for artificial intelligence applications. We created a reference architecture design for web applications that will be the template for all of our hands-on projects in part 2 of this book. Using this reference architecture, we recreated the Amazon Rekognition demo application using several AWS tools and services in the serverless style. We built the demo application's backend with AWS Chalice and *boto3* and leveraged AWS S3 and Amazon Rekognition to provide the business capabilities. Through the hands-on project, we showed you how architecture boundaries and good design allow for flexible application development and evolution. We also built a simple web user interface for the demo application with HTML, CSS, and JavaScript. Finally, we deployed the demo application as a serverless application to the AWS cloud.

Now that we have experience building a simple yet elegant intelligent-enabled application, we are ready to use the same architecture template and toolset to build more AI applications in part 2 of this book.

Further reading

You can refer to the following links for more information on the anatomy of a modern AI application:

- `http://www.cs.nott.ac.uk/~pszcah/G51ISS/Documents/NoSilverBullet.html`
- `https://developer.mozilla.org/en-US/docs/Web/HTTP/CORS`

2

Section 2: Building Applications with AWS AI Services

In this section, AWS offers a plethora of managed AI services that can be leveraged by applications without the efforts to gather and clean the training data, train and tune the custom models, and host and maintain the trained models. AWS has done the heavy lifting in these AI services. You will be able to design, develop, and deploy production-ready AI solutions quickly and bring them to market with speed. We will provide you not only with an in-depth understanding of these services, but also how best to integrate with them in the AI solutions for optimal speed of experimentation, architecture flexibility, and long-term maintenance.

This section comprises the following chapters:

- `Chapter 3`, *Detecting and Translating Text with Amazon Rekognition and Amazon Translate*
- `Chapter 4`, *Performing Speech-to-Text and Vice Versa with Amazon Transcribe and Amazon Polly*
- `Chapter 5`, *Extracting Information from Text with Amazon Comprehend*
- `Chapter 6`, *Building a Voice Chatbot with AWS Lex*

3
Detecting and Translating Text with Amazon Rekognition and Translate

In this chapter, we will build our first **Artificial Intelligence** (**AI**) application that solves a real-world problem, as opposed to a theoretical demonstration. We will build an application that can translate foreign texts appearing in pictures. We will do this by combining two AWS AI services, Amazon Rekognition and Amazon Translate. The application will use the reference architecture introduced in the previous chapter. In this hands-on project, not only will we be building intelligent capabilities for the current application, we will also be designing them to be reusable components that we can leverage in future hands-on projects.

We will cover the following topics:

- Detecting text in images with Amazon Rekognition
- Translating text using Amazon Translate
- Embedding intelligent capabilities into applications
- Building serverless AI applications with AWS services, RESTful APIs, and web user interface
- Discussing good design practices and build intelligent capabilities as reusable components

Making the world smaller

In this section of the book, we will start building intelligence-enabled solutions through hands-on projects. These projects will not only get you familiar with Amazon's AI services, they will also help you to strengthen your intuition on how to embed intelligent capabilities into applications to solve real-world problems. We'll start with an application that can make the world smaller.

When Google revealed a new feature in its Google Lens mobile app, users could just point their phones at something around their environment and get more information about it. Google Lens essentially brought search capabilities into the real world. One particular use case of this app was the real-time language translation of text. Users can point their camera at a street sign or a restaurant menu and get the translation back as an augmented reality camera feed on the phone's display. This feature alone can make the world more accessible to everyone.

We will be implementing this pictorial translation feature for our hands-on project with AWS AI services. Our application, we'll call it Pictorial Translator, will provide similar translation capabilities, albeit with a much less embellished user interface than Google Lens.

Understanding the architecture of Pictorial Translator

Following the architecture template defined in `Chapter 2`, *Anatomy of a Modern AI Application*, here is the architectural design for Pictorial Translator:

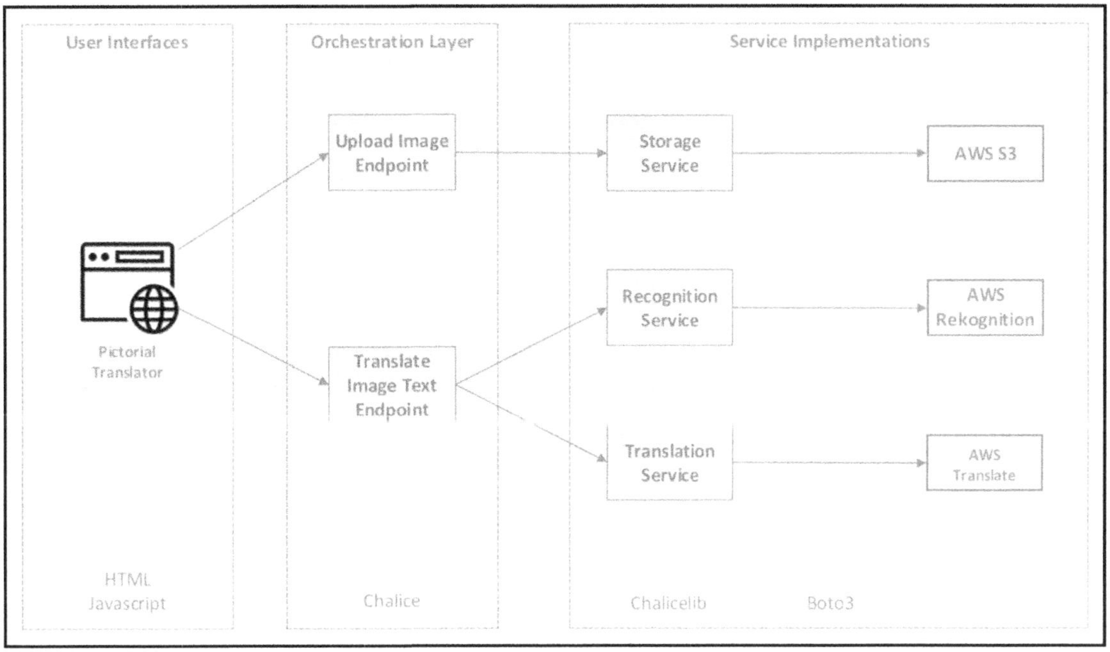

We will provide a web user interface for users to upload photos containing foreign text and then view the translation of the foreign text. The web user interface will interact with the **Orchestration Layer** containing two RESTful endpoints to handle the image upload and translation:

- **Upload Image Endpoint** will delegate the image upload to our **Storage Service**:
    - **Storage Service** provides an abstraction layer to **AWS S3**, where the uploaded photos will be stored, processed, and displayed from.
- **Translate Image Text Endpoint** will delegate the detection of text within the photos to our **Recognition Service** and the translation of the detected text to our **Translation Service**:
    - The **Recognition Service** provides an abstraction layer to the Amazon Rekognition service, more specifically, the text detection capability of Rekognition. We named our service **Recognition**, which is more generic and doesn't directly tie us in with **AWS Rekognition**.
    - The **Translation Service** provides an abstraction layer to the Amazon Translate service to perform the language translation.

The **Service Implememntation** might seem redundant to some readers. Why not just have the endpoints talk to the AWS services directly instead of talking through another layer of abstraction? There are many benefits to architecting the application this way. Here are a few examples:

- During development time, we can more easily build and test the application without dependency on AWS services. Any stub or mock implementation of these services can be used during development for speed, cost, and experimentation reasons. This lets us develop and iterate the application faster.
- When other services that provide better storage, recognition, or translation capabilities come along, our application can switch to those capabilities by swapping to a new service implementation with the same abstraction interface. The user interface and the endpoints will not need to be modified to leverage these better capabilities. This gives our application more flexibility to adapt to changes.
- This makes our code base more composable and reusable. The capabilities provided by these AWS services can be reused by other applications. These services are modular packages that can be more easily reused than the orchestration endpoints. The orchestration endpoints usually contain application-specific business logic that limits reuse.

Component interactions of Pictorial Translator

It's important to think through how the components of an application interact with each other and how the user experience will be influenced by our design choices before we dive into the implementation:

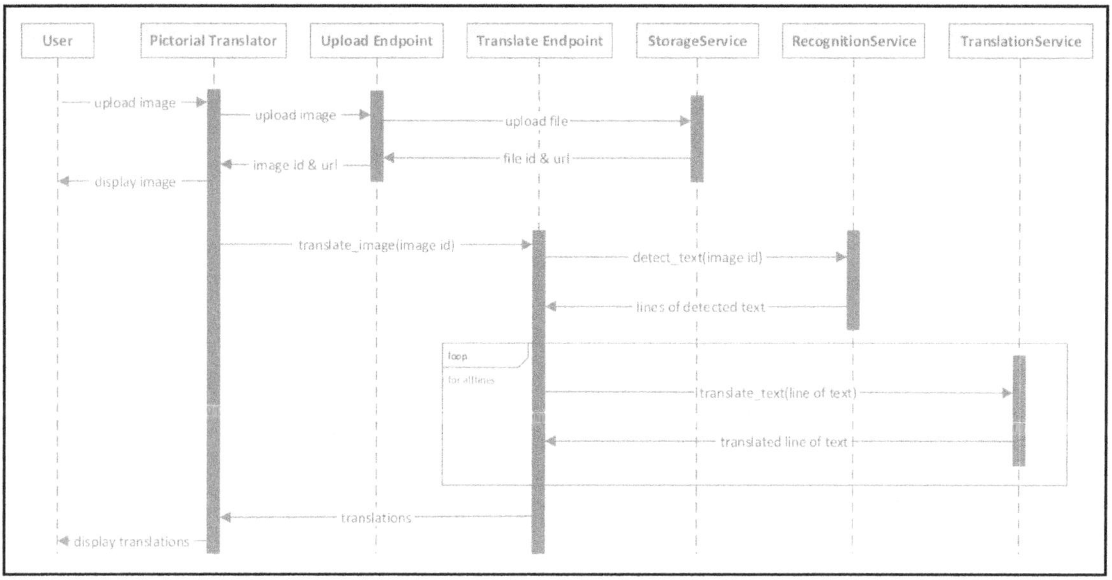

From the user's perspective, the application provides a sequential experience for uploading the image, viewing the uploaded images, and seeing the translated text. We made the design decision to ensure the user waits for each photo to be uploaded and processed (as opposed to bulk uploading many photos at once). This design decision is fine for our application, given our use case assumes that the users are at the physical locations waiting to see the translations before making decisions or taking actions.

Our Pictorial Translator application's interaction with the Upload Image Endpoint and `StorageService` is straightforward. The users' requests is essentially passed through to AWS S3 and back in a chain. Of course, the fact that the storage capability is provided by AWS S3 is shielded from both the endpoint and the application through the layers of abstraction. The photos will be stored in an S3 bucket, and the text detection and translation will be performed from the S3 bucket.

The translate image text endpoint simplifies some business logic from the Pictorial Translator application. Pictorial Translator is only sending the image ID to the translate image text endpoint and then receiving the translation for every line of text in the image. The translate image text endpoint does a couple of things behind the scenes. This endpoint is calling `detect_text()` in `RecognitionService` on the entire image, and then calling `translate_text()` in Translation Service multiple times for the lines of detected text. The endpoint will only call the Translation Service if the detected line of text meets a minimum confidence threshold.

Here, we made two design decisions:

- First, we translate text at the line level. The thinking is that the text we see in the real world is not always in the same context (for example, multiple street signs in the same photo) or even in the same language. The real-world results of this design decision need to be closely monitored in order to validate its user experience.
- Second, we only translate a line of text that `RecognitionService` is very confident about. The real world is messy, the user might upload photos containing text that's not relevant to the translation task (for example, street signs in a distance), or the user might upload photos not fit for quality text detection (for example, poor lighting and bad focus). We don't want to inundate the user with inaccurate translations, so our application took the approach to only translate high-quality text in the photos.

These are examples of design decisions AI practitioners should evaluate and validate when developing an intelligence-enabled application. Having a flexible architecture allows you to move through the iterations much faster.

Setting up the project structure

Let's create a similar base project structure with the steps outlined in `Chapter 2`, *Anatomy of a Modern AI Application*, including `pipenv`, `chalice`, and the web files:

1. In the terminal, we will create the `root` project directory and enter the following commands:

```
$ mkdir PictorialTranslator
$ cd PictorialTranslator
```

2. We will create placeholders for the web frontend by creating a directory named `Website` and, within this directory, create two files `index.html` and `scripts.js`:

```
$ mkdir Website
$ touch Website/index.html
$ touch Website/scripts.js
```

3. We will create a Python 3 virtual environment with `pipenv` in the project's `root` directory. Our Python portion of the project needs two packages, `boto3` and `chalice`. We can install them with the following commands:

```
$ pipenv --three
$ pipenv install boto3
$ pipenv install chalice
```

4. Remember that the Python packages installed via `pipenv` are only available if we activate the virtual environment. One way to do this is with the following command:

```
$ pipenv shell
```

5. Next, while still in the virtual environment, we will create the orchestration layer as an AWS `chalice` project named `Capabilities` with the following commands:

```
$ chalice new-project Capabilities
```

6. To create the `chalicelib` Python package, issue the following commands:

```
cd Capabilities
mkdir chalicelib
touch chalicelib/__init__.py
cd ..
```

The project structure for Pictorial Translator should look like the following:

```
Project Structure
------------
├── PictorialTranslator/
    ├── Capabilities/
        ├── .chalice/
            ├── config.json
        ├── chalicelib/
            ├── __init__.py
        ├── app.py
        ├── requirements.txt
    ├── Website/
        ├── index.html
        ├── script.js
    ├── Pipfile
    ├── Pipfile.lock
```

This is the project structure for Pictorial Translator. It contains the user interface, orchestration, and service implementation layers of the AI application architecture that we defined in `Chapter 2`, *Anatomy of a Modern AI Application*.

Implementing services

Now that we know what we are building, let's implement this application layer by layer, starting with the service implementations.

Recognition service – text detection

We are going to leverage the Amazon Rekognition service to provide the capability to detect text in an image. Let's first take a test drive of this capability using the AWS CLI. We will use a photo of a German street sign:

The source of the preceding photo is `https://www.freeimages.com/photo/german-one-way-street-sign-3-1446112`.

Since we will be using S3 to hold the photos, let's first upload this photo to an S3 bucket we created in `Chapter 1`, *Introduction to Artificial Intelligence on Amazon Web Services*. For instance, we will be uploading the image to our `contents.aws.ai` bucket. Once uploaded, to perform text detection on a photo with the name `german_street_sign.jpg` with the AWS CLI, issue the following command:

```
$ aws rekognition detect-text --image
S3Object=\{Bucket=contents.aws.ai,Name=german_street_sign.jpg\}
{
    "TextDetections": [
```

```
        {
            "DetectedText": "Einbahnstrabe",
            "Type": "LINE",
            "Id": 0,
            "Confidence": 99.16583251953125,
            "Geometry": {
                "BoundingBox": {
                    "Width": 0.495918333530426,
                    "Height": 0.06301824748516083,
                    "Left": 0.3853428065776825,
                    "Top": 0.4955403208732605
                },
                "Polygon": [
                    ...
                ]
            }
        },
        {
            "DetectedText": "Einbahnstrabe",
            "Type": "WORD",
            "Id": 1,
            "ParentId": 0,
            ...
        }
    ]
}
```

AWS CLI is a handy tool for examining the output formats of AWS services:

- Here, we see a JSON output from the text detection, with portions of the output truncated here for brevity.
- At the top level, we have an object surrounded by curly brackets, { and }. Within this top level object, we have a name-value pair with the name being `TextDetections` and the value being an array surrounded by square brackets, [and].
- Within this array are zero or more objects describing the detected texts. Looking at the detected text objects within the array, we see information such as `DetectedText`, `Type`, `Id`, `Confidence`, and `Geometry`.

In our photo, we have only one word. However, Rekognition returned two objects in the `TextDetections` array. That's because Rekognition returns two types of `DetectedText` as objects, `LINE` of text as well as all the `WORD` objects in that `LINE` of text as separate objects. The two objects we got back represent the `LINE` as well as the single `WORD` in that line. Notice the types of the two objects are different, and the ParentId of the second object (`WORD`) refers to `Id` of the first object (`LINE`), showing the parent/child relationship between lines and words.

We also see the `Confidence` level of the text detection we will use this later to filter which lines of text to translate. Rekognition is very confident with the word `Einbahnstrabe`, which has a `Confidence` score of `99.16583251953125`, with 100 being the maximum.

The `Geometry` name/value pair contains two systems to describe the location of the detected text in the image:

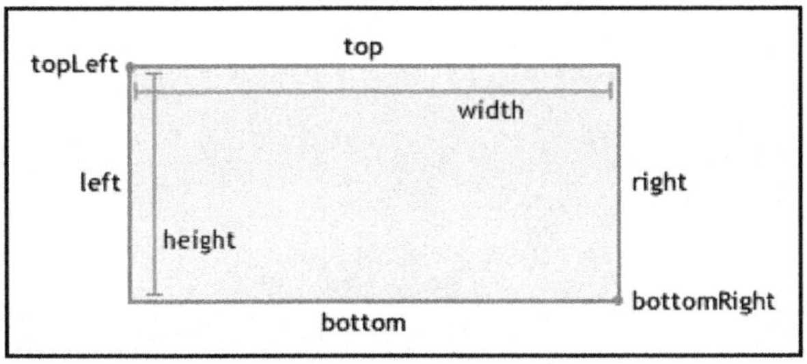

The previous diagrams explained the following:

- `BoundingBox` describes a coarse rectangle where the text is located. This system describes the `BoundingBox` with the coordinates of the top-left point of the rectangle, and the width and the height of the rectangle.
- These coordinates and measurements are all given in ratios for the image. For example, if the image is 700 x 200 pixels and the service returned left == 0.5 and top == 0.25, then the top-left point of the rectangle is at pixels (350, 50); 700 x 0.5 = 350 and 200 x 0.25 = 50.
- `Polygon` describes a set of points within the `BoundingBox` that gives a fine-grained polygon around the detected text. The *x* and y coordinates of each point are also using the same ratio system of the `BoundingBox` coordinates.

The information provided in `Geometry` is useful for tasks such as highlighting the text in the image or even overlaying other information on top of the image.

> Rekognition text detection seems to work well with alphabet-based languages such as English, German, and French, but doesn't work as well with character-based languages such as Chinese, Korean, and Japanese. This definitely limits the use cases of the application.

With these insights to the text detection output, let's implement our `RecognitionService`. Let's create a Python class named `RecognitionService` as shown in the following `recognition_service.py` file located in the `chalicelib` directory:

```
import boto3

class RecognitionService:
    def __init__(self, storage_service):
        self.client = boto3.client('rekognition')
        self.bucket_name = storage_service.get_storage_location()

    def detect_text(self, file_name):
        response = self.client.detect_text(
            Image = {
                'S3Object': {
                    'Bucket': self.bucket_name,
                    'Name': file_name
                }
            }
        )
        lines = []
        for detection in response['TextDetections']:
            if detection['Type'] == 'LINE':
                lines.append({
                    'text': detection['DetectedText'],
                    'confidence': detection['Confidence'],
                    'boundingBox': detection['Geometry']['BoundingBox']
                })

        return lines
```

In the preceding code, the following applies:

- The constructor, `__init__()`, creates a `boto3` client for the Rekognition service. The constructor also takes in a parameter for `storage_location` as the S3 bucket name in our implementation.
- The `detect_text()` method calls the `boto3` Rekognition client's `detect_text()` function and passes in the S3 bucket name and file key for the image. The `detect_text()` method then processes the output in the `TextDetections` array:
    - Here, we are only keeping the `LINE` detected text type and for each line we are storing the `DetectedText`, Confidence objects, and the `BoundingBox` coordinates.
    - Any client using the `detect_text()` method of the RecognitionService's will expect these pieces of information to be returned as a Python list with dictionaries (a key-value mapping) as `text`, `confidence`, and `boundingBox`.

Here, we adapted the AWS SDK input and output formats to our own `RecognitionService` interface contract. The rest of our application will expect the method parameters and return type of our `RecognitionService`. We essentially implemented the adapter design pattern. Even if we swap the AWS Rekognition service for a different one, as long as we adapt the new service to our interface contract, our application can interact with the new service without further modifications.

There are two ways to specify the image for text detection:

- One way is to provide an `S3Object` with the bucket name and object key.
- The other way is to provide the raw bits of the image.

For our application, the `S3Object` way works better.

Translation service – translating text

We are going to leverage the Amazon Translate service to provide the language translation capability. Again, let's take a test drive with this capability using the AWS CLI first. To perform a quick translation, let's copy the detected text from the previous section, `Einbahnstrabe` and issue the following command:

```
$ aws translate translate-text --text "Einbahnstrabe" --source-language-
code auto --target-language-code en
{
```

```
        "TranslatedText": "One way",
        "SourceLanguageCode": "de",
        "TargetLanguageCode": "en"
    }
```

We used `auto` as the source language; this tells Amazon Translate to automatically determine the language of the text. For the target language, we selected `en` for English.

The output of the Amazon Translate service is quite simple, it's just a JSON object with three name/value pairs. As we can see, Amazon Translate correctly determined `Einbahnstrabe` is a German word and its English translation is One way. This must be a photo of a `One Way` traffic sign.

TIP

The `auto` value for the source language is handy. However, there are situations where the source language cannot be determined with a high level of confidence. In those situations, AWS will throw a `DetectedLanguageLowConfidenceException`. This exception will contain the most likely source language. If your application can tolerate this low confidence, you can issue the translation request again with the source language specified in the exception.

Amazon Translate supports translation between numerous languages, and the list is growing. However, at the time of writing this book, there are still language pairs that are not supported. Check the AWS document on supported language pairs (`https://docs.aws.amazon.com/translate/latest/dg/pairs.html`) for the latest. If a request is issued to translate a language pair that's not supported, the AWS will throw an `UnsupportedLanguagePairException`.

Let's create a Python class named `TranslationService` as shown in the following, `translation_service.py` file located in the `chalicelib` directory:

```
import boto3

class TranslationService:
    def __init__(self):
        self.client = boto3.client('translate')

    def translate_text(self, text, source_language = 'auto',
target_language = 'en'):
        response = self.client.translate_text(
            Text = text,
            SourceLanguageCode = source_language,
            TargetLanguageCode = target_language
        )
```

```
        translation = {
            'translatedText': response['TranslatedText'],
            'sourceLanguage': response['SourceLanguageCode'],
            'targetLanguage': response['TargetLanguageCode']
        }

        return translation
```

In the preceding code, the following applies:

- The constructor, `__init__()`, creates a `boto3` client or is being sent to the Translate service.
- The `translate_text()` method calls the `boto3` Translate client's `translate_text()` function and passes in the text, source language, and target language. This method's `source_language` and `target_language` parameters have default values of `auto` and `en`, respectively.
- The `translate_text()` function then processes the output from the AWS SDK and returns as a Python dictionary with the `translatedText`, `sourceLanguage`, and `targetLanguage` keys. Once again, we adapted the AWS SDK input and output formats to our own *X* interface contract.

Amazon Translate service supports the concept of custom terminology. This feature allows developers to set up custom terminology to use during translation. This is useful for use cases where words and phrases in the source text are not part of the standard language such as company names, brands, and products. For example, "Packt" does not get translated correctly. To correct the translation, we can create a custom terminology in our AWS account by uploading a **Comma-Separated Values** (**CSV**) file with a mapping of "Packt" and to how it should be translated in various languages, as shown in the following:

```
en,fr,de,es
Packt, Packt, Packt, Packt
```

During translation, we can specify one or more of these custom terminologies with the TerminologyNames parameter. See the AWS documentation, `https://docs.aws.amazon.com/translate/latest/dg/how-custom-terminology.html, for more details.`

Storage service – uploading files

Let's create a Python class named `StorageService` as shown in the following, in the `storage_service.py` file located in the `chalicelib` directory:

```
import boto3

class StorageService:
    def __init__(self, storage_location):
        self.client = boto3.client('s3')
        self.bucket_name = storage_location

    def get_storage_location(self):
        return self.bucket_name

    def upload_file(self, file_bytes, file_name):
        self.client.put_object(Bucket = self.bucket_name,
                               Body = file_bytes,
                               Key = file_name,
                               ACL = 'public-read')

        return {'fileId': file_name,
                'fileUrl': "http://" + self.bucket_name +
".s3.amazonaws.com/" + file_name}
```

In the preceding code, the following applies:

- The constructor, `__init__()`, creates a `boto3` client or is being sent to the S3 service. The constructor also takes in a parameter for `storage_location` as the S3 bucket name in our implementation.
- The `get_storage_location()` method returns the S3 bucket name as the `storage_location`.
- The `upload_file()` method takes in the raw bytes of the file to be uploaded and the filename. This method then calls the `boto3` S3 client's `put_object()` function and passes in the bucket name, the raw bytes, key, and **Access Control List (ACL)** parameter.
- The first three parameters of `upload_file()` are self-explanatory. The ACL parameter specifies that the file will be publicly readable after it has been uploaded to the S3 bucket. Since the S3 bucket can serve static assets such as images and files, we will use S3 to serve the image in our web user interface.
- Our `upload_file()` method then returns the filename along with a URL to the uploaded file in S3. Since the ACL is set to `public-read`, anyone with this URL can see this file on the internet.

This class and its first two methods are exactly the same as `StorageService` we implemented in `Chapter 2`, *Anatomy of a Modern AI Application*. We are duplicating them here to make each hands-on project self-contained, but we are essentially just adding the `upload_file()` method to the `Chapter 2`, *Anatomy of a Modern AI Application*, `StorageService` implementation.

A recommendation on unit testing

Even though unit testing is beyond the scope of this book, we want to make a strong recommendation that you make writing unit tests a habit when developing applications that are intelligence-enabled or otherwise. Unit tests should be written for every layer of the application. Unit tests should be run often to execute functionalities and to catch bugs. Testing the application layer by layer will reduce the debugging time and effort by limiting the search space for the bugs. We wrote unit tests throughout the development of all hands-on projects in this book. As an example, the following is a unit test we wrote for `TranslationService`:

```
return files
import os, sys
import unittest

from chalicelib import translation_service

class TranslationServiceTest(unittest.TestCase):
    def setUp(self):
        self.service = translation_service.TranslationService()

    def test_translate_text(self):
        translation = self.service.translate_text('Einbahnstrabe')
        self.assertTrue(translation)
        self.assertEqual('de', translation['sourceLanguage'])
        self.assertEqual('One way', translation['translatedText'])

if __name__ == "__main__":
    unittest.main()
```

This is a simple unit test, but it allowed us to ensure the text translation is working before moving to the next layer. If something doesn't work in the application, we have some assurance that it is not caused by this service implementation.

Implementing RESTful endpoints

Now that the services are implemented, let's move to the orchestration layer with the RESTful endpoints.

Replace the contents of `app.py` in the `Chalice` project with the following code:

```
from chalice import Chalice
from chalicelib import storage_service
from chalicelib import recognition_service
from chalicelib import translation_service

#####
# chalice app configuration
#####
app = Chalice(app_name='Capabilities')
app.debug = True

#####
# services initialization
#####
storage_location = 'contents.aws.ai'
storage_service = storage_service.StorageService(storage_location)
recognition_service =
recognition_service.RecognitionService(storage_service)
translation_service = translation_service.TranslationService()

#####
# RESTful endpoints
#####
...
```

In the preceding code, the following applies:

- The first four lines of code handle the imports for `chalice` as well as our three services.
- The next two lines of code declare the `chalice` app with the name `Capabilities`, and turn on the debug flag. The `debug` flag tells chalice to output more useful information, which is helpful during development. You can turn this flag to `False` when deploying the application to production.
- The next four lines of code define the `storage_location` parameter as our S3 bucket, and then instantiate our storage, recognition, and translation services. The `storage_location` parameter should be replaced with your S3 bucket name.

Keep in mind that the `storage_location` parameter is more generic than an S3 bucket name. This parameter for both `StorageService` and `RecognitionService` can represent storage locations other than S3 buckets, for example, the NFS path or resource URI depending on the service implementation. This allows `StorageService` and `RecognitionService` to change the underlying storage technologies. However, in this design, `StorageService` and `RecognitionService` are coupled to use the same storage technology. There is an inherent assumption that `RecognitionService` can access the file uploaded through `StorageService` when performing the text detection task. We could have designed `StorageService` to return the raw bytes of the image and then pass it to the `RecognitionService`. This design would remove the same storage technology restriction, but it adds complexity and performance overhead. There are always trade-offs when it comes to design: you as an AI practitioner have to make the decisions on the trade-offs for your specific applications.

Translate the image text endpoint

We will start with the translate image text endpoint. The following code will continue with the Python code of `app.py`:

```
...
import json

...
#####
# RESTful endpoints
####
@app.route('/images/{image_id}/translated-text', methods = ['POST'], cors =
True)
def translate_image_text(image_id):
    """detects then translates text in the specified image"""
    request_data = json.loads(app.current_request.raw_body)
    from_lang = request_data['fromLang']
    to_lang = request_data['toLang']

    MIN_CONFIDENCE = 80.0

    text_lines = recognition_service.detect_text(image_id)

    translated_lines = []
    for line in text_lines:
        # check confidence
        if float(line['confidence']) >= MIN_CONFIDENCE:
            translated_line =
translation_service.translate_text(line['text'], from_lang, to_lang)
```

```
            translated_lines.append({
                'text': line['text'],
                'translation': translated_line,
                'boundingBox': line['boundingBox']
            })

    return translated_lines
```

In the preceding code, the following applies:

- The `translate_image_text()` function implements the `RESTful` endpoint.
- The annotation right above this function describes the HTTP request that can access this endpoint.
- In the `translate_image_text()` function, we first get the request data that contains the source language, `fromLang`, and target language, `toLang`, for the translation.
- Next, we call `RecognitionService` to detect text in the image and store the detected lines of text in `text_lines`.
- Then, for each line of text in `text_lines`, we check the confidence level of the detection. If the confidence level is above `MIN_CONFIDENCE`, which is set to `80.0`, then we perform the translation on that line of text.
- We then return the `text`, `translation`, and `boundingBox` to the caller as JSON (chalice automatically formats the contents in `translated_line` to JSON).

The following is an HTTP request to this RESTful endpoint. The `/images` path is treated as a collection resource in the RESTful convention, and `image_id` specifies a specific image within this collection:

```
POST <server url>/images/{image_id}/translate-text
{
    fromLang: "auto",
    toLang: "en"
}
```

To perform an action on the specific image specified by the `/images/{image_id}` URL, we use a `POST` HTTP request to a custom `translate-text` action. We have additional parameters as the JSON payload in the request body, `fromLang` and `toLang`, to specify the language codes of the translation. To read this RESTful HTTP request, we are performing `translate-text` action for an image in the `images` collection on `<server url>` with the specified `image_id`.

Let's test this endpoint out by running `chalice local` in the Python virtual environment as shown in the following, and then issue the following `curl` command and specify an image that has already been uploaded to our S3 bucket:

```
$ curl --header "Content-Type: application/json" --request POST --data
'{"fromLang":"auto","toLang":"en"}'
http://127.0.0.1:8000/images/german_street_sign.jpg/translate-text
[
 {
 "text": "Einbahnstrabe",
 "translation": {
 "translatedText": "One way",
 "sourceLanguage": "de",
 "targetLanguage": "en"
 },
 "boundingBox": {
 "Width": 0.495918333530426,
 "Height": 0.06301824748516083,
 "Left": 0.3853428065776825,
 "Top": 0.4955403208732605
 }
 }
]
```

This is the JSON that our web user interface will receive and use to display the translations to the user.

Upload the image endpoint

We are going to allow the clients of this endpoint to upload images using Base64 encoding. With Base64 encoding, we can translate binary data, such as image and audio, into ASCII string format and back. This method allows our application to upload images using the JSON payload in the HTTP request. Don't worry, you don't need to be familiar with Base64 to continue with the project implementation.

Let's have a look at the code of our endpoint function:

```
import base64
import json
...

@app.route('/images', methods = ['POST'], cors = True)
def upload_image():
    """processes file upload and saves file to storage service"""
    request_data = json.loads(app.current_request.raw_body)
```

```
    file_name = request_data['filename']
    file_bytes = base64.b64decode(request_data['filebytes'])

    image_info = storage_service.upload_file(file_bytes, file_name)

    return image_info
```

In the preceding code, the following applies:

- The `upload_image()` function implements the RESTful endpoint. The annotation right above it describes the HTTP request that can access this endpoint.
- In the `upload_image()` function, we use Base64 to decode the uploaded file in the JSON payload in the HTTP request and then upload it through our `StorageService`.
- In this function, we return to the caller the output of `StorageService.upload_file()` in JSON format.

The following is an HTTP request to this RESTful endpoint. Again, as shown in the following code block, `/images` is treated as a collection resource in the RESTful convention:

```
POST <server url>/images
```

To create a new resource within the collection, the RESTful convention uses the `POST` method to the `/images` collection resource.

With `chalice local` running, issue the following `curl` command to test the upload endpoint. We are using the `echo` command to send the JSON payload, including the Base64 encoding, to our endpoint. The file specified in the command must be on your local filesystem:

```
$ (echo -n '{"filename": "german_street_sign.jpg", "filebytes": "'; base64
/<file path>/german_street_sign.jpg; echo '"}') | curl --header "Content-
Type: application/json" -d @- http://127.0.0.1:8000/images
{
   "fileId":"germany_street_sign.jpg",
"fileUrl":"https://contents.aws.ai.s3.amazonaws.com/german_street_sign.jpg"
}
```

In the preceding code, the following applies:

- This is the JSON that our web user interface will receive. We get a `fileId` back; this ID can be used to specify the upload image in the `/images` collection resource.

- We also get a `fileUrl`, and the current `StorageService` implementation returns the S3 URL to the file, but this `fileUrl` is generic and not tied to any particular service.
- We will use this `fileUrl` to display the image in the web user interface.

At this point, you can go to your S3 bucket and see whether the file has been uploaded successfully.

Implementing the web user interface

Next, let's create a simple web user interface with HTML and JavaScript in the `index.html` and `script.js` files in the `Website` directory.

This is what the final web interface looks like:

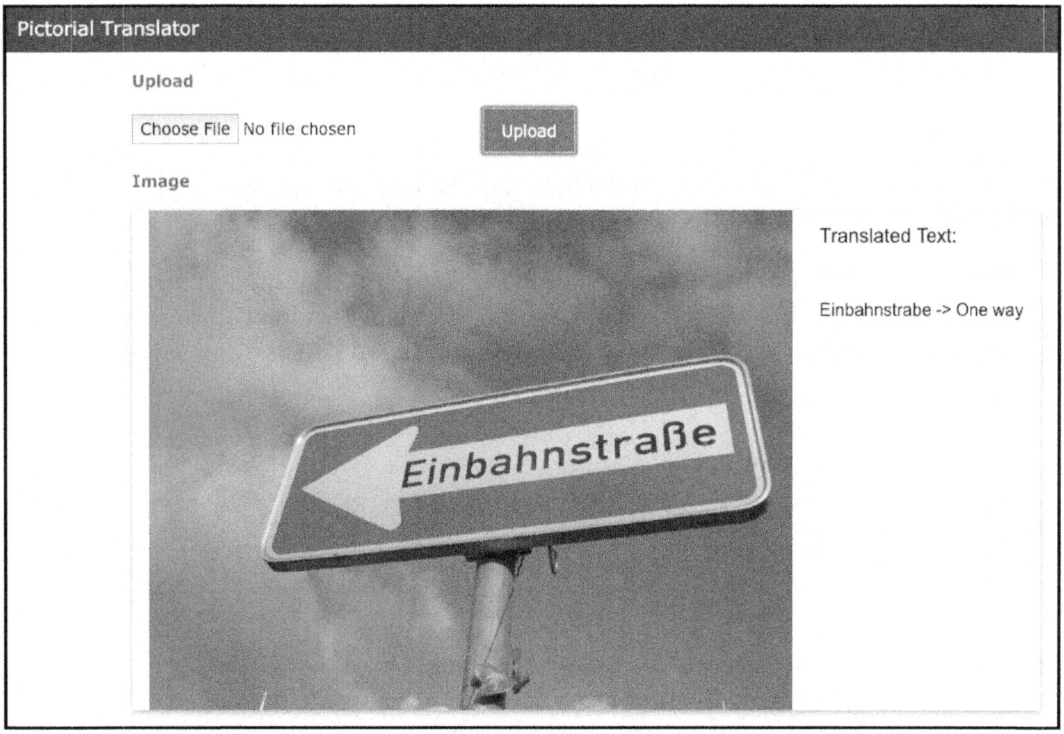

index.html

Let's create the web user interface with the `index.html` file, as shown in the following code block:

```
<!doctype html>
<html lang="en"/>

<head>
    <meta charset="utf-8"/>
    <meta name="viewport" content="width=device-width, initial-scale=1.0"/>

    <title>Pictorial Translator</title>

    <link rel="stylesheet" href="https://www.w3schools.com/w3css/4/w3.css">
    <link rel="stylesheet"
href="https://www.w3schools.com/lib/w3-theme-blue-grey.css">
</head>

<body class="w3-theme-14">
    <div style="min-width:400px">
        <div class="w3-bar w3-large w3-theme-d4">
            <span class="w3-bar-item">Pictorial Translator</span>
        </div>

        <div class="w3-container w3-content">
            <p class="w3-opacity"><b>Upload</b></p>
            <input id="file" type="file" name="file" accept="image/*"/>
            <input class="w3-button w3-blue-grey" type="submit"
value="Upload"
                   onclick="uploadAndTranslate()"/>

            <p class="w3-opacity"><b>Image</b></p>
            <div id="view" class="w3-panel w3-white w3-card w3-display-
container"
                 style="display:none;">
                <div style="float: left;">
                    <img id="image" width="600"/>
                </div>
                <div style="float: right;">
                    <h5>Translated Text:</h5>
                    <div id="translations"/>
                </div>
            </div>
        </div>
    </div>

    <script src="scripts.js"></script>
```

```
</body>

</html>
```

We are using standard HTML tags here, so the code of the web page should be easy to follow. Here are a few things to point out:

- We are using two `<input>` tags for the file chooser and the upload button. Typically, `<input>` tags are used inside HTML forms, but instead, we are running a JavaScript function, `uploadAndTranslate()`, when the upload button is clicked.
- The `<img>` tag, with the `image` ID, will be used to display the uploaded image. This ID will be used by JavaScript to add the image dynamically.
- The `<div>` tag, with the `translations` ID, will be used to display lines of detected text and their translations. This `id` will also be used by JavaScript to add the text and translation dynamically.

scripts.js

Let's create `scripts.js` as shown in the following. The JavaScript function is interacting with the endpoints and stitching together the overall user experience of the Pictorial Translator. Let's have a look at the following code:

1. First, define `serverUrl` as the address of `chalice local`.
2. We will also define a new `HttpError` to handle the exceptions that might occur during the HTTP requests.
3. Add this JavaScript class at the end of the `scripts.js` file:

```
"use strict";
const serverUrl = "http://127.0.0.1:8000";
...
class HttpError extends Error {
 constructor(response) {
        super(`${response.status} for ${response.url}`);
        this.name = "HttpError";
        this.response = response;
    }
}
```

4. Next, we will define four functions in `scripts.js`:

    - `uploadImage()`: This uploads the image via Base64 encoding to our `UploadImage()` endpoint.
    - `updateImage()`: This updates the user interface to display the uploaded image using the S3 URL.
    - `translateImage()`: This calls the translate image text endpoint to translate the text detected in the image.
    - `updateTranslations()`: This updates the user interface to display the translated texts.

These are sequential steps of the user experience. We broke them into individual functions to make the JavaScript code more modular and readable. Each function performs a specific task.

Let's have a look at the `uploadImage()` function, as shown in the following code block:

```
async function uploadImage() {
    // encode input file as base64 string for upload
    let file = document.getElementById("file").files[0];
    let converter = new Promise(function(resolve, reject) {
        const reader = new FileReader();
        reader.readAsDataURL(file);
        reader.onload = () => resolve(reader.result
            .toString().replace(/^data:(.*,)?/, ''));
        reader.onerror = (error) => reject(error);
    });
    let encodedString = await converter;

    // clear file upload input field
    document.getElementById("file").value = "";

    // make server call to upload image
    // and return the server upload promise
    return fetch(serverUrl + "/images", {
        method: "POST",
        headers: {
            'Accept': 'application/json',
            'Content-Type': 'application/json'
        },
        body: JSON.stringify({filename: file.name, filebytes:
encodedString})
    }).then(response => {
        if (response.ok) {
            return response.json();
```

```
            } else {
                throw new HttpError(response);
            }
        })
}
```

In the preceding code, the following applies:

- The `uploadImage()` function is creating a Base64-encoded string from the file input field in `index.html`.
    - This function is declared as async because we need to wait for the file to be read and encoded.
    - This function creates a JavaScript `Promise` function that uses a `FileReader` to read the file, and then converts the file content as Base64 with the `readAsDataURL()` function.
- This function clears the file input field after each upload, so the user can more easily upload another image.
- This function then sends the POST HTTP request with the JSON payload to our Upload Image Endpoint URL and returns `response.json`.

Let's have a look at the `updateImage()` function, as shown in the following code block:

```
function updateImage(image) {
    document.getElementById("view").style.display = "block";

    let imageElem = document.getElementById("image");
    imageElem.src = image["fileUrl"];
    imageElem.alt = image["fileId"];

    return image;
}
```

In the preceding code, the following applies:

- The `updateImage()` function makes the `<div>` tag with the `view` ID visible to display the image.
- This function finds the `<img>` tag with the `image` ID and sets the `src` attribute to the URL of the image file stored in S3.
- The `<img>` tag's `alt` attribute is set to the filename in case the image cannot be loaded for some reason.

The `alt` attribute makes web pages more accessible for more users, including the visually impaired. For more information on web page accessibility, search for `508 compliance`.

Lets, have a look at the `translateImage()` function, as shown in the following code block:

```
function translateImage(image) {
    // make server call to translate image
    // and return the server upload promise
    return fetch(serverUrl + "/images/" + image["fileId"] + "/translate-
text", {
        method: "POST",
        headers: {
            'Accept': 'application/json',
            'Content-Type': 'application/json'
        },
        body: JSON.stringify({fromLang: "auto", toLang: "en"})
    }).then(response => {
        if (response.ok) {
            return response.json();
        } else {
            throw new HttpError(response);
        }
    })
}
```

In the preceding code, the following applies:

- The `translateImage()` function sends the HTTP POST request, along with the JSON body, to our **Translate Image Text Endpoint** URL.
- The function then returns the response JSON with the translation texts.

Let's have a look at the `annotateImage()` function, as shown in the following code block:

```
function annotateImage(translations) {
    let translationsElem = document.getElementById("translations");
    while (translationsElem.firstChild) {
        translationsElem.removeChild(translationsElem.firstChild);
    }
    translationsElem.clear

    for (let i = 0; i < translations.length; i++) {
        let translationElem = document.createElement("h6");
        translationElem.appendChild(document.createTextNode(
            translations[i]["text"] + " -> " +
translations[i]["translation"]["translatedText"]
```

```
            ));
            translationsElem.appendChild(document.createElement("hr"));
            translationsElem.appendChild(translationElem);
        }
    }
```

In the preceding code, the following applies:

- The `updateTranslations()` function finds the `<div>` tag with the `translations` ID and removes any existing translations from the previous image.
- Then, it adds to the `<div>` tag for each line of text, a new `<h6>` tag to display the detected text as well as its translation.

All four functions are stitched together by the following `uploadAndTranslate()` function:

```
function uploadAndTranslate() {
    uploadImage()
        .then(image => updateImage(image))
        .then(image => translateImage(image))
        .then(translations => annotateImage(translations))
        .catch(error => {
            alert("Error: " + error);
        })
}
```

Notice how clear the sequence of events are in the `uploadAndTranslate()` function:

1. If the `updateImage()` function is successful, then run `updateImage()` with the image information.
2. Then, run the `translateImage()` function with the image information. If the `translateImage()` function is successful, then run `updateTranslations()`.
3. Catch any errors in this chain and display it in a pop-up modal.

The final project structure for the Pictorial Translator application should be as follows:

```
├── Capabilities
│   ├── app.py
│   ├── chalicelib
│   │   ├── __init__.py
│   │   ├── recognition_service.py
│   │   ├── storage_service.py
│   │   └── translation_service.py
│   └── requirements.txt
├── Pipfile
├── Pipfile.lock
```

```
└── Website
    ├── index.html
    └── scripts.js
```

Now, we have completed the implementation of the Pictorial Translator application.

Deploying Pictorial Translator to AWS

The deployment steps for the Pictorial Translator application are the same as the deployment steps of the Rekognition demonstration in `Chapter 2`, *Anatomy of a Modern AI Application*; we have included the steps here for completion:

1. First, let's tell `chalice` to perform policy analysis for us by setting `autogen_policy` to `false` in the `config.json` file in the `.chalice` directory of the project structure:

    ```
    {
      "version": "2.0",
      "app_name": "Capabilities",
      "stages": {
        "dev": {
          "autogen_policy": false,
          "api_gateway_stage": "api"
        }
      }
    }
    ```

2. Next, we create a new `policy-dev.json` file in the `.chalice` directory to manually specify the AWS services the project needs:

    ```
    {
     "Version": "2012-10-17",
     "Statement": [
     {
     "Effect": "Allow",
     "Action": [
     "logs:CreateLogGroup",
     "logs:CreateLogStream",
     "logs:PutLogEvents",
     "s3:*",
     "rekognition:*",
     "translate:*"
     ],
     "Resource": "*"
     }
    ```

```
    ]
  }
```

3. Next, we deploy the `chalice` backend to AWS by running the following command within the `Capabilities` directory:

```
$ chalice deploy
Creating deployment package.
Creating IAM role: Capabilities-dev
Creating lambda function: Capabilities-dev
Creating Rest API
Resources deployed:
  - Lambda ARN: arn:aws:lambda:us-
east-1:<UID>:function:Capabilities-dev
  - Rest API URL:
https://<UID>.execute-api.us-east-1.amazonaws.com/api/
```

When the deployment is complete, `chalice` will output a RESTful API URL that looks similar to `https://<UID>.execute-api.us-east-1.amazonaws.com/api/`, where the `<UID>` tag is a unique identifier string. This is the server URL your frontend app should hit to access the application backend running on AWS.

4. Next, we will upload the `index.html` and `scripts.js` files to this S3 bucket, and then set the permissions to publicly readable. Before we do that, we need to make a change in `scripts.js`, as shown in the following. Remember, the website will be running in the cloud now, and won't have access to our local HTTP server. Replace the local server URL with the one from our backend deployment:

```
"use strict";

const serverUrl =
"https://<UID>.execute-api.us-east-1.amazonaws.com/api";

...
```

Now the Pictorial Translator application is accessible for everyone on the internet to make our world smaller!

Discussing project enhancement ideas

At the end of each hands-on project in Part 2, we provide you with a few ideas to extend the intelligence-enabled application. Here are a couple of ideas to enhance the Pictorial Translator:

- Add voice read back for both original and translated texts. Voice read back for the original text will help users learn a foreign language. Voice read back of the translated text will help visually impaired users. AWS provides voice-generation capabilities with the Amazon Polly service.
- Create a native mobile app for better user experience. For example, a continuous camera scan for real-time pictorial translation. The mobile app can leverage the same two endpoints we created. The mobile app is just another frontend to the Pictorial Translator application.

Summary

In this chapter, we built a Pictorial Translator application to translate texts appearing in pictures. We leveraged Amazon Rekognition to first detect lines of text in pictures and then leveraged Amazon Translate to translate the detected texts. This is our first intelligence-enabled solution that solves a real-world problem. Building these solutions through hands-on projects helps to build your intuition for solving problems with AI capabilities. Along the way, we also discussed solution design decisions and trade-offs that must be validated against the real-world usages of our application. From an architectural perspective, not only did we build a working application, we architected it in a way that allows for reusable components that we can leverage in future hands-on projects.

In the next chapter, we will build more intelligence-enabled applications using additional AWS AI services. As we gain more experience building hands-on projects, pay close attention to the reusable opportunities created by our architecture design decisions.

Further reading

For more information on detecting and translating text with Amazon Rekognition and Amazon Translate, please refer to the following links:

- `https://www.androidauthority.com/google-lens-augmented-reality-785836/`
- `https://docs.aws.amazon.com/rekognition/latest/dg/API_DetectText.html`
- `https://www.cs.vu.nl/~eliens/assets/flex3/langref/flash/geom/Rectangle.html` (rectangle image)
- `https://en.wikipedia.org/wiki/Base64`

4
Performing Speech-to-Text and Vice Versa with Amazon Transcribe and Polly

In this chapter, we will continue to develop the skills and intuition required for real-world artificial intelligence applications. We will build an application that can translate spoken speech from one language to another. We will leverage Amazon Transcribe and Amazon Polly to perform speech-to-text and text-to-speech tasks. We will also demonstrate how our reference architecture allows us to reuse the service implementations we implemented in the previous chapter projects.

We will cover the following topics:

- Performing speech-to-text with Amazon Transcribe
- Performing text-to-speech with Amazon Polly
- Building serverless AI applications with AWS services, RESTful APIs, and web user interface
- Reusing existing AI service implementations within the reference architecture
- Discussing user experience and product design decisions

Technical requirements

This book's GitHub repository, which contains the source code for this chapter, can be found at `https://github.com/PacktPublishing/Hands-On-Artificial-Intelligence-on-Amazon-Web-Services`.

Technologies from science fiction

Google's recent entry into the headphone market, called the Pixel Buds, had a unique feature that wowed the reviewers. These headphones can translate conversations in real time for dozens of languages. This sounds like science fiction. What comes to mind is Star Trek's universal translator that allows Starfleet crews to communicate with almost any alien race. Even though the Pixel Buds are not as powerful as their science fiction counterpart, they are packed with some amazing **Artificial Intelligence** (**AI**) technologies. This product showcases what we can expect from AI capabilities to help us communicate with more people in more places.

We will be implementing a similar conversation translation feature using AWS AI services. Our application, modestly named the Universal Translator, will provide voice-to-voice translation between dozens of languages. However, our Universal Translator is not exactly real time and it only supports dozens of human languages.

Understanding the architecture of Universal Translator

Our Universal Translator application will provide a web user interface for the users to record a phrase in one language and then translate that phrase to another language. Here is the architecture design highlighting the layers and services of our application. The organization of the layers and components should be familiar to you from our previous projects:

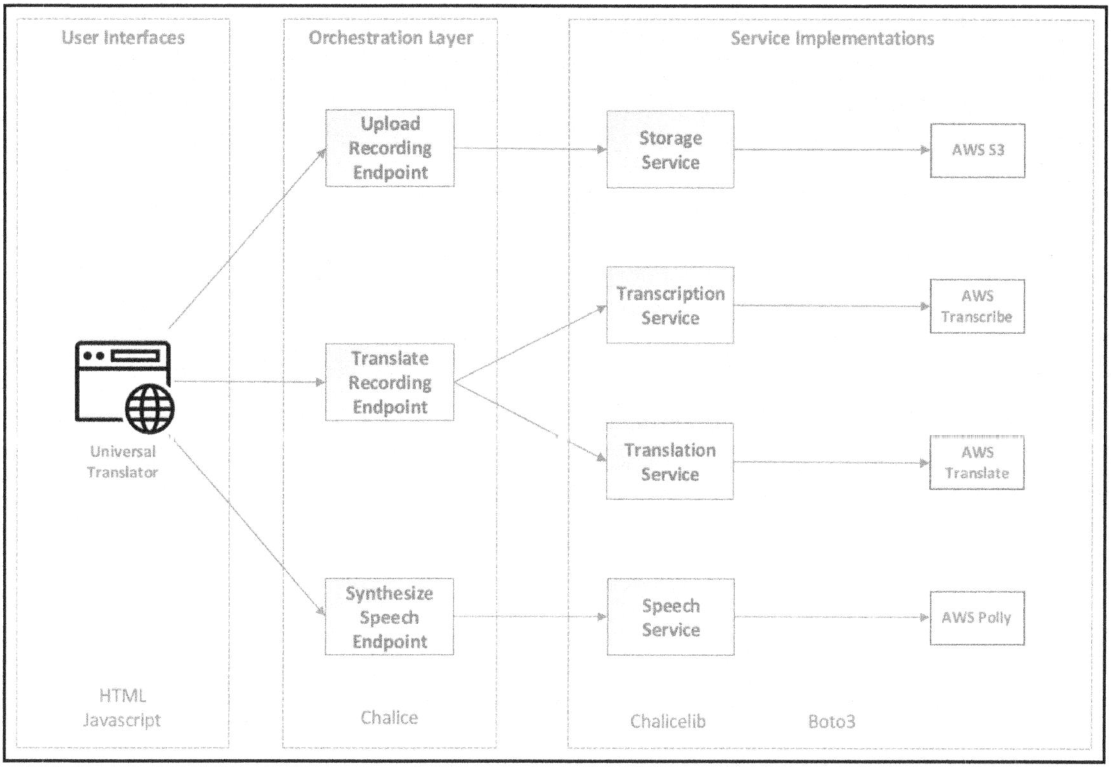

In this application, the web user interface will interact with three RESTful endpoints in the orchestration layer:

- **Upload Recording Endpoint** will delegate the audio recording upload to our Storage Service, which provides an abstraction layer to AWS S3.
- **Translate Recording Endpoint** will use both the Amazon Transcription Service and the Amazon Translation Service. It first gets the transcription of the audio recording, and then translates the transcription text to the target language. The transcription service and the translation service abstract the Amazon Transcribe and Amazon Translate services respectively.
- **Synthesize Speech Endpoint** will delegate the speech synthesis of the translated text to the Speech Service, which is backed by the Amazon Polly service.

As we will soon see in the project implementation, the Translation Service is reused from the Pictorial Translator project, without any modification. In addition, the upload file method in the Storage Service implementation is also reused from the previous projects. One of the benefits of separating the orchestration layer and the service implementations should be clear here. We can reuse and recombine various service implementations, without modification, by stitching them together in the orchestration layer. Each application's unique business logics are implemented in the orchestration layer while the capabilities are implemented without the knowledge of the application-specific business logic.

Component interactions of Universal Translator

The following diagram walks through how the different components will interact with each other to form the business logic workflow of the Universal Translator application:

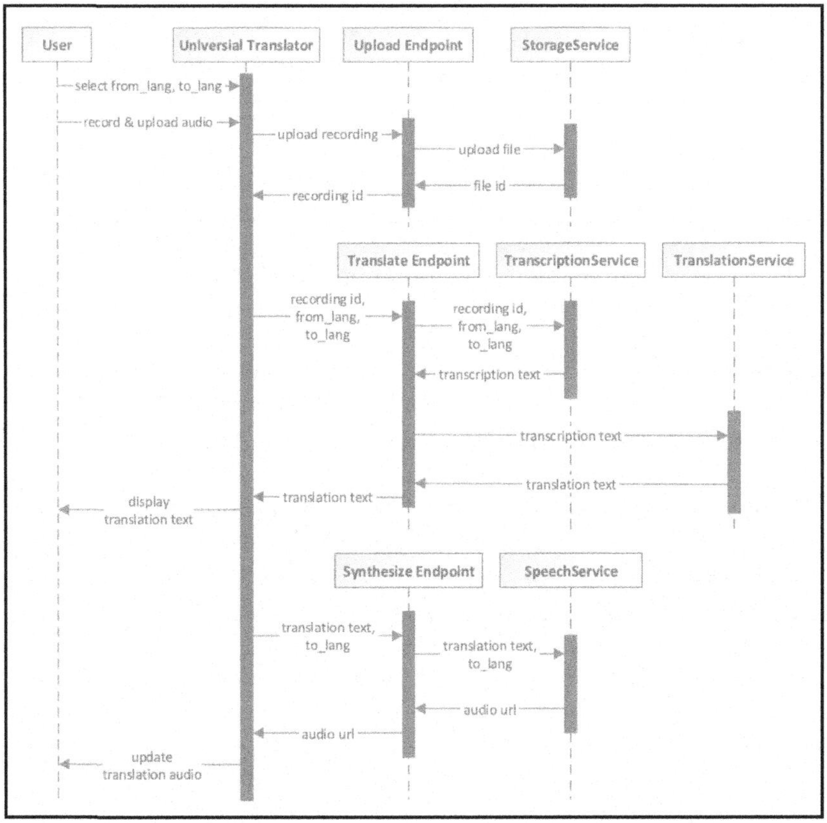

The following is from the user's perspective:

- The user first selects the source and target languages of the speech translation in the web user interface.
- The user then records a short audio speech with the on-screen controls.
- This recording can be played back from the web user interface. The user can use the playback feature to check the quality of the speech recording.
- When the user is satisfied with the recording, it can be uploaded for translation.
- Some time later, the web user interface will display both the transcription and translation texts in the web user interface.
- Finally, a synthesized speech of the translated text will be available for audio playback from the web user interface.

We decided to break the end-to-end translation process into three major steps:

1. Upload the audio recording.
2. Get the translation text.
3. Synthesize the speech.

This design decision allows the Universal Translator to display the translation text in the web user interface while the translation audio is being synthesized. This way, not only does the application appear more responsive to the user, but the user can also make use of the translation text in certain situations without waiting for the audio synthesis.

Setting up the project structure

Let's create a similar base project structure with the steps outlined in `Chapter 2`, *Anatomy of a Modern AI Application*, including `pipenv`, `chalice`, and the web files:

1. In the terminal, we will create the root project directory, and enter it with the following commands:

```
$ mkdir UniversalTranslator
$ cd UniversalTranslator
```

2. We will create placeholders for the web frontend by creating a directory named `Website`, and, within this directory, we will create the `index.html` and `scripts.js` files, as shown as follows:

```
$ mkdir Website
$ touch Website/index.html
$ touch Website/scripts.js
```

3. We will create a Python 3 virtual environment with `pipenv` in the project's `root` directory. Our Python portion of the project needs two packages, `boto3` and `chalice`. We can install them with the following commands:

```
$ pipenv --three
$ pipenv install boto3
$ pipenv install chalice
```

4. Remember that the Python packages installed via `pipenv` are only available if we activate the virtual environment. One way to do this is with the following command:

```
$ pipenv shell
```

5. Next, while still in the virtual environment, we will create the orchestration layer as an AWS `chalice` project named `Capabilities`, with the following commands:

```
$ chalice new-project Capabilities
```

6. To create the `chalicelib` Python package, issue the following commands:

```
cd Capabilities
mkdir chalicelib
touch chalicelib/__init__.py
cd ..
```

The initial project structure for Universal Translator should look like the following:

```
Project Structure
------------
├── UniversalTranslator/
    ├── Capabilities/
        ├── .chalice/
            ├── config.json
        ├── chalicelib/
```

```
            ├── __init__.py
        ├── app.py
        ├── requirements.txt
    ├── Website/
        ├── index.html
        ├── script.js
    ├── Pipfile
    ├── Pipfile.lock
```

This is the project structure for the Universal Translator; it contains a user interface, orchestration, and the service implementation layers of the AI application architecture that we defined in `Chapter 2`, *Anatomy of a Modern AI Application*.

Implementing services

Let's implement this application layer by layer, starting with the service implementations that contain the crucial AI capabilities that make the Universal Translator tick.

Transcription service – speech-to-text

In the Universal Translator, we are going to translate spoken words from one language to another. The first step of this translation process is to know which words were spoken. For this, we are going to use the Amazon Transcribe service. Amazon Transcribe uses deep learning based **Automatic Speech Recognition** (**ASR**) algorithms to generate text from speech.

Let's use the AWS CLI to understand how the Transcribe service works. Issue the following command to start a transcription:

```
$ aws transcribe start-transcription-job
  --transcription-job-name <jobname>
  --language-code en-US
  --media-format wav
  --media MediaFileUri=https://s3.amazonaws.com/contents.aws.a/<audio
file>.wav
  --output-bucket-name contents.aws.a
{
    "TranscriptionJob": {
        "TranscriptionJobName": "<jobname>",
        "TranscriptionJobStatus": "IN_PROGRESS",
        "LanguageCode": "en-US",
        "MediaFormat": "wav",
        "Media": {
```

```
                "MediaFileUri": "https://s3.amazonaws.com/<input bucket>/<audio
file>.wav"
            },
            "CreationTime": 1552752370.771
        }
}
```

Let's understand the parameters passed in the preceding command:

- The job name must be a unique ID for each transcription job.
- The language code tells the service which language the audio speech is in. Supported languages, at the time of this writing, are `"en-US"`, `"es-US"`, `"en-AU"`, `"fr-CA"`, `"en-GB"`, `"de-DE"`, `"pt-BR"`, `"fr-FR"`, and `"it-IT"`.
- The media format specifies the audio format of the speech; possible values are `"mp3"`, `"mp4"`, `"wav"`, and `"flac"`.
- The media parameter takes a URI to the audio recording, for example, an S3 URL.
- The output bucket name specifies in which S3 bucket the transcription output should be stored.

You will need to upload an audio recording to an S3 bucket for this command to work. You can use any available software tool to record an audio clip, or you can skip ahead to the *Speech Service* section of this chapter to learn how to generate speech audio with the Amazon Polly service.

Interestingly, we don't get the transcript in the output of this command. In fact, we can see that the transcription job we just started hasn't finished yet. In the output, `TranscriptionJobStatus` is still `IN_PROGRESS`. The Amazon Transcribe service follows an asynchronous pattern, which is commonly use for longer running tasks.

So how do we know the job has finished? There is another command as the following shows. We can issue this command to check the status of the job we just started:

```
$ aws transcribe get-transcription-job --transcription-job-name <jobname>
{
    "TranscriptionJob": {
        "TranscriptionJobName": "<jobname>",
        "TranscriptionJobStatus": "COMPLETED",
        "LanguageCode": "en-US",
        "MediaSampleRateHertz": 96000,
        "MediaFormat": "wav",
        "Media": {
            "MediaFileUri": "https://s3.amazonaws.com/<input bucket>/<audio
file>.wav"
```

```
        },
        "Transcript": {
            "TranscriptFileUri": "https://s3.amazonaws.com/<output
bucket>/jobname.json"
        },
        "CreationTime": 1552752370.771,
        "CompletionTime": 1552752432.731,
        "Settings": {
            "ChannelIdentification": false
        }
    }
}
```

In the preceding command:

- The `get-transcription-job` command takes in one parameter here, which is the unique job name that we specified when we started the job.
- When the job status becomes `"COMPLETED"`, `"TranscriptFileUri"` will point to the JSON output file sitting in the output bucket we specified earlier.

This JSON file contains the actual transcription; here's an excerpt:


```
{
   "jobName":"jobname",
   "accountId":"...",
   "results":{
      "transcripts":[
         {
            "transcript":"Testing, testing one two three"
         }
      ],
      "items":[
         ...
      ]
   },
   "status":"COMPLETED"
}
```


This is the JSON output we need to parse in our service implementation to extract the transcription text.

The Transcription Service is implemented as a Python class:

- The constructor, `__init__()`, creates a `boto3` client to the Transcribe service. The constructor also takes in the Storage Service as a dependency for later use.
- The `transcribe_audio()` method contains the logic to work with the Amazon Transcribe service.
- The `extract_transcript()` method is a helper method that contains the logic to parse the transcription JSON output from the Transcribe service.

```
import boto3
import datetime
import time
import json

class TranscriptionService:
    def __init__(self, storage_service):
        self.client = boto3.client('transcribe')
        self.bucket_name = storage_service.get_storage_location()
        self.storage_service = storage_service

    def transcribe_audio(self, file_name, language):
        ...

    @staticmethod
    def extract_transcript(transcription_output):
        ...
```

Before we dive deeper into the implementation of the `"transcribe_audio()"` and `"extract_transcript()"` methods, let's first take a look at the APIs available for Transcribe in the `boto3` SDK.

As with the AWS CLI commands, the Amazon Transcribe APIs follow the same asynchronous pattern. We can call `"start_transcription_job()"` with `"TranscriptionJobName"`, which is the unique identifier for the transcription job. This method invokes the transcription process; however, it does not return the transcription text when the API call finishes. The `"start_transcription_job()"` API call also returns a `"TranscriptionJobStatus"` field within its response, which can be one of three values, `"IN_PROGRESS"`, `"COMPLETED"`, or `"FAILED"`. We can check on the transcription process with the API call to `"get_transcritpion_job()"` with the previously specified `"TranscriptionJobName"` to check on the job status.

When the job is completed, the transcription text is placed in an S3 bucket. We can either specify an S3 bucket with "OutputBucketName" when calling "start_transcription_job()" or Amazon Transcribe will place the transcription output in a default S3 bucket with a presigned URL to access the transcription text. If the job failed, another "FailureReason" field in the response of "start_transcription_job()" or "get_transcription_job()" will provide the information about why the job failed.

> This asynchronous pattern is commonly used for longer running processes. Instead of blocking the API caller until the process is completed, it allows the caller to perform other tasks and check back on the process later. Think about the customer experience of ordering an item on Amazon.com. Instead of making the customer wait on the website for the item to be packaged, shipped, and delivered, the customer is immediately shown the confirmation message that the order has been placed, and the customer can check on the order status (with a unique order ID) at a later time.

The "transcribe_audio()" method in the TranscriptionService class works around this asynchronous pattern of the Amazon Transcribe APIs:

```
def transcribe_audio(self, file_name, language):
    POLL_DELAY = 5

    language_map = {
        'en': 'en-US',
        'es': 'es-US',
        'fr': 'fr-CA'
    }

    job_name = file_name + '-trans-' +
datetime.datetime.now().strftime("%Y%m%d%H%M%S")

    response = self.client.start_transcription_job(
        TranscriptionJobName = job_name,
        LanguageCode = language_map[language],
        MediaFormat = 'wav',
        Media = {
            'MediaFileUri': "http://" + self.bucket_name +
".s3.amazonaws.com/" + file_name
        },
        OutputBucketName = self.bucket_name
    )

    transcription_job = {
```

```
            'jobName': response['TranscriptionJob']['TranscriptionJobName'],
            'jobStatus': 'IN_PROGRESS'
        }
        while transcription_job['jobStatus'] == 'IN_PROGRESS':
            time.sleep(POLL_DELAY)
            response = self.client.get_transcription_job(
                TranscriptionJobName = transcription_job['jobName']
            )
            transcription_job['jobStatus'] = response['TranscriptionJob']
                                                    ['TranscriptionJobStatus']

        transcription_output = self.storage_service.get_file(job_name +
    '.json')
        return self.extract_transcript(transcription_output)
```

The following is an overview of the preceding "`transcribe_audio()`" implementation:

- We used a simple Python dictionary to store three pairs of language codes. The abbreviations "en", "es", and "fr" are the language codes used by our Universal Translator, and they are mapped to the language codes used by Amazon Transcribe, "en-US", "es-US", and "fr-CA" respectively.
- This particular mapping is limited to only three languages to simplify our project. However, it does demonstrate the technique for abstracting the language codes, an implementation detail used by third-party services from our application. This way, regardless of the underlying third-party services, we can always standardize the language codes used by our application.
- We generated a unique name for each transcription job, called "`job_name`". This name combines the audio filename and a string representation of the current time. This way, even if the method is called on the same file multiple times, the job name still remains unique.
- This method then calls "`start_transcription_job()`" with the unique "`job_name`", language code, media format, the S3 URI where the recording is located, and finally the output bucket name.
- Even though the Transcribe API is asynchronous, we designed our "`transcribe_audio()`" method to be synchronous. To make our synchronous method work with Transcribe's asynchronous APIs, we added a wait loop. This loop waits for the `POLL_DELAY` seconds (set at 5 seconds) and then calls the "`get_transcription_job()`" method repeatedly to check on the job status. The loop runs while the job status is still "`IN_PROGRESS`".

- Finally, when the job completes or fails, we grab the contents of the JSON output file from the specified S3 bucket via the Storage Service. This is why we needed the Storage Service as a dependency in the constructor. We then parse the transcription output with an "`extract_transcript()`" helper method.

Next, we implement the "`extract_transcript()`" helper method, previously used by the "`transcribe_audio()`" method to parse the Amazon Transcribe output:

```
@staticmethod
def extract_transcript(transcription_output):
    transcription = json.loads(transcription_output)

    if transcription['status'] != 'COMPLETED':
        return 'Transcription not available.'

    transcript = transcription['results']['transcripts'][0]['transcript']
    return transcript
```

We have seen the JSON output format earlier with the transcription job we issued with the AWS CLI. This helper method encapsulates the logic to parse this JSON output. It first checks if the job completed successfully, and, if not, the method returns an error message as the transcription text; otherwise, it returns the actual transcription text.

Translation Service – translating text

Just like in `Chapter 3`, *Detecting and Translating Text with Amazon Rekognition and Translate*, the Pictorial Translator application, we are going to leverage the Amazon Translate service to provide the language translation capability. As stated earlier, we can reuse the same implementation of the translation service that we used in the Pictorial Translator project:

```
import boto3

class TranslationService:
    def __init__(self):
        self.client = boto3.client('translate')

    def translate_text(self, text, source_language = 'auto',
target_language = 'en'):
        response = self.client.translate_text(
            Text = text,
            SourceLanguageCode = source_language,
            TargetLanguageCode = target_language
        )
```

```
        translation = {
            'translatedText': response['TranslatedText'],
            'sourceLanguage': response['SourceLanguageCode'],
            'targetLanguage': response['TargetLanguageCode']
        }

        return translation
```

The preceding code is the exact same implementation of `TranslationService` from the previous project. For completion, we include this code here. For more details on its implementation and design choices, refer to `Chapter 3`, *Detecting and Translating Text with Amazon Rekognition and Translate*.

Speech Service – text-to-speech

Once we have the translation text, we are going to leverage the Amazon Polly service to generate a spoken version of the translation.

Before we dive into the implementation, let's generate a short audio speech using this service with the following AWS CLI command:

```
$ aws polly start-speech-synthesis-task
  --output-format mp3
  --output-s3-bucket-name <bucket>
  --text "testing testing 1 2 3"
  --voice-id Ivy
{
    "SynthesisTask": {
        "TaskId": "e68d1b6a-4b7f-4c79-9483-2b5a5932e3d1",
        "TaskStatus": "scheduled",
        "OutputUri": "https://s3.us-east-1.amazonaws.com/<bucket>/<task
id>.mp3",
        "CreationTime": 1552754991.114,
        "RequestCharacters": 21,
        "OutputFormat": "mp3",
        "TextType": "text",
        "VoiceId": "Ivy"
    }
}
```

This command has four mandatory parameters:

- The output format is the audio format:
    - For audio stream, this can be `"mp3"`, `"ogg_vorbis"`, or `"pcm"`.
    - For speech marks, this will be `"json"`.

- The output S3 bucket name is where the generated audio file will be placed.
- The text is the text to be used for the text-to-speech synthesis.
- The voice ID specifies one of many voices available in Amazon Polly. The voice ID indirectly specifies the language, as well as a female or male voice. We used Ivy, which is one of the female voices for US English.

The Amazon Polly service follows a similar asynchronous pattern we saw earlier with Amazon Transcribe. To check on the status of the task we just started, we issue the following AWS CLI command:

```
$ aws polly get-speech-synthesis-task --task-id
e68d1b6a-4b7f-4c79-9483-2b5a5932e3d1
{
    "SynthesisTask": {
        "TaskId": "e68d1b6a-4b7f-4c79-9483-2b5a5932e3d1",
        "TaskStatus": "completed",
        "OutputUri": "https://s3.us-east-1.amazonaws.com/<bucket>/<task
id>.mp3",
        "CreationTime": 1552754991.114,
        "RequestCharacters": 21,
        "OutputFormat": "mp3",
        "TextType": "text",
        "VoiceId": "Ivy"
    }
}
```

In the preceding command, we have the following:

- The "get-speech-synthesis-task" command takes in just one parameter, the task ID that was passed back in the output of the "start-speech-synthesis-task" command.
- When the job status becomes "completed", the "OutputUri" will point to the audio file generated in the S3 bucket we specified earlier.
- The audio filename is the task ID with the specified audio format file extension, for example,"e68d1b6a-4b7f-4c79-9483-2b5a5932e3d1.mp3" for the MP3 format.

Our Speech Service implementation is a Python class with a constructor, "__init__()", and a method named synthesize_speech(). Here is its implementation as follows:

```
import boto3
import time

class SpeechService:
    def __init__(self, storage_service):
```

```
        self.client = boto3.client('polly')
        self.bucket_name = storage_service.get_storage_location()
        self.storage_service = storage_service

    def synthesize_speech(self, text, target_language):
        POLL_DELAY = 5
        voice_map = {
            'en': 'Ivy',
            'de': 'Marlene',
            'fr': 'Celine',
            'it': 'Carla',
            'es': 'Conchita'
        }

        response = self.client.start_speech_synthesis_task(
            Text = text,
            VoiceId = voice_map[target_language],
            OutputFormat = 'mp3',
            OutputS3BucketName = self.bucket_name
        )

        synthesis_task = {
            'taskId': response['SynthesisTask']['TaskId'],
            'taskStatus': 'inProgress'
        }

        while synthesis_task['taskStatus'] == 'inProgress'\
                or synthesis_task['taskStatus'] == 'scheduled':
            time.sleep(POLL_DELAY)

            response = self.client.get_speech_synthesis_task(
                TaskId = synthesis_task['taskId']
            )

            synthesis_task['taskStatus'] =
response['SynthesisTask']['TaskStatus']
            if synthesis_task['taskStatus'] == 'completed':
                synthesis_task['speechUri'] =
response['SynthesisTask']['OutputUri']
self.storage_service.make_file_public(synthesis_task['speechUri'])
                return synthesis_task['speechUri']

        return ''
```

The constructor creates a boto3 client for the Amazon Polly service, and takes in StorageService as a dependency for later use.

In the synthesize_speech() method, we used the Python voice_map dictionary to store five pairs of language codes. The language codes used by our Universal Translator application are "en", "de", "fr", "it", and "es". Instead of language codes, Amazon Polly uses voice ids which are associated with languages as well as female/male voices. The following is an excerpt of Polly voice mappings:

Language	**Female ID(s)**	**Male ID(s)**
English, British (en-GB)	Amy, Emma	Brian
German (de-DE)	Marlene, Vicki	Hans
French (fr-FR)	Celine, Lea	Mathieu
Italian (it-IT)	Carla, Bianca	Giorgio
Spanish, European (es-ES)	Conchita, Lucia	Enrique

The voice_map dictionary in this method stored the first female voice ID of each language that the Universal Translator supports. This design choice is to simplify our project implementation. For a more polished voice-to-voice translation application, the developer can choose to support more languages and to provide customizations on the different voices. Again, "voice_map" abstracts third party service implementation details, the Amazon Polly voice ids, from our application.

Our choices of supported languages are not completely arbitrary here. We specifically picked US English, US Spanish, and Canadian French for the input voices of Amazon Transcribe, and a European variant of the output voices of Amazon Polly. We are targeting customers from North America who are traveling to Europe with our Universal Translator, at least for this **MVP** (**minimal viable product**) version.

The Amazon Polly service APIs follow the same asynchronous pattern as its AWS CLI commands, with the "start_speech_synthesis_task()" and "get_speech_synthesis_task()" API calls. The implementation to synthesize speech looks very similar to the transcription implementation. Once again, we call the "start_speech_synthesis_task()" method to start the long-running process, and then use a while loop to make our method implementation synchronous. This loop waits for the POLL_DELAY seconds (set at 5 seconds) and then calls the "get_speech_synthesis_task()" method to check on the job status, which can be "scheduled", "inProgress", "completed", and "failed". The loop runs while the status is still "scheduled" or "inProgress".

Notice that, even amongst AWS APIs, the status values are not consistent from service to service. Our speech and transcription services shielded all these implementation details from the rest of our application. In the event that we want to swap in a different speech or transcription service implementation, the changes are isolated in the service implementation layer.

Finally, when the task has the status of `"completed"`, we grab the S3 URI of the synthesized audio translation. By default, the file in the S3 bucket will not be publicly accessible, and our web user interface will not be able to play the audio translation. Therefore, before we return the S3 URI, we used our Storage Service `"make_file_public()"` method to make the audio translation public. We will take a look at how that's done in the Storage Service implementation next.

Storage Service – uploading and retrieving a file

Most of the Storage Service implementation should look familiar from the previous chapter. The `__init__()`, constructor, the `"get_storage_location()"` method, and the `"upload_file()"` method are all exactly the same as in our previous implementations. We added two new methods to extend the functionalities of `StorageService`.

Here is the complete implementation:

```
import boto3

class StorageService:
    def __init__(self, storage_location):
        self.client = boto3.client('s3')
        self.bucket_name = storage_location

    def get_storage_location(self):
        return self.bucket_name

    def upload_file(self, file_bytes, file_name):
        self.client.put_object(Bucket = self.bucket_name,
                               Body = file_bytes,
                               Key = file_name,
                               ACL = 'public-read')

        return {'fileId': file_name,
                'fileUrl': "http://" + self.bucket_name +
".s3.amazonaws.com/" + file_name}

    def get_file(self, file_name):
        response = self.client.get_object(Bucket = self.bucket_name, Key =
```

```
file_name)

        return response['Body'].read().decode('utf-8')

    def make_file_public(self, uri):
        parts = uri.split('/')
        key = parts[-1]
        bucket_name = parts[-2]

        self.client.put_object_acl(Bucket = bucket_name,
                                   Key = key,
                                   ACL = 'public-read')
```

Let's have a look at the two new class methods:

- The `get_file()` method takes a filename and returns that file's content as a string. We accomplish this by using the `boto3` S3 client to get the object by key (filename) from the bucket name (Storage Service's storage location), and then decode the file content as a UTF-8 string.
- The `make_file_public()` method takes a file URI and changes the **Access Control List** (**ACL**) of the target file to allow public access. Since our Storage Service is backed by AWS S3, the method assumes the URI is an S3 URI and parses it accordingly to extract the bucket name and key. With the bucket name and key, it then changes the object's ACL to `'public-read'`.

All of the methods within the Storage Service are designed to be generic, so that they are more likely to be reused by different applications.

Implementing RESTful endpoints

Now that the services are implemented, let's move on to the orchestration layer with the RESTful endpoints. Since all of the real work is done by the service implementations, the endpoints are used to stitch the capabilities together and to provide HTTP access for the user interface layer to use these capabilities. The implementation code, therefore, is concise and easy to understand.

The `app.py` file contains the RESTful endpoint implementations. Here's a snippet from `app.py` that includes the imports, configuration, and initialization code:

```
from chalice import Chalice
from chalicelib import storage_service
from chalicelib import transcription_service
from chalicelib import translation_service
```

```
from chalicelib import speech_service

import base64
import json

#####
# chalice app configuration
#####
app = Chalice(app_name='Capabilities')
app.debug = True

#####
# services initialization
#####
storage_location = 'contents.aws.ai'
storage_service = storage_service.StorageService(storage_location)
transcription_service =
transcription_service.TranscriptionService(storage_service)
translation_service = translation_service.TranslationService()
speech_service = speech_service.SpeechService(storage_service)


#####
# RESTful endpoints
#####
...
```

We will discuss each endpoint implementation in `app.py` in detail in the next few sections.

Translate recording endpoint

The Translate Recording endpoint is an HTTP POST endpoint that takes JSON parameters in the request's body. This endpoint takes the recording ID as a parameter, and uses a JSON body to pass in the source and target languages of the translation:

```
@app.route('/recordings/{recording_id}/translate-text', methods = ['POST'],
cors = True)
def translate_recording(recording_id):
    """transcribes the specified audio then translates the transcription
text"""
    request_data = json.loads(app.current_request.raw_body)
    from_lang = request_data['fromLang']
    to_lang = request_data['toLang']

    transcription_text =
transcription_service.transcribe_audio(recording_id, from_lang)
```

```
        translation_text =
translation_service.translate_text(transcription_text,
                                                            target_language =
to_lang)

        return {
            'text': transcription_text,
            'translation': translation_text
        }
```

The annotation right above this function describes the HTTP request that can access the endpoint:

```
POST <server url>/recordings/{recording_id}/translate-text
{
    "fromLang": <SOURCE LANGUAGE>,
    "toLang": <TARGET LANGUAGE>
}
```

Let's look at the preceding code:

- The annotation right above the "`transcribe_recording()`" describes the HTTP POST request that can access the endpoint.
- The function first gets the request data that contains the source language, "`fromLang`", and target language, "`toLang`", for the translation.
- The "`transcribe_recording()`" function calls to the Transcription Service to transcribe the audio recording.
- Next, this function calls the Translation Service to translate the transcription text.
- Finally, this function returns a JSON object containing both the transcription text and the translation information.

Let's test this endpoint out by running `chalice local` in the Python virtual environment, and then issue the following `curl` command that specifies an audio clip that has already been uploaded to our S3 bucket:

```
$ curl --header "Content-Type: application/json" --request POST --data
'{"fromLang":"en","toLang":"de"}'
http://127.0.0.1:8000/recordings/<recording id>/translate-text
[
    {
        "text": "<transcription>",
        "translation": {
            "translatedText": "<translation>",
            "sourceLanguage": "en",
            "targetLanguage": "de"
```

```
            }
        }
    ]
```

The `<recording id>` identifies the filename of the audio file in our S3 bucket.

This is the JSON that our web user interface will receive and use to display the translation to the user.

Synthesize speech endpoint

The Synthesize Speech endpoint is an HTTP POST endpoint that takes JSON parameters in the request's body. This endpoint uses JSON to pass in the target language and the text to be converted into speech. Even though Universal Translator is designed to translate short phrases, the text used to perform text-to-speech on can potentially be long, depending on the application. We are using a JSON payload here, as opposed to the URL parameters, because there's a limit to the length of URLs. This design decision makes the endpoint more reusable for other applications in the future. It is also a good practice to keep the URLs of your application short and clean:

```
@app.route('/synthesize_speech', methods = ['POST'], cors = True)
def synthesize_speech():
    """performs text-to-speech on the specified text / language"""
    request_data = json.loads(app.current_request.raw_body)
    text = request_data['text']
    language = request_data['language']

    translation_audio_url = speech_service.synthesize_speech(text,
language)

    return {
        'audioUrl': translation_audio_url
    }
```

The annotation right above this function describes the HTTP request that can access this endpoint:

```
POST <server url>/synthesize_speech
{
    "text": <TEXT>,
    "language": <LANGUAGE>
}
```

In the preceding code, we have the following:

- The `synthesize_speech()` function parses the request body as JSON data to get the text and the language for the speech synthesis.
- The function then calls the Speech Service's `synthesize_speech()` method.
- The function then returns the URL to the audio file. Remember that we already made this audio file publicly accessible before `synthesize_speech()` returned.

Let's test this endpoint out by running `chalice local` in the Python virtual environment, and then issue the following `curl` command to pass in the JSON payload:

```
$ curl --header "Content-Type: application/json" --request POST --data
'{"text":"Dies ist ein Test des Amazons Polly Service.","language":"de"}'
http://127.0.0.1:8000/synthesize_speech
{
  "audioUrl": "https://s3.us-east-1.amazonaws.com/<bucket>/<task id>.mp3"
}
```

This is the JSON that our web user interface will receive and use to update the audio player for the translation speech.

Upload recording Endpoint

This endpoint is essentially the same as the Upload Image Endpoint from `Chapter 3`, *Detecting and Translating Text with Amazon Rekognition and Translate*, Pictorial Translator application. It uses the same two functions that we implemented in the project without modification. The only change is the `@app.route` annotation, where we created a different HTTP POST endpoint, `/recordings`, that takes uploads via Base64 encoding:

```
@app.route('/recordings', methods = ['POST'], cors = True)
def upload_recording():
    """processes file upload and saves file to storage service"""
    request_data = json.loads(app.current_request.raw_body)
    file_name = request_data['filename']
    file_bytes = base64.b64decode(request_data['filebytes'])

    file_info = storage_service.upload_file(file_bytes, file_name)

    return file_info
```

For completion, we include the code for both the endpoint and its helper function here. For more details on their implementations, refer to `Chapter 3`, *Detecting and Translating Text with Amazon Rekognition and Translate.*

Implementing the Web User Interface

Next, let's create a simple web user interface with HTML and JavaScript in the `index.html` and `scripts.js` files in the `Website` directory.

This is what the final web interface looks like:

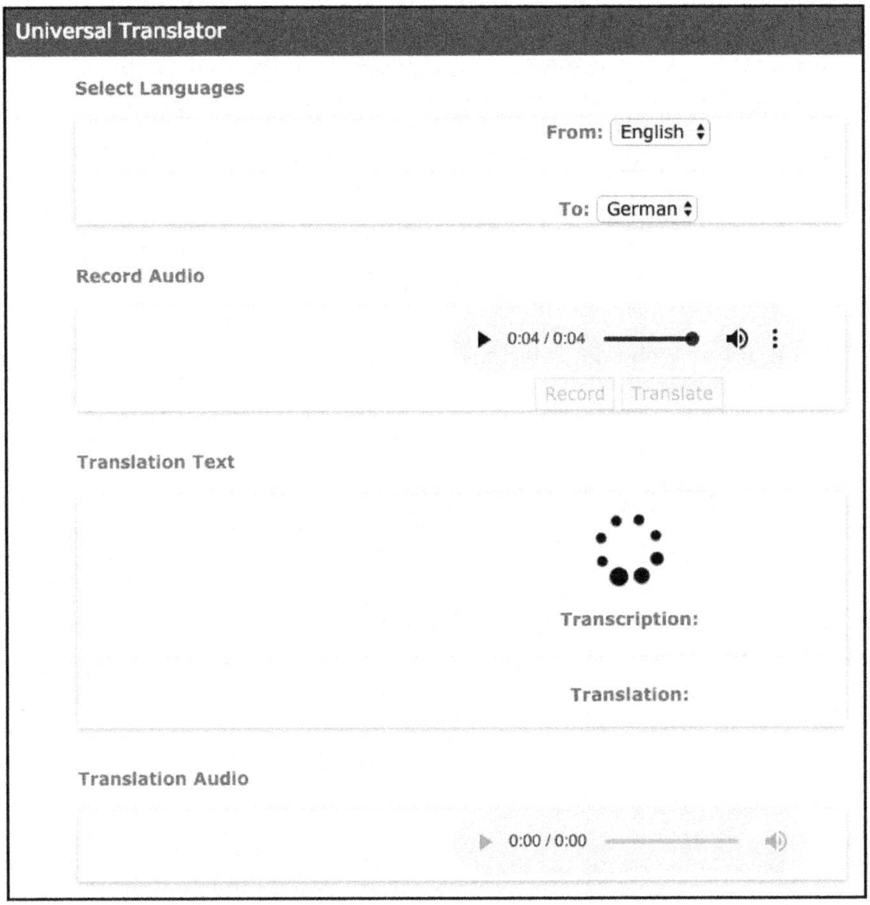

In this application, the user first selects the languages to translate from and to in the **Select Languages** section. The user then records a short speech in the **Record Audio** section. In this section, the user can also playback the recording to check for quality. Then the translation process kicks off. When the translation text becomes available, it is displayed to the user in the **Translation Text** section. Then the text-to-speech generation process is started. When the generated audio translation becomes available, the audio player controls are enabled to allow playback of the translation.

We made the design decision to treat the steps of every translation as sequential, meaning only one translation can be performed at a time. There is a certain amount of wait time for each end-to-end translation, mostly due to the speed of Amazon Transcribe and Amazon Polly services. There are a few techniques to improve the user experience during the wait time:

- A most important technique is actually letting the user know that the application is processing. We employed spinners in the **Translation Text** and **Translation Audio** sections while the application is processing. The fact that we are displaying spinners gives the clue to the user that these steps are not instantaneous.
- Another technique we employed is breaking up the text translation and audio translation steps. Even though the total amount of processing time stays about the same, the user sees progress and intermediate results. Psychologically, this significantly reduces the perception of the wait time for the user.
- We could also reduce the `POLL_DELAY` in our Transcription Service and Speech Service implementations. Currently, the `POLL_DELAY` is set to 5 seconds in both. This results in some delay after the processing is completed, on average 2.5 seconds of delay in each step and on average 5 seconds in total. We can certainly reduce the delay. However, there is a tradeoff here: shorter `POLL_DELAY` will result in more AWS API calls to `"get_transcription_job()"` and `"get_speech_synthesis_task()"` functions.
- Finally, we could use real-time services for faster processing if they are available. For example, Amazon Transcribe now supports real-time transcription with a feature called Streaming Transcription. This feature enables applications to pass in live audio streams and receive text transcripts in real time. Unfortunately, at the time of this writing, this feature is not available in the Python AWS SDK. A flexible architecture will allow future service implementations, AWS-based or otherwise, to be more easily swapped in for long term evolution of the application.

index.html

Following is the `index.html` file. We are using standard HTML tags here, so the code of the web page should be easy to follow:

```
<!doctype html>
<html lang="en"/>

<head>
    <meta charset="utf-8"/>
    <meta name="viewport" content="width=device-width, initial-scale=1.0"/>

    <title>Universal Translator</title>

    <link rel="stylesheet" href="https://www.w3schools.com/w3css/4/w3.css">
    <link rel="stylesheet"
href="https://www.w3schools.com/lib/w3-theme-blue-grey.css">
    <link rel="stylesheet"
href="https://cdnjs.cloudflare.com/ajax/libs/font-awesome/4.7.0/css/font-aw
esome.min.css">
</head>

<body class="w3-theme-14">
    <div style="min-width:400px">
        <div class="w3-bar w3-large w3-theme-d4">
            <span class="w3-bar-item">Universal Translator</span>
        </div>

        ...
    </div>

    <script
src="https://github.com/streamproc/MediaStreamRecorder/releases/download/1.
3.4/MediaStreamRecorder.js"></script>
   <script src="scripts.js"></script>
</body>

</html>
```

This code snippet shows the frame and the title of the web user interface:

- In addition to the W3 stylesheets we have used in previous projects, we also included the Font-Awesome CSS for the spinners.
- At the bottom of `index.html`, we have included `MediaStreamRecorder.js` for the audio recording functionality in the web user interface.

- The rest of the `index.html` code snippet goes inside the top level `<div>` tag within the `<body>`

```
...
    <div class="w3-container w3-content">
        <p class="w3-opacity"><b>Select Languages</b></p>
        <div class="w3-panel w3-white w3-card w3-display-container
        w3-center">
            <div>
                <b class="w3-opacity">From:</b>
                <select id="fromLang">
                    <option value="en">English</option>
                    <option value="es">Spanish</option>
                    <option value="fr">French</option>
                </select>
                <hr>
                <b class="w3-opacity">To:</b>
                <select id="toLang">
                    <option value="de">German</option>
                    <option value="fr">French</option>
                    <option value="it">Italian</option>
                    <option value="es">Spanish</option>
                </select>
            </div>
        </div>
    </div>

    <div class="w3-container w3-content">
        <p class="w3-opacity"><b>Record Audio</b></p>
        <div class="w3-panel w3-white w3-card w3-display-container
        w3-center">
            <div>
                <audio id="recording-player" controls>
                    Your browser does not support the audio
                    element...
                </audio>
            </div>
            <div>
                <input type="button" id="record-toggle"
                value="Record"
                       onclick="toggleRecording()"/>
                <input type="button" id="translate"
                 value="Translate"
                       onclick="uploadAndTranslate()" disabled/>
            </div>
        </div>
    </div>
...
```

In this code snippet, we have the following:

- We created the `Select Languages` and **Record Audio** sections of the web user interface.
- In the **Select Languages** section, we hardcoded the supported `fromLang` and `toLang` in `dropdown` lists.
- In the **Record Audio** section, we used the `<audio>` tag to create an audio player with a couple of input buttons to control the recording and translation functions.
- Most of the dynamic behaviors are implemented in `scripts.js`.

To continue with the `index.html` code, execute the following command:

```
...
        <div class="w3-container w3-content">
            <p class="w3-opacity"><b>Translation Text</b></p>
            <div class="w3-panel w3-white w3-card w3-display-container
            w3-center">
                <p id="text-spinner" hidden>
                    <i class="fa fa-spinner w3-spin" style="font-
                    size:64px"></i>
                </p>
                <p class="w3-opacity"><b>Transcription:</b></p>
                <div id="transcription"></div>
                <hr>
                <p class="w3-opacity"><b>Translation:</b></p>
                <div id="translation"></div>
            </div>
        </div>

        <div class="w3-container w3-content">
            <p class="w3-opacity"><b>Translation Audio</b></p>
            <div class="w3-panel w3-white w3-card w3-display-container
            w3-center">
                <p id="audio-spinner" hidden>
                    <i class="fa fa-spinner w3-spin" style="font-
                     size:64px"></i>
                </p>
                <audio id="translation-player" controls>
                    Your browser does not support the audio element...
                </audio>
            </div>
        </div>
...
```

In this code snippet, we have the following:

- We created the `Translation Text` and **Translation Audio** sections of the web user interface.
- In the **Translation Text** section, we placed a spinner that's initially hidden from view and a couple of `<div>` that will be used to display the translation results.
- In the **Translation Audio** section, we placed another spinner that's also initially hidden from view, along with an audio player that will be used to play back the translation audio.

scripts.js

The following is the `scripts.js` file. Much of the Universal Translator's dynamic behaviors are implemented in JavaScript. `scripts.js` is interacting with the endpoints and stitching together the overall user experience of the application:

```
"use strict";

const serverUrl = "http://127.0.0.1:8000";

...

class HttpError extends Error {
    constructor(response) {
        super(`${response.status} for ${response.url}`);
        this.name = "HttpError";
        this.response = response;
    }
}
```

This snippet defines the `serverUrl` as the address of `chalice local`. It also defines the `HttpError` to handle the exceptions that might occur during the HTTP requests:

```
let audioRecorder;
let recordedAudio;

const maxAudioLength = 30000;
let audioFile = {};

const mediaConstraints = {
 audio: true
};

navigator.getUserMedia(mediaConstraints, onMediaSuccess, onMediaError);
```

```
function onMediaSuccess(audioStream) {
 audioRecorder = new MediaStreamRecorder(audioStream);
 audioRecorder.mimeType = "audio/wav";
 audioRecorder.ondataavailable = handleAudioData;
}

function onMediaError(error) {
 alert("audio recording not available: " + error.message);
}

function startRecording() {
 recordedAudio = [];
 audioRecorder.start(maxAudioLength);
}

function stopRecording() {
 audioRecorder.stop();
}

function handleAudioData(audioRecording) {
 audioRecorder.stop();
 audioFile = new File([audioRecording], "recorded_audio.wav", {type:
"audio/wav"});

 let audioElem = document.getElementById("recording-player");
 audioElem.src = window.URL.createObjectURL(audioRecording);
}
```

This code snippet follows the recommended audio recording implementation from `https://github.com/intercom/MediaStreamRecorder` which we will not cover. There are a few details to point out:

- Universal Translator supports upto 30 seconds of audio recording, defined in the `maxAudioLength` constant. This length should be sufficient for translation of short phrases.
- The audio recording format is set to `audio/wav`, which is one of the formats supported by Amazon Transcribe.
- When the audio recording is completed, we perform two tasks:
    - We place the recorded bits in a JavaScript File object with the filename `recorded_audio.wav`; this will be the filename of the uploaded recording to S3. Since the recordings all have the same filename, a previously uploaded recording will be replaced when a new recording is uploaded.

- We update the audio player in the **Record Audio** section with an Object URL to the recorded audio for playback.

```
let isRecording = false;

function toggleRecording() {
    let toggleBtn = document.getElementById("record-toggle");
    let translateBtn = document.getElementById("translate");

    if (isRecording) {
        toggleBtn.value = 'Record';
        translateBtn.disabled = false;
        stopRecording();
    } else {
        toggleBtn.value = 'Stop';
        translateBtn.disabled = true;
        startRecording();
    }

    isRecording = !isRecording;
}
```

The `toggleRecording` function in `scripts.js` makes the first input button beneath the audio player a toggle button. This toggle button starts or stops the audio recording with the `MediaStreamRecorder` implementation preceding.

Next, we define five functions:

- `uploadRecording()`: Uploads the audio recording via Base64 encoding to our Upload Recording Endpoint
- `translateRecording()`: Calls our Translate Recording Endpoint to translate the audio recording
- `updateTranslation()`: Updates the **Translation Text** section with the returned transcription and translation texts
- `synthesizeTranslation()`: Calls our Synthesize Speech Endpoint to generate audio speech of the translation text
- `updateTranslationAudio()`: Updates the audio player in the **Translation Audio** section with the audio speech URL to enable playback

These functions correspond to the sequential steps of the translation user experience. We broke them into individual functions to make the JavaScript code more modular and readable; each function performs a specific task. Let's go through the implementation details of these functions.

Let's have a look at the `uploadRecording()` function as shown in the following code block:

```
async function uploadRecording() {
    // encode recording file as base64 string for upload
    let converter = new Promise(function(resolve, reject) {
        const reader = new FileReader();
        reader.readAsDataURL(audioFile);
        reader.onload = () => resolve(reader.result
            .toString().replace(/^data:(.*,)?/, ''));
        reader.onerror = (error) => reject(error);
    });
    let encodedString = await converter;

    // make server call to upload image
    // and return the server upload promise
    return fetch(serverUrl + "/recordings", {
        method: "POST",
        headers: {
            'Accept': 'application/json',
            'Content-Type': 'application/json'
        },
        body: JSON.stringify({filename: audioFile.name, filebytes:
encodedString})
    }).then(response => {
        if (response.ok) {
            return response.json();
        } else {
            throw new HttpError(response);
        }
    })
}
```

In the preceding code, we have the following:

- The `uploadRecording()` function creates a Base64 encoded string from the File object that's holding the audio recording.
- This function formats the JSON payload to include the `filename` and `filebytes` that our endpoint is expecting.
- It then sends the HTTP POST request with the JSON payload to our Upload Recording Endpoint URL and returns the response JSON.

- This is almost the same code as the `uploadImage()` function in the Pictorial Translator application; the only difference is the File is coming from the audio recorder.

Let's have a look at the `translateRecording()` function as shown in the following code block:

```
let fromLang;
let toLang;

function translateRecording(audio) {
    let fromLangElem = document.getElementById("fromLang");
    fromLang = fromLangElem[fromLangElem.selectedIndex].value;
    let toLangElem = document.getElementById("toLang");
    toLang = toLangElem[toLangElem.selectedIndex].value;

    // start translation text spinner
    let textSpinner = document.getElementById("text-spinner");
    textSpinner.hidden = false;

    // make server call to transcribe recorded audio
    return fetch(serverUrl + "/recordings/" + audio["fileId"] +
"/translate-text", {
        method: "POST",
        headers: {
            'Accept': 'application/json',
            'Content-Type': 'application/json'
        },
        body: JSON.stringify({fromLang: fromLang, toLang: toLang})
    }).then(response => {
        if (response.ok) {
            return response.json();
        } else {
            throw new HttpError(response);
        }
    })
}
```

In the preceding code, we have the following:

- The `translateRecording()` function first grabs the values of the languages from the `fromLang` and `toLang` dropdowns in the web user interface.
- The function then starts the spinner, signaling the start of the translation process to the user. It then calls our Translate Recording Endpoint and waits for the response.

Let's have a look at the `updateTranslation()` function as shown in the following code block:

```
function updateTranslation(translation) {
    // stop translation text spinner
    let textSpinner = document.getElementById("text-spinner");
    textSpinner.hidden = true;

    let transcriptionElem = document.getElementById("transcription");
transcriptionElem.appendChild(document.createTextNode(translation["text"]))
;

    let translationElem = document.getElementById("translation");
translationElem.appendChild(document.createTextNode(translation["translatio
n"]
["translatedText"]));

    return translation
}
```

In the preceding code, the following applies:

- When the Translate Recording Endpoint responds, the `updateTranslation()` function hides the spinner.
- The function then updates the `Translation Text` section with the transcription and translation texts.

Let's have a look at the `synthesizeTranslation()` function as shown in the following code block:

```
function synthesizeTranslation(translation) {
    // start translation audio spinner
    let audioSpinner = document.getElementById("audio-spinner");
    audioSpinner.hidden = false;

    // make server call to synthesize translation audio
    return fetch(serverUrl + "/synthesize_speech", {
        method: "POST",
        headers: {
            'Accept': 'application/json',
            'Content-Type': 'application/json'
        },
        body: JSON.stringify({text:
translation["translation"]["translatedText"], language: toLang})
    }).then(response => {
        if (response.ok) {
            return response.json();
```

```
            } else {
                throw new HttpError(response);
            }
        })
}
```

In the preceding code, we have the following:

- The `synthesizeTranslation()` function starts the spinner to signal the start of the speech synthesis process to the user.
- This function then calls the Synthesize Speech Endpoint and waits for the response. Remember this endpoint is expecting JSON parameters, which it is setting in the `fetch()` call.

Let's have a look at the `updateTranslationAudio()` function as shown in the following code block:

```
function updateTranslationAudio(audio) {
    // stop translation audio spinner
    let audioSpinner = document.getElementById("audio-spinner");
    audioSpinner.hidden = true;

    let audioElem = document.getElementById("translation-player");
    audioElem.src = audio["audioUrl"];
}
```

In the preceding code, we have the following:

- When the Synthesize Speech Endpoint responds, the `updateTranslationAudio()` function stops the audio synthesis spinner.
- This function then updates the audio player with the URL of the synthesized translation audio.

All preceding five functions are stitched together by the `uploadAndTranslate()` function as follows:

```
function uploadAndTranslate() {
    let toggleBtn = document.getElementById("record-toggle");
    toggleBtn.disabled = true;
    let translateBtn = document.getElementById("translate");
    translateBtn.disabled = true;

    uploadRecording()
        .then(audio => translateRecording(audio))
        .then(translation => updateTranslation(translation))
        .then(translation => synthesizeTranslation(translation))
```

```
            .then(audio => updateTranslationAudio(audio))
            .catch(error => {
                alert("Error: " + error);
            })

        toggleBtn.disabled = false;
    }
```

Notice how clear the sequence of events are in the `uploadAndTranslate()` function. By way of a final step in this function, we enable the record toggle button so that the user can start the next translation.

The final project structure for the Universal Translator application should be as follows:

```
├── Capabilities
│   ├── app.py
│   ├── chalicelib
│   │   ├── __init__.py
│   │   ├── speech_service.py
│   │   ├── storage_service.py
│   │   ├── transcription_service.py
│   │   └── translation_service.py
│   └── requirements.txt
├── Pipfile
├── Pipfile.lock
└── Website
    ├── index.html
    └── scripts.js
```

Now, we have completed the implementation of the Universal Translator application.

Deploying the Universal Translator to AWS

The deployment steps for the Universal Translator application is the same as the deployment steps of the projects in the previous chapters. We include them here for completion.

1. First, let's tell Chalice to perform policy analysis for us by setting `"autogen_policy"` to `false` in the `config.json` file in the `.chalice` directory of the project structure:

```
{
  "version": "2.0",
  "app_name": "Capabilities",
  "stages": {
```

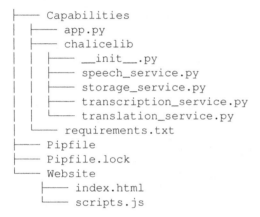

```
        "dev": {
          "autogen_policy": false,
          "api_gateway_stage": "api"
        }
      }
    }
```

2. Next, we create a new file `policy-dev.json` in the `chalice` directory to manually specify the AWS services the project needs:

```
    {
     "Version": "2012-10-17",
     "Statement": [
     {
     "Effect": "Allow",
     "Action": [
     "logs:CreateLogGroup",
     "logs:CreateLogStream",
     "logs:PutLogEvents",
     "s3:*",
     "translate:*",
     "transcribe:*",
     "polly:*"
     ],
     "Resource": "*"
     }
     ]
    }
```

3. Next, we deploy the Chalice backend to AWS by running the following command within the `Capabilities` directory:

```
$ chalice deploy
Creating deployment package.
Creating IAM role: Capabilities-dev
Creating lambda function: Capabilities-dev
Creating Rest API
Resources deployed:
  - Lambda ARN: arn:aws:lambda:us-
east-1:<UID>:function:Capabilities-dev
  - Rest API URL:
https://<UID>.execute-api.us-east-1.amazonaws.com/api/
```

When the deployment is complete, Chalice will output a RESTful API URL that looks similar to `https://<UID>.execute-api.us-east-1.amazonaws.com/api/` where the `<UID>` is a unique identifier string. This is the server URL your frontend app should hit to access the application backend running on AWS.

4. Next we will upload the `index.html` and `scripts.js` files to this S3 bucket, and then set the permissions to publicly readable. Before we do that, we need to make a change in `scripts.js` as shown in the following. Remember, the website will be running in the cloud now, and won't have access to our local HTTP server. Replace the local server URL with the one from our backend deployment:

```
"use strict";
const serverUrl =
"https://<UID>.execute-api.us-east-1.amazonaws.com/api";
...
```

Now the Universal Translator application is accessible to everyone on the Internet!

Discussing the project enhancement ideas

At the end of each hands-on project in Part 2, we provide you with a few ideas to extend the intelligence-enabled application. Here are a couple of ideas to enhance the Universal Translator:

- Allow users to save default source language and output voice preferences within the application. The user is likely to use his or her native language as the source language and may prefer the translated speech to match the his or her gender and voice.
- Add real-time transcription with Amazon Transcribe's Streaming Transcription feature. This feature can greatly reduce the user's wait time for the voice translation. At the time of this writing, the Python SDK does not support this feature, so your implementation will need a different SDK. Our architecture does support a polyglot system, a system written in multiple languages.
- The Universal Translator and the Pictorial Translator both provide translation capabilities. These two forms of translation capability can be combined into a single application for travelers and students, especially a mobile app that's always with the user in the real-world.

Summary

In this chapter, we built a Universal Translator application to translate spoken speech from one language to another. We combined speech-to-text, language translation, and text-to-speech capabilities from AWS AI services, including Amazon Transcribe, Amazon Translate, and Amazon Polly. This hands-on project continued our journey as AI practitioners to develop the skills and intuition for real-world AI applications. Along the way, we also discussed user experience and product design decisions of our Universal Translator application. Additionally, we demonstrated clean code reuse of Translation Service and Storage Service in the reference architecture defined in `Chapter 2`, *Anatomy of a Modern AI Application*.

In the next chapter, we will leverage more AWS AI services to create solutions that can simplify our lives. Being an AI practitioner is not just about knowing which services or APIs to use, but is also about being skilled in fusing good product and architecture designs with AI capabilities.

References

For more information on Performing Speech-to-Text and Vice-versa with Amazon Transcribe and Amazon Polly, please refer to the following links:

- `https://www.verizonwireless.com/wireless-devices/accessories/google-pixel-buds/`
- `https://www.washingtonpost.com/news/the-switch/wp/2017/11/15/i-tried-out-googles-translating-headphones-heres-what-i-found/?utm_term=.1cef17d669e2`
- `https://github.com/intercom/MediaStreamRecorder`

5

Extracting Information from Text with Amazon Comprehend

In this chapter, we will build an application that can automatically extract contact information from photos of business cards. With this application, we aim to reduce tedious manual work by using automation. We will use Amazon Rekognition to detect text in the business card photos and then use Amazon Comprehend to extract structured information such as the name, address, and phone number. We will demonstrate that the goal of automation is not always full autonomy; there is some value in keeping the human component in the solution.

In this chapter, we will cover the following topics:

- Understanding the role of Artificial Intelligence in our workplaces
- Performing information extraction with Amazon Comprehend and Amazon Comprehend Medical
- Storing and retrieving data in AWS DynamoDB
- Building serverless AI applications with AWS services, RESTful APIs, and web user interface
- Reusing existing AI service implementations within the reference architecture
- Discussing human-in-the-loop interface design in automation solutions

Technical requirements

This book's GitHub repository, which contains the source code for this chapter, can be found at `https://github.com/PacktPublishing/Hands-On-Artificial-Intelligence-on-Amazon-Web-Services`.

Working with your Artificial Intelligence coworker

Artificial Intelligence (**AI**) is advancing the progress of automation in our lives. When most people think about intelligent automation they think of smart thermostats, vacuum robots, or autonomous vehicles that help us live better. There are also tremendous opportunities for us to use intelligent automation to help us work better. AI can complement human labor in the workplace to provide value for businesses, contribute to economic growth, and redirect human labor toward creative work. One area hungry for automation progress is manual back office processes. There are many tasks still fulfilled by humans behind the scenes when we deposit checks, when we sign up for services, and when we buy things online.

There certainly are concerns about losing jobs to automation; however, we have also observed improved worker morale when menial efforts are automated. Most of the manual back office processes are tedious and repetitive. For example, there are people whose jobs involve reading through multiple documents, identifying certain pieces of information within them, and then manually entering the information into computer systems. These back-office document processing tasks are also called "swivel-chair" processes because the workers are constantly swiveling in their chairs to switch between the documents and the computer screens. We could use AI to automate the documentation process by reading the documents using **Optical Character Recognition** (**OCR**) and then extracting information using **Natural Language Processing** (**NLP**).

However, automating document processing is not trivial. Paper documents must be scanned first. Depending on the quality of the document image, the complexity of the document structure, or even handwritten text within the documents, it can be difficult to guarantee processing accuracy. For certain business environments and use cases, anything less than 100% accuracy is not acceptable. In such cases, automation developers must design with failover to manual intervention in mind so that humans can step in and take over. For example, an automation solution can extract the dollar amount on a check during a bank deposit. Inaccuracies during this business process can have major consequences for the bank customer. To ensure the correct dollar amount is deposited, the automation solution could extract the value and then show the extracted amount to a human operator before the deposit is completed. This solution leverages AI capabilities to automate the task but also allows humans to intervene in the event of errors.

In this chapter, we will be implementing an application, Contact Organizer, to automate document processing. More specifically, this application helps us extract contact information from scanned business cards. To ensure accuracy, our application will provide a human-in-the-loop user interface so that automatically extracted information can be reviewed and corrected by the user before it is saved. This human-in-the-loop user interface is a popular approach because it improves automation accuracy with human judgement.

Understanding the Contact Organizer architecture

The Contact Organizer application will provide a web user interface for users so that they can upload an image of a business card. The contact information will be extracted and categorized by the application. The automatically extracted contact information will then be displayed to the user in the web user interface. The user can review and correct the information before saving it to a permanent contact store.

The following diagram shows the architecture's design, highlighting the layers and services of the Contact Organizer application. The following architecture design should look very familiar by now; the layers and components follow the same reference architecture template we defined in `Chapter 2`, *Anatomy of a Modern AI Application*:

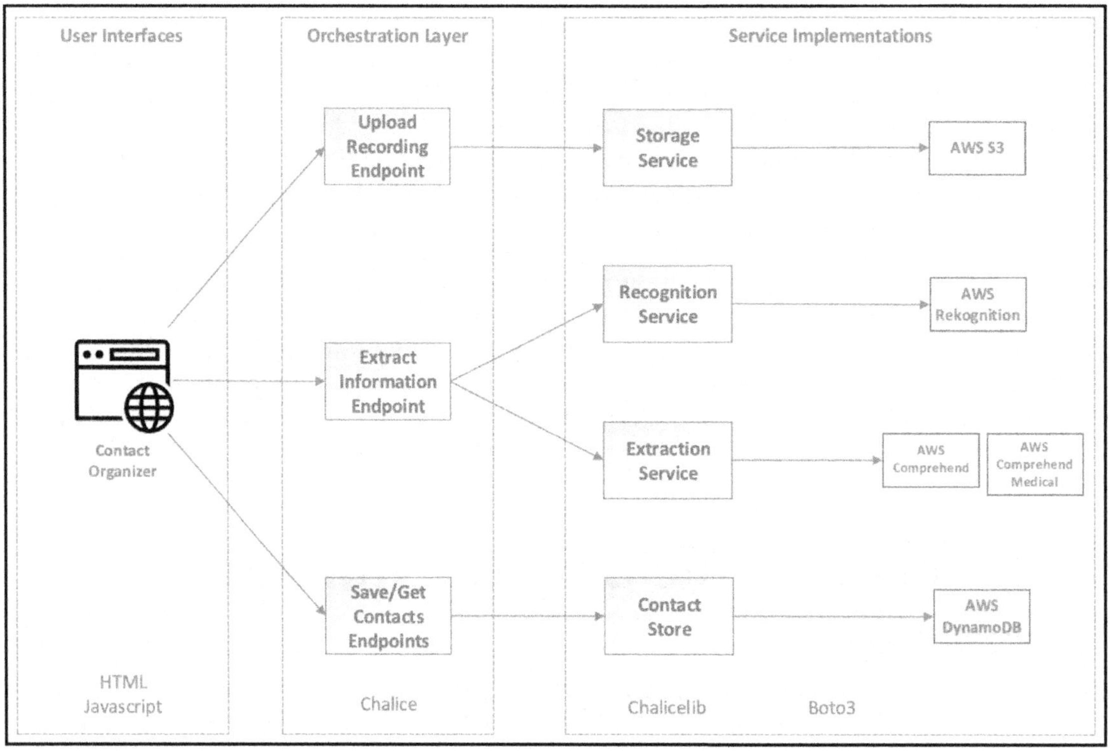

In this application, the web user interface will interact with three RESTful endpoints in the orchestration layer:

- **Upload Recording Endpoint** will delegate the image upload to our **Storage Service**.
- **Extract Information Endpoint** will use the **Recognition Service** and **Extraction Service**:
    - The Recognition Service is reused from `Chapter 3`, *Detecting and Translating Text with Amazon Rekognition and Translate,* when we looked at the Pictorial Translator project.
    - The Extraction Service will use both Amazon Comprehend and Amazon Comprehend Medical to extract and categorize the diverse contact information such as name, address, and phone number.
- **Save/Get Contacts Endpoints** will write to/read from the **Contact Store**, which is backed by the AWS DynamoDB NoSQL database.

In Contact Organizer, there are several opportunities for us to reuse components we already implemented in previous projects. In the orchestration layer, we can reuse the Upload Recording Endpoint. In the service implementation layer, we can reuse the Storage and Recognition services.

Component interactions in Contact Organizer

The following interaction diagram walks through the Contact Organizer's business logic workflow between the application's components:

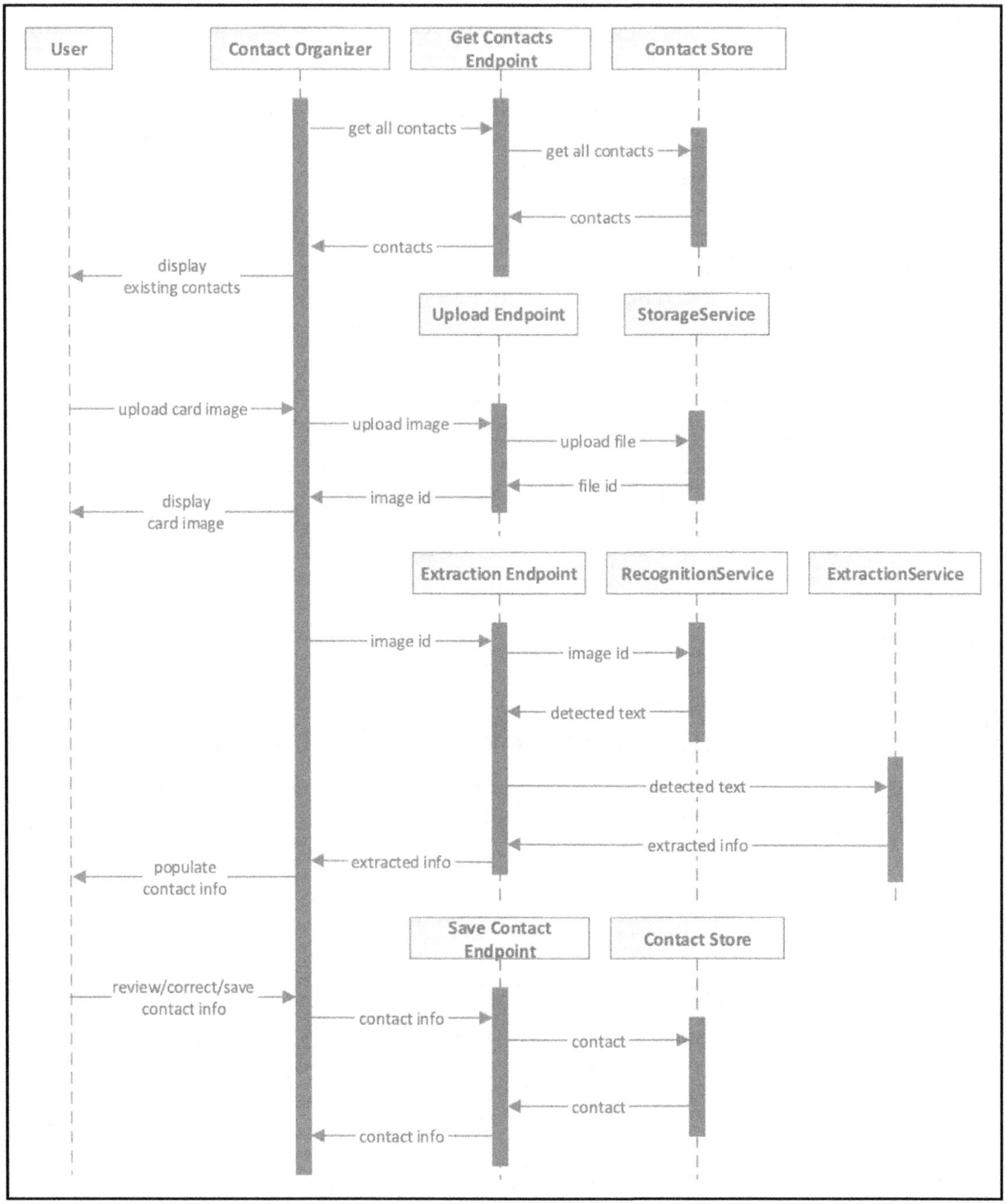
User
Contact Organizer
Get Contacts Endpoint
Contact Store
get all contacts
get all contacts
contacts
contacts
display existing contacts
Upload Endpoint
StorageService
upload card image
upload image
upload file
file id
image id
display card image
Extraction Endpoint
RecognitionService
ExtractionService
image id
image id
detected text
detected text
extracted info
extracted info
populate contact info
Save Contact Endpoint
Contact Store
review/correct/save contact info
contact info
contact
contact
contact info

From the user's perspective, we have the following:

1. When the Contact Organizer web user interface first loads, it will get and display all of the existing contacts.
2. The user can then upload a photo of a business card via the web user interface.
3. After the upload is completed, two steps are kicked off:
    1. The uploaded business card image is displayed in the user interface.
    2. The automated contact information extraction process is started.
4. When the information extraction is completed, the extracted information is displayed to the user for review and correction.
5. After the user has reviewed and corrected the information, the contact information can be persisted after the user clicks the **Save** button.

We designed the Contact Organizer to have a human-in-the-loop user interface, as follows:

1. The uploaded business card image is displayed back to the user so that they can see the original contact information.
2. The automatically extracted contact information is also displayed to the user, along with the business card image.
3. The user has the option to change or correct any of the extracted information from the user interface.
4. The user has to explicitly click the **Save** button, which acts as confirmation from a human that the contact information is correct.

TIP

This human-in-the-loop user interface should not just be an afterthought in an intelligence-enabled solution either. Our rule of thumb for evaluating the design of such interfaces is that the solution should be fully functional, even if the AI capabilities are not present alongside the user interface.

Setting up the project structure

Create a similar base project structure to the one we outlined in `Chapter 2`, *Anatomy of a Modern AI Application*, including `pipenv`, `chalice`, and the web files:

1. In the terminal, we will create the `root` project directory and enter it with the following commands:

```
$ mkdir ContactOrganizer
$ cd ContactOrganizer
```

2. We will create placeholders for the web frontend by creating a directory named `Website`. Within this directory, we will create two files, `index.html` and `scripts.js`, as shown in the following code:

```
$ mkdir Website
$ touch Website/index.html
$ touch Website/scripts.js
```

3. We will create a Python 3 virtual environment with `pipenv` in the project's root directory. Our Python portion of the project needs two packages, `boto3` and `chalice`. We can install them with the following commands:

```
$ pipenv --three
$ pipenv install boto3
$ pipenv install chalice
```

4. Remember that the Python packages that are installed via `pipenv` are only available if we activate the virtual environment. One way to do this is with the following command:

```
$ pipenv shell
```

5. Next, while still in the virtual environment, we will create the orchestration layer as an AWS Chalice project named `Capabilities` with the following commands:

```
$ chalice new-project Capabilities
```

6. To create the `chalicelib` Python package, issue the following commands:

```
cd Capabilities
mkdir chalicelib
touch chalicelib/__init__.py
cd ..
```

The initial project structure for Contact Organizer should look as follows:

```
Project Structure
------------
├── ContactOrganizer/
    ├── Capabilities/
        ├── .chalice/
            ├── config.json
        ├── chalicelib/
            ├── __init__.py
        ├── app.py
        ├── requirements.txt
    ├── Website/
```

```
        ├── index.html
        ├── script.js
    ├── Pipfile
    ├── Pipfile.lock
```

This project structure for Contact Organizer contains the user interface, orchestration, and service implementations layers of the AI application architecture that we defined in `Chapter 2`, *Anatomy of a Modern AI Application.*

Implementing services

Let's implement the Contact Organizer layer-by-layer, starting with the service implementations that contain crucial AI capabilities. Many of the capabilities we need for this project, such as detecting text in images and handling file uploads, were implemented in previous projects. Services with truly new capabilities are the Extraction Service and Contact Store.

Recognition Service – text detection

Once again, we are going to leverage the Amazon Rekognition Service to provide the capability to detect text in an image. We can reuse the exact same implementation of our Recognition Service from the Pictorial Translator project in `Chapter 3`, *Detecting and Translating Text with Amazon Rekognition and Translate,* as shown in the following code:

```
import boto3

class RecognitionService:
    def __init__(self, storage_location):
        self.client = boto3.client('rekognition')
        self.bucket_name = storage_location

    def detect_text(self, file_name):
        response = self.client.detect_text(
            Image = {
                'S3Object': {
                    'Bucket': self.bucket_name,
                    'Name': file_name
                }
            }
        )

        lines = []
        for detection in response['TextDetections']:
```

```
        if detection['Type'] == 'LINE':
            lines.append({
                'text': detection['DetectedText'],
                'confidence': detection['Confidence'],
                'boundingBox': detection['Geometry']['BoundingBox']
            })

    return lines
```

For more details on its implementation and the design choices of the Recognition Service, refer to `Chapter 3`, *Detecting and Translating Text with Amazon Rekognition and Translate.*

> There is a new Amazon Textract service that can automatically extract text and data from scanned documents. Amazon Textract might work just as well for extracting text from business cards, but there are a few things to consider. Even though business cards are document-like, our application is processing photos of business cards, not scanned images.
>
> Amazon Textract is generally available now; replacing AWS Rekognition because of its text extraction capability will make a good feature enhancement exercise for this hands-on project. Think about which components and interactions would be impacted by this change in our architecture.

Extraction Service – contact information extraction

We are going to leverage Amazon Comprehend to extract the contact information from the text that's detected on the business cards. First, let's explore this service using the AWS CLI.

The Contact Organizer needs to extract information from our business cards. Typically, text on business cards contains information such as the person's name, job title, organization, address, phone number, email, and so on.

The following is example text from a made-up contact:

```
AI Enterprise Inc.
John Smith
Senior Software Engineer
123 Main Street Washington D.C. 20001
john.smith@aienterprise.com
(202) 123-4567
```

Let's see what Amazon Comprehend can extract from this example text. Issue the following AWS CLI command:

```
$ aws comprehend detect-entities --language-code en --text "AI Enterprise
Inc. John Smith Senior Software Engineer 123 Main Street Washington D.C.
20001 john.smith@aienterprise.com (202) 123-4567"
{
    "Entities": [
        {
            "Score": 0.8652380108833313,
            "Type": "ORGANIZATION",
            "Text": "AI Enterprise Inc",
            ...
        },
        {
            "Score": 0.9714182019233704,
            "Type": "PERSON",
            "Text": "John Smith",
            ...
        },
        {
            "Score": 0.9006084203720093,
            "Type": "LOCATION",
            "Text": "123 Main Street Washington D.C.",
            ...
        },
        {
            "Score": 0.48333245515823364,
            "Type": "DATE",
            "Text": "20001",
            ...
        },
        {
            "Score": 0.998563826084137,
            "Type": "OTHER",
            "Text": "john.smith@aienterprise.com",
            ...
        },
        {
```

```
                "Score": 0.9999305009841919,
                "Type": "OTHER",
                "Text": "(202) 123-4567",
                ...
            }
        ]
    }
```

Amazon Comprehend extracted some pieces of information, including the organization (`ORGANIZATION`), the person's name (`PERSON`), and the address (`LOCATION`). However, AWS Comprehend extracted the email and the phone number as `OTHER`, incorrectly extracted the zip code as a `DATE`, and failed to extract the job title.

Even though the extraction results are not perfect, they can still be leveraged by our Contact Organizer application to reduce manual effort on the part of users.

There is a way to improve upon these information extraction results. Amazon offers another variant of the Comprehend service called AWS Comprehend Medical. This variant of the service specializes in extracting information from various medical documents.

One of its features is the extraction of **Protected Health Information** (**PHI**) such as name, age, address, phone number, and email. We can leverage this feature for our business card information extraction task.

Let's see how this feature performs with the same example text we looked at previously. Issue the follow AWS CLI command:

```
aws comprehendmedical detect-phi --text "AI Enterprise Inc. John Smith
Software Engineer 123 Main Street Washington D.C. 20001
john.smith@aienterprise.com (202) 123-4567"
{
    "Entities": [
        {
            "Text": "AI Enterprise Inc",
            "Category": "PROTECTED_HEALTH_INFORMATION",
            "Type": "ADDRESS",
            ...
        },
        {
            "Text": "John Smith",
            "Category": "PROTECTED_HEALTH_INFORMATION",
            "Type": "NAME",
            ...
        },
        {
            "Text": "Software Engineer",
            "Category": "PROTECTED_HEALTH_INFORMATION",
```

```
                "Type": "PROFESSION",
                ...
            },
            {
                "Text": "123 Main Street Washington D.C. 20001",
                "Category": "PROTECTED_HEALTH_INFORMATION",
                "Type": "ADDRESS",
                ...
            },
            {
                "Text": "john.smith@aienterprise.com",
                "Category": "PROTECTED_HEALTH_INFORMATION",
                "Type": "EMAIL",
                ...
            },
            {
                "Text": "(202) 123-4567",
                "Category": "PROTECTED_HEALTH_INFORMATION",
                "Type": "PHONE_OR_FAX",
                ...
            }
        ]
    }
```

Amazon Comprehend Medical extracted much of the same information as its non-medical counterpart. In addition, it extracted the job title (`PROFESSION`), the phone number (`PHONE_OR_FAX`), and the email (`EMAIL`). The extracted address (`ADDRESS`) also seems more accurate than the non-medical variant. When we combine the results from both variants of the Comprehend service, we are able to extract the contact information on typical business cards.

With these insights, let's implement our Extraction Service. Let's create a Python class named `ExtractionService` in the `extraction_service.py` file located in the `chalicelib` directory:

```
import boto3
from collections import defaultdict
import usaddress

class ExtractionService:
    def __init__(self):
        self.comprehend = boto3.client('comprehend')
        self.comprehend_med = boto3.client('comprehendmedical')

    def extract_contact_info(self, contact_string):
        ...
```

This code excerpt shows the imports the service needs, as well as the constructor method, that instantiates two `boto3` clients for the Amazon Comprehend and the Amazon Comprehend Medical services, respectively.

Now let's see how the `extract_contact_info()` method is implemented with these two services:

```
def extract_contact_info(self, contact_string):
    contact_info = defaultdict(list)

    # extract info with comprehend
    response = self.comprehend.detect_entities(
        Text = contact_string,
        LanguageCode = 'en'
    )

    for entity in response['Entities']:
        if entity['Type'] == 'PERSON':
            contact_info['name'].append(entity['Text'])
        elif entity['Type'] == 'ORGANIZATION':
            contact_info['organization'].append(entity['Text'])

    # extract info with comprehend medical
    response = self.comprehend_med.detect_phi(
        Text = contact_string
    )

    for entity in response['Entities']:
        if entity['Type'] == 'EMAIL':
            contact_info['email'].append(entity['Text'])
        elif entity['Type'] == 'PHONE_OR_FAX':
            contact_info['phone'].append(entity['Text'])
        elif entity['Type'] == 'PROFESSION':
            contact_info['title'].append(entity['Text'])
        elif entity['Type'] == 'ADDRESS':
            contact_info['address'].append(entity['Text'])

    # additional processing for address
    address_string = ' '.join(contact_info['address'])
    address_parts = usaddress.parse(address_string)

    for part in address_parts:
        if part[1] == 'PlaceName':
            contact_info['city'].append(part[0])
        elif part[1] == 'StateName':
            contact_info['state'].append(part[0])
        elif part[1] == 'ZipCode':
```

```
            contact_info['zip'].append(part[0])

    return dict(contact_info)
```

In the preceding code, we can see the following:

- The `extract_contact_info()` method calls both variants of Amazon Comprehend through `boto3`. The results from both calls are processed and stored in the `contact_info` dictionary.
- `contact_info` is declared as a `defaultdict(list)`, which is a dictionary data structure where the values are defaulted to an empty list.

In practice, multiple results may be extracted for a given type. For example, two phone numbers can be extracted from a single business card. This can happen for three reasons, as we have observed in our use cases:

- The first reason applies when there are actually multiple pieces of information for a given type. For example, when there is a phone number and a fax number on a business card.
- The second reason is that the information is a composite of simpler pieces of information. For example, many job titles actually include role names, job levels, and specialties.
- The third reason is inaccuracies during the extraction process by the Amazon Comprehend service. For example, the zip code in the address may be mistakenly categorized as the phone number.

The two calls to the two variants of AWS Comprehend are as follows:

- The first call is to the `detect_entities()` function of the Amazon Comprehend client. From the response, we store the name and organization in `contact_info`.
- The second call is to the `detect_phi()` function of the Amazon Comprehend Medical client. From the response, we store the email, phone number, job title, and address in `contact_info`.

If there are multiple results for each of these types, they are appended to the corresponding list in the `defaultdict(list)` data structure.

AWS Comprehend extracts the address as a single piece of information. However, it would be more useful to store the various pieces of the address, such as city, state, and zip code, separately. This will make organizing, searching, and displaying contact information easier. In the `extract_contact_info()` method, we also use a Python package named `usaddress` to try and parse out the subcomponents of the address and then store them separately in the `contact_info` data structure.

Finally, the `extract_contact_info()` method returns `contact_info` as a standard Python dictionary.

> In the Contact Organizer application, the user uploads a photo of a business card. Then, the application tries to detect text with AWS Rekognition and feeds the detected text to AWS Comprehend to try to extract information. There is also a post-processing step for the address to parse out the city, state, and zip code.
>
> We can think of this process as a pipeline with multiple sequential steps; the output of a previous step feeds into the next step as input. Just like a game of telephone, the final result may be mangled by the output quality of any of the steps. The accuracy of the extraction depends on the quality of the photo, the detection accuracy of text in the photo, the extraction accuracy of information from the text, and the parsing accuracy of the post-processing.

Contact Store – save and retrieve contacts

After the user saves the contact information in the Contact Organizer, they should be able to retrieve this information. Retrieving data requires data persistence.

In Contact Organizer, we will be leveraging AWS DynamoDB, a highly scalable NoSQL database in the cloud. DynamoDB fits well with our serverless architecture because developers do not need to manage database servers. Instead, developers can create tables that scale with demand automatically. We will be storing and retrieving contact information using a DynamoDB table.

Let's create a Contacts table using the AWS Web Console:

1. Go to the **DynamoDB** dashboard page and click on the **Create table** button:

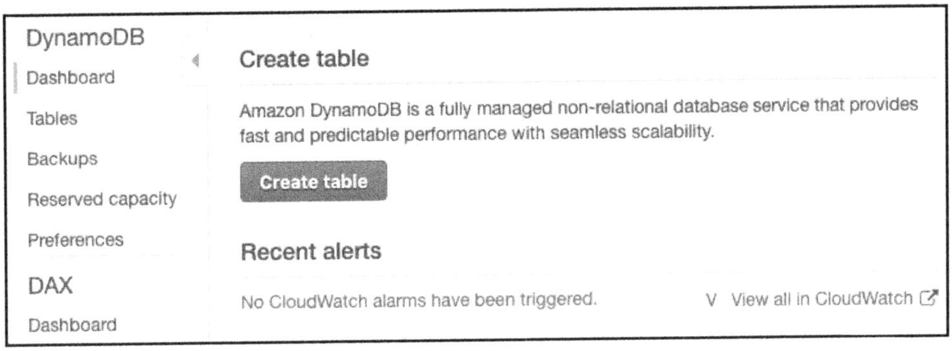

2. On the **Create DynamoDB table** page, set the table name to **Contacts** and set the primary key to **name**. Since **DynamoDB** is a NoSQL or document database, we do not need to specify the entire database table schema a priori:

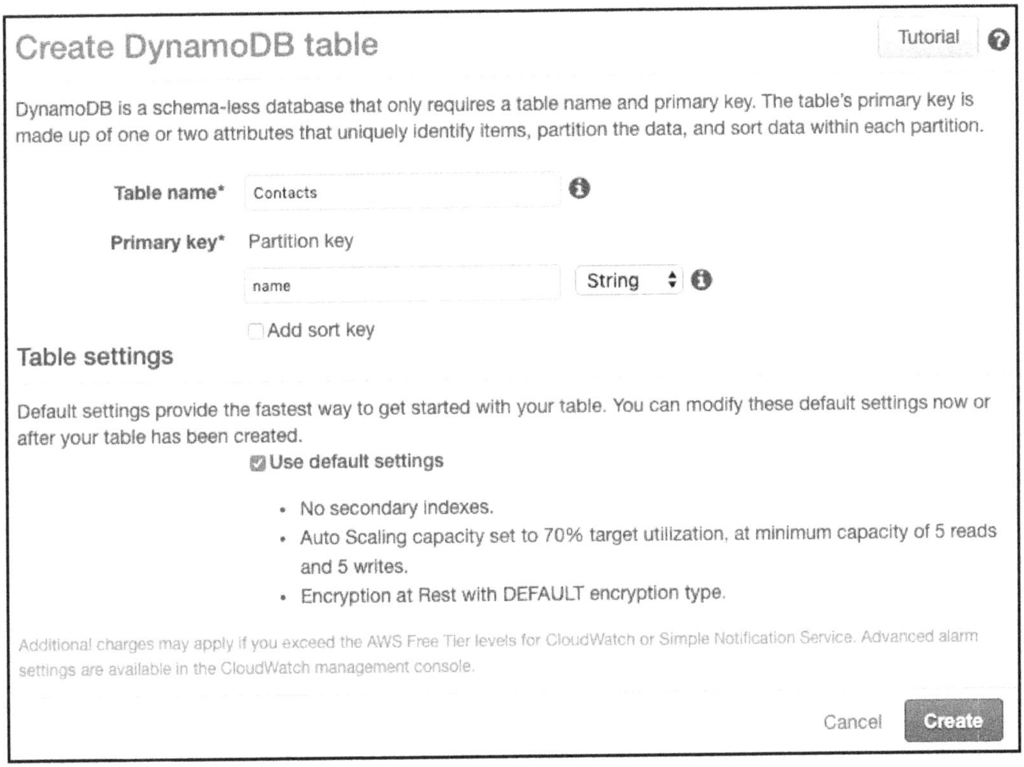

3. Finish the table setup by choosing the **Use default settings** option and clicking **Create**.

That's it! You just created a web-scale database that can handle more than 10 trillion requests per day. The best thing is, you don't have to manage it!

> **TIP**
>
> For this simple project, we used the AWS Web Console to create a database table. For enterprise-grade applications, we recommend following the best practices in line with **Infrastructure as Code (IaC)**, where infrastructure should be provisioned and managed automatically through code or configuration rather than by using a manual setup such as with AWS Web Console.
>
> The benefits include fast recovery from catastrophic events, rapid experimentation of features, and documentation of the system environment setup, to name only a few. Boto3 allows you to write Python code to create and configure DynamoDB tables. AWS CloudFormation also allows for the automatic creation and configuration of DynamoDB and many more AWS services.

Now with the `Contacts` table created, let's implement our `ContactStore` service. Create a Python class named `ContactStore` in the `contact_store.py` file, which is located in the `chalicelib` directory:

```
import boto3

class ContactStore:
    def __init__(self, store_location):
        self.table = boto3.resource('dynamodb').Table(store_location)

    def save_contact(self, contact_info):
        response = self.table.put_item(
            Item = contact_info
        )
        # should return values from dynamodb however,
        # dynamodb does not support ReturnValues = ALL_NEW
        return contact_info

    def get_all_contacts(self):
        response = self.table.scan()

        contact_info_list = []
        for item in response['Items']:
            contact_info_list.append(item)

        return contact_info_list
```

In the preceding code, we have the following:

- The constructor, `__init__()`, creates a `boto3` source for DynamoDB in order to get our `Contacts` table. The constructor takes in a parameter for `store_location` as the table name in our implementation.
- The `save_contact()` method takes a Python dictionary data structure containing the contact information and stores the contact using the `put_item()` function, which takes in the item to be put into the table.
- In `save_contact()`, we are returning the `contact_info` data object to the caller. We are trying to conform to the RESTful API convention: when an API creates a new resource (contact), it should return the updated resource (contact):
    - The RESTful convention recommends returning the new representation of the resources' state after their creation. For example, a new ID might have been created for the resource. However, the `put_item()` function in `boto3` currently does not return the new values of the resource. This is fine for Contact Organizer, since we chose to use the "name" as the key or the ID for the contact.
- The `get_all_contacts()` method retrieves all the contacts that have been saved in DynamoDB using the `scan()` function. With only the table name provided, the `scan()` function returns all the items in the table.

Storage Service – uploading and retrieving a file

We can reuse the exact same implementation of `StorageService` from previous projects. We are only providing the methods we need for the current project, as follows:

```
import boto3

class StorageService:
    def __init__(self, storage_location):
        self.client = boto3.client('s3')
        self.bucket_name = storage_location
    def upload_file(self, file_bytes, file_name):
        self.client.put_object(Bucket = self.bucket_name,
                               Body = file_bytes,
                               Key = file_name,
                               ACL = 'public-read')

        return {'fileId': file_name,
                'fileUrl': "http://" + self.bucket_name +
".s3.amazonaws.com/" + file_name}
```

For more details on the implementation and design choices, refer to `Chapter 3`, *Detecting and Translating Text with Amazon Rekognition and Translate.*

Implementing RESTful endpoints

Let's move on to the orchestration layer so that we can stitch together the various capabilities we implemented in the services. The RESTful endpoints provide HTTP access for the user interface layer to access business capabilities.

As we stated previously, the orchestration layer should be concise and easy to understand. RESTful endpoints should only be concerned with orchestrating the services to form a higher-level business logic and handling HTTP protocol specifics.

> TIP
>
> One way to evaluate whether the orchestration layer or RESTful endpoints are well designed in terms of separation of concerns is to check package imports. Does the orchestration layer need to import packages from the services?
>
> For example, in our projects, do the RESTful endpoints import a `boto3` that interacts with AWS? They shouldn't.
>
> Typically, RESTful endpoints will import service implementations (`storage_service` and `recognition_service`), programming framework-related packages (`chalice`), and protocol-related packages (`JSON` and `CGI`).

Replace the contents of `app.py` in the Chalice project with the following code:

```
from chalice import Chalice
from chalicelib import storage_service
from chalicelib import recognition_service
from chalicelib import extraction_service
from chalicelib import contact_store

import base64
import json


#####
# chalice app configuration
#####
app = Chalice(app_name='Capabilities')
app.debug = True
```

```
#####
# services initialization
#####
storage_location = 'contents.aws.ai'
storage_service = storage_service.StorageService(storage_location)
recognition_service =
recognition_service.RecognitionService(storage_location)
extraction_service = extraction_service.ExtractionService()
store_location = 'Contacts'
contact_store = contact_store.ContactStore(store_location)


#####
# RESTful endpoints
#####
...
```

The preceding code excerpt handles all package imports, the Chalice app configuration, and the instantiation of our four services.

Extract Image Information endpoint

The `extract_image_info()` function implements the RESTful endpoint. Use the following code to continue with the Python code in `app.py`:

```
@app.route('/images/{image_id}/extract-info', methods = ['POST'], cors =
True)
def extract_image_info(image_id):
    """detects text in the specified image then extracts contact
information from the text"""
    MIN_CONFIDENCE = 70.0

    text_lines = recognition_service.detect_text(image_id)

    contact_lines = []
    for line in text_lines:
        # check confidence
        if float(line['confidence']) >= MIN_CONFIDENCE:
            contact_lines.append(line['text'])

    contact_string = '   '.join(contact_lines)
    contact_info = extraction_service.extract_contact_info(contact_string)

    return contact_info
```

The annotation right above this function describes the HTTP request that can access this endpoint:

```
POST <server url>/images/{image_id}/extracted-info
```

In the preceding code, we have the following:

- In the `extract_image_info()` function, we call `RecognitionService` to detect text in the image and store the detected lines of text in `text_lines`.
- Then, we build a string, `contact_string`, that contains all of the lines of detected text with a confidence level is above `MIN_CONFIDENCE`, which is set to `70.0`:
    - This `contact_string` is built by joining the detected text with three spaces in between. We chose three spaces as the delimiter because detected lines are more likely to be related information, and we are hinting that relationship to the extraction service with the extra spaces.
- We then call the `extract_contact_info()` method of the Extraction Service and return the contact info. Remember that `extract_contact_info()` not only calls two variants of the Amazon Comprehend service, it also uses the `usaddress` Python package to parse out the individual parts of an address.

Let's test this endpoint out by running `chalice local` in the Python virtual environment and then issue the following `curl` command. Then, we will specify an image that has already been uploaded to our S3 bucket:

```
curl -X POST http://127.0.0.1:8000/images/<uploaded image>/extract-info
{
    "organization":[
        "<organization>"
    ],
    "name":[
        "<name>"
    ],
    "title":[
        "<title>"
    ],
    "address":[
        "<address>"
    ],
    "phone":[
        "<phone>"
    ],
    "email":[
```

```
            "<email>"
        ]
    }
```

This is the JSON that our web user interface will receive and use to display translations to the user.

Save contact and get all contacts endpoints

The save contact and get all contacts endpoints deal with the saving and retrieval of contacts through the Contact Store service:

```
@app.route('/contacts', methods = ['POST'], cors = True)
def save_contact():
    """saves contact information to the contact store service"""
    request_data = json.loads(app.current_request.raw_body)

    contact = contact_store.save_contact(request_data)

    return contact


@app.route('/contacts', methods = ['GET'], cors = True)
def get_all_contacts():
    """gets all saved contacts in the contact store service"""
    contacts = contact_store.get_all_contacts()

    return contacts
```

Their implementations are pretty simple:

- The `save_contact()` function gets the contact information from the JSON parameters in the request's body. This method then saves the contact using the Contact Store. The following code is the HTTP request that can access this endpoint:

```
POST <server url>/contacts
{
    "name": <NAME>,
    "organization": <ORGANIZATION>,
    "title": <TITLE>,
    "address": <ADDRESS>,
    "city": <CITY>,
    "state": <STATE>,
    "zip": <ZIP>,
    "phone": <PHONE>,
```

```
        "email": <EMAIL>
    }
```

- The `get_all_contacts()` method retrieves all of the saved contacts using the Contact Store. The following code is the HTTP request that can access this endpoint:

  ```
  GET <server url>/contacts
  ```

Let's test these endpoints together with a pair of `curl` commands:

```
$ curl --header "Content-Type: application/json" --request POST --data
'{"name": "John Smith", "organization": "AI Enterprise Inc.", "title":
"Senior Software Engineer", "address": "123 Main Street", "city":
"Washington D.C.", "zip": "20001", "phone": "(202) 123-4567", "email":
"john.smith@aienterprise.com"}' http://127.0.0.1:8000/contacts
{
 "name":"John Smith",
 "Organization":
 ...

$ curl http://127.0.0.1:8000/contacts
[
 {
 "city":"Washington D.C.",
 "zip":"20001",
 "organization":"AI Enterprise Inc.",
 "address":"123 Main Street",
 "email":"john.smith@aienterprise.com",
 "phone":"(202) 123-4567",
 "name":"John Smith",
 "title":"Senior Software Engineer"
 }
]
```

We can see the following:

- The first `POST` command gets the contact representation back as a response to conform to the RESTful convention.
- The second `GET` command gets a list of contacts with the one contact we just saved.

These are the JSON formats that are used to interact with the web user interface.

Upload image endpoint

We are reusing the exact same implementation of the upload image endpoint from the Pictorial Translator project. For more implementation details and design choices for this code snippet. Please refer to `Chapter 3`, *Detecting and Translating Text with Amazon Rekognition and Translate*:

```
@app.route('/images', methods = ['POST'], cors = True)
def upload_image():
    """processes file upload and saves file to storage service"""
    request_data = json.loads(app.current_request.raw_body)
    file_name = request_data['filename']
    file_bytes = base64.b64decode(request_data['filebytes'])

    image_info = storage_service.upload_file(file_bytes, file_name)

    return image_info
```

Now the Contact Organizer's orchestration layer is complete.

Implementing the web user interface

Next, we will create a simple web user interface with HTML and JavaScript in the `index.html` and `scripts.js` files in the `Website` directory.

The following screenshot shows the final web user interface:

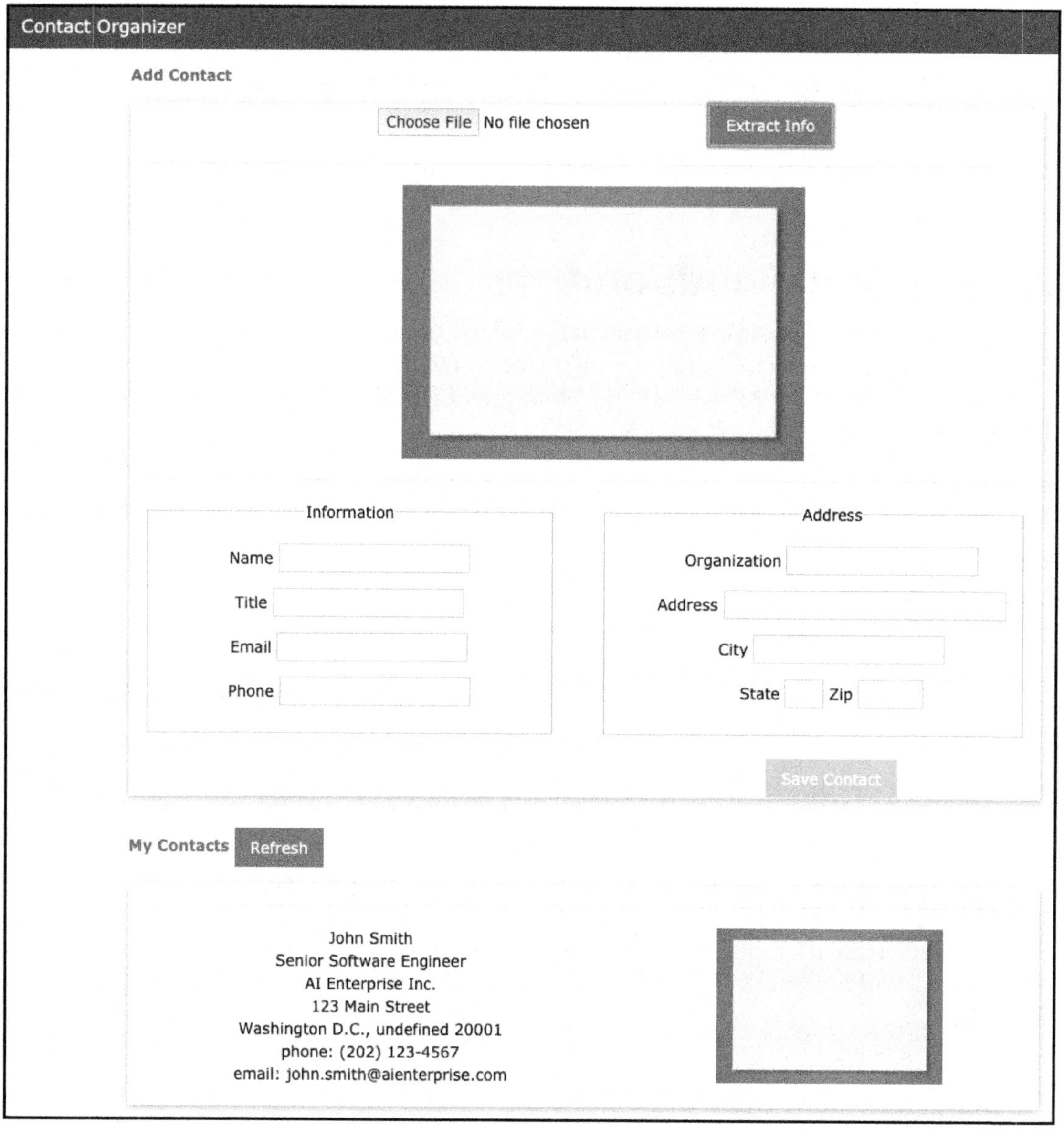

In the Contact Organizer, the user uploads a photo of a business card and the application will do its best to detect the text on the card and extract diverse information from the detected text. The application then populates the input fields with the extracted information for the user to review and modify.

> If multiple pieces of information were extracted for a certain type, the Contact Organizer populates the input field for that type with all the available information. For example, if multiple phone numbers were extracted, then the phone input field will be populated with all the phone numbers that are available.
> This design decision assumes that it is easier for a user to delete surplus information than to type in missing information. This assumption sounds valid; however, it should be validated with the target audience of the application through surveys or user studies. Fine-tuning these design decisions for human-in-the-loop user interfaces gives an application a slight edge over the competition.

Even though we would like an application such as the Contact Organizer to automatically extract and save all of the information on the business card, the aim of the Contact Organizer is to reduce menial effort as much as possible, while still keeping the user in the loop to ensure information accuracy.

> TIP
> The human-in-the-loop user interface has another important benefit. Because a human is involved in correcting any mistakes that are made by intelligent automation, this is an opportunity to capture training data that can be used to improve the automation technology in the future. Users are essentially providing training examples to the machine learning algorithm. Remember, better data always wins!

Index.html

We are using standard HTML tags here, so the code for the web page should be easy to follow:

```
<!doctype html>
<html lang="en"/>

<head>
    <meta charset="utf-8"/>
    <meta name="viewport" content="width=device-width, initial-scale=1.0"/>

    <title>Contact Organizer</title>
```

```
    <link rel="stylesheet" href="https://www.w3schools.com/w3css/4/w3.css">
    <link rel="stylesheet"
href="https://www.w3schools.com/lib/w3-theme-blue-grey.css">
</head>

<body class="w3-theme-14" onload="retrieveAndDisplayContacts()">
    <div style="min-width:400px">
        <div class="w3-bar w3-large w3-theme-d4">
            <span class="w3-bar-item">Contact Organizer</span>
        </div>

        ...

        <div class="w3-container w3-content">
            <p>
                <b class="w3-opacity">My Contacts</b>
                <input class="w3-button w3-blue-grey" type="submit"
                       value="Refresh"
onclick="retrieveAndDisplayContacts()"/>
            </p>
            <div class="w3-panel w3-white w3-card w3-display-container w3-
center">
                <div id="contacts"/>
            </div>
        </div>

    </div>

    <script src="scripts.js"></script>
</body>

</html>
```

This preceding HTML code snippet includes the top and bottom portions of the web user interface:

- When the web page initially loads, it calls a JavaScript function, `retrieveAndDisplayContacts()`, to load existing contacts from the server. This is done in the `<body>` tag's onload attribute.

- After the contacts are returned from the server, the `retrieveAndDisplayContacts()` function then updates `<div id="contacts"/>` to display the existing contacts to the user.
- The application also provides a **Refresh** button for the user to reload the contacts from the server at any time:

```
...
<div class="w3-container w3-content">
    <p class="w3-opacity"><b>Add Contact</b></p>
    <div class="w3-panel w3-white w3-card w3-display-container w3-center">
        <div>
            <input id="file" type="file" name="file" accept="image/*"/>
            <input class="w3-button w3-blue-grey" type="submit"
                   value="Extract Info" onclick="uploadAndExtract()"/>
            <hr>
        </div>
        <div id="view" style="display: none;">
            <img id="image" width="400"/>
            <hr>
        </div>
        <div class="w3-display-container w3-left" style="width:45%">
            <fieldset>
                <legend>Information</legend>
                <p>
                    <label for="name">Name</label>
                    <input id="name" type="text" name="name"/>
                </p>
                <p>
                    <label for="title">Title</label>
                    <input id="title" type="text" name="title"/>
                </p>
                <p>
                    <label for="email">Email</label>
                    <input id="email" type="email" name="email"/>
                </p>
                <p>
                    <label for="phone">Phone</label>
                    <input id="phone" type="tel" name="phone"/>
                </p>
            </fieldset>
        </div>
        <div class="w3-display-container w3-right" style="width:50%">
            <fieldset>
                <legend>Address</legend>
                <p>
                    <label for="organization">Organization</label>
                    <input id="organization" type="text"
```

```
                    name="organization"/>
            </p>
            <p>
                <label for="address">Address</label>
                <input id="address" type="text" name="address"
                 size="30"/>
            </p>
            <p>
                <label for="city">City</label>
                <input id="city" type="text" name="city"/>
            </p>
            <p>
                <label for="state">State</label>
                <input id="state" type="text" name="state" size="3"/>
                <label for="zip">Zip</label>
                <input id="zip" type="text" name="zip" size="6"/>
            </p>
        </fieldset>
        <br>
        <input class="w3-button w3-blue-grey" type="submit" id="save"
               value="Save Contact" onclick="saveContact()" disabled/>
    </div>
  </div>
</div>
...
```

This code snippet contains the Contact Organizer's human-in-the-loop interface so that it can add new contacts.

There are a few things to point out, as follows:

- We are providing an image upload interface that's similar to previous projects. We are displaying the uploaded image of a business card to the user. This way, the user can view the business card while reviewing and correcting the contact information.
- We are providing two columns of input fields for the various contact information types.
- We are providing a Save contact button for the user so that they can explicitly save contact information. The Save contact button is initially disabled until the application receives the extracted information from the server.

scripts.js

The first part of the Contact Organizer's `scripts.js` file is the same implementation of image upload from the Pictorial Translator project:

```
"use strict";

const serverUrl = "http://127.0.0.1:8000";

class HttpError extends Error {
    constructor(response) {
        super(`${response.status} for ${response.url}`);
        this.name = "HttpError";
        this.response = response;
    }
}

async function uploadImage() {
    // encode input file as base64 string for upload
    let file = document.getElementById("file").files[0];
    let converter = new Promise(function(resolve, reject) {
        const reader = new FileReader();
        reader.readAsDataURL(file);
        reader.onload = () => resolve(reader.result
            .toString().replace(/^data:(.*,)?/, ''));
        reader.onerror = (error) => reject(error);
    });
    let encodedString = await converter;

    // clear file upload input field
    document.getElementById("file").value = "";

    // make server call to upload image
    // and return the server upload promise
    return fetch(serverUrl + "/images", {
        method: "POST",
        headers: {
            'Accept': 'application/json',
            'Content-Type': 'application/json'
        },
        body: JSON.stringify({filename: file.name, filebytes:
encodedString})
    }).then(response => {
        if (response.ok) {
            return response.json();
        } else {
            throw new HttpError(response);
        }
```

```
        })
    }

    function updateImage(image) {
        document.getElementById("view").style.display = "block";

        let imageElem = document.getElementById("image");
        imageElem.src = image["fileUrl"];
        imageElem.alt = image["fileId"];

        return image;
    }
```

In the preceding code, we implemented the `uploadImage()` and `updateImage()` functions, which we will need later:

```
    function extractInformation(image) {
        // make server call to extract information
        // and return the server upload promise
        return fetch(serverUrl + "/images/" + image["fileId"] + "/extract-
    info", {
            method: "POST"
        }).then(response => {
            if (response.ok) {
                return response.json();
            } else {
                throw new HttpError(response);
            }
        })
    }

    function populateFields(extractions) {
        let fields = ["name", "title", "email", "phone", "organization",
    "address", "city", "state", "zip"];
        fields.map(function(field) {
            if (field in extractions) {
                let element = document.getElementById(field);
                element.value = extractions[field].join(" ");
            }
            return field;
        });
        let saveBtn = document.getElementById("save");
        saveBtn.disabled = false;
    }

    function uploadAndExtract() {
        uploadImage()
            .then(image => updateImage(image))
```

```
        .then(image => extractInformation(image))
        .then(translations => populateFields(translations))
        .catch(error => {
            alert("Error: " + error);
        })
}
```

In the preceding code snippet, we implement the following:

- The `extractInformation()` function, which calls the Extract Information endpoint
- The `populateFields()` function, which fills input fields with extracted contact information
- The `uploadAndExtract()` function chains, along with the `uploadImage()`, `updateImage()`, `extractInformation()`, and `populateFields()` functions, to compose the business logic flow when the user clicks on the **Extract Info** button:

```
function saveContact() {
    let contactInfo = {};

    let fields = ["name", "title", "email", "phone",
"organization", "address", "city", "state", "zip"];
    fields.map(function(field) {
        let element = document.getElementById(field);
        if (element && element.value) {
            contactInfo[field] = element.value;
        }
        return field;
    });
    let imageElem = document.getElementById("image");
    contactInfo["image"] = imageElem.src;

    // make server call to save contact
    return fetch(serverUrl + "/contacts", {
        method: "POST",
        headers: {
            'Accept': 'application/json',
            'Content-Type': 'application/json'
        },
        body: JSON.stringify(contactInfo)
    }).then(response => {
        if (response.ok) {
            clearContact();
            return response.json();
        } else {
```

```
                    throw new HttpError(response);
                }
            })
        }
```

In the preceding code snippet, the following things occur:

1. The `saveContact()` function gets a value from every input field and then creates the `contactInfo` data structure. This function then sends the data in `contactInfo` to the server for persistence.
2. If the response from the server is `ok`, it means the contact has been saved.
3. Then, this function calls the `clearContact()` function to clear the values of the input fields and the image display.

The following is the code for the `clearContact()` helper function:

```
function clearContact() {
    let fields = ["name", "title", "email", "phone", "organization",
"address", "city", "state", "zip"];
    fields.map(function(field) {
        let element = document.getElementById(field);
        element.value = "";
        return field;
    });

    let imageElem = document.getElementById("image");
    imageElem.src = "";
    imageElem.alt = "";

    let saveBtn = document.getElementById("save");
    saveBtn.disabled = true;
}
```

The `clearContact()` helper function from the preceding code prepares the user interface to process another business card. Let's have a look at the following code:

```
function retrieveContacts() {
    // make server call to get all contacts
    return fetch(serverUrl + "/contacts", {
        method: "GET"
    }).then(response => {
        if (response.ok) {
            return response.json();
        } else {
            throw new HttpError(response);
        }
```

```
        })
}

function displayContacts(contacts) {
    ...
}

function retrieveAndDisplayContacts() {
    retrieveContacts()
        .then(contacts => displayContacts(contacts))
        .catch(error => {
            alert("Error: " + error);
        })
}
```

In the preceding code snippet, the following occurs:

1. The `retrieveContacts()` function calls the server to retrieve all existing contacts.
2. The `displayContacts()` function takes the contacts and displays them at the bottom of the Contacts Organizer user interface.
3. The `retrieveAndDisplayContacts()` function chains together the business logic flow when the web interface is initially loaded or when the user clicks on the **Refresh** button:

```
function displayContacts(contacts) {
    let contactsElem = document.getElementById("contacts")
    while (contactsElem.firstChild) {
        contactsElem.removeChild(contactsElem.firstChild);
    }

    for (let i = 0; i < contacts.length; i++) {
        let contactElem = document.createElement("div");
        contactElem.style = "float: left; width: 50%";
contactElem.appendChild(document.createTextNode(contacts[i]["name"]
));
        contactElem.appendChild(document.createElement("br"));
contactElem.appendChild(document.createTextNode(contacts[i]["title"
]));
        contactElem.appendChild(document.createElement("br"));
contactElem.appendChild(document.createTextNode(contacts[i]["organi
zation"]));
        contactElem.appendChild(document.createElement("br"));
contactElem.appendChild(document.createTextNode(contacts[i]["addres
s"]));
        contactElem.appendChild(document.createElement("br"));
        contactElem.appendChild(document.createTextNode(
```

```
                contacts[i]["city"] + ", " + contacts[i]["state"] + "
" + contacts[i]["zip"]
            ));
            contactElem.appendChild(document.createElement("br"));
            contactElem.appendChild(document.createTextNode("phone: " +
contacts[i]["phone"]));
            contactElem.appendChild(document.createElement("br"));
            contactElem.appendChild(document.createTextNode("email: " +
contacts[i]["email"]));

            let cardElem = document.createElement("div");
            cardElem.style = "float: right; width: 50%";
            let imageElem = document.createElement("img");
            imageElem.src = contacts[i]["image"];
            imageElem.height = "150";
            cardElem.appendChild(imageElem);

            contactsElem.appendChild(document.createElement("hr"));
            contactsElem.appendChild(contactElem);
            contactsElem.appendChild(imageElem);
            contactsElem.appendChild(document.createElement("hr"));
        }
    }
```

This code snippet shows the gory details of generating HTML to display a list of contacts, the contact information, and the business card image.

> As you can see in the `displayContacts()` function, there is a lot of JavaScript code being used to generate HTML. Using a combination of business logic and display logic is considered bad practice.
>
> We highly recommend leveraging a JavaScript framework such as Angular, React, or Vue to better implement the **Model View Control** (**MVC**) design pattern for the user interface. To limit the scope of this book, we had no choice but to deal with code ugliness in our hands-on projects.

Deploying the Contact Organizer to AWS

The deployment steps for the Contact Organizer application are similar, but slightly different from, the deployment steps in the previous projects we covered. Let's get started:

1. For the Contact Organizer, we need to add additional Python packages to the AWS Lambda environment. We do this by adding two packages to the `requirements.txt` file:
    - The `usaddress` package is used to parse the various parts of the address, such as city, state, zip, and so on.
    - The `boto3` package is specified here because we need a specific version. At the time of writing, the `boto3` version in the AWS Lambda environment does not support the `comprehendmedical` service; we need a newer version for this project:

    ```
    usaddress==0.5.10
    boto3==1.9.224
    ```

2. Next, let's tell Chalice to perform a policy analysis for us by setting `"autogen_policy"` to `false` in the `config.json` file in the `.chalice` directory of the project structure:

    ```
    {
      "version": "2.0",
      "app_name": "Capabilities",
      "stages": {
        "dev": {
          "autogen_policy": false,
          "api_gateway_stage": "api"
        }
      }
    }
    ```

3. Next, we create a new file, `policy-dev.json`, in the `.chalice` directory to manually specify the AWS services the project needs:

    ```
    {
     "Version": "2012-10-17",
     "Statement": [
     {
     "Effect": "Allow",
     "Action": [
     "logs:CreateLogGroup",
     "logs:CreateLogStream",
     "logs:PutLogEvents",
    ```

```
"s3:*",
"rekognition:*",
"comprehend:*",
"comprehendmedical:*",
"dynamodb:*"
],
"Resource": "*"
}
]
}
```

4. Next, we deploy the Chalice backend to AWS by running the following command within the `Capabilities` directory:

```
$ chalice deploy
Creating deployment package.
Creating IAM role: Capabilities-dev
Creating lambda function: Capabilities-dev
Creating Rest API
Resources deployed:
  - Lambda ARN: arn:aws:lambda:us-
east-1:<UID>:function:Capabilities-dev
  - Rest API URL:
https://<UID>.execute-api.us-east-1.amazonaws.com/api/
```

When the deployment is complete, Chalice will output a RESTful API URL that looks similar to `https://<UID>.execute-api.us-east-1.amazonaws.com/api/`, where `<UID>` is a unique identifier string. This is the server URL your frontend app should hit to access the application backend running on AWS.

5. Next, we will upload the `index.html` and `scripts.js` files to this S3 bucket, then set the permissions as `publicly readable`. Before we do that, we need to make a change in `scripts.js`, as follows. Remember, the website will be running in the cloud now and won't have access to our local HTTP server. Replace the local server URL with the one from our backend deployment:

```
"use strict";

const serverUrl =
"https://<UID>.execute-api.us-east-1.amazonaws.com/api";

...
```

Now the Contact Organizer application is publicly accessible to everyone on the internet.

> As it is implemented in this chapter, the Contact Organizer shows anyone who has the URL for the application all of the saved contact information. We do not recommend leaving any personally identifiable information out in the open on the internet.
> One way to protect this information is to add authentication and authorization features to Contact Organizer. These features are beyond the scope of this book, but they are interesting enhancements for this project.

Discussing the project enhancement ideas

At the end of each hands-on project in Part 2, we provide you with a few ideas to extend our intelligence-enabled application. The following are a couple of ideas for enhancing the Contact Organizer:

- Use the Amazon Textract service to create another implementation of the Recognition Service. Textract provides an **Optical Character Recognition** (**OCR**) capability that's much better suited for documents with a large amount of text. Depending on the business card's appearance, environment lighting, and photo quality, Textract might provide better text detection performance.
- The intelligent capabilities and the user interface we created for Contact Organizer can also be used for other use cases, such as data extraction from business documents, summarizing school notes, and categorizing customer requests. The raw text doesn't even need to come from images; other sources can include emails, phone calls, and even social media. Think about use cases where you might use a similar human-in-the-loop user interface and intelligent capabilities.

Summary

In this chapter, we built a Contact Organizer application that can extract contact information from uploaded photos of business cards. We used two variants of the Amazon Comprehend service, Amazon Comprehend and Amazon Comprehend Medical, to extract different types of contact information. The Contact Organizer has a human-in-the-loop user interface, where the user can review and correct automatically extracted information before saving it to the Contact Store. We noted that the human-in-the-loop user interface should provide business value, even if AI capabilities are not present in the solution. As AI practitioners, we don't always have to provide fully automated solutions—there is value in providing intelligent assistive solutions, which can be much more feasible to build and maintain as long as they are well designed with the human component in mind.

In the next chapter, we will build an AI solution that can communicate with us using natural conversational interfaces. We will be using AI technologies that are at the heart of the popular Alexa smart speakers.

Further reading

For more information on extracting information from text with Amazon Comprehend, please refer to the following links:

- `https://www.mckinsey.com/featured-insights/future-of-work/ai-automation-and-the-future-of-work-ten-things-to-solve-for`
- `https://builtin.com/artificial-intelligence/examples-ai-in-industry`

6
Building a Voice Chatbot with Amazon Lex

In this chapter, we will build a chatbot that allows the user to search for information and perform actions using voice or text conversations. This chatbot offers a more intuitive interface for humans to interact with computers. We will use Amazon Lex to build a custom AI capability to understand requests in natural language, to ask for missing inputs, and to fulfill tasks. We will provide guidance on the Amazon Lex development paradigm, including its conventions and norms.

In this chapter, we will cover the following topics:

- Building conversational interfaces with Amazon Lex
- Implementing task fulfillment logics with AWS Lambda
- Adding a RESTful API in front of Amazon Lex custom AI capability
- Discussing design concerns for conversational interfaces

Understanding the friendly human-computer interface

The intelligent personal assistant, sometimes called the **chatbot**, is rapidly appearing in more and more products with which we interact. The most prominent of these products are smart speakers, such as Amazon Echo and Google Home. Interacting with machines using your voice used to be the stuff of science fiction. Nowadays, fun facts and jokes are just an *Alexa* or *Hey Google* away. The tasks we can ask these intelligent assistants to perform include media control, information search, home automation, and administrative tasks, such as emails, to-dos, and reminders.

The capability of the intelligent personal assistant can be integrated into many more types of devices and platforms than just smart speakers. These include mobile operating systems such as Android and iOS, instant messaging apps such as Facebook Messenger, and company websites such as restaurants (to take orders) and banks (to check account balances). There are two main methods of interaction: through text or voice. This intelligent assistant capability is a combination of several AI technologies. For both interaction methods, **Natural Language Processing** (**NLP**) is needed to interpret and match the text to supported questions or commands. For voice interaction, speech-to-text and text-to-speech are needed to enable voice communication, which is something we have had hands-on experience with in Amazon Transcribe and Amazon Polly, respectively.

It may appear that these intelligent assistants are performing tasks such as getting answers to questions, placing orders, and automating our homes. But behind the scenes, these tasks are almost always fulfilled by traditional APIs and services. What we actually get with the intelligent assistant capability is a more flexible human-computer interface. Leveraging this new capability is not simply slapping a fancy voice interface on top of an existing application. When designing intelligent assistants, it's important to understand the use cases and operating environments where the intelligent assistant can provide a better user experience. Not all applications should have such interfaces; for example, use cases requiring precise inputs or dense outputs, noisy operating environments, and workflows that are long and complex.

In this chapter, we will be implementing an intelligent assistant, called Contact Assistant, for searching contact information. The contact assistant will work with the same contact data store we created for the contact organizer project in `Chapter 5`, *Extracting Information from Text with Amazon Comprehend*. We will also add a RESTful API in front of the contact assistant, giving us multiple applications to leverage its capabilities. The way this intelligent assistant is designed makes it most useful out in the field, for example, when a traveling salesman is driving to a client and needs to get the client's contact information verbally. Instead of performing the searches through a web application running in a browser, this use case is better suited to be a mobile application with a driver-friendly user interface. This mobile application and its user interface are beyond the scope of this book, but may turn out to be interesting hands-on projects for some of you.

Contact assistant architecture

The architecture for the contact assistant project includes the following:

- An orchestration layer
- A service implementation layer

The following architecture does not include the user interface layer, since we will not be implementing the mobile or web application that connects to the contact assistant. Instead, we will be focusing our efforts on developing a custom AI capability, an intelligent assistant bot, using the Amazon Lex platform. Let's have a look at a screenshot of the following architecture:

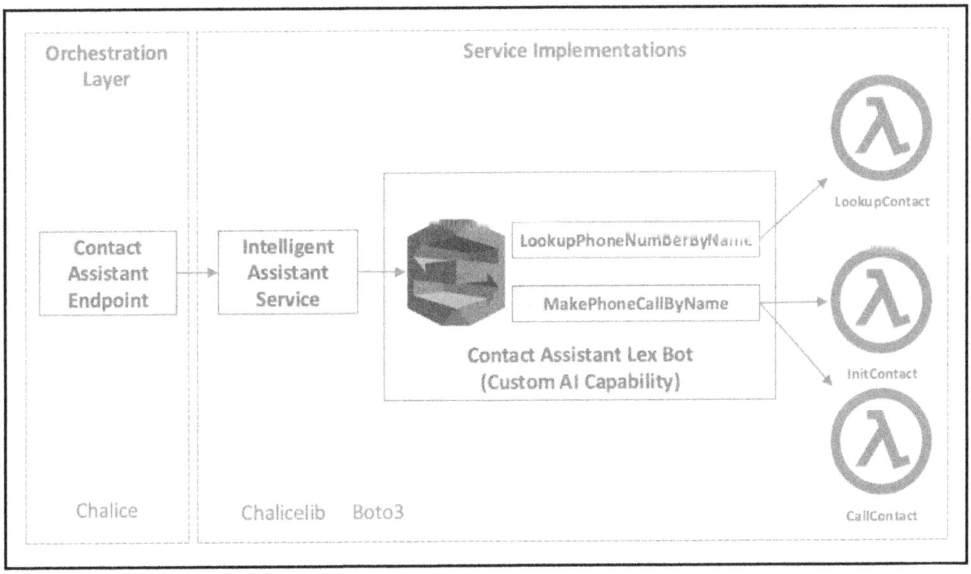

The contact assistant architecture includes the following:

- In the orchestration layer, we will build a **Contact Assistant Endpoint** that provides a RESTful interface to access our contact assistant's capabilities.
- In the service implementation layer, we will build a service, called the **intelligent assistant service**, that shields implementation details of our custom AI capability, including its Amazon Lex implementation details. This way, when we want to reimplement the contact assistant bot with a different chatbot technology, only the intelligent assistant service needs to be modified.

In previous chapters, we built our own services, such as Recognition Service and Speech Service, that connect to AWS AI capabilities such as Rekognition and Polly, respectively. Just like these services are shielding implementation details of the AWS AI services, the intelligent assistant service is shielding implementation details of our custom AI capability built on top of Amazon Lex.

- The contact assistant bot will be able to perform two tasks, `LookupPhoneNumberByName` and `MakePhoneCallByName`. This bot leverages Amazon Lex's underlying AI capabilities to interpret the user's verbal commands, and then performs the tasks using AWS Lambda functions. These Lambda functions implement the fulfillment of the tasks, looking up phone numbers and making phone calls.
- Contact Assistant will be looking up contact information stored in the same DynamoDB table that we used in `Chapter 5`, *Extracting Information from Text with Amazon Comprehend*, in the contact organizer application. In the spirit of reuse, we will be reusing the contact store implementation that connects to the DynamoDB table. More specifically, the Lambda functions will delegate the contact searches to the contact store. The fact that the contact information is stored in a DynamoDB table is transparent to the contact assistant.

Understanding the Amazon Lex development paradigm

Amazon Lex is a development platform for building intelligent assistants or chatbots. With Amazon Lex, we are building our own custom intelligent assistant capabilities. Lex itself provides many AI capabilities, including **Automatic Speech Recognition** (**ASR**) and **Natural Language Understanding** (**NLU**), that are useful for building conversational interfaces. However, developers must follow Lex's development constructs, conventions, and norms to leverage these underlying AI capabilities.

These Amazon Lex conversational interfaces are built from Lex's specific building blocks:

- **Bot**: A Lex bot can perform a set of related tasks through the custom conversational interfaces. A bot organizes the related tasks into a unit for development, deployment, and execution.
    - For example, to make the tasks available to the applications, they are deployed or published as a bot and the application must specify the bot name in order to access the available tasks.
- **Intent**: An intent represents an automated task the users want to perform. An intent belongs to a specific AWS account rather than a specific bot and can be used by different bots in the same AWS account. This design decision makes them more reusable.

- **Sample utterance**: An utterance is a typed or spoken phrase in natural language that the user might say to invoke an automated task. Amazon Lex encourages developers to provide multiple utterances to make the conversational interface more flexible for the users.
    - For example, a user might either say *What's the weather like today?*, or *Tell me about the weather today?* to check the weather report. Amazon Lex uses advanced NLU to understand the intent of the user.
    - Given the previous two sample utterances, Amazon Lex also uses the NLU capability to handle variations of the utterances. Lex can understand *Tell me what the weather's like today?* even if the exact phrase is not provided.
- **Slot**: An automated task may require zero or more slots (parameters) to complete. For example, the date and the location are parameters used to fetch the weather report the user is interested in. In the conversational interface, Lex asks the user to provide all of the required slots.
    - For example, the location can be defaulted to the user's home address if not specified.
- **Slot type**: Each slot has a type. Similar to a parameter type in programming languages, a slot type restricts input space and simplifies verification to make the conversational interface more user friendly. In verbal communication in particular, knowing the types of slots can help the AI technologies more accurately determine the typed or spoken texts.
    - There are numerous built-in slot types, such as Number, City, Airport, Language, and Musician, to name but a few. Developers can also create custom slot types specific to their applications.
- **Prompt and response**: A prompt is a question in which Lex asks the users to either provide input to a slot, or to confirm the input provided. A response is a message to inform the user about the result of the task, such as the weather report.
    - The design of prompts and responses for conversational interfaces should take into account the use case, communication modality (text or speech), and the operating environment. The design should get user confirmation while not overburdening users with unnecessary communication.

- **Session attributes**: Amazon Lex provides mechanisms to keep contextual data that can be shared across intents in the same session.
    - For example, if a user just asked for the weather report for a city and then follows up with a question, *How's the traffic there?*, the session context should be able to infer that *there* means the city reference in the previous intent. This type of contextual information can be stored in Lex's session attributes for developers to build smarter bots.

The Amazon Lex platform focuses on building conversational interfaces; fulfillment of the automated tasks is delegated to AWS Lambda. There are two built-in hook types for developers to integrate lambda functions:

- **Lambda initialization and validation**: This hook allows developers to write AWS Lambda functions to validate the user inputs. For example, the lambda function can verify a user's inputs from a data source and with more complex business logic.
- **The fulfillment lambda function**: This hook allows developers to write AWS Lambda code that performs the task. With this lambda hook, developers can tap into AWS services, API endpoints, and much more to write the business logic for tasks such as checking the weather, ordering a pizza, and sending messages.

Setting up the contact assistant bot

Now that we understand the Amazon Lex's development paradigm and terminology, let's put them to use by building a bot with both the conversational interface and the fulfillment business logic. We will be building the contact assistant using the AWS Console. Observe the following steps:

1. Navigate to the **Amazon Lex** page and click on the **Create** button.
2. On the **Create your bot** page, select **Custom bot** to create our own bot instead of building from a sample bot.
3. For the **Bot name** field, enter `ContactAssistant`.
4. For the **Output voice**, select **Joanna**. Currently, Lex only supports US English.
5. For the **Session timeout**, enter **5 min**. This is the maximum idle time before the contact assistant closes a session.
6. For the **IAM role**, leave it as the default **AWSServiceRoleForLexBots**.
7. Select **No** for COPPA; the contact assistant is designed for a traveling salesman, not children.

8. Click on the **Create** button.

The **Create your bot** page should have the following settings after the preceding steps have been carried out:

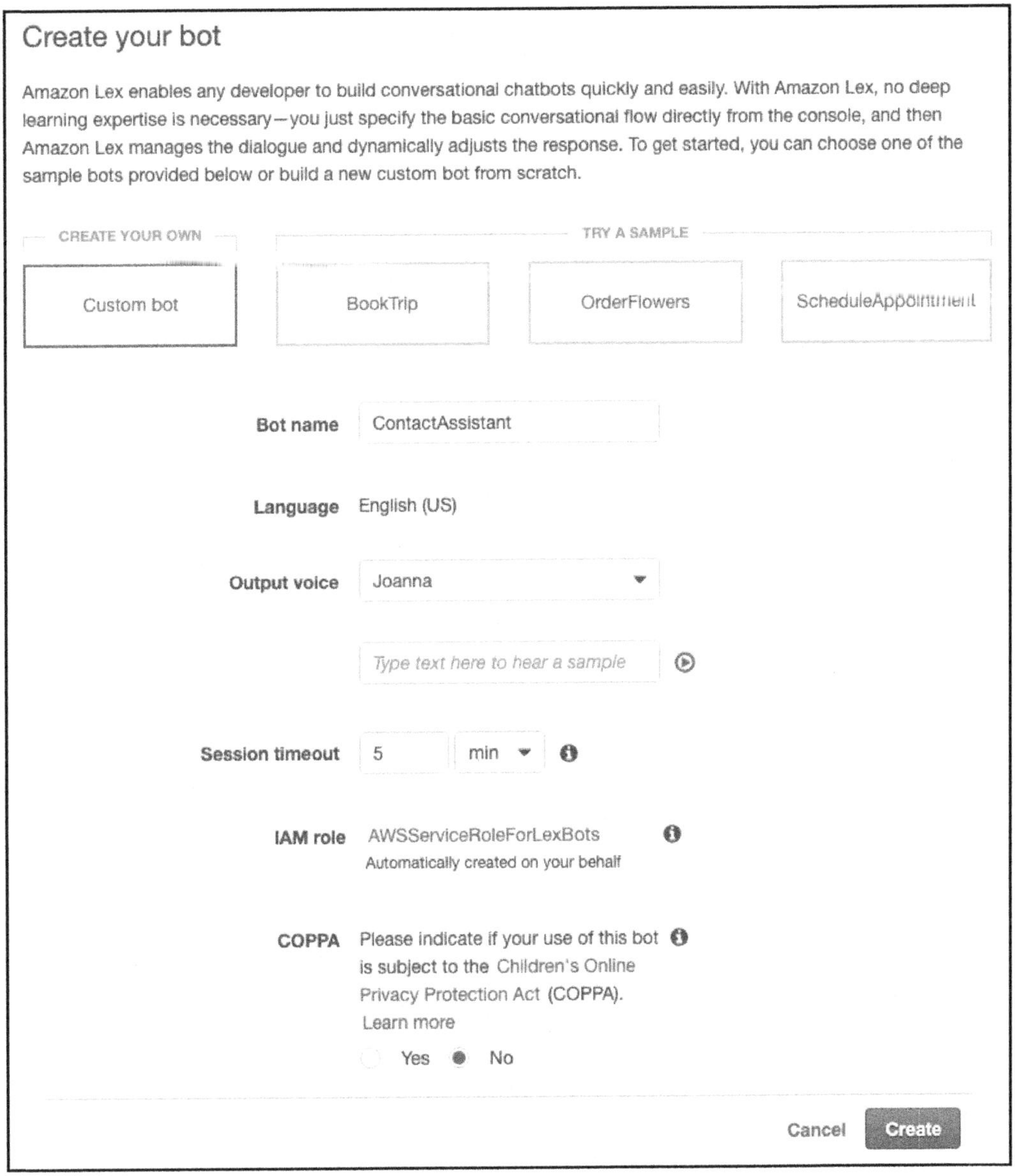

9. Once the contact assistant has been created, you will be taken to the development console for Lex, similar to the one shown in the following screenshot:

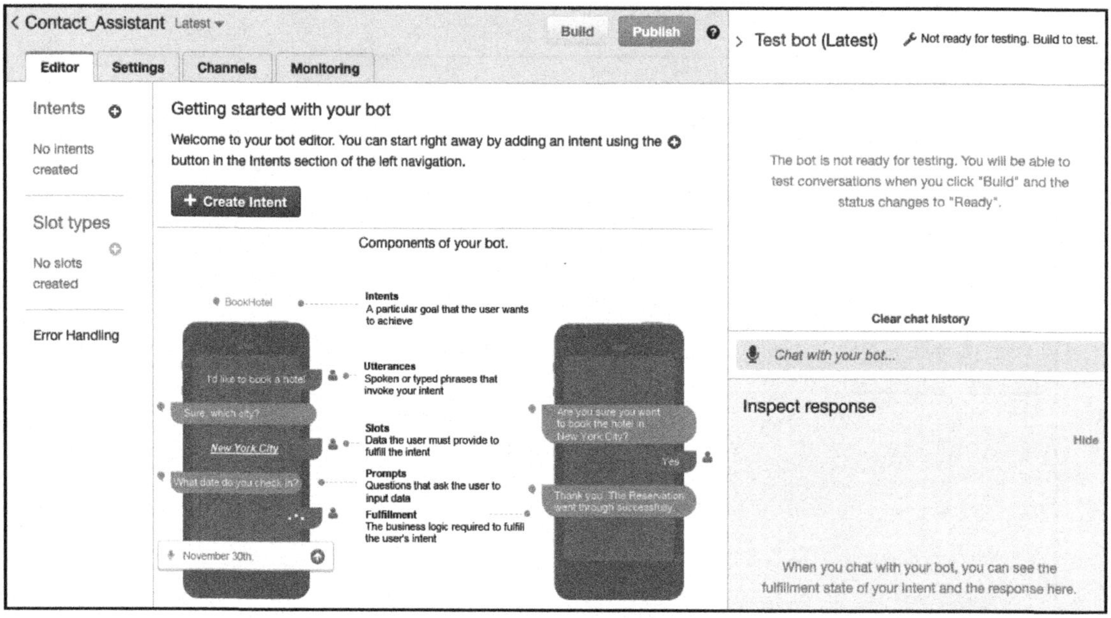

Let's familiarize ourselves with the Lex development console:

1. The bot's name can be found in the top-left corner, **Contact_Assistant**.
2. There are a pair of disabled buttons for **Build** and **Publish** in the top-right corner.
3. Below the bot name and buttons are the tabs for **Editor**, **Settings**, **Channels**, and **Monitoring** screens. We will perform most of our bot development in the **Editor** tab.
4. With the **Editor** tab selected, we see that no **Intents** or **Slot types** have been added to the contact assistant.
5. In the top-right corner of the screen, there is a **Test bot** sidebar that can be expanded (shown in the diagram) to reveal a chat interface. This chat interface is used to issue verbal commands to the bot under development. The chat interface is currently disabled. The bot needs to be built, with at least one intent created.
6. Finally, Click on the **Create Intent** button to build our first intent.

The LookupPhoneNumberByName intent

Our first intent allows the user to look up a contact's phone number by stating the contact's first and last names. This intent is essentially a search feature built on top of the contact store, but with a conversational interface.

> TIP: We recommend designing each intent to focus on a narrow use case, and building up multiple intents to expand the bot's use cases.

The `LookupPhoneNumberByName` intent has very focused inputs and outputs, but we can build many related intents, such as `LookupAddressByName` and `LookupContactNamesByState`. Even though we can consider the `LookupPhoneNumberByName` intent as a search feature to a data source, it requires a different design thinking.

Let's highlight a few design differences when comparing this intent to a more conventional search feature on a web application:

- In a web interface, we would provide the user with several search parameters, such as name, organization, and location. In a conversational interface, we would want to limit the number of search parameters, or inputs, for each intent. In a voice chatbot in particular, prompting and confirming all of the inputs might be cumbersome.
- In a web interface, we would return many pieces of information about the contact and display them on the screen. In a conversational interface, we need to consider the modality. If this is a text chatbot, we might be able to get away with displaying multiple pieces of information. But, if this is a voice chatbot, then reading a long list of information to the user might create a cognitive burden.

Sample utterances and slots for LookupPhoneNumberByName

When designing a new intent, all stakeholders, not just developers, must carefully think through the conversational flow between the user and the bot. Let's start with the sample utterances.

The intelligent assistant is a likely replacement for existing communication channels to users, such as phone calls to customer representatives, inquiry emails for product issues, and text chats with technical agents. It's common practice to use recordings of user conversations from these existing channels to design the conversational flow of the intelligent assistant. These recordings provide the most accurate reflection of your users' interactions with the products; they are a good starting point for designing the utterances and the prompts.

Sample utterances are phrases that invoke the intent to perform an automated task. Here are a few sample utterances for our `LookupPhoneNumberByName` intent:

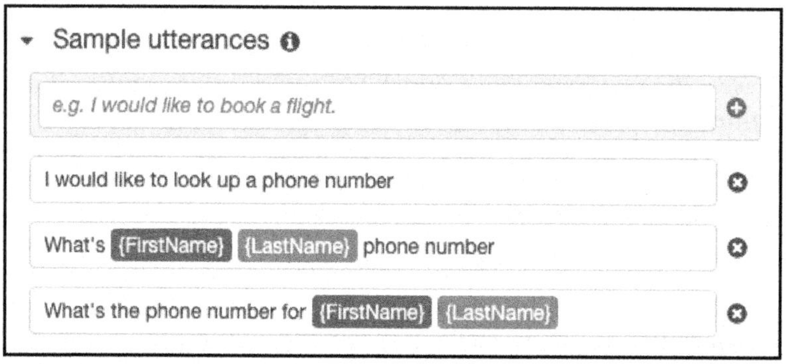

As we can see in the preceding screenshot, two of the sample utterances naturally included slots or input parameters, **{FirstName}** and **{LastName}**, in the conversation flow. This way users can provide some or all of the inputs needed to fulfill the task when it is invoked.

For `LookupPhoneNumberByName`, we need both the **{FirstName}** and **{LastName}** to look up a phone number as they are both required. Let's have a look at the following screenshot of slots:

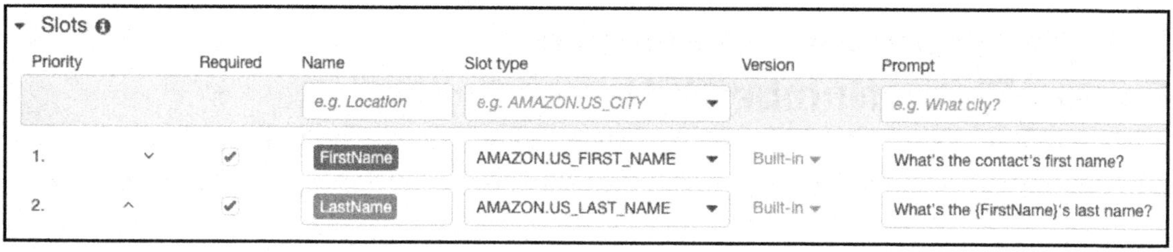

As shown in the preceding screenshot, for the slot types, there are built-in **AMAZON.US_FIRST_NAME** and **AMAZON.US_LAST_NAME** types. As we noted previously, specifying the most relevant and specific types for the inputs makes natural language understanding and value validation much easier for the underlying AI technologies.

What if the user did not provide the inputs to the slots? For example, what if the user spoke the first sample utterance, *I would like to look up a phone number*. Each slot must have one or more prompts to ask the user for the input value if it was not provided in the invoking utterance. For `{FirstName}` and `{LastName}`, we used `What's the contact's first name?` and `What's the {FirstName}'s last name?`, respectively. Notice that the prompt for `{LastName}` included the slot value for `{FirstName}`. This can make the conversation flow more natural and human-like.

To add more than one prompt for a slot, click on the gear icon to edit the slot's settings. Here, you can add additional prompts, set the **Maximum number of retries** to elicit this input, and corresponding utterances, as follows:

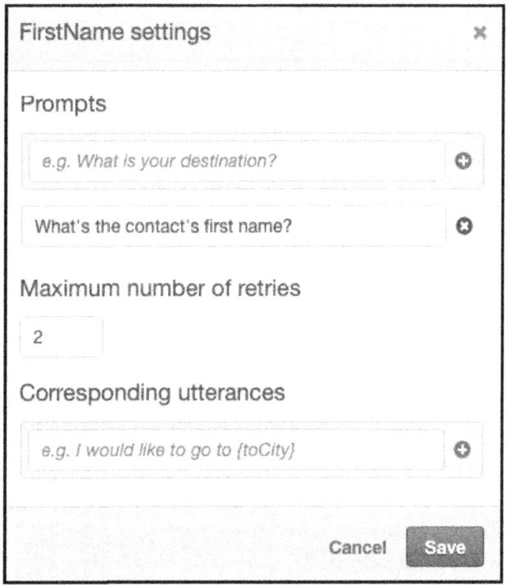

The bot will select from this list of prompts to ask the user for the slot. The bot will attempt the prompts up to two times before giving up.

Confirmation prompt and response for LookupPhoneNumberByName

To complete the conversational flow design, let's move on to the confirmation prompt and response. Both of these are optional, but they can greatly improve the behavior and user experience of the intelligent assistant.

The following is a screenshot of a confirmation prompt. A confirmation prompt is an opportunity to inform the user about the action about to be taken. At this point, values for all of the required slots and potentially optional slots have been elicited:

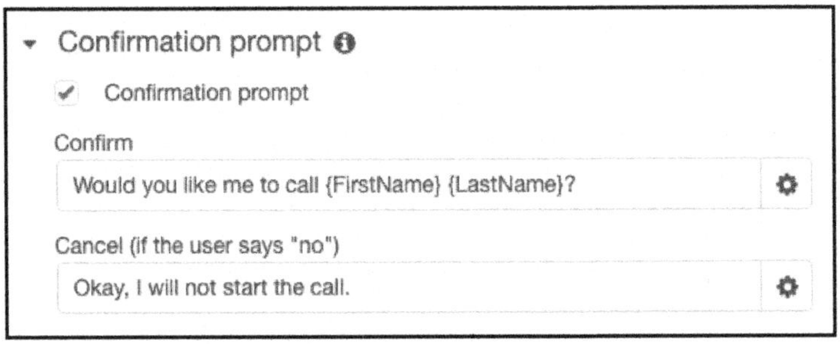

We are able to use `{FirstName}` and `{LastName}` in the confirmation message. It's a good design to read or display back the values for the `{FirstName}` and `{LastName}` slots; this confirms with the user that the bot understood the inputs correctly. Natural language conversations can be ambiguous at times. Let's take a look at this example conversation:

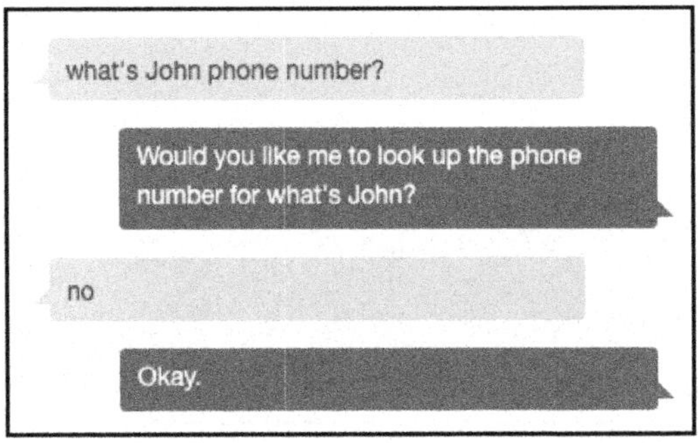

Do you spot the issue? One of our sample utterances is **What's {FirstName} {LastName} phone number**. However, the user invoked the intent without providing a `{LastName}`. Our bot interpreted *what's* as the `{FirstName}`, and `John` as the `{LastName}`. By reading back the input values with the confirmation prompt, the user can notice and correct the input error before the action is taken.

We will skip fulfillment of the task for now and move on to the response. In the following screenshot, the response for the `LookupPhoneNumberByName` intent closes out the task by displaying or reading the phone number for the contact:

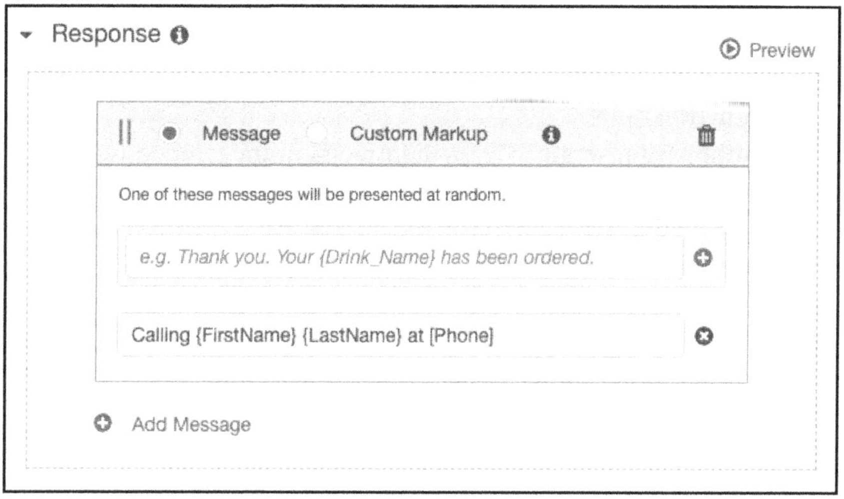

`[Phone]` is a session attribute that is holding the phone number for the contact. It will be set in the fulfillment lambda function. We will cover how that's implemented later in the chapter.

This intent is used to query for information. Providing the information in the response will feel natural to users. There are also intents that will perform a task without the need to provide information back to the users. In such cases, it is still a good idea to respond to the users of the outcome of the task.

Now, we have completed the conversational interface for our first intent. Next, we will implement the AWS Lambda function that will perform the task asked of our intelligent assistant.

Fulfillment for LookupPhoneNumberByName using AWS Lambda

To perform any fulfillment action with the intelligent assistant, developers need to invoke AWS Lambda functions. The *Fulfillment* section provides a hook to an existing lambda function. Let's implement a lambda function called **LookupPhoneNumberByName** to search for the phone number of a contact by his or her first and last names.

In contrast to previous projects, where we used AWS Chalice to develop and deploy the lambda code and AWS permissions, we will be using the AWS Lambda console page to create the `LookupPhoneNumberByName` function. Here are the steps:

1. Navigate to the AWS Lambda service from AWS Console, and then click on the **Create function** button.
2. Select **Author from scratch**. We will implement the lambda function without any blueprints or sample applications.
3. Name the function `LookupPhoneNumberByName`.
4. Select the **Python 3.7** runtime to match the language version for our other hands-on projects.
5. Choose **Create a new role with basic Lambda permissions to create a role**. We will need to add additional policies later to connect to additional AWS services.
6. Click the **Create function** button.

The settings on the **Create function** page should look similar to the following screenshot:

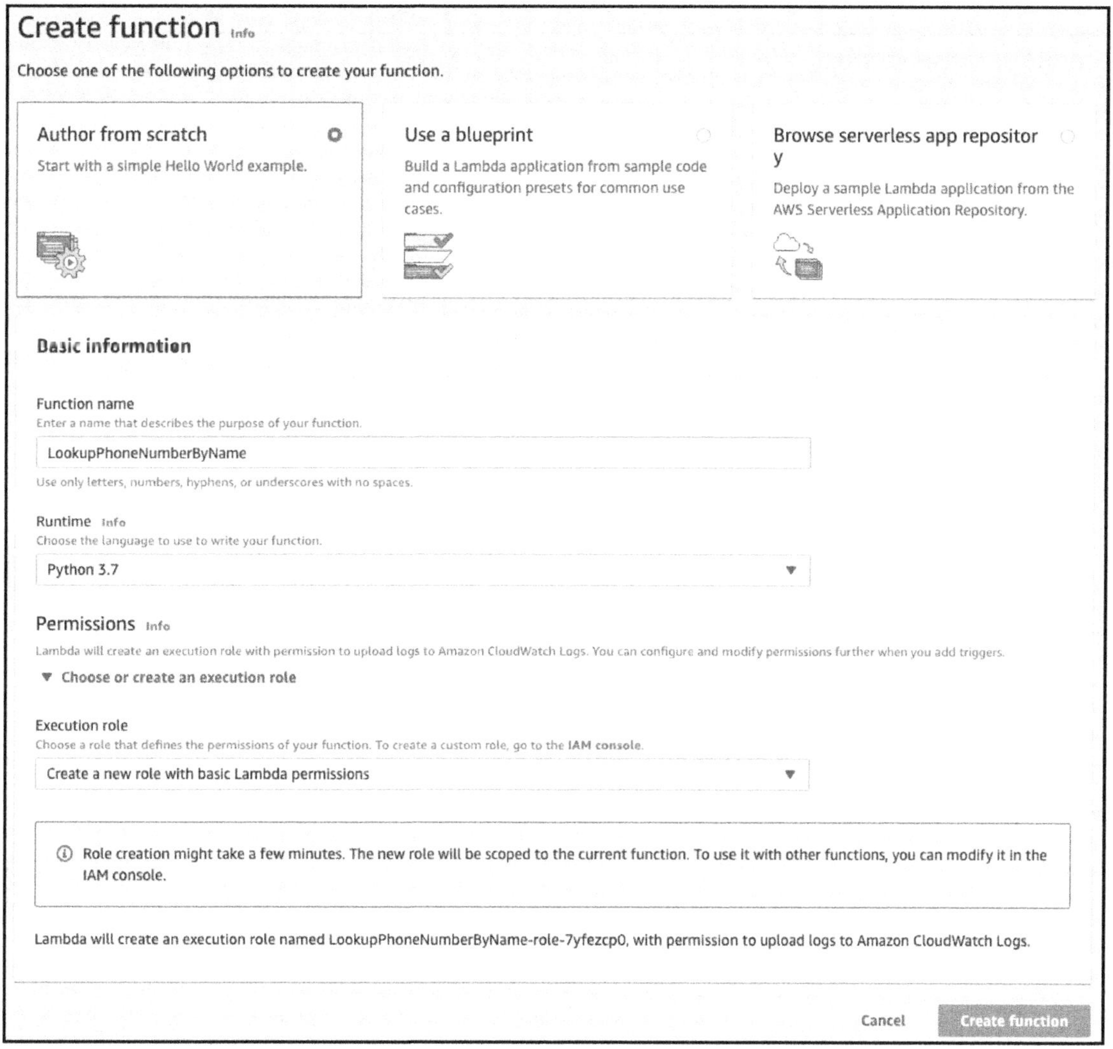

After the lambda function and its execution role have been created, you will see a development console similar to this one:

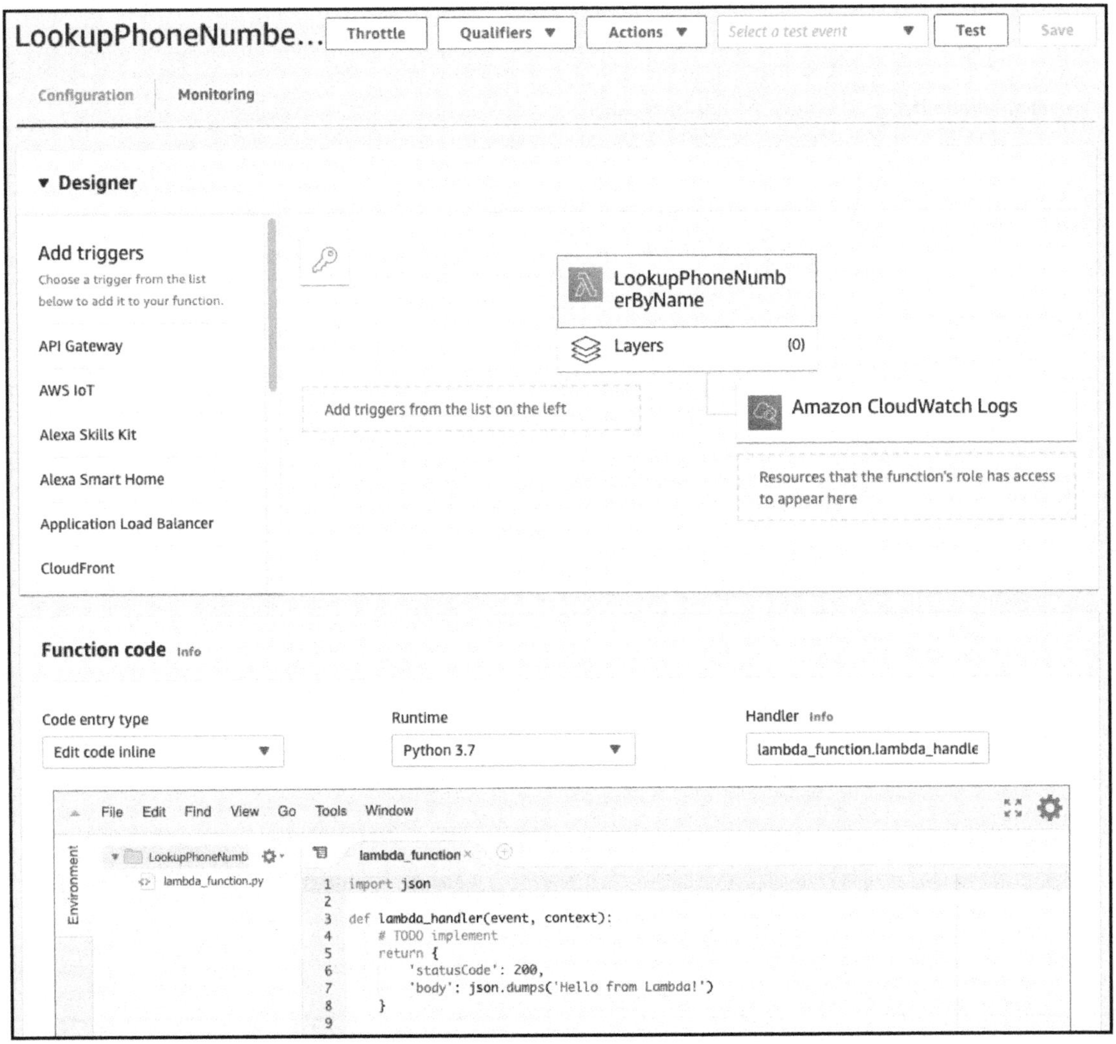

The preceding screenshot demonstrates the following:

- In the **Designer** section, we can add triggers to invoke this lambda function. For Lex bots, we do not need to select a trigger.
- We also see that the `LookupPhoneNumberByName` function has access to CloudWatch logs. Any outputs or error messages from the execution of this function will be written to CloudWatch, and we can view those logs from the **CloudWatch** console page. This will be useful while developing and debugging the function.
- In the **Function code** section, we can choose **Edit code inline**, modify the function runtime, and change the **Handler** function name. The handler function specifies the Python file and function name that constitute the entry point to our lambda function.
- Beneath the three lambda configuration fields, we have the inline code editor. Here, we can create additional source files and edit the code for each source file.

Our lambda function will need to interact with the same DynamoDB that stores the contact information from the contact organizer application. We can leverage the existing contact store and then add a new function to query for contact information with the help of the following steps:

1. Right-click within the left panel of the inline editor and then select **New File.**
2. Name the file `contact_store.py`.
3. Replace the content of `contact_store.py` with the contact store implementation from `Chapter 5`, *Extracting Information from Text with Amazon Comprehend.*
4. Add `get_contact_by_name()` after the existing function implementation:

```
import boto3

class ContactStore:
    def __init__(self, store_location):
        self.table =
boto3.resource('dynamodb').Table(store_location)

    ...

    def get_contact_by_name(self, name):
        response = self.table.get_item(
            Key = {'name': name}
        )

        if 'Item' in response:
```

```
        contact_info = response['Item']
    else:
        contact_info = {}

    return contact_info
```

The preceding code includes the following elements:

- The `get_contact_by_name()` method retrieves a single contact by its unique identifier, which is the name. In this method, we are calling DynamoDB's `get_item()` function. The response from `get_item()` contains a dictionary. If the item key exists, then we get a return value containing the contact information.
- Here, we are getting an item from the DynamoDB table by key. The key is the name of the contact, first name, and last name, separated by a space. This code will be executed in the Python 3.7 lambda runtime environment. In this environment, the `boto3` package is already installed.

DynamoDB IAM role for LookupPhoneNumberByName

Since this code will need to connect to DynamoDB, we need to add a policy to our lambda function's execution role:

1. Navigate to the IAM page from AWS Console.
2. Click on **Roles** on the left-hand panel.
3. From the list of roles, find and click on the **LookupPhoneNumberByName-role-<unique id>** role for our lambda function.
4. Click on the **Attach policies** button.
5. Find and select the **AmazonDynamoDBFullAccess** policy, and then click on the **Attach policy** button.

Now, let's have a look at the following screenshot:

Now, our LookupPhoneNumberByName lambda function can access DynamoDB. The AmazonDynamoDBFullAccess policy is fine for our hands-on projects, but, for real production application, you should fine-tune the policy to limit the number of permissions granted.

Fulfillment lambda function for LookupPhoneNumberByName

In the lambda editor window, open the existing lambda_function.py file and replace its content with the following implementation:

```
import contact_store

store_location = 'Contacts'
contact_store = contact_store.ContactStore(store_location)

def lex_lambda_handler(event, context):
    intent_name = event['currentIntent']['name']
    parameters = event['currentIntent']['slots']
    attributes = event['sessionAttributes'] if event['sessionAttributes']
is not None else {}

    response = lookup_phone(intent_name, parameters, attributes)

    return response

def lookup_phone(intent_name, parameters, attributes):
    first_name = parameters['FirstName']
    last_name = parameters['LastName']

    # get phone number from dynamodb
    name = (first_name + ' ' + last_name).title()
    contact_info = contact_store.get_contact_by_name(name)

    if 'phone' in contact_info:
        attributes['Phone'] = contact_info['phone']
        attributes['FirstName'] = first_name
        attributes['LastName'] = last_name
        response = intent_success(intent_name, parameters, attributes)
    else:
        response = intent_failure(intent_name, parameters, attributes,
'Could not find contact information.')

    return response
```

```
# Amazon lex helper functions
...
```

In the preceding code, the following takes place:

- We first initialize the contact store with the DynamoDB table contacts.
- In the `lambda_handler()` function, we are extracting the intent name, the slots, and the attributes from the event object passed in. The event object is passed in to our Amazon Lex bot when the fulfillment hook is triggered. All of the slot input values, as well as the session attributes, will be included in this event object.
- `lambda_handler()` then calls the `lookup_phone()` function that uses the contact store to retrieve the contact information.
- In the `lookup_phone()` function, we are constructing the item key from the `FirstName` and `LastName` slot values. The item key must be `FirstName` and `LastName` separated by a space, with the correct capitalization.
    - For example, the first name `john` and the last name `smith` will result in the item key `John Smith`; the first letter of each part of the name is capitalized.
    - We are using the `title()` function to ensure correct capitalization, irrespective of how the user inputs the names.

If we are able to retrieve a contact with those names, we will save the contact's phone number, first name, and last name in the session attributes. This is how the phone number is passed back to be displayed or spoken in this intent's response. We will cover why the first name and last name are saved in the session attributes in a later section of this chapter.

If we are successful at fulfilling the lookup, we respond with `intent_success()`, otherwise, we respond with `intent_failure()` with an explanation message. These are helper functions that encapsulate some of Amazon Lex's specific response formats.

Amazon Lex helper functions

The Amazon Lex helper functions format the responses to what Lex is expecting. We have four helper functions here:

- `intent_success()` indicates that the intent has been successfully fulfilled, and any session attributes are passed back to Lex as `sessionAttributes`.
- `intent_failure()` indicates that the intent was not fulfilled successfully. This response also includes an explanation message.

- `intent_elicitation()` asks the Lex bot to elicit a value for the specified parameter name. This elicitation might be due to missing slot values or invalid slot values. This helper function is useful when we create custom `Lambda initialization and validation` logic.
- `intent_delegation()` indicates that the lambda function has completed its obligation and directs Lex to choose the next course of action based on the bot's configuration.

We only used the first two helper functions for this `LookupPhoneNumberByName` intent. Here is the code implementation:

```
# Amazon lex helper functions
def intent_success(intent_name, parameters, attributes):
    return {
        'sessionAttributes': attributes,
        'dialogAction': {
            'type': 'Close',
            'fulfillmentState': 'Fulfilled'
        }
    }

def intent_failure(intent_name, parameters, attributes, message):
    return {
        'dialogAction': {
            'type': 'Close',
            'fulfillmentState': 'Failed',
            'message': {
                'contentType': 'PlainText',
                'content': message
            }
        }
    }

def intent_delegation(intent_name, parameters, attributes):
    return {
        'sessionAttributes': attributes,
        'dialogAction': {
            'type': 'Delegate',
            'slots': parameters,

        }
    }

def intent_elicitation(intent_name, parameters, attributes,
parameter_name):
    return {
```

```
            'sessionAttributes': attributes,
            'dialogAction': {
                'type': 'ElicitSlot',
                'intentName': intent_name,
                'slots': parameters,
                'slotToElicit': parameter_name
            }
        }
```

> Even though the `lambda_function.py` file is relatively short, we still applied a few clean code practices. We organized all of the AWS Lambda- and Amazon Lex-specific implementation details into the `lambda_handler()` function and the Amazon Lex helper functions.
>
> For example, how are the slots from the Lambda event object and the response format to Amazon Lex to be retrieved? This way, the `lookup_phone()` function is free from those platform specific details and, hence, is more likely to be reusable on other platforms. The `lookup_phone()` function only requires `intent_name` to be a string, and the parameters and attributes to be dictionaries.

Save the lambda function implementation by clicking on the **Save** button in the top-right corner of the lambda development console.

The intent fulfillment for LookupPhoneNumberByName

Now, let's add this lambda function to the fulfillment hook:

1. Go to the Amazon Lex development console and, under **Fulfillment**, select **LookupPhoneNumberByName** from the **Lambda function** list, as shown in the following screenshot:

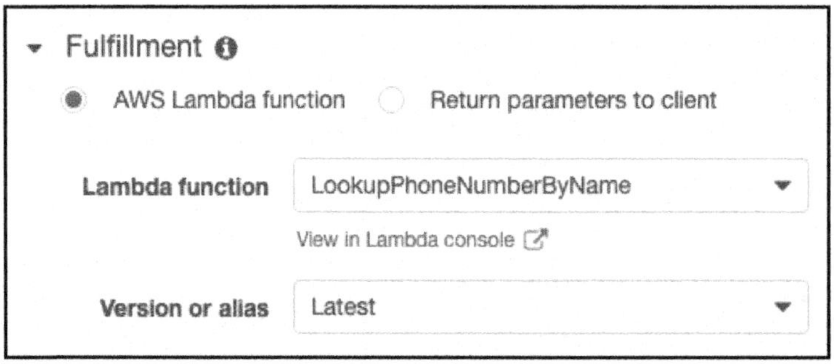

2. As shown in the following screenshot, Amazon Lex will ask for permission to invoke this lambda function. Click **OK** to grant permission:

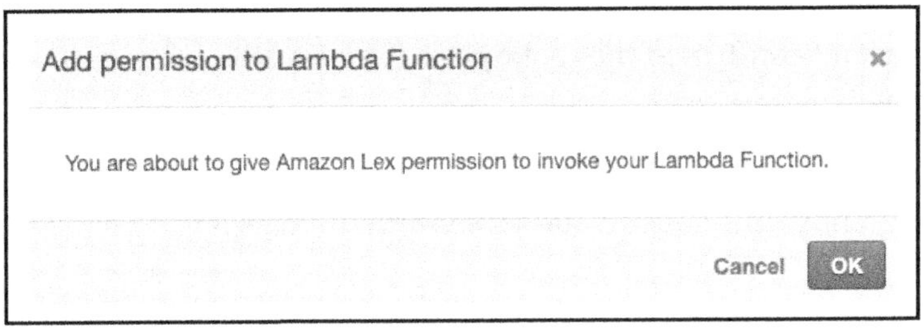

3. In the Lex development console, click on the **Save Intent** button at the bottom of the page, and then click on the **Build** button in the top-right corner of the page. It will take a few seconds for our first Lex bot to build.

Test conversations for LookupPhoneNumberByName

Now, we are ready to build and test our first intent. In the **Test bot** panel on the right of the page, issue a few variations of the sample utterances and follow the conversation with the contact assistant. Here is a sample conversation:

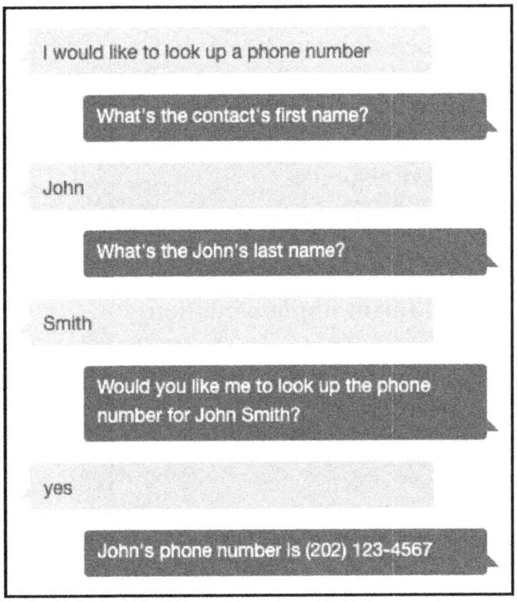

In the preceding conversation, the following happened:

- The utterance did not include the slots, and our contact assistant prompted for the first and last names
- The assistant confirmed the lookup for **John Smith** before proceeding with fulfillment
- The response included the contact's first name and the phone number

Now, think through how this conversation plays out, both as a text chat and as a voice conversation.

Here is another sample conversation:

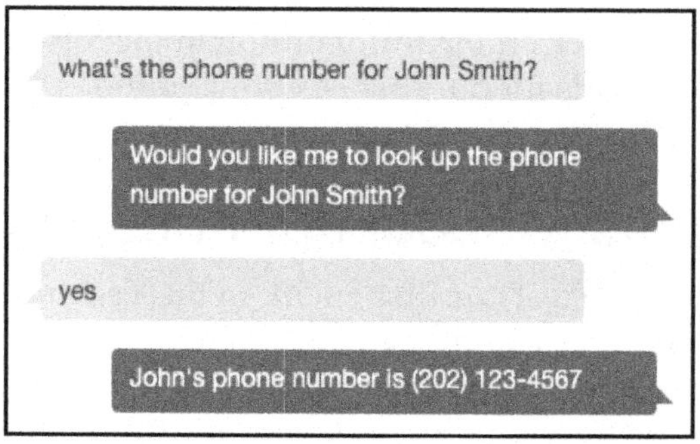

In the preceding conversation, the following happened:

- The utterance included both of the required slots
- This time, our contact assistant only had to confirm the lookup before proceeding with the fulfillment and response
- The user can also respond **no** to the confirmation prompt to cancel the fulfillment

Congratulations! You just completed your first intelligent assistant with a conversation interface and AWS Lambda fulfillment implementation.

The test bot panel's chat interface also supports voice inputs. You can use the microphone icon to issue the utterances and responses via voice.

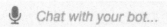

In the test bot chat interface, the response from Lex will always be in text.

The MakePhoneCallByName intent

Next, we will create a second intent for our contact assistant, called **MakePhoneCallByName**. The task performed by this intent should be obvious from its name; it can phone the contacts. However, we will not be implementing the phone call functionality in this project.

The goal as regards implementing this second intent is to demonstrate how multiple intents of an intelligent assistant can interact and collaborate. We want to design the conversational interface of `MakePhoneCallByName` to be able to function independently, but also to be able to function in conjunction with the `LookupPhoneNumberByName` intent.

To make this intent collaboration concrete, imagine that the user just looked up the phone number of a contact and then decided to make a call to this contact. Should the second intent start over with the first name and last name slot elicitations? Or would it be more fluid and natural to know that the user wants to call the same contact that the assistant just looked up? Of course, the latter. After `LookupPhoneNumberByName` was fulfilled successfully, and then the user utters `Call him` or `Call her`, `MakePhoneCallByName` should just know who `him` or `her` is referring to based on the context of prior conversations. This is where session attributes can help to maintain the context.

Sample utterances and lambda initialization/validation for MakePhoneCallByName

We'll start by adding a new intent from the Lex development console by clicking on the blue plus button next to **Intents** on the left-hand panel, as shown in the following screenshot:

1. Select **Create intent**, name it `MakePhoneCallByName`, and then click on **Add**.

2. Let's create a few sample utterances for this intent. The first utterance **Call {FirstName} {LastName}** provides the values for the two required slots. For the other utterances, the intent should try its best to get the slot values from the conversation context if possible:

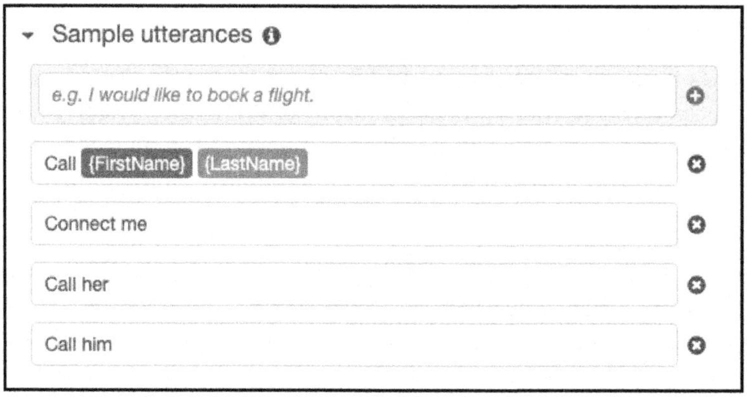

To do this, we will use the second type of AWS Lambda hook from Amazon Lex, lambda initialization and validation. The following steps will create the hook:

1. In the **Lambda initialization and validation** section, check the box for **Initialization and validation code hook.**
2. Go to the AWS Lambda page from AWS Console and create a lambda function named `InitContact` from scratch for Python 3.7.
3. Create a new default lambda execution role. We do not need the **AmazonDynamoDBFullAccess** policy for this lambda function.
4. In the inline function code editor, replace the `lambda_function.py` file contact with the following implementation:

```
def lex_lambda_handler(event, context):
    intent_name = event['currentIntent']['name']
    parameters = event['currentIntent']['slots']
    attributes = event['sessionAttributes'] if
event['sessionAttributes'] is not None else {}

    response = init_contact(intent_name, parameters, attributes)

    return response

def init_contact(intent_name, parameters, attributes):
    first_name = parameters.get('FirstName')
    last_name = parameters.get('LastName')
```

```
    prev_first_name = attributes.get('FirstName')
    prev_last_name = attributes.get('LastName')

    if first_name is None and prev_first_name is not None:
        parameters['FirstName'] = prev_first_name

    if last_name is None and prev_last_name is not None:
        parameters['LastName'] = prev_last_name

    if parameters['FirstName'] is not None and
parameters['LastName'] is not None:
        response = intent_delegation(intent_name, parameters,
attributes)
    elif parameters['FirstName'] is None:
        response = intent_elicitation(intent_name, parameters,
attributes, 'FirstName')
    elif parameters['LastName'] is None:
        response = intent_elicitation(intent_name, parameters,
attributes, 'LastName')

    return response

# lex response helper functions
...
```

In the preceding code, the following takes place:

- In the `init_contact()` function, we check whether `FirstName` and `LastName` are missing from the slots coming from the utterance. If so, we then check whether `FistName` and `LastName` exist in the session attributes.
    - Do you recall that we saved `FirstName` and `LastName` to the session attributes in the fulfillment implementation for the `LookupPhoneNumberByName` intent? We are retrieving those saved values here.
- If both `FirstName` and `LastName` are set, then we respond back to Lex with a delegation response.
    - The delegation response tells Lex that initialization and validation are complete, and that the bot should continue with its execution based on its configuration, including fulfillment.
- If either `FirstName` or `LastName` is still missing its value, then we respond back with an elicitation response.
    - The elicitation response will trigger the prompt for the missing slot that was configured for the bot.

Save the lambda function, and then go back to the Amazon Lex development console:

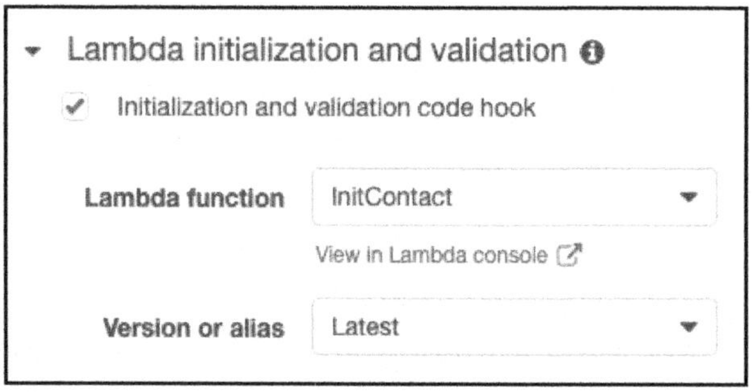

Select **InitContact** for the **Lambda initialization and validation** function.

Slots and confirmation prompt for MakePhoneCallByName

The slots configuration for the `MakePhoneCallByName` intent can be exactly the same as the configuration for `LookupPhoneNumberByName`. See the details in the following screenshot:

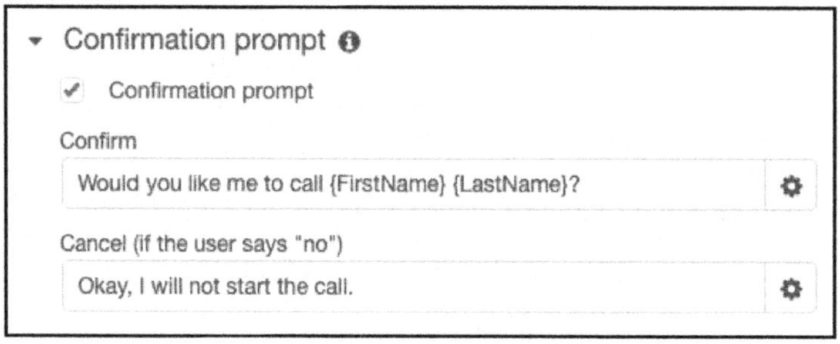

Both slots are required, and are set to the built-in `AMAZON.US_FIRST_NAME` and `AMAZON.US_LAST_NAME` types.

The **Confirmation prompt** can be tailored for making phone calls, as shown in the following screenshot:

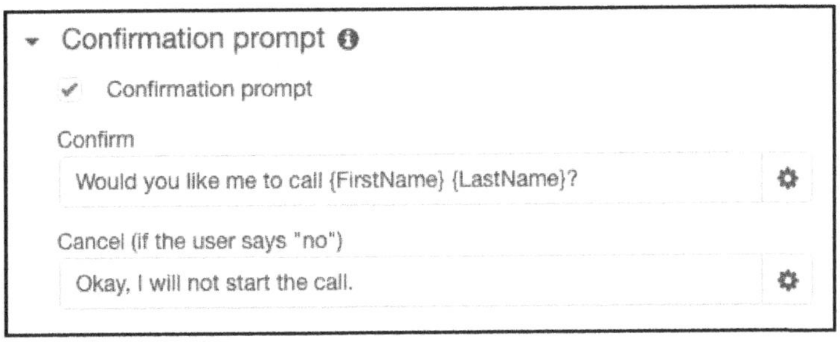

Both the **Confirm** and **Cancel** messages are tailored to the `MakePhoneCallByName` intent.

Fulfillment and response for MakePhoneCallByName

We could implement a new lambda function to fulfill the contact lookup and phone call functionalities. But, since we are not actually making phone calls in this project, the business logic of the fulfillment lambda function will be the same as the contact lookup function we already implemented.

In fact, for this project, **Fulfillment** can be handled by the **LookupPhoneNumberByName** lambda function, as shown in the following screenshot:

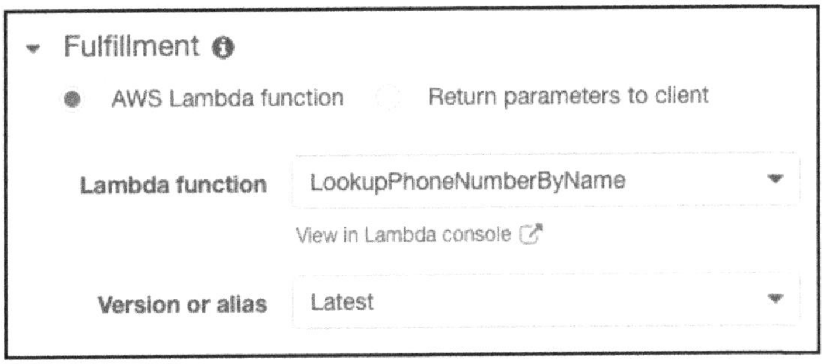

Finally, the **Response** configuration can also be tailored to make phone calls, as follows:

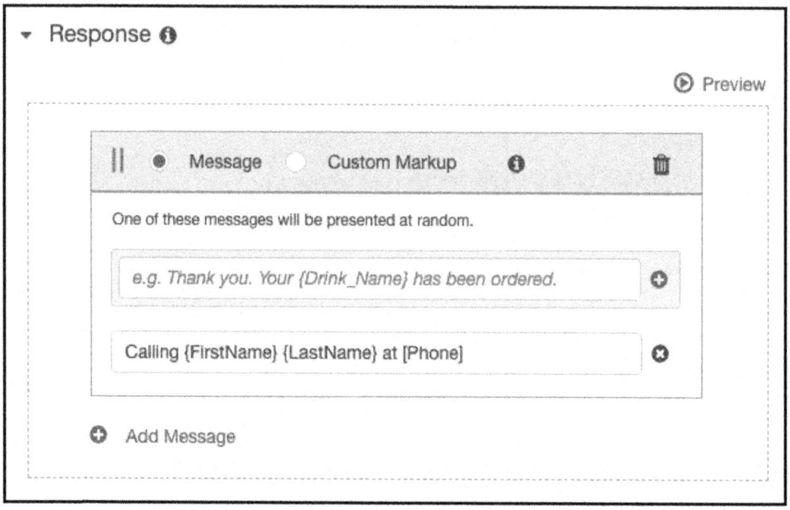

Now, click on the **Save Intent** button on the bottom of the Lex development console, and then click on the **Build** button in the top-right corner of the development console.

Test conversations for MakePhoneCallByName

In the **Test bot** panel on the right-hand side of the page, issue a few variations of the sample utterances and follow the conversation with the contact assistant. Here is a sample conversation:

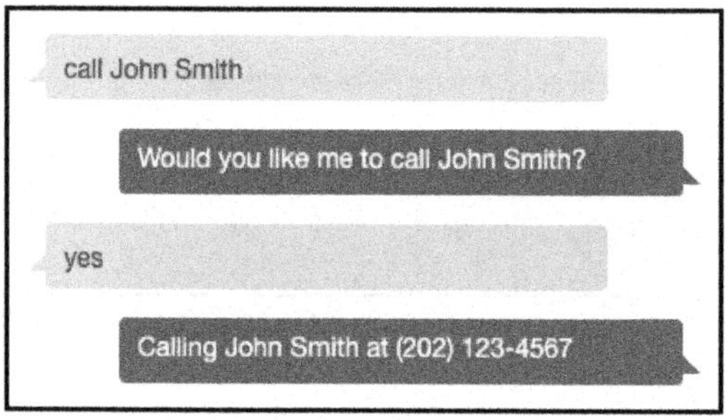

The preceding conversation demonstrates that the `MakePhoneCallByName` intent can function independently without running the `LookupPhoneNumberByName` intent first.

Here is another sample conversation:

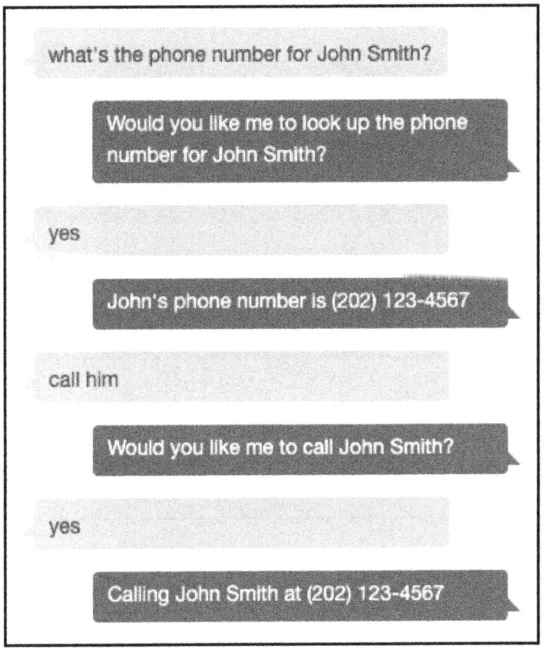

The preceding conversation shows the power of context:

- The user first asked for John Smith's phone number with the `LookupPhoneNumberByName` intent.
- Then, the user requested to `call him`.
- At this point, our `InitContact` lambda function grabbed the `FirstName` and `LastName` from the session attributes and confirmed whether John Smith is the contact to call.
    - The confirmation prompt is important here, since the contact assistant is inferring the contact. We do not want to automatically make awkward calls to the wrong contact; it is better to confirm with the user first before taking action.

Click on **Clear chat history** before issuing the next utterance. This will clear the session and its stored attributes. Continue the sample conversation with the following:

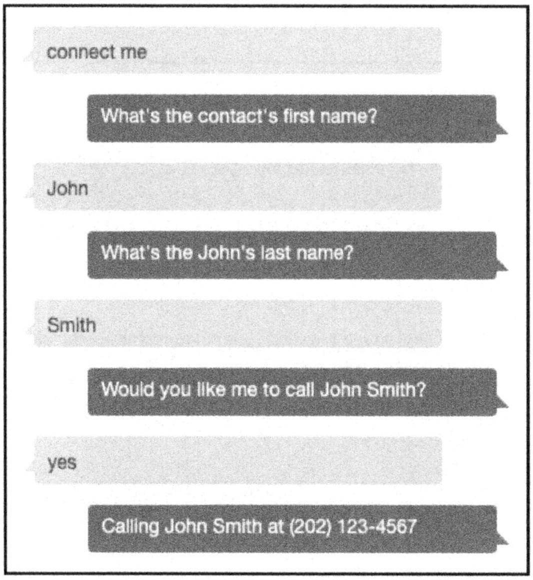
connect me
What's the contact's first name?
John
What's the John's last name?
Smith
Would you like me to call John Smith?
yes
Calling John Smith at (202) 123-4567

In this conversation, the following took place:

- The user started with an utterance without any slots. On this occasion, however, there was no previous conversational context saved in the session attributes.
- The `InitContact` lambda function was not able to retrieve a first and last name; therefore, it responds with intent elicitations.
- It's important to test our intelligent assistant to handle all possible orders and combinations of intents and utterances. This quality assurance becomes more difficult as more intents share the session attributes.

Congratulations! Our contact assistant just became more intelligent with context awareness.

Deploying the contact assistant bot

We can now publish the contact assistant as a custom intelligent assistant capability.

Click on the **Publish** button on the top right of the Lex development console and set **Alias** to **Production**:

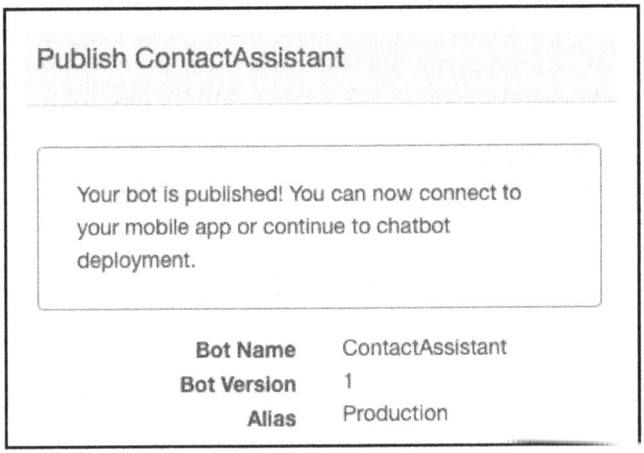

The preceding screenshot shows that the contact assistant is now published. Once the contact assistant is published, the applications can start to leverage it through various integration methods, including the boto3 SDK.

Integrating the contact assistant into applications

Next, we will create the layers to integrate the contact assistant capability into applications. As mentioned at the beginning of this chapter, we will not implement any application; we will only implement the service and RESTful endpoint layers.

As with previous hands-on projects, we will be using Python, Pipenv, Chalice, and boto3 as part of the technology stack. Let's create a project structure first.

1. In the terminal, we will create the `root` project directory and enter it with the following commands:

```
$ mkdir ContactAssistant
$ cd ContactAssistant
```

2. We will create a Python 3 virtual environment with `Pipenv` in the project's `root` directory. Our Python portion of the project requires two packages, `boto3` and `chalice`. We can install them with the following commands:

```
$ pipenv --three
$ pipenv install boto3
$ pipenv install chalice
```

3. Remember that the Python packages installed via `pipenv` are only available if we activate the virtual environment. One way to do this is by means of the following command:

```
$ pipenv shell
```

4. Next, while still in the virtual environment, we will create the orchestration layer as an AWS Chalice project named `Capabilities` with the following commands:

```
$ chalice new-project Capabilities
```

5. To create the `chalicelib` Python package, issue the following commands:

```
cd Capabilities
mkdir chalicelib
touch chalicelib/__init__.py
cd ..
```

The initial project structure should look like the following:

```
Project Structure
------------
├── ContactAssistant/
    ├── Capabilities/
        ├── .chalice/
            ├── config.json
        ├── chalicelib/
            ├── __init__.py
        ├── app.py
        ├── requirements.txt
    ├── Pipfile
    ├── Pipfile.lock
```

The project structure is slightly different to those structures created in previous chapters. This project structure contains the orchestration and service implementations layers, but does not include a web user interface.

Intelligent assistant service implementation

The contact assistant is backed by a Lex bot in the current implementation, but good architecture design should have the flexibility to change implementations easily. The service implementation serves to shield the Lex implementation details from the client applications.

Create a Python file in `chalicelib` with the name `intelligent_assistant_service.py`, as shown in the following screenshot:

```
import boto3

class IntelligentAssistantService:
    def __init__(self, assistant_name):
        self.client = boto3.client('lex-runtime')
        self.assistant_name = assistant_name

    def send_user_text(self, user_id, input_text):
        response = self.client.post_text(
            botName = self.assistant_name,
            botAlias = 'Production',
            userId = user_id,
            inputText = input_text
        )

     return response['message']
```

In the preceding code, the following takes place:

- `IntelligentAssistantService` is a generic implementation that can be configured to work with different intelligent assistants, and not just the contact assistant.
- The `__init__()` constructor takes in the assistant name to configure itself for a particular intelligent assistant at creation time. The constructor creates a `boto3` client for `lex-runtime`, which can communicate with published Lex bots.
- `IntelligentAssistantService` implements the `send_user_text()` method to send text chat messages to the assistants. This method takes in a `user_id` and the `input_text` from the application, and uses the `post_text()` function from `lex-runtime` to send the input text.
    - `user_id` is an ID created by the client application. A Lex bot can have multiple conversations with different users at once. This `user_id` identifies a user; in other words, it identifies a chat session.

> There is also a `post_content()` function from `lex-runtime` for sending both text and speech inputs. In addition to `botName`, `botAlias`, and `userId`, the `post_content()` function also requires the `contentType` and `inputStream` parameters to be set. `contentType` can be either audio or text, with a few supported audio formats. `inputStream` contains the byte stream for the audio or text contents. If the application would like to receive an audio response from the Lex bot, the `accept` parameter should be set to one of the audio output formats supported. The supported audio input and output formats are implementation details of Lex. Any format conversions for the audio inputs and outputs should be performed in this service implementation to hide those details from the client applications.

Contact assistant RESTful endpoint

Let's have a look at the following steps:

1. Now, let's build a quick RESTful endpoint to the contact assistant in `app.py`. This way, we can test our `IntelligentAssistantService` with `curl` commands:

```
from chalice import Chalice
from chalicelib import intelligent_assistant_service

import json

#####
# chalice app configuration
#####
app = Chalice(app_name='Capabilities')
app.debug = True

#####
# services initialization
#####
assistant_name = 'ContactAssistant'
assistant_service =
intelligent_assistant_service.IntelligentAssistantService(assistant
_name)

#####
# RESTful endpoints
#####
@app.route('/contact-assistant/user-id/{user_id}/send-text',
```

```
methods = ['POST'], cors = True)
def send_user_text(user_id):
    request_data = json.loads(app.current_request.raw_body)

    message = assistant_service.send_user_text(user_id,
request_data['text'])

    return message
```

The RESTful endpoint implementation is short and simple:

- The initialization code binds our generic `IntelligentAssistantService` implementation to the contact assistant
- The RESTful endpoint itself takes in the `user_id` through the URL and the input text as JSON in the request body

2. Start the `chalice local` environment with the following command in the terminal:

```
$ chalice local
Restarting local dev server.
Found credentials in shared credentials file: ~/.aws/credentials
Serving on http://127.0.0.1:8000
```

3. Now, we can have a conversation with our contact assistant using the `curl` commands:

```
$ curl --header "Content-Type: application/json" --request POST --
data '{"text": "Call John Smith"}'
http://127.0.0.1:8000/contact-assistant/user-id/me/send-text
> Would you like me to call John Smith?

$ curl --header "Content-Type: application/json" --request POST --
data '{"text": "Yes"}'
http://127.0.0.1:8000/contact-assistant/user-id/me/send-text
> Calling John Smith at (202) 123-4567
```

In the preceding conversation, the following takes place:

- The first `curl` command issues the intent `Call John Smith`, which includes both slots required for the first and last names of the contact.
- The response is a confirmation from the contact assistant, *Would you like me to call John Smith?*
- The second `curl` command continues the conversation by replying, *Yes*.
- The contact assistant then responds with, *Calling John Smith at (202) 123-4567.*

The applications that will leverage the capabilities of the contact assistant will provide the appropriate user interface to best facilitate the conversation, for example, a mobile app for a traveling salesman. The application will pass the verbal communication between the users and the contact assistant using the RESTful endpoint.

Summary

In this chapter, we built the contact assistant, a chatbot that allows the user to search for contact information using a voice or text conversational interface. We built the contact assistant's conversational interface using Amazon Lex. We learned the development paradigm of Amazon Lex to build a custom AI capability, including concepts such as intents, utterances, prompts, and confirmations. The contact assistant supports two intents, `LookupPhoneNumberByName` and `MakePhoneCallByName`. The task fulfillment of these intents is implemented using AWS Lambda. We also designed these two intents to be context aware by using Amazon Lex's session attributes; being context aware reduces the cognitive burden of the user and makes the chatbot smarter.

Amazon Lex is the last of the AWS AI services that we will cover in this book. In the next part of the book, we will cover AWS ML services to train customer AI capabilities using machine learning.

Further reading

For more information on building a voice chatbot with Amazon Lex, you can refer to the following links:

`https://restechtoday.com/smart-speaker-industry/`

`https://www.lifewire.com/amazon-alexa-voice-assistant-4152107`

`https://www.nngroup.com/articles/intelligent-assistants-poor-usability-high-adoption/`

3

Section 3: Training Machine Learning Models with Amazon SageMaker

In this section, you will learn how to design, develop, and deploy an enterprise-level machine learning solution in AWS. Also, an in-depth understanding of the challenges involved with wrangling big data and data parallelization and model deployment will be addressed at length. We'll illustrate these concepts by discussing a few real-world case studies.

This section comprises the following chapters:

- `Chapter 7`, *Working with Amazon SageMaker*
- `Chapter 8`, *Creating Machine Learning Inference Pipelines*
- `Chapter 9`, *Discovering Topics in Text Collection*
- `Chapter 10`, *Classifying Images using Amazon SageMaker*
- `Chapter 11`, *Sales Forecasting with Deep Learning and Auto Regression*

7
Working with Amazon SageMaker

In the last few chapters, you have learned about readily-available **Machine Learning** (**ML**) APIs that solve business challenges. In this chapter, we will deep dive into AWS SageMaker—the service that is used to build, train, and deploy models seamlessly when the ML APIs do not completely meet your requirements. SageMaker increases the productivity of data scientists and machine learning engineers by abstracting away the complexity involved in provisioning compute and storage.

This is what will we cover in this chapter:

- Processing big data through Spark EMR
- Conducting training in Amazon SageMaker
- Deploying trained models and running inference
- Runninghyperparameter optimization
- Understanding SageMaker experimentation service
- Bring your own model – SageMaker, MXNet, and Gluon
- Bring your own container – R Model

Technical requirements

For the following sections, we will employ the book rating dataset known as `goodbooks-10k` to illustrate all of the topics outlined previously. The dataset consists of 6 million ratings on 10,000 books from 53,424 users. More details on the goodbooks-10k dataset can be found `https://www.kaggle.com/zygmunt/goodbooks-10k#books.csv`.

In the `folder` associated with this chapter, you will find two CSV files:

- `ratings.csv`: Contains book ratings, user IDs, book IDs, and rating
- `books.csv`: Contains book attributes, including title

It is now time to wrangle big data to create a dataset for modeling.

Preprocessing big data through Spark EMR

The design pattern to execute models in SageMaker is to read the data placed in S3. The data may not be readily consumable most of the time. If the datasets required are large, then wrangling the data in the Jupyter notebook may not be practical. In such cases, Spark EMR clusters can be employed to conduct operations on big data.

Wrangling a big dataset in Jupyter notebooks results in out-of-memory errors. Our solution is to employ AWS EMR (Elastic MapReduce) clusters to conduct distributed data processing. Hadoop will be used as the underlying distributed filesystem while Spark will be used as the distributed computing framework.

Now, to run commands against the EMR cluster to process big data, AWS offers EMR notebooks. EMR notebooks provide a managed notebook environment, based on Jupyter Notebook. These notebooks can be used to interactively wrangle large data, visualize the same, and prepare analytics-ready datasets. Data engineers and data scientists can employ a variety of languages, Python, SQL, R, and Scala, to process large volumes of data. These EMR notebooks can also be saved periodically to a persistent data store, S3, so the saved work can be retrieved later. One of the critical components of Amazon EMR architecture is the Livy service. It is an open source REST interface for interacting with Spark clusters without the need for Spark client. The Livy service enables communication between the EMR notebook and EMR cluster, where the service is installed.

The following architecture diagram details how EMR notebooks communicate with Spark EMR clusters to process large data:

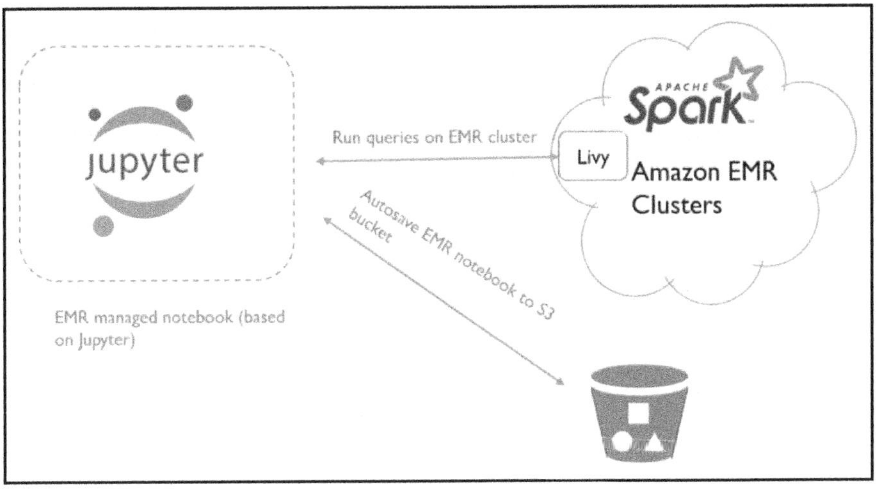

Now that we've looked at how EMR clusters interact with EMR notebooks to process big data interactively, let's begin by creating an EMR notebook and cluster, as shown in the following:

1. Navigate to **Amazon EMR** under **Services** and click on **Notebooks**.
2. In the **Create notebook** page, enter **Notebook name** and **Description**, as shown in the following screenshot:

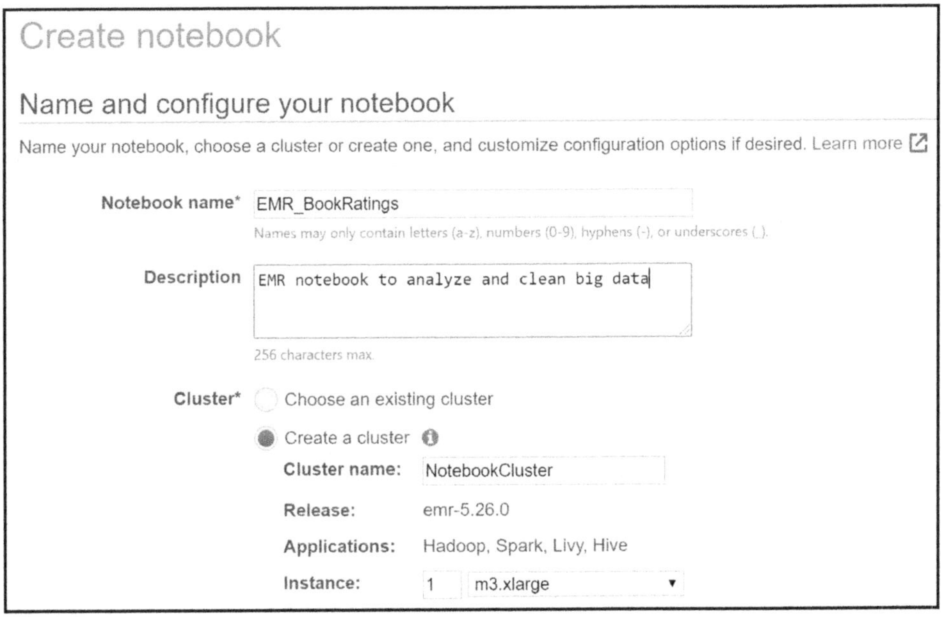

3. Next, select the option **Create a cluster**, enter **Cluster name**, and select **Instance** type and number. As you can see in the preceding screenshot, the EMR cluster comes with **Hadoop**, **Spark**, **Livy**, and **Hive** applications.
4. Now, let's review the policies of EMR role and EC2 instance profile and enter the S3 location where EMR notebooks will be saved, as in the following:

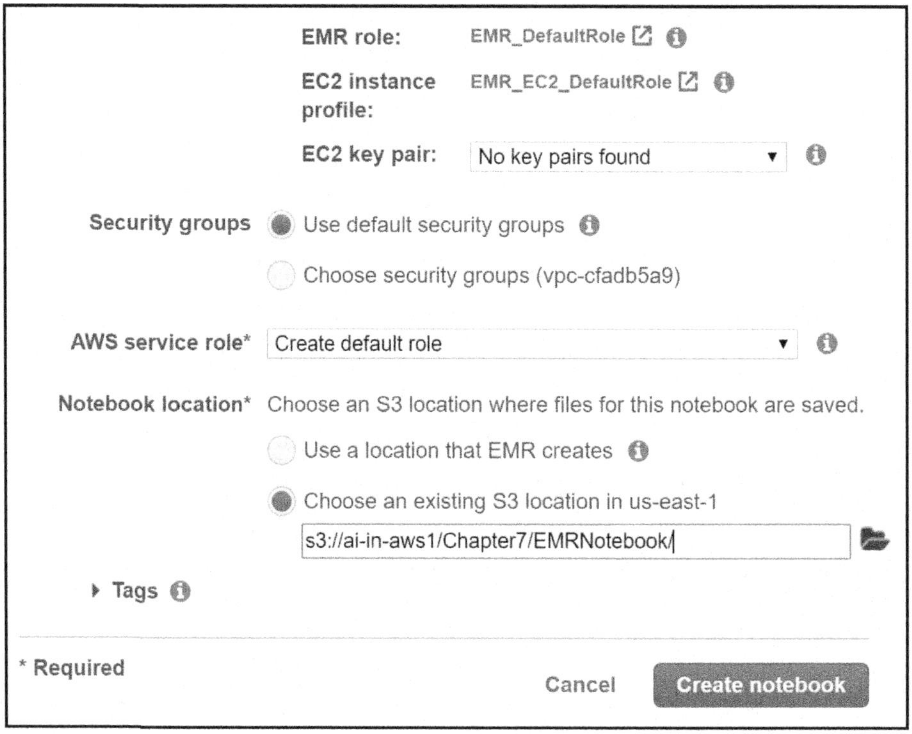

From the preceding visual, we can see the following:

- The EMR role is used to give the EMR service access to other AWS services (for example, EC2).
- The EMR EC2 instance profile further enables EC2 instances launched by EMR to have access to other AWS services (for example, S3).
- We configured appropriate security groups around the EMR cluster to allow communication between the EMR notebook and master node of the EMR cluster.

- We also assigned a service role to the EMR cluster, so it can interact with other AWS services.
- Also, EMR notebooks are saved to the designated S3 location when you click on **Save** in EMR notebooks.

5. Now, click on **Create notebook** to launch a new EMR notebook. The notebook and cluster will start provisioning, as shown in the following:

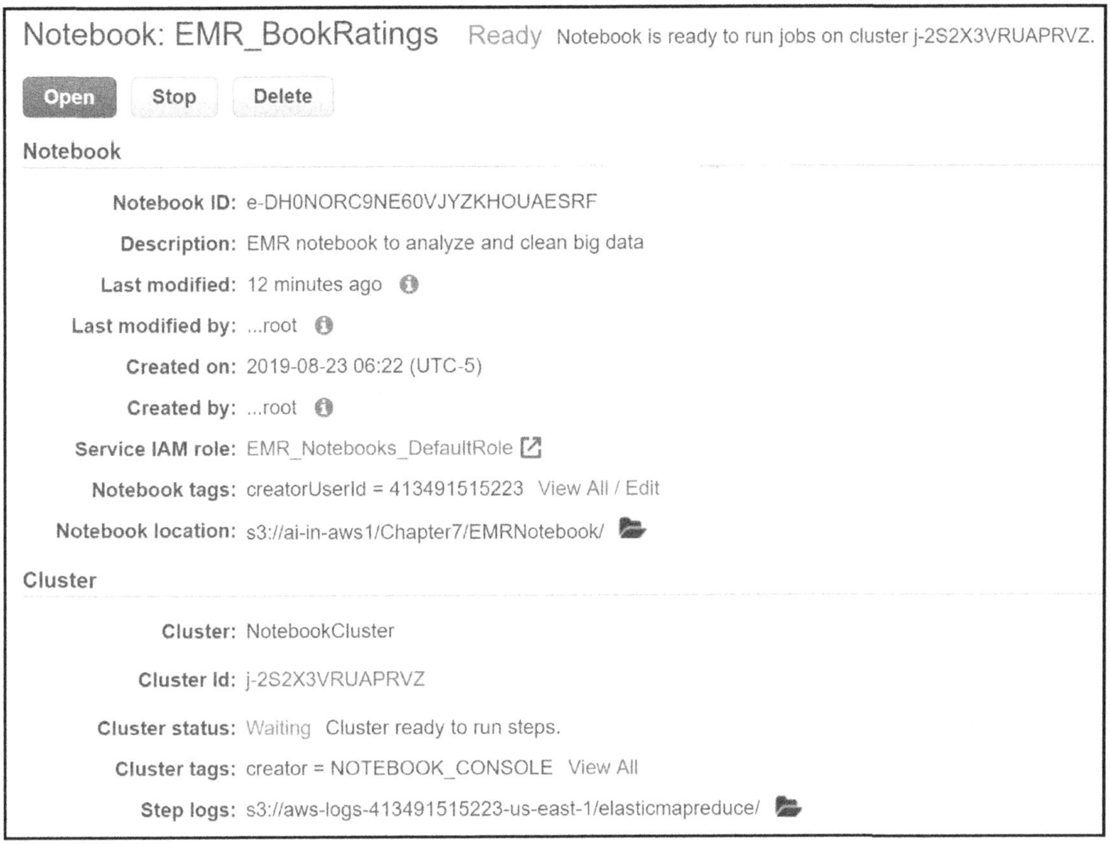

6. Once the EMR notebook and cluster are provisioned, click on **Open** to open the notebook. We will use the EMR notebook to create a dataset that will be used to recommend books to users via the **object2vec** algorithm, which is a built-in SageMaker algorithm used to predict the affinity of a user toward a book.

In the EMR notebook, we do five things:

1. Read the ratings and books CSV files.
2. Analyze the ratings dataset to understand the number of ratings by user and book.
3. Filter the original ratings dataset to only include ratings, where it contains users who have rated more than 1% of books and books that have been rated by at least 2% of the users.
4. Create indexes (starting with zero) for both users and books in the ratings dataset—this is required to train the `object2vec` algorithm.
5. Write (in parquet format) the resulting ratings dataset, which also includes the book title, to relevant S3 bucket. The ratings dataset will then have a rich history of user preferences, along with the popularity of books.

In the following code block, we will whittle down 6 million ratings to ~1 million:

```
# Filter ratings by selecting books that have been rated by at
least 1200 users and users who have rated at least 130 books
fil_users = users.filter(F.col("count") >= 130)
fil_books = books.filter(F.col("count") >= 1200)
```

In the preceding code, we filtered ratings to include users who have rated at least 130 books and books that have been rated by at least 1,200 users.

6. Once the ratings dataset is prepared, we'll persist it to S3 bucket, as shown in the following:

	Name ▼	Last modified ▼	Size ▼	Storage class ▼
☐	🗋 _SUCCESS	Jan 30, 2019 2:49:44 PM GMT-0600	0 B	Standard
☐	🗋 part-00000-70be57fc-191f-4624-a9df-af0edc3536aa-c000.snappy.parquet	Jan 30, 2019 2:49:20 PM GMT-0600	32.4 KB	Standard
☐	🗋 part-00001-70be57fc-191f-4624-a9df-af0edc3536aa-c000.snappy.parquet	Jan 30, 2019 2:49:20 PM GMT-0600	27.1 KB	Standard
☐	🗋 part-00002-70be57fc-191f-4624-a9df-af0edc3536aa-c000.snappy.parquet	Jan 30, 2019 2:49:20 PM GMT-0600	31.7 KB	Standard
☐	🗋 part-00003-70be57fc-191f-4624-a9df-af0edc3536aa-c000.snappy.parquet	Jan 30, 2019 2:49:20 PM GMT-0600	35.0 KB	Standard
☐	🗋 part-00004-70be57fc-191f-4624-a9df-af0edc3536aa-c000.snappy.parquet	Jan 30, 2019 2:49:20 PM GMT-0600	28.8 KB	Standard
☐	🗋 part-00005-70be57fc-191f-4624-a9df-af0edc3536aa-c000.snappy.parquet	Jan 30, 2019 2:49:21 PM GMT-0600	34.1 KB	Standard
☐	🗋 part-00006-70be57fc-191f-4624-a9df-af0edc3536aa-c000.snappy.parquet	Jan 30, 2019 2:49:21 PM GMT-0600	38.6 KB	Standard
☐	🗋 part-00007-70be57fc-191f-4624-a9df-af0edc3536aa-c000.snappy.parquet	Jan 30, 2019 2:49:21 PM GMT-0600	28.5 KB	Standard
☐	🗋 part-00008-70be57fc-191f-4624-a9df-af0edc3536aa-c000.snappy.parquet	Jan 30, 2019 2:49:21 PM GMT-0600	39.2 KB	Standard

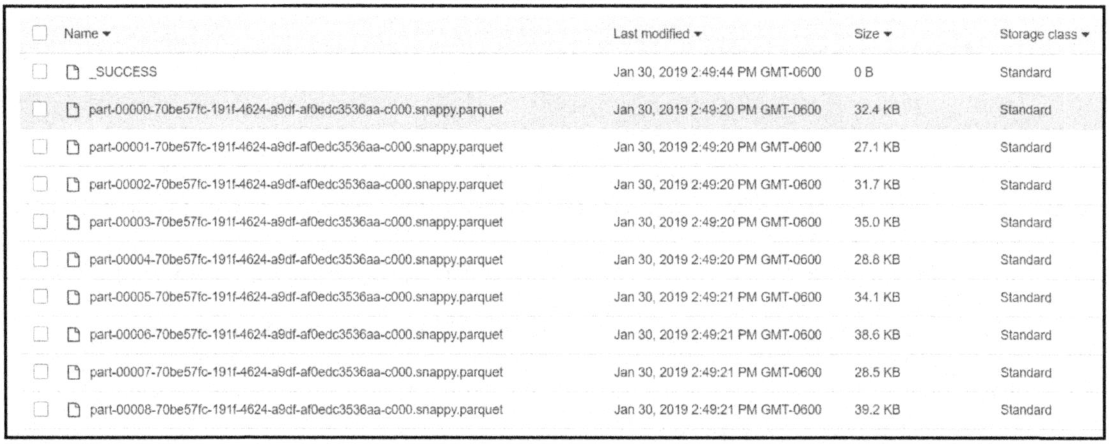

From the preceding screenshot, the following is understood:

- Since the data is parallel processed on the EMR cluster, the output contains several `parquet` files.
- Apache Parquet is an open source compressed columnar storage format in the Apache Hadoop ecosystem.
- Compared to the traditional approach where data is stored in a row-oriented approach, Parquet allows us to be more efficient in terms of storage and performance.
- Stop the notebook and terminate the cluster after you are done storing the processed dataset in S3 to avoid unnecessary costs.

Now, we are ready to understand the built-in `object2vec` algorithm and start training the model.

Conducting training in Amazon SageMaker

Let's begin by spending a few minutes understanding how the `object2vec` algorithm works. It is a multi-purpose algorithm that can create lower dimensional embeddings of higher dimensional objects. This process is known as dimensionality reduction, most commonly implemented through a statistical procedure called **Principal Component Analysis** (**PCA**). However, Object2Vec uses neural networks to learn these embeddings.

Some of the common applications of these embeddings include customer segmentation and product search. In the case of customer segmentation, similar customers appear closer in the lower dimensional space. A customer can be defined through multiple attributes such as name, age, home address, and email address. With regards to product search, because product embeddings capture the semantics of the underlying data, any combination of search terms can be used to retrieve the target product. The embedding of these search terms (semantics) should just match that of the product.

Let's look at how Object2Vec works.

Learning how Object2Vec Works

Object2vec can learn embeddings of pairs of objects. In our case, the higher the rating of the book, the stronger the relationship between the user and the book. The idea is that users with similar tastes are likely to rate similar books higher. Object2vec approximates the book rating by using embeddings of users and books. The closer a user is to some books, the higher the rating given by that user to the books. We provide the algorithm with (`user_ind` and `book_ind`) pairs; for each such pair, we also provide a **label** that tells the algorithm whether the user and book are similar or not. The **label** in our case is the book rating. Therefore, the trained model can be used to predict the rating of a book for a given user such as the book; in this case, the one which has never been rated by the user.

Following is the conceptual diagram of how `object2vec` works:

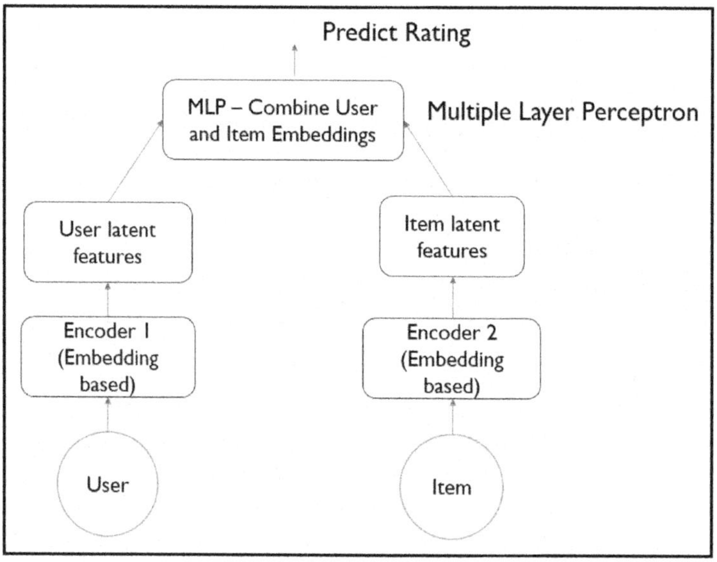

From the preceding visual, we can see the following:

- We can see that the user and item or book embeddings are concatenated, which are then passed to the **Multiple Layer Perceptron** (**MLP**).
- User and book embeddings are created from a one-hot encoded representation of user and book indexes respectively.
- Through supervised learning, MLP can learn the weights of the network and these weights can be used to predict score or rating of user-book pair.

To further understand the inner workings of `object2vec`, see the following screenshot:

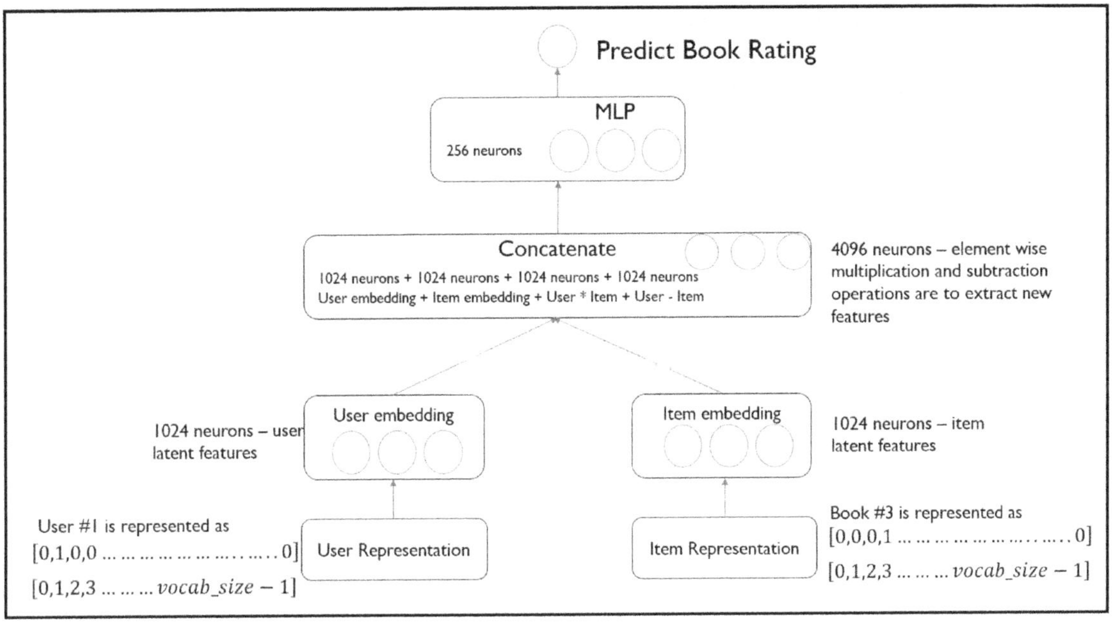

From the preceding visual, we can see the following:

- Object2vec starts with representing user and book with one-hot encoding. To explain, in our case, a user can be represented with an array of the size 12,347, which means that there are a total of 12,347 unique users in the dataset.
- User #1 can be represented by denoting 1 at position 1, while all of the other positions in the array have zeros.
- Books can also be represented in a comparable manner.
- It is time to now reduce the dimensionality of these representations. Therefore, the algorithm uses an embedding layer with 1,024 neurons, each for a user and a book.
- Object2vec further extracts additional features by conducting element-wise multiplication and subtraction between 1,024 user embedding neurons and 1,024 item embedding neurons.

In other words, the user and book embeddings are compared in different ways. Overall, we will then have 4,096 neurons when all of the neurons from the previous layers are merged. The algorithm then uses a single perceptron layer with 256 neurons. This perceptron layer is then fully connected to the output layer with one neuron. This one neuron will then predict the rating of a book given by a user.

It is now time to train the Object2Vec algorithm

Training the Object2Vec algorithm

Now that we have an understanding of how the algorithm works, let's dive into the training process:

1. **Data processing**: Feed data in the form of JSON lines; random shuffle the data for optimal performance. As you will see later, we send data in the format of `user index, book index, label=rating`.
2. **Model training**: We pass both training and validation data to the algorithm. There are multiple hyperparameters that we can configure to fine-tune the model's performance. We will review them in the upcomings sections. The objective function, in our case, is to minimize the **Mean Squared Error** (**MSE**). The error is the difference between the label (actual value) and the predicted rating.

Once the model has been trained, we will deploy it as an endpoint for inference.

In data processing, we will do the following:

1. First, we will read the ratings dataset stored in `parquet` format on the S3 bucket, as shown in the following code:

```
s3 = s3fs.S3FileSystem()

s3_bucket = 's3://ai-in-aws1/'
input_prefix = 'Chapter7/object2vec/bookratings.parquet'
dataset_name = s3_bucket + input_prefix

df_bkRatngs = pq.ParquetDataset(dataset_name,
filesystem=s3).read_pandas().to_pandas()
```

In the preceding code, we can see the following:

- `s3fs` is a Python library that is based on boto3, an AWS SDK for Python. `s3fs` provides a filesystem interface for S3.
- We use the `pyarrow` Python library to read partitioned `parquet` files from a designated s3 bucket.
- Specifically, we call the `ParquetDataset()` function by passing in the dataset name and filesystem.

2. After reading the dataset, we display it to ensure that the data is read correctly, as shown in the following screenshot:

	book_id	user_id	rating	title	book_ind	user_ind
0	1159	32773	5	Stones from the River	80	6320
1	1159	47984	4	Stones from the River	80	9777
2	1159	29097	3	Stones from the River	80	5444
3	1159	5657	3	Stones from the River	80	10959
4	1159	19404	4	Stones from the River	80	2756

Then, we load the dataframe in a format required by the `Object2Vec` algorithm. For each user-book pair and rating label, we create an entry in a data list by calling the `load_df_data()` function. Please refer to the source code attached to this chapter for details.

In model training, we start by partitioning the dataset into training, validation, and test sets. For each of the sets, we call the `write_data_list_to_jsonl()` function to create `.jsonl` (JSON lines) files, the format required by `object2vec`. A sample `jsonl` file is shown in the following screenshot:

```
{"in0": [1832], "in1": [392], "label": 4.0}
{"in0": [3093], "in1": [233], "label": 3.0}
{"in0": [3412], "in1": [385], "label": 4.0}
{"in0": [828], "in1": [561], "label": 5.0}
{"in0": [4267], "in1": [194], "label": 4.0}
{"in0": [11478], "in1": [504], "label": 5.0}
{"in0": [3858], "in1": [555], "label": 4.0}
{"in0": [6739], "in1": [144], "label": 4.0}
{"in0": [11708], "in1": [183], "label": 4.0}
```

1. Then, we upload the prepared datasets to the designated S3 bucket.

2. We obtain a Docker image of the Object2Vec algorithm, as follows:

```
container = get_image_uri(boto3.Session().region_name,
'object2vec')
```

In the preceding code, we can see the following:

- To get the **Uniform Resource Identifier** (**URI**) of the `object2vec` Docker image, we called the `get_image_uri()` function by passing the region name of the local SageMaker session and the name of the algorithm as input.
- The `get_image_uri()` function is part of the SageMaker Python SDK.

After obtaining the `uri` of the `object2vec` algorithm, we define the hyperparameters, as follows:

- **Encoder network**: This includes the following:
    - `enc0_layers`: This is the number of layers in the encoder network.
    - `enc0_max_seq_len`: This is the maximum number of sequences sent to the encoder network (in this case, only one user sequence is sent to the network).
    - `enc0_network`: This defines how embeddings are handled. In this case, since we address one user embedding at a time, no aggregation is necessary.
    - `enc0_vocab_size`: This defines the first encoder vocabulary size. It represents the number of users in the dataset.

  Since there are two encoders in the network, the same hyperparameters apply for encoder 1. For encoder 1, the vocabulary size needs to be defined appropriately, which is the number of books in the dataset—`enc1_vocab_size: 985`.

- **MLP**: This includes the following:
    - `mlp_dim`: This is the number of neurons in the MLP layers. In our experiment, we set it to 256.
    - `mlp_layers`: This is the number of layers in the MLP network. We use a single layer in our experiment.
    - `mlp_activation`: This is the activation function for MLP layers. In our experiment, we use the **Rectified Linear Unit** (**ReLU**) activation function for faster convergence and to avoid vanishing gradient issues. Note that the ReLU activation function is given by $y = max(0, x)$.

- **The following instances control how** `object2vec` **is trained:**
    - `epochs`: This is the number of backward and forward passes. We use 10 in our case.
    - `mini_batch_size`: This is the number of training examples to process before updating weights. We use 64.
    - `early_stopping_patience`: This is the maximum number of bad epochs (epochs where loss does not improve) that are executed before stopping. We use 2.
    - `early_stopping_tolerance`: This is the improvement in loss function required between two consecutive epochs for training to continue. This is after the number of patience epochs conclude. We use 0.01 for this parameter.
- **Others** includes the following:
    - `optimizer`: This is the optimization algorithm to arrive at optimal network parameters. In this experiment, we use adaptive moment estimation, also known as Adam. It computes the individual learning rate for each parameter. Parameters pertaining to features or inputs with sparse data go through large updates relative to the ones with dense data. Also, Adam computes individual momentum changes for each of the parameters. Remember that, during backpropagation, it is important to navigate in the right direction for faster convergence. Momentum changes help to navigate in the correct direction.
    - `output_layer`: This defines whether the network is a classifier or a regressor. In this case, since the network is trying to learn to rate, we define the output layer as a mean squared error (linear).

After the hyperparameters have been defined, we fit the `object2vec` estimator to the prepared datasets (train and validation), as shown in the following code:

```
# create object2vec estimator
regressor = sagemaker.estimator.Estimator(container, role,
train_instance_count=1,
 train_instance_type='ml.m5.4xlarge', output_path=output_path,
sagemaker_session=sess)

# set hyperparameters
regressor.set_hyperparameters(**static_hyperparameters)

# train and tune the model
regressor.fit(input_paths)
```

In the preceding code, we are doing the following:

1. We begin by creating an `object2vec` estimator by passing the Docker image, current execution role, number, and type of training instances, and current `sagemaker` session.
2. We then set hyperparameters for the newly created `object2vec` estimator using the `set_hyperparameters()` function.
3. Then, we fit the model to the training and validation datasets using the `fit()` function of the `Estimator` object.
4. The duration of training depends on the training instance type and the number of instances. For one `m5.4xlarge` machine learning instance, it took 2 hours to complete 10 epochs.

To monitor the training job in progress, navigate to the **Training** section on the left-hand side of the SageMaker service. Click on **Training Jobs** and then on the job name of your current job. After, navigate to the **monitor** section to see the training job's progress, as shown in the following screenshot:

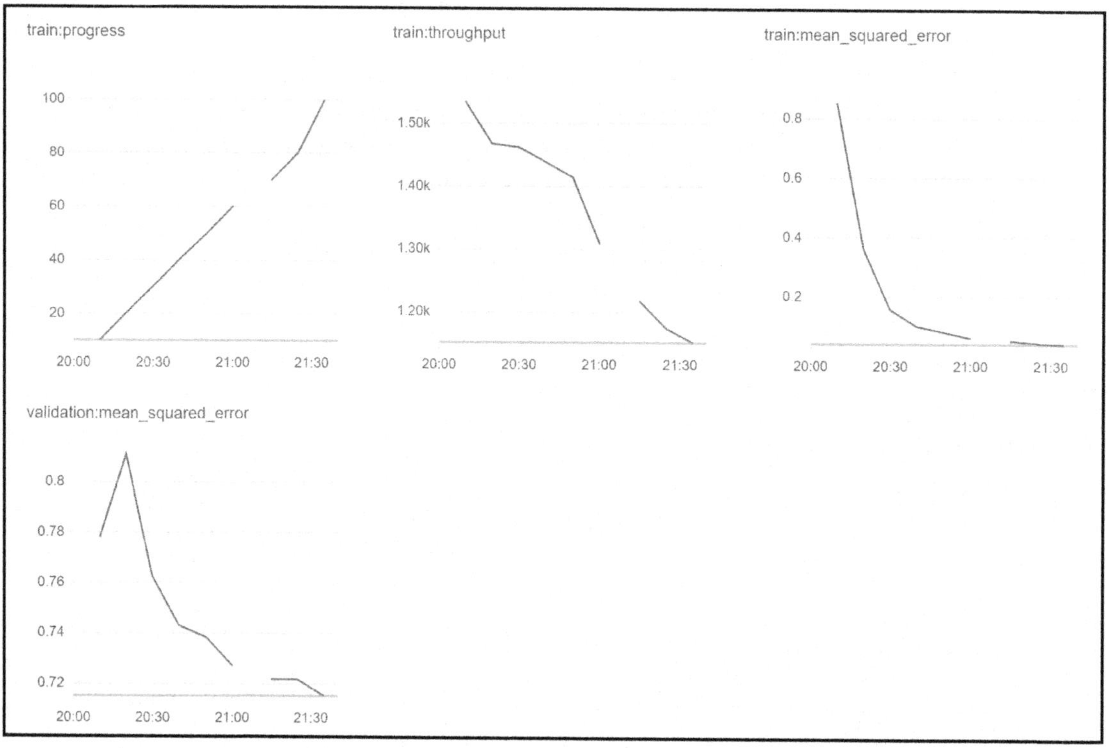

As you can see in the preceding screenshot, as the training MSE decreases, the validation MSE also decreases—although, in the validation dataset, the decrease in error is not as steep as the decrease in the training dataset. The training throughput can also be monitored through this dashboard.

Now that the training is done, let's deploy the trained model as an endpoint for inference.

Deploying the trained Object2Vec and running inference

Now, let's deploy the trained `object2vec` model. The SageMaker SDK offers methods so that we can seamlessly deploy trained models:

1. First, we will create a model from the training job using the `create_model()` method of the SageMaker `Estimator` object, as shown in the following code:

```
from sagemaker.predictor import json_serializer, json_deserializer

# create a model using the trained algorithm
regression_model =
regressor.create_model(serializer=json_serializer,
 deserializer=json_deserializer,content_type='application/json')
```

   To the `create_model()` method, we passed the type of serializers and deserializers to be used for the payload at the time of inference.

2. Once the model has been created, it can be deployed as an endpoint via the `deploy()` method of the SageMaker `Model` object, as shown in the following code:

```
# deploy the model
predictor = regression_model.deploy(initial_instance_count=1,
instance_type='ml.m4.xlarge')
```

   To the `deploy()` method, we have specified the number and type of instances that you have to launch to host the endpoint.

3. Once the `object2vec` model has been deployed as an endpoint, we can navigate to the **Endpoints** section under the **Inference** grouping (present on the left navigation menu under the SageMaker service). The status of the deployed endpoint can be viewed here, as shown in the following screenshot:

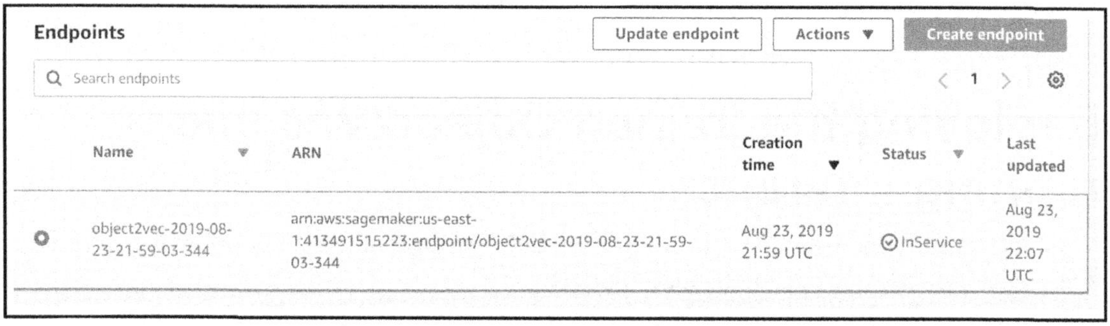

Now that we have the `object2vec` endpoint available, let's run inference.

4. We will create the `RealTimePredictor` object (the SageMaker Python SDK) by passing the endpoint name, along with the type of serialization and deserialization for the input and output, respectively. See the following code on how to initialize the `RealTimePredictor` object:

```
from sagemaker.predictor import RealTimePredictor, json_serializer,
json_deserializer

predictor =
RealTimePredictor(endpoint='object2vec-2019-08-23-21-59-03-344',
sagemaker_session=sess, serializer=json_serializer,
deserializer=json_deserializer, content_type='application/json')
```

You can change the endpoint name to reflect your current endpoint (the first argument of the `RealTimePredictor` object).

5. We then invoke the `predict()` method of `RealTimePredictor`, as shown in the following code:

```
# Send data to the endpoint to get predictions

prediction = predictor.predict(test_data)
print("The mean squared error on test set is %.3f"
%get_mse_loss(prediction, test_label))
```

In the preceding code, remember that `test_data` should be in a format that's consumable by `object2vec`. We use the `data_list_to_inference_format()` function to transform the test data into two components: instances and label. For details on this function, please see the source code associated with this chapter. Check out the following screenshot to see how the test data should be structured:

```
infer_data :  {'instances': ({'in0': [8488], 'in1': [725]}, {'in0': [3917], 'in1': [550]}, {'in0': [6106], 'in1': [193]},
{'in0': [2257], 'in1': [52]}, {'in0': [3783], 'in1': [555]}, {'in0': [11195], 'in1': [832]}, {'in0': [864], 'in1': [228]},
{'in0': [4856], 'in1': [626]}, {'in0': [10875], 'in1': [626]}, {'in0': [2203], 'in1': [46]}, {'in0': [9206], 'in1': [478]}
{'in0': [4678], 'in1': [123]}, {'in0': [6899], 'in1': [0]}, {'in0': [8491], 'in1': [294]}, {'in0': [1869], 'in1': [1]}, {'
```

As shown in the preceding screenshot, the inputs for 0 (`in0`) and 1 (`in1`) should have the indexes of the user and book, respectively. As for the test label, we produce a data list of ratings for each of the associated user-book pairs, as shown in the following screenshot:

```
label : (5.0, 1.0, 5.0, 3.0, 3.0, 4.0, 3.0, 4.0, 2.0, 4.0, 4.0, 5.0, 4.0, 5.0, 5.0, 3.0, 3.0, 5.0, 4.0, 5.0, 4.0, 3.0, 5.0,
4.0, 4.0, 5.0, 5.0, 4.0, 3.0, 4.0, 4.0, 3.0, 2.0, 3.0, 3.0, 5.0, 4.0, 3.0, 3.0, 3.0, 3.0, 3.0, 3.0, 4.0, 5.0, 3.0, 4.0, 3.0,
5.0, 4.0, 3.0, 4.0, 4.0, 4.0, 3.0, 5.0, 5.0, 4.0, 2.0, 5.0, 5.0, 5.0, 5.0, 5.0, 3.0, 4.0, 5.0, 5.0, 3.0, 4.0, 1.0, 5.0, 4.0,
5.0, 3.0, 5.0, 1.0, 4.0, 3.0, 5.0, 3.0, 4.0, 5.0, 3.0, 4.0, 5.0, 4.0, 4.0, 3.0, 2.0, 5.0, 4.0, 2.0, 2.0, 3.0, 5.0, 5.0, 3.0,
5.0, 2.0)
```

As shown in the preceding screenshot, we pass the first 100 user-book pairs from the test dataset to the `predict()` method of `RealTimePredictor`. The result is an MSE of 0.110.

6. Now, let's compare this MSE with the MSE from the naive options of computing book ratings:

    - **Baseline 1**: For each user-book pair in the test dataset, compute the rating, which is the average book ratings across all of the users, as shown in the following code:

    ```
    train_label = [row['label'] for row in copy.deepcopy(train_list)]
    bs1_prediction = round(np.mean(train_label), 2)
    print("The validation mse loss of the Baseline 1 is
    {}".format(get_mse_loss(len(test_label)*[bs1_prediction],
    test_label)))
    ```

To compute the average rating across all users, we do the following:

- We iterate through all of the ratings in the training dataset to create a labels list, `train_label`.
- `train_label` is then used to compute the mean. To calculate the MSE, in the `get_mse_loss()` function, the average rating across all of the users is subtracted from each of the ratings in `test_label`.
- The error is then squared and averaged across all of the test users. Please see the attached source code for details. The MSE from this option is 1.13.

- **Baseline 2**: For each user-book pair in the test dataset, we compute the rating, which is the average book rating for that user (that is, the average rating across all books rated by the user), as shown in the following code:

```
def bs2_predictor(test_data, user_dict):
  test_data = copy.deepcopy(test_data['instances'])
  predictions = list()
  for row in test_data:
    userID = int(row["in0"][0])
```

In the `bs2_predictor()` function, we passed the test data and user dictionary from the training dataset as inputs. For each user in the test data, if they exist in the training dataset, we computed the average book rating across all of the books rated by them. If they do not exist in the training dataset, we just get the average rating across all of the users, as shown in the following code:

```
 if userID in user_dict:
   local_books, local_ratings = zip(*user_dict[userID])
   local_ratings = [float(score) for score in local_ratings]
   predictions.append(np.mean(local_ratings))
 else:
   predictions.append(bs1_prediction)

return predictions
```

In the preceding `bs2_predictor()` function, the `zip(*)` function is used to return lists of books and ratings for each user. `bs1_prediction` is the average rating across all of the users in the training dataset. The MSE from this option is 0.82.

As we can see, an MSE of 0.110 from `object2vec` is better than the baselines:

- **Baseline 1 MSE**: 1.13, where the predicted book rating is the global average book rating across all users
- **Baseline 2 MSE**: 0.82, where the predicted book rating is the average book rating by user

Now that we have trained and evaluated the built-in SageMaker algorithm, `object2vec`, it is time to understand the features that SageMaker offers so that we can automate hyperparameter tuning.

Running hyperparameter optimization (HPO)

It takes data scientists numerous hours and experiments to arrive at an optimal set of hyperparameters that are required for best model performance. This process is mostly based on trial and error.

Although `GridSearch` is one of the techniques that is traditionally used by data scientists, it suffers from the curse of dimensionality. For example, if we have two hyperparameters, with each taking five possible values, we're looking at calculating objective function 25 times (5 x 5). As the number of hyperparameters grows, the number of times that the objective function is computed blows out of proportion.

Random Search addresses this issue by randomly selecting values of hyperparameters, without doing an exhaustive search of every single combination of hyperparameters. This `paper` by Bergstra et al. claims that a random search of the parameter space is guaranteed to be more effective than a grid search.

The idea is that some parameters have much less effect than others on the objective function. This is reflected by the number of values that are picked for each parameter in the grid search. Random Search enables the exploration of more values for each parameter, given several trials. The following is a diagram that illustrates the difference between grid search and random search:

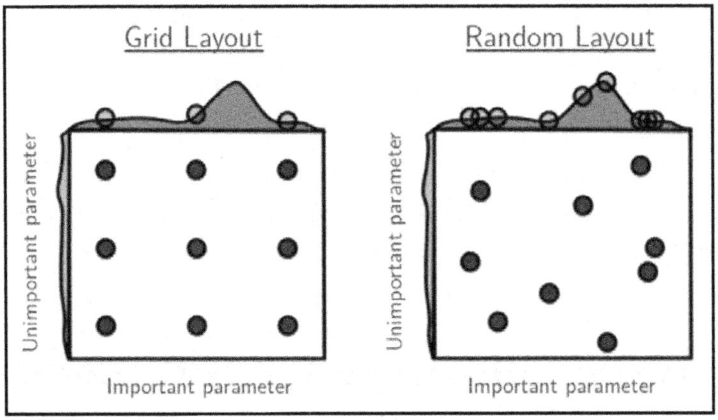

As you can see from the preceding screenshot, in a random search, we can test more values for important parameters, resulting in increased performance from training a model.

Neither of these techniques automate the process of hyperparameter optimization. **Hyperparameter Optimization** (**HPO**), from SageMaker, automates the process of selecting the optimal combination of hyperparameters. Here is how the tool works:

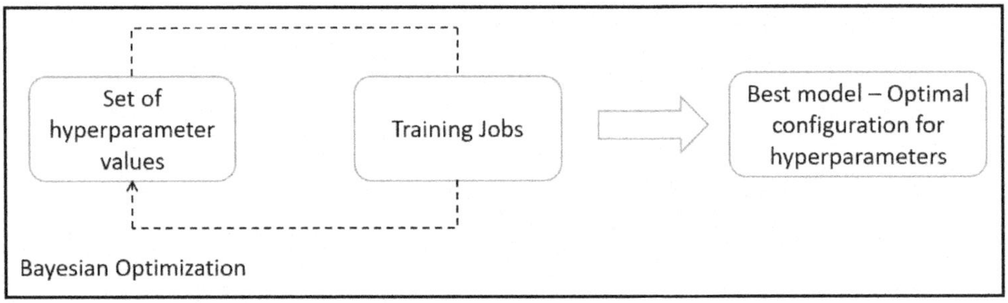

Take a look at the following points:

- HPO uses a Bayesian technique to iteratively select a combination of hyperparameters to train the algorithm.
- HPO picks the next set of hyperparameters, given the performance of the model and the configuration of hyperparameters in all of the historical steps.

- Also, it employs an *acquisition function* to determine where the next best opportunity is to lower the cost function.
- After a specified number of iterations, you will arrive at an optimal configuration of hyperparameters producing the best model.

For the `object2vec` algorithm, let's select the hyperparameters that we want to tune:

- `learning_rate`: Controls the speed with which weights in the neural network are optimized
- `dropout`: The percent of the neurons in a layer that are ignored in forward and backward passes
- `enc_dim`: The number of neurons to generate user/item embedding
- `mlp_dim`: The number of neurons in the MLP layer
- `weight_decay`: A factor to prevent overfitting (L2 regularization—causes the weight to decay in proportion to the factor specified)

We will use the `HyperparameterTuner` class from the `sagemaker` Python SDK to create tuning jobs. The goal of the tuning jobs is to reduce the MSE for the validation dataset. Depending on your budget and time, you can choose the number of training jobs you want to run. In this case, I chose to run 10 jobs, with only one job running at a given moment. You can choose to run multiple jobs in parallel.

To instantiate hyperparameter tuning jobs, we will need to do the following:

- Define the hyperparameters to tune and specify the objective function, as shown in the following code:

```
tuning_job_name = "object2vec-job-{}".format(strftime("%d-%H-%M-
%S", gmtime()))

hyperparameters_ranges = {
"learning_rate": ContinuousParameter(0.0004, 0.02),
"dropout": ContinuousParameter(0.0, 0.4),
"enc_dim": IntegerParameter(1000, 2000),
"mlp_dim": IntegerParameter(256, 500),
"weight_decay": ContinuousParameter(0, 300) }

objective_metric_name = 'validation:mean_squared_error'
```

As shown in the preceding code, we defined the ranges for each of the hyperparameters. For the objective function, we specified it as the mean squared error in the validation dataset:

- Define an estimator to train the `object2vec` model.
- Define the `HyperparameterTuner` job by passing the estimator, the objective function and type, and the maximum number of jobs to run, as shown here:

```
tuner = HyperparameterTuner(regressor, objective_metric_name,
hyperparameters_ranges, objective_type='Minimize', max_jobs=5,
max_parallel_jobs=1)
```

  The `HyperparameterTuner` object takes the estimator (named `regressor`) as one of the inputs. The estimator should be initialized with hyperparameters, along with the number and type of instances to be launched. Please see the associated source code for this chapter.

- Fit the tuner to the training and validation datasets, as shown in the following code:

```
tuner.fit({'train': input_paths['train'], 'validation':
input_paths['validation']}, job_name=tuning_job_name,
include_cls_metadata=False)
tuner.wait()
```

To the `fit` method of `hyperparameterTuner`, we pass the location of training and validation datasets. We wait for the tuner to finish running all of the jobs.

The following screenshot shows a few training jobs with a different set of hyperparameters that have been executed by `HyperparameterTuner`:

	Name	Status	Objective metric value	Creation time	Training Duration
○	object2vec-job-03-18-19-21-010-0a4f6531	Completed	3.1846425533294678	Feb 03, 2019 20:11 UTC	10 minute(s)
○	object2vec-job-03-18-19-21-009-6be1cd71	Completed	3.1857500076293945	Feb 03, 2019 20:00 UTC	7 minute(s)
○	object2vec-job-03-18-19-21-008-59d2ab63	Completed	3.184649705886841	Feb 03, 2019 19:50 UTC	7 minute(s)
○	object2vec-job-03-18-19-21-007-7783d580	Completed	3.19575834274292	Feb 03, 2019 19:35 UTC	12 minute(s)
○	object2vec-job-03-18-19-21-006-ccca4715	Completed	3.18619704246521	Feb 03, 2019 19:23 UTC	10 minute(s)
○	object2vec-job-03-18-19-21-005-40851de2	Completed	3.1850974559783936	Feb 03, 2019 19:12 UTC	7 minute(s)
○	object2vec-job-03-18-19-21-004-52ed057a	Completed	3.1856284141540527	Feb 03, 2019 19:03 UTC	6 minute(s)
○	object2vec-job-03-18-19-21-003-72db6efe	Completed	3.1868464946746826	Feb 03, 2019 18:50 UTC	8 minute(s)
○	object2vec-job-03-18-19-21-002-f9ea778f	Completed	3.1856629848480225	Feb 03, 2019 18:32 UTC	15 minute(s)

With each job, you can look at the hyperparameters that were used and the value of the objective function.

To look at the best job with the lowest MSE, navigate to the **Best job** tab, as shown in the following screenshot:

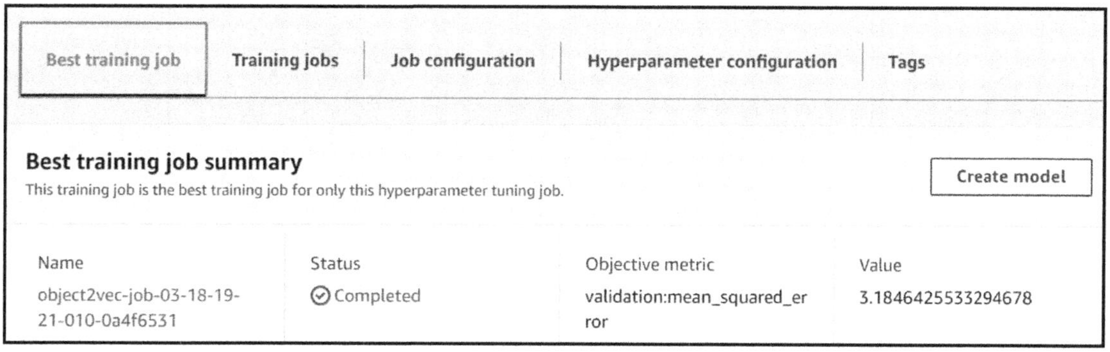

After the jobs are executed, you can run analytics on the results from hyperparameter optimization to answer questions, such as how does the MSE vary as the tuning jobs are being executed? You can also look at whether there is a correlation between the MSE and hyperparameters being tuned, such as the learning rate, dropout, weight decay, and the number of dimensions for both the encoder and `mlp`.

In the following code, we plot how the MSE changes as the training jobs are being executed:

```
objTunerAnltcs = tuner.analytics()
dfTuning = objTunerAnltcs.dataframe(force_refresh=False)
p = figure(plot_width=500, plot_height=500, x_axis_type = 'datetime')
p.circle(source=dfTuning, x='TrainingStartTime', y='FinalObjectiveValue')
show(p)
```

In the preceding code, we create an analytics object from `HyperparameterTuner`, which we created earlier. We then obtain a DataFrame from the analytics object—the DataFrame contains the metadata of all of the training jobs that were executed by the tuner. We then plot the MSE against time.

In the following diagram, we track how the MSE varies with the training time:

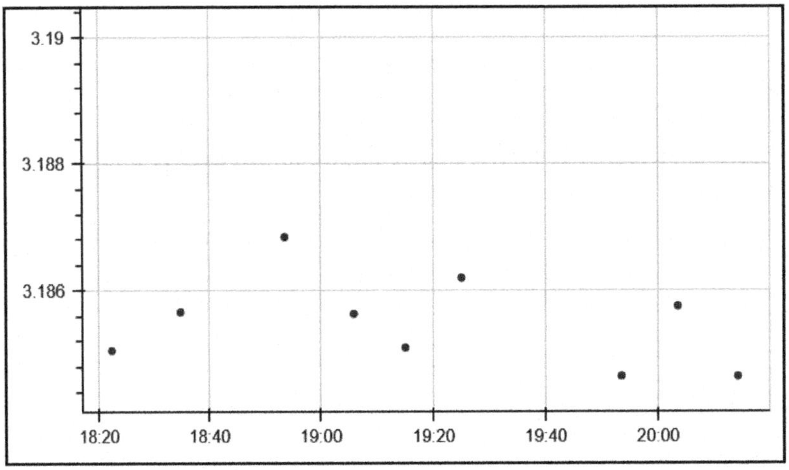

As you can see, the plot is very bumpy. If you increase the number of training jobs, perhaps the hyperparameter tuning job will converge.

It is time to look at another important feature of SageMaker, that is, the experiment service or search.

Understanding the SageMaker experimentation service

The goal of experiment management with SageMaker Search is to accelerate the model's development and experimentation phase, improving the productivity of data scientists and developers, while also reducing the overall time to market machine learning solutions.

The machine learning life cycle (continuous experimentation and tuning) states that when you initiate the training of a new learning algorithm, to improve model performance, you conduct hyperparameter tuning. With each iteration of the tuning, you will need to check how the model's performance is improving.

This leads to hundreds and thousands of experiments and model versions. The whole process slows down the selection of a final optimized model. Additionally, it is critical to monitor the performance of a production model. If the predictive performance of the model is degrading, it is important to know how the real-life data is different from the data that's used during training and validation.

SageMaker's Search tackles all of the challenges we highlighted previously by providing the following features:

- **Organizing, tracking, and evaluating model training experiments**: Creating leaderboards for winning models, cataloging model training runs, and comparing models by performance metrics such as training loss and validation accuracy
- **Seamlessly searching and retrieving the most relevant training runs**: Runs that can be searched by key attributes, which can be the training job name, status, start time, last modified time, and failure reason, among other things
- **Tracking the lineage of a deployed model in a live environment**: Tracking the training data used, values of the hyperparameters specified, resulting model performance, and version of the model deployed

Let's illustrate the features of SageMaker Search:

1. Navigate to **Search** on the left navigation pane of the Amazon SageMaker service.
2. Search for experiments that have been conducted using the `object2vec` algorithm:
    1. In the **Search** pane, under **Property**, select **AlgorithmSpecification.TrainingImage**.
    2. Under **Operator**, select **Contains**.
    3. Under **Value**, select **object2vec**, as shown in the following code:

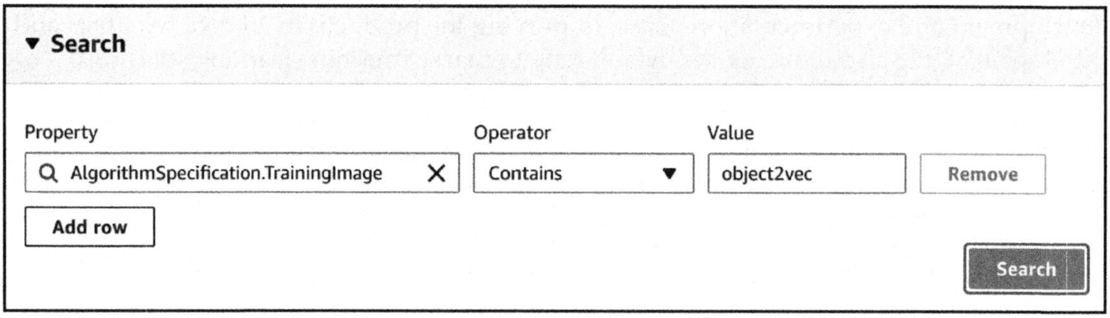

You can also search for experiments programmatically using `boto3`, the AWS SDK for Python, as shown here:

```
sgmclient = boto3.client(service_name='sagemaker')
results = sgmclient.search(**search_params)
```

In the preceding code, we instantiated the `sagemaker` client by passing the service name.

3. We will then call the search function of the SageMaker client by passing search parameters, as shown in the following code:

```
search_params={ "MaxResults": 10, "Resource": "TrainingJob",
"SearchExpression": {
 "Filters": [{"Name":
"AlgorithmSpecification.TrainingImage","Operator":
"Equals","Value": "Object2Vec"}]},
 "SortBy": "Metrics.validation:mean_squared_error",
 "SortOrder": "Descending"}
```

In the preceding code block, we defined search parameters such as the type of resource to search for the maximum number of results to show, search expression, and sort by and order. We pass the search parameters that were defined to the search function of the SageMaker client to retrieve results:

To find the winning training job, do the following:

1. Search for the experiments, as we discussed earlier. We can search based on several attributes, such as fields related to `TrainingJob`, `TuningJob`, `AlgorithmSpecification`, `InputDataConfiguration`, and `ResourceConfiguration`.
2. Once the relevant experiments have been retrieved, we can sort them by objective metrics to find the winning training job.

To deploy the best mode, follow these steps:

1. Click on the winning training job and click on the **Create Model** button at the top.
2. Specify the location of model artifacts and registry path of the inference image, among other details, to create a model. Once the model have been created, navigate to **Models** under the **Inference** section (the left navigation menu) of the SageMaker service.
3. You will find two options: **Create batch transform job** and **create endpoint**. For real-time inference, click on **create endpoint** and provide configuration details.

To track the lineage of a deployed model, do the following:

1. Choose **Endpoints** in the left navigation pane and select the endpoint of the winning model.
2. Scroll to the **Endpoint Configuration Settings** to locate the hyperlink to the **Training Job** that was used to create the endpoint.
3. Once the hyperlink has been clicked, you should see details on the model and training job, as shown in the following screenshot:

Model name	Training job	Variant name	Instance type	Elastic Inference	Initial instance count	Initial weight
object2vec-2019-02-03-22-28-12-576	object2vec-2019-02-03-22-14-21-943	AllTraffic	ml.m4.xlarge	-	1	1

You can also programmatically track the lineage of a deployed model:

1. Use `boto3` to get the endpoint configuration by calling the `describe_endpoint_config()` function of the SageMaker client.
2. From the configuration, select the model name to retrieve the Model Data URL.
3. Retrieve a training job from the Model Data URL. By doing this, from a deployed endpoint, we can trace back to the training job.

Let's now turn our attention to how SageMaker allows data scientists to bring their own machine learning and deep learning libraries to AWS.

Bring your own model – SageMaker, MXNet, and Gluon

This section focuses on how SageMaker allows you to bring your own deep learning libraries to the Amazon Cloud and still utilize the productivity features of SageMaker to automate training and deployment at scale.

The deep learning library we will bring in here is Gluon:

- Gluon is an open source deep learning library jointly created by AWS and Microsoft.
- The primary goal of the library is to allow developers to build, train, and deploy machine learning models in the cloud.

In the past, a tremendous amount of research has been conducted on recommender systems. In particular, Deep Structured Semantic models attempt to capture information from attributes, such as product image, title, and description. Extracting semantic information from these additional characteristics will solve the cold start problem in the space of recommender systems. In other words, when there is not much consumption history for a given user, a recommender system can propose products similar to the minimal products that are purchased by the user.

Let's see how pretrained word embeddings, available via the `gluonnlp` library, can be used in SageMaker to find books similar to the books that a user likes, that is, recommended books whose titles are semantically similar to titles of books that a user likes.

To do this, we will look at the same book ratings dataset we used in the previous sections of this chapter:

1. Let's begin by installing the prerequisites:
    - `mxnet`: This is a deep learning framework.
    - `gluonnlp`: This builds on top of MXNet. It is an open source deep learning library for **natural language processing** (**NLP**).
    - `nltk`: This is a Python natural language toolkit.
2. Next, we will read the filtered book ratings dataset that we created in the *Conduct Training in Amazon SageMaker* section. Then, we will obtain unique book titles from the dataset.
3. From each of the book titles, remove words with punctuation marks, numbers, and other special characters and only retain words that contain alphabets, as shown in the following code:

```
words = []

for i in df_bktitles['BookTitle']:
    tokens = word_tokenize(i)
    words.append([word.lower() for word in tokens if
word.isalpha()])
```

   In the preceding code block, we can see the following:

    - We iterate through each of the book titles and create tokens by calling the `word_tokenize()` function from `nltk.tokenize`.
    - For each title, we only retain words containing alphabets by calling the `isapha()` method on word strings. In the end, we have a list of lists called `words`.

4. Next, we will count the frequency of tokens across all of the book titles, as shown in the following:

```
counter =
nlp.data.count_tokens(itertools.chain.from_iterable(words))
```

   In the preceding code, we can see the following:

    - To compute the frequency of tokens, we called the `count_tokens()` function from `gluonnlp.data` by passing the words list to it.
    - `counter` is a dictionary containing tokens (keys) and associated frequencies (values).

5. Load the pre-trained word embedding vectors that were trained using fastText—a library from the Facebook AI Research lab that's used to learn word embeddings. Then, tie the word embeddings to each of the words in a book title, as shown here:

    ```
    vocab = nlp.Vocab(counter)
    fasttext_simple = nlp.embedding.create('fasttext',
    source='wiki.simple')
    vocab.set_embedding(fasttext_simple)
    ```

    In the preceding code block, we can see the following:

    - We created the indexes of tokens that can be attached to token embeddings by instantiating the `Vocab` class.
    - We then instantiated word/token embeddings by passing embedding type as `fasttext`.
    - We called the `set_embedding()` method of the `Vocab` object to attach pre-trained word embedding to each of the tokens.

6. Now, we create the embedding of a book title by averaging across individual word embeddings, as shown here:

    ```
    for title in words:
    title_arr = ndarray.mean(vocab.embedding[title], axis=0,
    keepdims=True)
    title_arr_list = np.append(title_arr_list, title_arr.asnumpy(),
    axis=0)
    ```

    In the preceding code, we can see the following:

    - We iterated through each of the book titles and computed its embedding by averaging across all of the embeddings of the words in the title. This is done by calling the `mean()` method of the `ndarray` object, an *n*-dimensional array.
    - We then created an array, `title_arr_list`, of title embeddings by using the `append()` method of the `numpy` module.

7. It is now time to plot book titles—first, we will reduce the dimensions of the embeddings from 300 dimensions to 2. Note that the shape of `title_arr_list` is 978 x 300. This means that the array has 978 unique book titles and each title is represented by a vector that's 300 in size. We will use the **T-distributed Stochastic Neighbor Embedding** (**TSNE**) algorithm to reduce the dimensionality but still retain its original meaning—that is, the distance between titles in a higher dimensional space is going to be the same as the distance between titles in a lower dimensional space. To go to a lower dimensional space for the title, we instantiate the `TSNE` class from the `sklearn` library, as shown in the following code:

```
tsne = TSNE(n_components=2, random_state=0)
Y = tsne.fit_transform(title_arr_list)
```

In the preceding code block, we called the `fit_transform()` method of the `TSNE` object to return the transformed version of embedding.

After we get the transformed embedding, we will do a scatter plot with one dimension on the *x*-axis and another dimension on the *y*-axis, as shown in the following diagram:

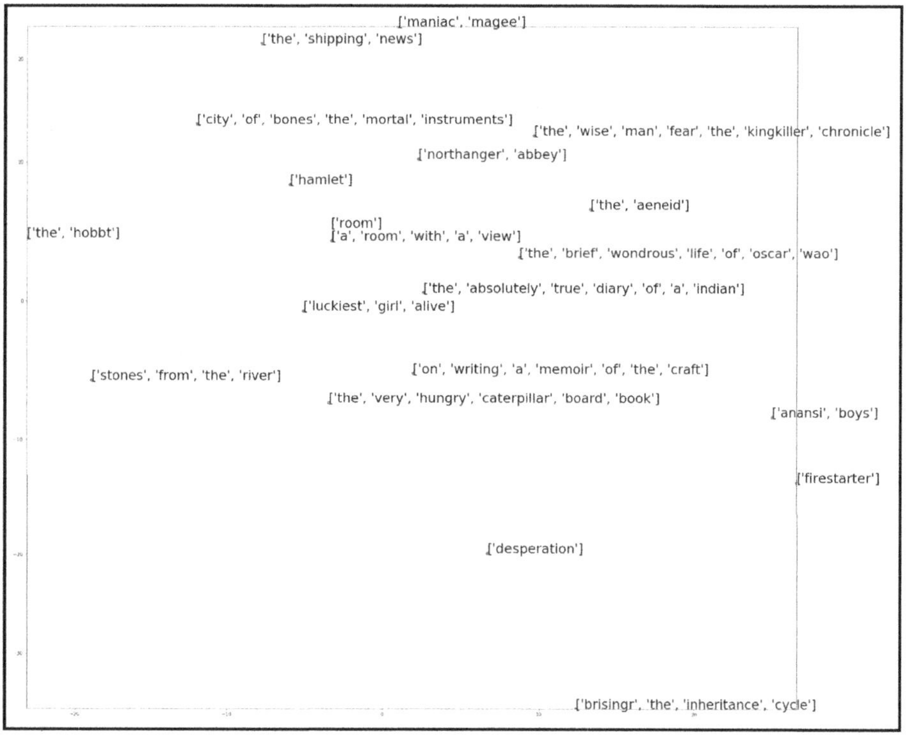

The proximity of book titles implies that they are semantically similar. For example, titles such as *Room* and *A Room with a View* seem to talk about the same subject room. These titles are located together in the lower dimensional space.

In this section, you learned how to bring pretrained word embeddings from fastText via the MXNet deep learning library to SageMaker. It is also possible to also train neural networks that have been built using the MXNet deep learning library from scratch. The same capabilities of SageMaker, such as training and deployment, are equally available for both built-in and custom algorithms.

Now that we have walked through how to bring your machine and/or deep learning library to SageMaker, it is time to look at how to bring your own container.

Bring your own container – R model

In this section, we will illustrate the process of bringing your own Docker container to Amazon SageMaker. Particularly, we will focus on training and hosting R models seamlessly in Amazon SageMaker. Rather than reinventing the wheel in terms of building ML models using SageMaker's built-in algorithms, data scientists and machine learning engineers can reuse the work that they've done in R in SageMaker.

The following is the architecture regarding how different AWS components interact to train and host R models:

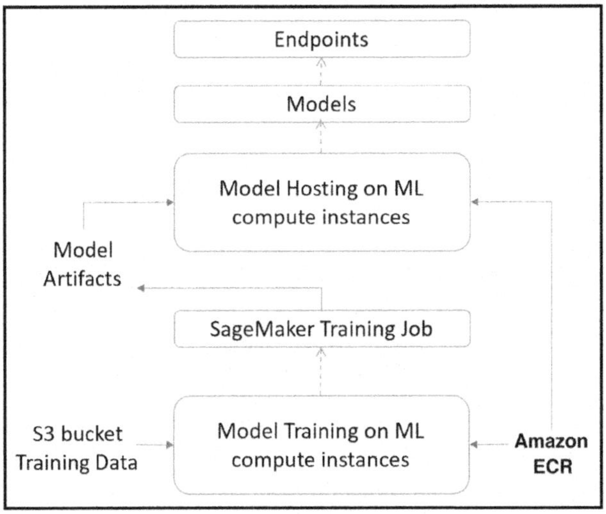

To follow the preceding architectural diagram, we start with Amazon **Elastic Container Registry** (**ECR**):

1. We create a Docker image containing an underlying operating system, prerequisites to train a recommender algorithm in R, and R code for training and scoring the **User-Based Collaborative Filtering** (**UBCF**) recommender algorithm.
2. The created Docker image is then published to Amazon ECR. Remember that the training data for both SageMaker built-in and custom algorithms sits in the S3 bucket.
3. To start a training job in SageMaker, you designate the location of the training data and Docker registry path (in ECR) of the training image.
4. During training, the appropriate R functions are triggered to train the UBCF algorithm. The training happens on SageMaker's machine learning compute instances.
5. The resulting trained models known as model artifacts, are saved to the designated location on the S3 bucket.

As for hosting the trained model, SageMaker requires two things:

- Model artifacts
- The Docker registry path of the inference image

To create an inference endpoint, the following takes place:

1. SageMaker will create a model by passing the Docker registry path of the inference image of the R model and model artifacts.
2. Once the SageMaker model has been created, SageMaker launches machine learning to compute instances by instantiating the Docker inference image.
3. The compute instances will have R code for inference available as a RESTful API.

In this section, we will look at the same book ratings dataset we used in the previous sections of this chapter, goodbooks-10k. Our goal is to suggest the top five books to users who are not part of the training dataset. We will use the `recommenderlab` R package to measure the cosine distance between users (UBCF). For our target user, we will pick 10 users/neighbors from the training set based on cosine similarity.

To estimate the top five book recommendations for the target user, the UBCF algorithm uses two things:

- Target user preferences for some books in the collection
- The trained model

With the help of a trained model, we will compute ratings for books that the target user has never rated before. The top five books (among all of the books in the dataset) with the highest ratings are proposed to a given user. The trained model fills in ratings for all the books and for all of the users in the training dataset, as shown in the following:

	BK1	BK2	BK3	BK4	BK5	Similarity(i, A)
A*	3	3.72	5	3.7	2	1
B	2	3				0.29
C	5	4	3			0.73
D	1		2	3		0.60
E	2		1	5	2	0.32

During the training process, UBCF computes the missing ratings. Let's assume that we want to fill in missing ratings for user A. User A has only rated **book #1 (BK1)** and **book #3 (BK3)**. To compute ratings for books 2, 4, and 5, the UBCF algorithm does the following:

- It computes the cosine similarity between user A and the rest of the users in the training dataset. To compute the similarity between user A and B, we do the following:

    1. If users A and B have common books that they've rated, multiply the ratings by the book.
    2. Add these ratings across all of the common books.
    3. Then, divide the result by the norm of vectors represented by users A and B.

- Given a similarity score for users B through E relative to A, compute the rating for a given new book by taking the weighted average of ratings given by users B through E for that book:

    1. For example, to compute the rating for book #2 for user A, we multiply a rating of 3 given by user B for book #2 by a similarity score of 0.29 and multiply a rating of 4 given by user C for book #2 by a similarity score of 0.73. We add these two factors together.
    2. We then add the two similarity score of 0.29 and 0.73.
    3. Finally, we divide the results from 1 with 2.

Now that we have looked at the training and hosting architecture for custom containers in SageMaker and discussed the use case, let's begin the implementation:

1. The first step is to define the Dockerfile by highlighting the requirements to run the R code. The requirements are an underlying operating system, the R version, the R packages, and the location of the R logic for training and inference. Create and publish a Docker image to the **EC2 Container Registry** (**ECR**).

   The following Dockerfile defines the specifications for training and hosting R model:

   ```
   FROM ubuntu:16.04

   RUN apt-get -y update --allow-unauthenticated && apt-get install -y
   --no-install-recommends \
    wget \
    r-base \
    r-base-dev \
    ca-certificates
   ```

   In the preceding code block, we can see the following:

   - We defined the version of the Ubuntu operating system to install.
   - We also specified that we need R installed.
   - Additionally, we have specified the R packages that need to be in place for the `Recommender` algorithm to work, as shown in the following code:

   ```
   RUN R -e "install.packages(c('reshape2', 'recommenderlab',
   'plumber', 'dplyr', 'jsonlite'), quiet = TRUE)"

   COPY Recommender.R /opt/ml/Recommender.R
   COPY plumber.R /opt/ml/plumber.R

   ENTRYPOINT ["/usr/bin/Rscript", "/opt/ml/Recommender.R", "--no-
   save"]
   ```

   In the preceding code, we can see the following:

   - We copied the training (`Recommender.R`) and inference (`plumber.R`) code to the appropriate location.
   - Later, we specified an entry point (code to run) after the Docker image is instantiated.

Now that the Dockerfile has been compiled, it is time to create a Docker image and push it to ECR, as shown here:

```
Docker build -t ${algorithm_name}.
Docker tag ${algorithm_name} ${fullname}
Docker push ${fullname}
```

In the preceding code, we can see the following:

- To build the Docker image locally, we run the `Docker build` command by passing the image name to the local SageMaker instance.
- The Dockerfile from the local directory (`"."`) is leveraged.
- After tagging the Docker image, we then push it to ECR with the `Docker push` command.

2. The next step is to create a SageMaker training job, listing training dataset, the latest Docker image for training, and infrastructure specifications. The model artifacts from the training job are stored in the relevant S3 bucket. This is very similar to running any training job on SageMaker.

Let's understand the R functions that are triggered during training:

- Remember that the `Recommender.R` code gets executed when ML compute instances are launched as part of the training.
- Depending on the command-line arguments that are passed, either the `train()` function or `serve()` function is executed, as shown in the following code:

```
args <- commandArgs()
if (any(grepl('train', args))) {
 train()}
if (any(grepl('serve', args))) {
 serve()}
```

- If the command-line argument contains the `train` keyword, the `train()` function gets executed. The same logic holds true for the `serve` keyword.

During training, SageMaker copies the training dataset from the S3 bucket to ML compute instances. After we prepare training data for model fitting, we call the `Recommender` method (the `recommenderlab` R package) by specifying the number of users in the training set, the type of recommender algorithm, and the type of output (top N book recommendations), as shown in the following:

```
rec_model = Recommender(ratings_mat[1:n_users], method = "UBCF",
param=list(method=method, nn=nn))
```

In the preceding code block, we can see the following:

- We train the model on 270 users and 973 books.
- The entire dataset contains 275 users.

Please refer to the source code attached to this chapter. Once the UBCF algorithm has been trained, the resulting model is saved in the designated location on the ML compute instance, which is then pushed to the specified location on the S3 bucket (model output path).

3. The third step is to host the trained model as an endpoint (RESTful API). SageMaker will need to create a model before provisioning an endpoint. Model artifacts and Docker images from training are required to define a SageMaker model. Note that the Docker image that was used for training is also used for inference. The SageMaker endpoint takes infrastructure specifications for ML compute instances as input, along with the SageMaker model. Again, this process of creating an endpoint in SageMaker for custom containers is the same as that for built-in algorithms.

Let's understand the R functions that are triggered during inference.

The following R function is run when SageMaker sends the `serve` command at the time of inference, as shown in the following code:

```
# Define scoring function
serve <- function() {
 app <- plumb(paste(prefix, 'plumber.R', sep='/'))
 app$run(host='0.0.0.0', port=8080)}
```

In the preceding code, we can see the following:

- We have used the plumber R package to turn R functions into REST endpoints.
- R functions that will need to be converted in to REST APIs are decorated with appropriate comments.
- We used the `plumb()` method to host the `plumber.R` code as an endpoint.

For each of the HTTP requests that's sent to the endpoint, the appropriate function is called, as shown here:

```
load(paste(model_path, 'rec_model.RData', sep='/'), verbose = TRUE)
pred_bkratings <- predict(rec_model, ratings_mat[ind], n=5)
```

In the preceding code, we can see the following:

- At the time of inference, we load the trained model by calling the `load()` method and passing the path to the model artifacts.
- We then call the `predict()` method by specifying the name of the trained model, the new user vector or book preferences, and the number of books to recommend.
- Note that the ratings matrix, `ratings_mat`, contains all 275 users and their ratings, where present, for books. In this case, we are interested in user #272. Remember that, in the dataset for this section, we have a total of 275 users and 973 books.

4. The fourth step is to run model inference, as shown here:

```
payload = ratings.to_csv(index=False)

response = runtime.invoke_endpoint(EndpointName='BYOC-r-endpoint-
<timestamp>', ContentType='text/csv', Body=payload)

result = json.loads(response['Body'].read().decode())
```

In the preceding code, we can see the following:

- We captured the entire dataset of 275 users in a CSV file called **payload**.
- We then pass the payload file as input to the `invoke_endpoint()` method of the SageMaker runtime, along with the endpoint name and content type.

The endpoint responds with results, as shown in the following:

```
                    The Dark Tower (The Dark Tower, #7)
                                A Tree Grows in Brooklyn
The Return of the King (The Lord of the Rings,...
                                             Fight Club
                                             Life of Pi
```

By doing this, we have seen how seamless it is to bring your own container to SageMaker to train and host models, reusing training and scoring (inference) logic that's been written in other languages.

Summary

In this chapter, you've learned how to process big data to create an analytics-ready dataset. You've also seen how SageMaker automates most of the steps of the machine learning life cycle, enabling you to build, train, and deploy models seamlessly. Additionally, we've illustrated some of the productivity features, such as hyperparameter optimization and experimentation service, which enable data scientists to run multiple experiments and deploy the winning model. Finally, we have looked at bringing our own models and containers to the SageMaker ecosystem. Through bringing our own models based on open source machine learning libraries, we can readily build solutions based on open source frameworks, while still leveraging all of the capabilities of the platform. Similarly, by bringing our own container, we can readily port solutions, written in other programming languages besides Python, to SageMaker.

Learning all of the aforementioned aspects of Amazon SageMaker enables data scientists and machine learning engineers to decrease speed-to-market machine learning solutions.

In the next chapter, we will cover how to create training and inference pipelines so that models can be trained and deployed for efficiently running inferences (by creating reusable components).

Further reading

For extended examples and details on working with SageMaker, please refer to the following AWS blogs:

- https://github.com/awslabs/amazon-sagemaker-examples
- https://aws.amazon.com/blogs/machine-learning/introduction-to-amazon-sagemaker-object2vec/
- https://aws.amazon.com/blogs/machine-learning/amazon-sagemaker-now-comes-with-new-capabilities-for-accelerating-machine-learning-experimentation/

8
Creating Machine Learning Inference Pipelines

The data transformation logic that is used to process data for model training is the same as the logic that's used to prepare data for obtaining inferences. It is redundant to repeat the same logic twice.

The goal of this chapter is to walk you through how SageMaker and other AWS services can be employed to create **machine learning** (**ML**) pipelines that can process big data, train algorithms, deploy trained models, and run inferences, all while using the same data processing logic for model training and inference.

In this chapter, we will cover the following topics:

- Understanding the architecture of the inference pipeline in SageMaker
- Creating features using Amazon Glue and SparkML
- Identifying topics by training NTM in SageMaker
- Running online as opposed to batch inference in SageMaker

Let's look at the technical requirements for this chapter.

Technical requirements

To illustrate the concepts that we will cover in this chapter, we will use the `ABC Millions Headlines` dataset. This dataset contains approximately a million news headlines. In the `github` repository associated with this chapter, you should find the following files:

- `abcnews-date-text.zip`: The input dataset
- `libraries-mleap`: MLeap libraries (includes a `.jar` file and a Python wrapper for the `.jar`)

Let's begin by looking at the architecture of an inference pipeline.

Understanding the architecture of the inference pipeline in SageMaker

There are three major components of the inference pipeline we are building:

- Data preprocessing
- Model training
- Data preprocessing (from *Step 1*) and inference

The following is the architectural diagram—the steps we are going to walk through are applicable to big data:

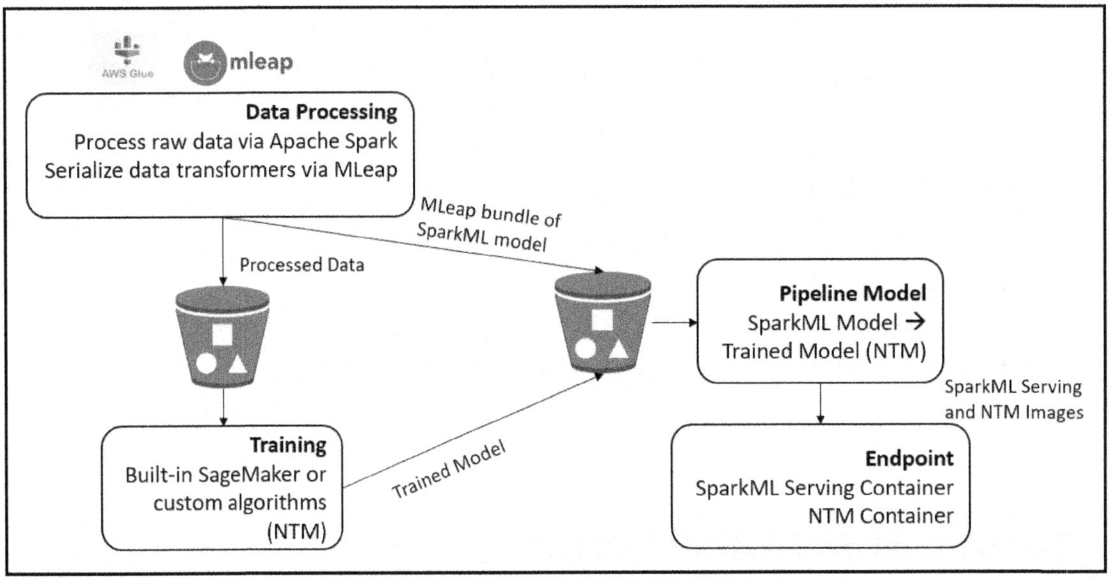

In the first step of the pipeline, we execute data processing logic on Apache Spark via AWS Glue. The Glue service is called from a SageMaker Notebook instance.

> Amazon Glue is a fully managed, serverless **Extract, Transform, and Load (ETL)** service that's used to wrangle big data. ETL jobs are run on an Apache Spark environment where Glue provisions, the configuration and scale the resources that are required to run the jobs.

The data processing logic, in our case, includes creating tokens/words from each of the news headlines, removing stop words, and counting the frequency of each of the words in a given headline. The ETL logic is serialized into an MLeap bundle, which can be used at the time of inference for data processing. Both the serialized SparkML model and processed input data are stored in an S3 bucket.

> MLeap is an open source Spark package that's designed to serialize Spark-trained transformers. Serialized models are used to transform data into the desired format.

In the second step, the **neural topic model** (**NTM**) algorithm is trained on the processed data to discover topics.

In *Step 3*, both the SparkML and trained NTM models are used to create a pipeline model, which is used to execute the models in the specified sequence. SparkML serves a docker container, and the NTM docker container is provisioned as an endpoint for real-time model predictions. The same pipeline model can be used to run inferences in batch mode, that is, score multiple news headlines in one go, discovering topics for each of them.

It is now time to delve globally into *Step 1*—how to invoke Amazon Glue from a SageMaker Notebook instance for big data processing.

Creating features using Amazon Glue and SparkML

To create features in a big data environment, we will use PySpark to write data preprocessing logic. This logic will be part of the Python `abcheadlines_processing.py` file. Before we review the logic, we need to walk through some prerequisites.

Walking through the prerequisites

1. Provide SageMaker Execution Role access to the Amazon Glue service, as follows:

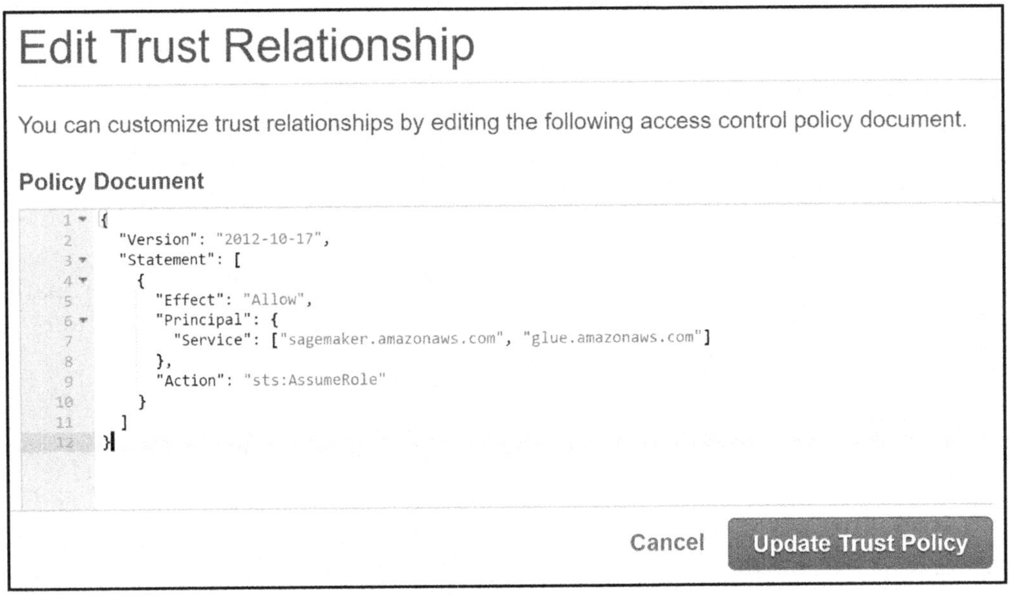
Edit Trust Relationship
You can customize trust relationships by editing the following access control policy document.
Policy Document
{
"Version": "2012-10-17",
"Statement": [
{
"Effect": "Allow",
"Principal": {
"Service": ["sagemaker.amazonaws.com", "glue.amazonaws.com"]
},
"Action": "sts:AssumeRole"
}
]
}
Cancel
Update Trust Policy

Obtaining a SageMaker Execution Role by running the get_execution_role() method of the SageMaker session object

2. On the IAM Dashboard, click on **Roles** on the left navigation pane and search for this role. Click on the **Target Role** to navigate to its **Summary** page. Click on the **Trust Relationships** tab to add `AWS Glue` as an additional trusted entity. Click on **Edit trust relationship** to add the following entry to `"Service" key: "glue.amazonaws.com"`.
3. Upload MLeap binaries to the appropriate location on the S3 bucket, as follows. The binaries can be found in the source code for this chapter:

```
python_dep_location = sess.upload_data(path='python.zip',
bucket=default_bucket, key_prefix='sagemaker/inference-
pipeline/dependencies/python')

jar_dep_location =
sess.upload_data(path='mleap_spark_assembly.jar',
bucket=default_bucket, key_prefix='sagemaker/inference-
pipeline/dependencies/jar')
```

4. We will use the `upload_data()` method of the SageMaker Session object to upload MLeap binaries to the appropriate location on the S3 bucket. We will need the `MLeap` Java package and the Python wrapper, MLeap, to serialize SparkML models. Similarly, we will upload the input data, that is, `abcnews-date-text.zip`, to the relevant location on the S3 bucket.

Now we'll review the data preprocessing logic in `abcheadlines_processing.py`.

Preprocessing data using PySpark

The following data preprocessing logic is executed on a Spark cluster. Let's go through the steps:

1. We will begin by gathering arguments sent by the SageMaker Notebook instance, as follows:

```
args = getResolvedOptions(sys.argv, ['S3_INPUT_BUCKET',
 'S3_INPUT_KEY_PREFIX',
 'S3_INPUT_FILENAME',
 'S3_OUTPUT_BUCKET',
 'S3_OUTPUT_KEY_PREFIX',
 'S3_MODEL_BUCKET',
 'S3_MODEL_KEY_PREFIX'])
```

We will use the `getResolvedOptions()` utility function from the AWS Glue library to read all the arguments that were sent by the SageMaker notebook instance.

2. Next, we will read the news headlines, as follows:

```
abcnewsdf = spark.read.option("header","true").csv(('s3://' +
os.path.join(args['S3_INPUT_BUCKET'], args['S3_INPUT_KEY_PREFIX'],
args['S3_INPUT_FILENAME'])))
```

We use `spark`, which is the active SparkSession, to read the `.csv` file that contains the relevant news headlines.

3. Next, we retrieve 10% of the headlines and define the data transformations. We can process all 1,000,000 headlines using distributed computing from Apache Spark. We will, however, illustrate the concepts behind using AWS Glue from a SageMaker notebook instance by using a sample of the dataset:

```
abcnewsdf = abcnewsdf.limit(hdl_fil_cnt)

tok = Tokenizer(inputCol="headline_text", outputCol="words")
swr = StopWordsRemover(inputCol="words", outputCol="filtered")
ctv = CountVectorizer(inputCol="filtered", outputCol="tf",
vocabSize=200, minDF=2)
idf = IDF(inputCol="tf", outputCol="features")
```

`hdl_fil_cnt` is 10% of the total number of headlines. `abcnewsdf` contains around 100,000 headlines. We use `Tokenizer`, `StopWordsRemover`, `CountVectorizer`, and the **inverse document frequency (IDF)** transformer and estimator objects from `pyspark.ml.feature` to transform the headline text, as follows:

1. First, `Tokenizer` transforms the headline text into a list of words.
2. Second, `StopWordsTokenizer` removes stop words from the list of words produced by `Tokenizer`.
3. Third, `CountVectorizer` takes the output from the previous step to calculate word frequency.
4. Lastly, IDF, an estimator, computes the inverse document frequency factor for each of the words (IDF is given by $tf_{i,j} * log(\frac{N}{df_i})$, where $t_{i,j}$ is the term frequency of term i in headline j, N is the total number of headlines, and df_i is the number of headlines containing term i). Words that are unique to a headline are much more important than those that appear frequently in other headlines.

For more information on `Estimator` and `Transformer` objects in Spark ML, please refer to Spark's documentation at `https://spark.apache.org/docs/latest/ml-pipeline.html`.

4. Next, we will stitch all the transformer and estimator stages together into a pipeline and transform the headlines into feature vectors. The width of a feature vector is 200, as defined by `CountVectorizer`:

```
news_pl = Pipeline(stages=[tok, swr, ctv, idf])
news_pl_fit = news_pl.fit(abcnewsdf)
news_ftrs_df = news_pl_fit.transform(abcnewsdf)
```

In the preceding code, we use the `Pipeline` object from `pyspark.ml` to tie data transformations together. We also call the `fit()` method on the `Pipeline` object, `news_pl`, to create `PipelineModel`. `news_pl_fit` will have learned the IDF factor for each of the words in the news headlines. When the `transform()` method is invoked on `news_pl_fit`, the input headlines are transformed into feature vectors. Each headline will be represented by a vector that's 200 in length. `CountVectorizer` picks the top 200 words ordered by word frequency across all the headlines. Note that the processed headlines will be stored in the `features` column, as indicated by the `outputCol` parameter of the IDF Estimator stage.

5. Now we save the resulting feature vectors in `.csv` format, as follows:

```
news_save = news_formatted.select("result")
news_save.write.option("delimiter",
"\t").mode("append").csv('s3://' +
os.path.join(args['S3_OUTPUT_BUCKET'],
args['S3_OUTPUT_KEY_PREFIX']))
```

To save the processed headlines in `.csv` format, the `features` column needs to be in a simple string format. The CSV file format does not support storing arrays or lists in a column. We will define a user-defined function, `get_str`, to convert a feature vector into a string of comma-separated tf-idf numbers. Please look at the source code associated with this chapter for additional details. The resulting `news_save` DataFrame will be saved to a designated location on the S3 bucket as a `.csv` file. The following screenshot shows the format of the `.csv` file:

0	0	0	0	0	0	0	0	0	0	0	0	0	0	0	0	0	0	0
0	0	0	0	0	0	0	0	0	0	0	0	4.481468	0	0	0	0	0	0
0	0	0	0	0	0	0	0	0	0	0	0	0	0	0	0	0	0	0
0	0	0	0	0	0	0	0	0	0	0	0	0	0	0	0	0	0	0
0	0	0	0	0	0	0	0	0	0	0	0	0	0	0	0	0	0	0
0	0	0	0	0	0	0	0	0	0	0	0	0	0	0	0	0	0	0
0	0	0	0	0	0	0	0	0	0	0	0	0	0	0	0	0	0	0
0	0	0	0	0	0	0	0	0	0	0	0	0	0	0	0	0	0	0
0	0	0	0	0	3.909462	3.935557	0	0	0	0	0	0	0	0	0	0	0	0
0	0	0	0	0	0	0	0	0	0	0	0	0	0	0	0	0	0	0
0	0	0	0	0	0	3.935557	0	0	0	0	0	0	0	0	0	0	0	0
0	0	0	0	0	0	0	0	0	0	0	0	0	0	0	0	0	0	0
0	0	0	0	0	0	0	0	0	0	0	0	0	0	0	0	0	0	0
0	0	0	0	0	0	0	0	0	0	0	0	0	0	0	0	0	0	0
0	0	0	0	0	0	0	4.037008	0	0	0	0	0	0	0	0	0	0	4.550232

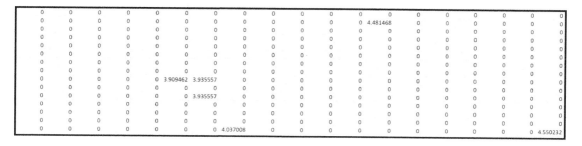

6. Similarly, we will also save the vocabulary into a separate text file.
7. Now it's time to serialize `news_pl_fit` and push it to an S3 bucket, as follows:

```
 SimpleSparkSerializer().serializeToBundle(news_pl_fit,
"jar:file:/tmp/model.zip", news_ftrs_df)
s3.Bucket(args['S3_MODEL_BUCKET']).upload_file('/tmp/model.tar.gz',
file_name)
```

In the preceding code block, we use the `serializetoBundle()` method of the `SimpleSparkSerializer` object from the MLeap `pyspark` library to serialize `news_pl_fit`. We will convert the format of the serialized model from a `.zip` into a `tar.gz` before uploading it to the S3 bucket.

Now let's walk through the process of running `abcheadlines_processing.py` through an AWS Glue job.

Creating an AWS Glue job

Now we will create a Glue job using `Boto3`, which is the AWS SDK for Python. This SDK allows Python developers to create, configure, and manage AWS services.

Let's create a Glue job by providing the following specifications:

```
response = glue_client.create_job(
    Name=job_name,
    Description='PySpark job to featurize the ABC News Headlines dataset',
    Role=role,
    ExecutionProperty={
        'MaxConcurrentRuns': 1
    },
```

In the preceding code block, we call the `create_job()` method of the AWS Glue client by passing in the job name, description, and role. We also specify how many concurrent we want to execute.

Now let's look at the command that's sent by Glue to the Spark cluster:

```
Command={
'Name': 'glueetl',
'ScriptLocation': script_location
},
```

In the preceding code, we define the command name and location of the Python script containing the data preprocessing logic, that is, `abcheadlines_processing.py`.

Now let's look at which binaries need to be configured in order to serialize SparkML models:

```
DefaultArguments={
'--job-language': 'python',
'--extra-jars' : jar_dep_location,
'--extra-py-files': python_dep_location
},)
```

In the preceding code, we define a default language so that we can preprocess big data, the locations of the MLeap `.jar` file, and the Python wrapper of MLeap.

Now that we have created the Glue job, let's run it:

```
job_run_id = glue_client.start_job_run(JobName=job_name,
                                        Arguments = {
                                         '--S3_INPUT_BUCKET':
s3_input_bucket,
                                         '--S3_INPUT_KEY_PREFIX':
s3_input_key_prefix,
                                         '--S3_INPUT_FILENAME': s3_input_fn,
                                         '--S3_OUTPUT_BUCKET':
s3_output_bucket,
                                         '--S3_OUTPUT_KEY_PREFIX':
s3_output_key_prefix,
                                         '--S3_MODEL_BUCKET':
s3_model_bucket,
                                         '--S3_MODEL_KEY_PREFIX':
s3_model_key_prefix
                                        })
```

We invoke the `start_job_run()` method of the AWS Glue client by passing the name of the Glue job we created earlier, along with the arguments that define the input and location locations.

We can get the status of the Glue job as follows:

```
job_run_status =
glue_client.get_job_run(JobName=job_name,RunId=job_run_id)['JobRun']['JobRu
nState']
```

We will receive the following output:

```
RUNNING
RUNNING
RUNNING
RUNNING
SUCCEEDED
```

We invoke the `get_job_run()` method of the AWS Glue client and pass in the name of the Glue job whose status we want to check.

To check the status of the AWS Glue job, you can also navigate to the AWS Glue service from the **Services** menu. Under the **ETL** section in the left-hand navigation menu, click on **Jobs**. Select a job name to look at the details of that Glue job:

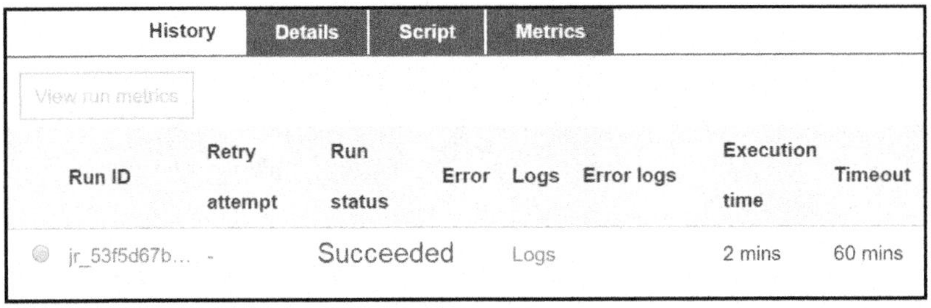

Now we will uncover topics that are in the ABC News Headlines dataset by fitting NTM to it.

Identifying topics by training NTM in SageMaker

Perform the following steps to train the NTM model:

1. Read the processed ABC News Headlines dataset from the output folder on the designated S3 bucket, as follows:

   ```
   abcnews_df = pd.read_csv(os.path.join('s3://', s3_output_bucket,
   f.key))
   ```

   We use the `read_csv()` function from the pandas library to read the processed news headlines into a DataFrame. The DataFrame contains 110,365 headlines and 200 words.

2. Then, we split the dataset into three parts—train, validation, and test—as follows:

```
vol_train = int(0.8 * abcnews_csr.shape[0])

train_data = abcnews_csr[:vol_train, :]
test_data = abcnews_csr[vol_train:, :]

vol_test = test_data.shape[0]
val_data = test_data[:vol_test//2, :]
test_data = test_data[vol_test//2:, :]
```

In the preceding code block, we take 80% of the data for training, 10% for validation, and the remaining 10% for testing.

3. Upload the train, validation, and test datasets to the appropriate location on the S3 bucket. We also need to upload the vocabulary text file that was created by the AWS Glue job to the auxiliary path. SageMaker's built-in algorithm uses the auxiliary path to provide additional information while training. In this case, our vocabulary contains 200 words. However, the feature vector from the previous section does not know the word name; it does, however, know the word index. Therefore, after the NTM is trained, so that SageMaker can output significant words that correspond to a topic, it needs a vocabulary text file.
4. The next step is to define the NTM Estimator object from SageMaker by passing the number and type of compute instances and the Docker NTM image to a SageMaker session. Estimators are learning models that are suitable for the data.
5. Now we are ready to train the NTM algorithm, as follows:

```
ntm_estmtr_abc.fit({'train': s3_train, 'validation': s3_val,
'auxiliary': s3_aux})
```

To train the NTM algorithm, we use the `fit()` method of the `ntm` Estimator object by passing the location of the train, test, and auxiliary datasets. Since we have a whole new chapter, `Chapter 9`, *Discovering Topics in Text Collection*, dedicated to understanding how the NTM algorithm works, we will save the model training details for later.

1. The following is the model's output—we've configured the model so that it retrieves five topics:

```
International Politics and Conflict
[0.40, 0.94] defends decision denies war anti pm warns un bush
report iraq calls public australia minister backs wins tas plans
chief

Sports and Crime
```

```
[0.52, 0.77] clash top win world tour test pakistan back record cup
killed title final talks england set australia us still pm

Natural Disasters and Funding
[0.45, 0.90] urged indigenous water power take call lead boost
final residents get wa act funds england centre fire help plan
funding

Protest and Law Enforcement
[0.51, 0.72] new record says found strike set win cup south police
fire us go pay court plan rise australia bid deal

Crime
[0.54, 0.93] charged dies murder man charges crash death dead car
two woman accident face charge found attack police injured court
sydney
```

There are two numbers at the beginning of each topic—kld and recons. We will go into each of these losses in the next chapter. But for now, understand that the first fraction reflects the loss in creating embedded news headlines, while the second fraction reflects the reconstruction loss (that is, creating headlines from embeddings). The smaller the losses, the better the topic clusters.

For each of the topics we've discovered, we manually label the topics based on the word groupings.

Now we are ready to look at inference patterns. Inferences can be obtained both in real-time and batch mode.

Running online versus batch inferences in SageMaker

In real-world production scenarios, we typically come across two situations:

- Running inferences in real-time or in online mode
- Running inferences in batch or in offline mode

To illustrate this, in the case of using a recommender system as part of a web/mobile app, real-time inferences can be used when you want to personalize item suggestions based on in-app activity. The in-app activity, such as items you browsed, items left in your shopping cart and not checked out, and so on, can be sent as input to an online recommender system.

On the other hand, if you want to present item suggestions to your customers even before they engage with your web/mobile app, then you can send data related to their historical consumption behavior to an offline recommender system so that you can obtain item suggestions for your entire customer base in one shot.

Let's look at how real-time predictions are run.

Creating real-time predictions through an inference pipeline

In this section, we will build a pipeline where we reuse the serialized SparkML model for data preprocessing and employ a trained NTM model to derive topics from preprocessed headlines. SageMaker's Python SDK provides classes such as `Model`, `SparkMLModel`, and `PipelineModel` to create an inference pipeline that can be used to conduct feature processing and then score processed data using the trained algorithm.

Let's walk through the steps for creating an endpoint that can be used for real-time predictions:

1. Create a `Model` from the NTM training job (the one we created in the previous section), as follows:

```
ntm_model = Model(model_data=modeldataurl, image=container)
```

   Here, we create the `Model` object that's present in the `sagemaker.model` module. We pass in the location of the trained NTM model and the Docker registry path of the NTM inference image.

2. Create a SparkML `Model` representing the learned data preprocessing logic, as follows:

```
sparkml_data = 's3://{}/{}/{}'.format(s3_model_bucket,
s3_model_key_prefix, 'model.tar.gz')
sparkml_model = SparkMLModel(model_data=sparkml_data,
env={'SAGEMAKER_SPARKML_SCHEMA' : schema_json})
```

   We define `sparkml_data` as the location of the serialized `PipelineModel` from the `pyspark.ml` package. Remember that `PipelineModel` contains three transformers (`Tokenizer`, `StopWordsRemover`, and `CountVectorizer`) and one estimator (IDF) from the data preprocessing we did in the previous section. Then, we create a `SparkMLModel` object, `sparkml_model`, by passing the location of the trained Spark `PipelineModel` and schema of input data for inference.

3. Create a `PipelineModel`, encompassing and sequencing the `sparkml_model` (data preprocessing) and `ntm_model` as follows:

   ```
   sm_model = PipelineModel(name=model_name, role=role,
   models=[sparkml_model, ntm_model])
   ```

   We create a `PipelineModel` object from the `sagemaker.pipeline` module by passing in the model name, the `sagemaker` execution role, and the sequence of models we want to execute.

4. Now it's time to deploy the `PipelineModel`, as follows:

   ```
   sm_model.deploy(initial_instance_count=1,
   instance_type='ml.c4.xlarge', endpoint_name=endpoint_name)
   ```

We will invoke the `deploy()` method on `sm_model` to deploy the model as an endpoint. We pass the number and type of instances we need to host the endpoint, along with the endpoint's name, to the deployed model.

Now it's time to pass a sample headline from the test dataset to the newly created endpoint. Let's walk through the steps:

1. First, we create a `RealTimePredictor` object from the `sagemaker.predictor` module, as follows:

   ```
   predictor = RealTimePredictor(endpoint=endpoint_name,
   sagemaker_session=sess, serializer=json_serializer,
    content_type=CONTENT_TYPE_JSON, accept=CONTENT_TYPE_CSV)
   ```

   We define the `RealTimePredictor` object by passing the name of the endpoint created previously, the current SageMaker session, the serializer (this defines how the input data is encoded when transmitting it to an endpoint), and the request and response content types.

2. Then we invoke the `predict()` method of the `RealTimePredictor` object, `predictor`, as follows:

   ```
   predictor.predict(payload)
   ```

We call the `predict()` method of `predictor`, initialized as the `RealTimePredictor` object, by passing a sample headline from the test dataset as part of the `json` payload, as follows:

```
payload = {
    "schema": {
        "input": [
        {
            "name": "headline_text",
            "type": "string"
        },
    ],
    "output":
        {
            "name": "features",
            "type": "double",
            "struct": "vector"
        }
    },
    "data": [
        ["lisa scaffidi public hearing possible over expenses
scandal"]
            ]
}
```

The payload variable contains two keys, `schema` and `data`. The `schema` key contains the input and output structure of `SparkMLModel`, while the `data` key contains a sample headline whose topics we want to discover. If we choose to override the SageMaker `sparkml` schema we specified while initializing `SparkMLModel`, we can pass the new schema. The following is the output from scoring a news headline:

```
{"predictions":[{"topic_weights":[0.5172129869,0.0405323133,0.2246916145,0.
1741439849,0.0434190407]}]}
```

We can see that the headline has three prominent topics: International Politics and Conflict, followed by Funding/Expenses related challenges and Law Enforcement.

A little bit of context—Lisa Scaffidi was the Lord Mayor of Perth, Western Australia. She was charged with inappropriate use of her position—failure to declare gifts and travel worth tens of thousands of dollars. Therefore, this headline aptly has a mixture of topics: International Politics and Conflict (51%), followed by Funding/Expenses-related challenges (22%) and then by Law Enforcement (17%).

Now let's look at inferring topics for a batch of headlines.

Creating batch predictions through an inference pipeline

In this section, we will turn our attention from real-time predictions to batch predictions. To address the need to deploy trained models in offline mode, SageMaker offers Batch Transform. Batch Transform is a newly released high-performance and throughput feature where inferences can be obtained for the entire dataset. Both the input and output data is stored in an S3 bucket. The *Batch Transform* service manages the necessary compute resources to score the input data, given the trained model.

This following diagram shows how the *Batch Transform* service works:

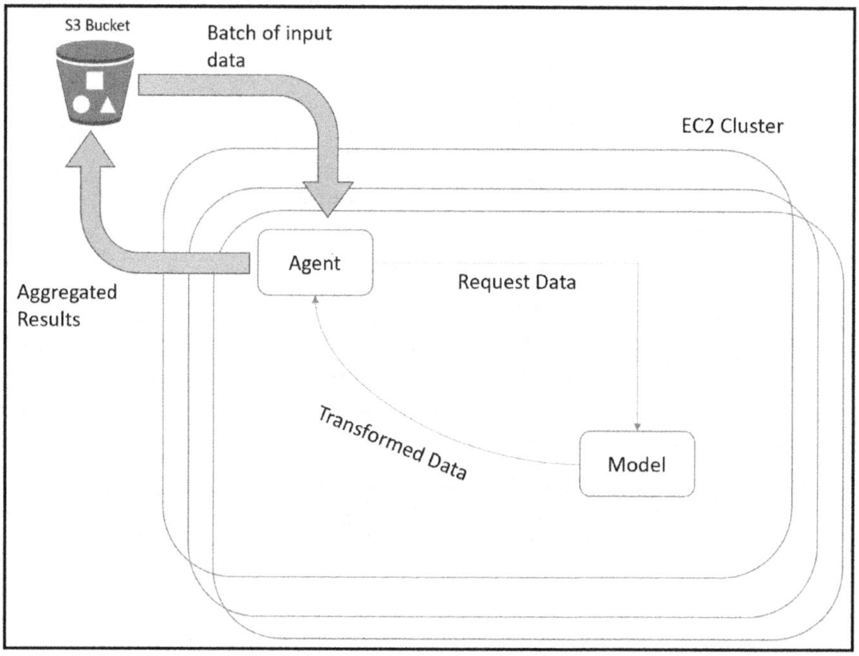

In the preceding diagram, we can see the following steps:

1. The Batch Transform service ingests large volumes of input data (from the S3 bucket) through an agent.
2. The role of the Batch Transform agent is to orchestrate communication between the trained model and the S3 bucket, where input and output data is stored.

3. Once the request data is available to the agent, it sends it to the trained model, which transforms news headlines and generates topics.
4. The inferences or topics that are produced are deposited back in the designated S3 bucket by the intermediate agent.

Let's go through the steps for running a Batch Transform job:

1. Define the path to the S3 bucket where the input and output data is stored, along with the name of the `PipelineModel` we created in the previous section. The name of the `PipelineModel` can be obtained either programmatically or through the AWS console (navigate to the SageMaker service on the left navigation pane; then, under **Inference**, click on **Models**).
2. Create a `Transformer` object from the `sagemaker.transformer` module, as follows:

```
transformer = sagemaker.transformer.Transformer(
 model_name = model_name,
 instance_count = 1,
 instance_type = 'ml.m4.xlarge',
 strategy = 'SingleRecord',
 assemble_with = 'Line',
 output_path = output_data_path,
 base_transform_job_name='serial-inference-batch',
 sagemaker_session=sess,
 accept = CONTENT_TYPE_CSV
)
```

   Here, we define the compute resources that are required to run the pipeline model, for example, the EC2 instance type and number. Then, we define and assemble a strategy, that is, how to batch records (single or multiple records) and how to assemble the output. The Current SageMaker session and output content type defined by `accept` are also provided.

3. Invoke the `transform()` method of the transformer object we created in the previous step, as follows:

```
transformer.transform(data = input_data_path,
                      job_name = job_name,
                      content_type = CONTENT_TYPE_CSV,
                      split_type = 'Line')
```

We define the path to the input data, the name of the Batch Transform job, the input content type, and how the input records are separated (news headlines are separated by line, in this case). Next, we wait for the batch inference to be run on all the input data. The following is an excerpt from the output that was produced:

Headline	Topic 1	Topic 2	Topic 3	Topic 4	Topic 5
gower warns of french resistance	0.6014835	0.1155266	0.0977373	0.0810384	0.1042142
greens seek inquiry into jockey offer allegations	0.1023946	0.1208197	0.3941616	0.0770099	0.3056142
gregan put on notice horan	0.3041118	0.2034628	0.1746403	0.1478757	0.1699095
gungahlin roadwork delays slow other upgrades	0.3041118	0.2034628	0.1746403	0.1478757	0.1699095
hackers use sony bmg software to hide in pcs	0.3041118	0.2034628	0.1746403	0.1478757	0.1699095
health service faces funding cut	0.2284847	0.0780824	0.3143376	0.2452072	0.1338882
henry takes all blacks into new era	0.2866432	0.2429818	0.2257657	0.1718663	0.0727429
heritage council rejects camberwell station listing	0.3061328	0.0676769	0.3875068	0.0698637	0.1688199
heroin addict gets 20 years for taxi drivers murder	0.1621254	0.2586859	0.3177063	0.0604307	0.2010518
hodge in form with century against windies	0.3041118	0.2034628	0.1746403	0.1478757	0.1699095
hodge justifies test call up	0.057705	0.3068286	0.3168347	0.1368421	0.1817897
hodge tunes up with half century	0.3041118	0.2034628	0.1746403	0.1478757	0.1699095
hope for aussie on death row not lost labor	0.3925557	0.0913394	0.2443132	0.1058502	0.1659415
hope for health service funding to continue	0.2246623	0.0857421	0.3201226	0.2495116	0.1199614
hospital emergency service delay creates angst	0.1115589	0.1981474	0.2989576	0.156964	0.2343721
hunter man in running for senior of the year award	0.1235819	0.145608	0.1249724	0.1957543	0.4100834
ideas aplenty for harbourside project area	0.3041118	0.2034628	0.1746403	0.1478757	0.1699095
indonesian police say gunfire killed azahari	0.0507304	0.306136	0.1548292	0.140412	0.3478923
iran frees detained aussie british couple	0.1752351	0.3295657	0.1308063	0.0907015	0.2736915

Remember that we have uncovered five topics: International Politics and Conflict, Sports and Crime, Natural Disasters and Funding, Protest and Law Enforcement, and Crime. For each news headline, the NTM algorithm predicts the probability that the headline contains topics 1 through 5. Thus, each headline will be represented by a mixture of five topics.

For example, in the *Indonesian police say gunfire killed azahari* headline, crime-related topics are predominant. The topics are very relevant since the headline has to do with the murder of Azahari, the mastermind behind the 2002 Bali bombing.

By completing this section, we have successfully looked at two different patterns for running inferences in SageMaker.

Summary

In this chapter, we have learned how to reuse data preprocessing logic for training and inference and how to run online as opposed to offline inferences. We started by understanding the architecture of the machine learning inference pipeline. Then, we used the ABC News Headlines dataset to illustrate big data processing through AWS Glue and SparkML. Then, we discovered topics from the news headlines by fitting the NTM algorithm to processed headlines. Finally, we walked through real-time as opposed to batch inferences by utilizing the same data preprocessing logic for inference. Through the inference pipeline, data scientists and machine learning engineers can increase speed with which ML solutions are marketed.

In the next chapter, we'll do a deep dive into **Neural Topic Models** (**NTMs**).

Further reading

The following reading material is intended to enhance your understanding of what was covered in this chapter:

- **Pipeline models in Spark**: `https://blog.insightdatascience.com/spark-pipelines-elegant-yet-powerful-7be93afcdd42`
- **Batch Transform**: `https://docs.aws.amazon.com/sagemaker/latest/dg/how-it-works-batch.html`
- **Topic modeling**: `https://medium.com/ml2vec/topic-modeling-is-an-unsupervised-learning-approach-to-clustering-documents-to-discover-topics-fdfbf30e27df`
- **Transformers in Spark**: `https://spark.apache.org/docs/1.6.0/ml-guide.html#transformers`

9 Discovering Topics in Text Collection

One of the most useful ways to understand text is through topics. The process of learning, recognizing, and extracting these topics is called topic modeling. Understanding broad topics in text has several applications. It can be used in the legal industry to surface themes from contracts. (Rather than manually reviewing mountains of contracts for certain provisions, through unsupervised learning, themes or topics can surface). Furthermore, it can be used in the retail industry to identify broad trends in social media conversations. These broad trends can then be used for product innovation—to introduce new merchandise into online and physical stores, to inform others of product assortment, and so on.

In this chapter, we are going to learn how to synthesize topics from long-form text (text that's longer than 140 characters). We will review the techniques of topic modeling and understand how the **Neural Topic Model** (**NTM**) works. We will then look at training and deploying NTM in SageMaker.

In this chapter, we will cover the following topics:

- Reviewing topic modeling techniques
- Understanding how the Neural Topic Model works
- Training NTM in SageMaker
- Deploying NTM and running inference

Technical requirements

To illustrate the concepts in this chapter, we will use the **Bag of Words** (`https://archive.ics.uci.edu/ml/datasets/bag+of+words`) dataset from the **UCI Machine Learning Repository** (`http://archive.ics.uci.edu/ml`). The dataset contains information on Enron emails, such as email IDs, word IDs, and their count, which is the number of times a particular word appeared in a given email.

In the GitHub repository (`https://github.com/PacktPublishing/Hands-On-Artificial-Intelligence-on-Amazon-Web-Services/tree/master/Ch9_NTM`) associated with this chapter, you should find the following files:

- `docword.enron.txt.gz` (`https://github.com/PacktPublishing/Hands-On-Artificial-Intelligence-on-Amazon-Web-Services/blob/master/Ch9_NTM/data/docword.enron.txt.gz`): Contains Email ID and Word ID
- `vocab.enron.txt` (`https://github.com/PacktPublishing/Hands-On-Artificial-Intelligence-on-Amazon-Web-Services/tree/master/Ch9_NTM/data/vocab.enron.txt`): Contains the actual words that are part of the dataset

Let's begin by looking at topic modeling techniques.

Reviewing topic modeling techniques

In this section, we look at several linear and non-linear learning techniques when it comes to topic modeling. Linear techniques include Latent Semantic Analysis (two approaches - Singular Vector Decomposition and Non-negative Matrix Factorization), probabilistic Latent Semantic Analysis, and Latent Dirichlet Allocation. On the other hand, non-linear techniques include LDA2Vec and the Neural Variational Document Model.

In the case of **Latent Semantic Analysis (LSA)**, topics are discovered by approximating documents into a smaller number of topic vectors. A collection of documents is represented by document-word matrix:

- In its simplest form, the document word matrix consists of raw counts, which is the frequency with which a given word occurs in a given document. Since this approach doesn't account for the significance of each word in the document, we replace raw counts with the **tf-idf** (**term frequency-inverse document frequency**) score.

- Through tf-idf, words that occur frequently within the document in question, but less frequently across all the other documents, will have a higher weight. Given that the matrix of documents and words is sparse and noisy, dimensionality must be reduced to obtain meaningful relationships between documents and words via topics.
- Reducing dimensionality can be done through truncated **SVD** (**Singular Value Decomposition**), where the document-word matrix is broken down into three different matrices, that is, document topic (*U*), word-topic (*V*), and singular values matrix (*S*), where singular values represent the strength of the topics, as shown in the following diagram:

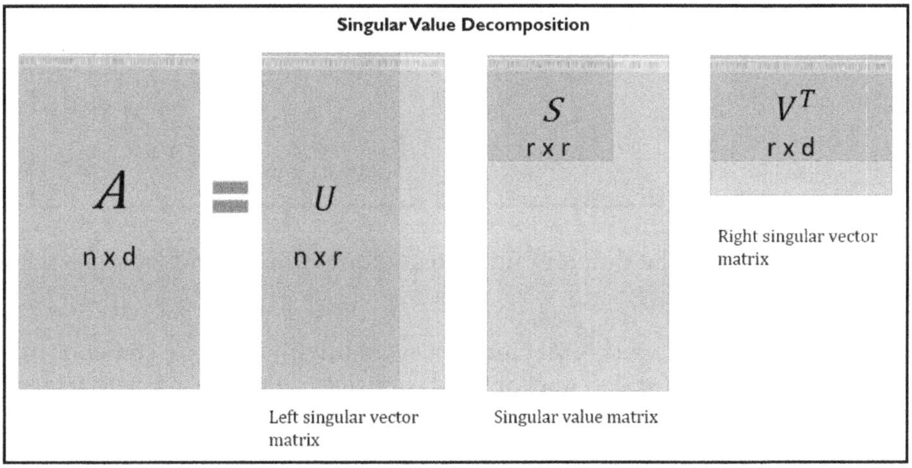

This decomposition is unique. To represent documents and words in a lower-dimensional space, only *T* largest singular values are chosen (a subset of the matrix, as shown in the preceding diagram), and only the first *T* columns of *U* and *V* are retained. *T* is a hyperparameter and can be adjusted to reflect the number of topics we want to find. In linear algebra, any *m x n* matrix *A* can be decomposed as follows:

- $A * V = U * S$, where *U* is called the left singular vector, *V* is called the right singular vector, and *S* is called the **singular value matrix**.

For information on how to compute singular values, as well as left and right singular vectors for a given matrix, refer to `https://machinelearningmastery.com/singular-value-decomposition-for-machine-learning/ intuitive explanation—reconstruct matrix from SVD.`

- Therefore, we get, $A = U * S * V^T$.

Besides SVD, you can also conduct matrix factorization through (**non-negative matrix factorization** (**NMF**). NMF belongs to linear algebra algorithms and is used to identify a latent structure in the data. Two non-negative matrices are used to approximate the document-term matrix, as shown in the following diagram (terms and words are used interchangeably):

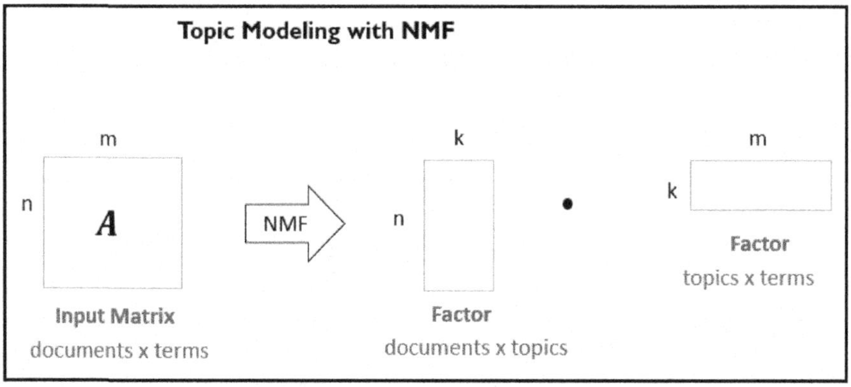

Let's compare and contrast the different linear techniques of LSA and look at a variant of LSA that offers more flexibility:

- The difference between NMF and SVD is that with SVD, we can end up with negative component (left and/or right) matrices, which is not natural for interpreting textual representation. NMF, on the other hand, generates non-negative representations for performing LSA.
- The drawback of LSA, in general, is that it has fewer interpretable topics and a less efficient representation. Additionally, it is a linear model and cannot be used to model non-linear dependencies. The number of latent topics is limited by the rank of the matrix.

Probabilistic LSA (**pLSA**): The whole idea of pLSA is to find a probabilistic model of latent topics that can generate documents and words we can observe. Therefore, the joint probability, that is, the probability of finding a combination of documents and words, $P(D, W)$, can be written as follows:

$$P(D, W) = \sum_{Z} P(Z) * P(D|Z) * P(W|Z)$$

Here, *D*=Document, *W*=Word, and *Z*=Topic.

Let's look at how pLSA works and an example of when it is not adequate:

- We can see how pLSA is similar to LSA in that *P(Z)* corresponds to a singular value matrix, *P(D | Z)* corresponds to a left singular vector, and *P(W | Z)* corresponds to a right singular vector from SVD.
- The number one disadvantage with this approach is that we cannot readily generalize it for new documents. LDA addresses this issue.

Latent Dirichlet Allocation (**LDA**): While LSA and pLSA are used for semantic analysis or information retrieval, LDA is used for topic mining. In simple terms, you uncover topics based on the word frequency across a collection of documents:

- For a collection of documents, you designate the number of topics you want to uncover. This number can be adjusted depending on the performance of LDA on unseen documents.
- Then, you tokenize the documents, remove any stop words, retain words that appear a certain number of times across the corpus, and conduct stemming.
- To begin with, for each word, you assign a random topic. You then compute the topic mixture by document, that is, the number of times each topic appears in the document. You also compute the word mixture by topic across the corpus, that is, the number of times each word appears in the topic.
- Iteration/Pass 1: For each word, you then reassign a topic after navigating through the entire corpus. The topic is reassigned based on other topic assignments by document. Let's say a document is represented by the following topic mixture: topic 1 - 40%, topic 2 - 20%, and topic 3 - 40% and the first word in the document is assigned to topic 2. The word in question appears across these topics (the entire corpus) in the following manner: topic 1 - 52%, topic 2 - 42%, and topic 3 - 6%. In the document, we reassign the word from topic 2 to topic 1 because the word represents topic 1 (40%*52%) more than topic 2 (20%*42%). This process is repeated for all the documents. By the end of pass 1, you will have covered each of the words in the corpus.
- We go through several passes or iterations across the entire corpus for each word until no further reassignment is necessary.
- In the end, we have a few designated topics, with each topic represented by keywords.

Up until now, we have looked at linear techniques for topic modeling. Now, it's time to turn our attention to non-linear learning. Neural network models for topic modeling are much more flexible, allowing new capabilities to be added (for example, creating contextual words for an input/target word).

Lda2vec is a superset of word2vec and LDA models. It is a variation of the skip-gram word2vec model. Lda2Vec can be used for a variety of applications, such as predicting contextual words given a word (known as a pivot or target word), including learning topic vectors for topic modeling.

Lda2vec is similar to **Neural Variational Document Models** (**NVDM**) in terms of producing topic embeddings or vectors. However, NVDM adopts a much cleaner and flexible approach to topic modeling by creating document vectors using neural networks, where a word-to-word relationship is completely disregarded.

NVDM (**Neural Variational Document Model**) is a flexible generative document modeling process where we learn about multiple representations of documents through topics (hence the word *variational*—meaning multiple—in NVDM):

- NVDM is based on the **Variational Autoencoder** (**VAE**) framework, which uses one neural network to encode (that is, an encoder) a collection of documents and a second one to decode (that is, a decoder) the compressed representation of documents. The goal of this process is to look at the best way to approximate information in a corpus. The autoencoder is optimized by minimizing two types of losses:
    - **Loss with Decoding** (the **reconstruction error**): Reconstruct the original document from topic embeddings.
    - **Loss with Encoding** (the **Kullback Leibler or KL Divergence**): Build a stochastic representation of the input document or topic embeddings. KL divergence measures information that's lost when encoding a bag-of-words representation of documents.

Now, let's do a delve into the Neural Topic Model, an implementation of NVDM from AWS. Although AWS offers a readily consumable API, AWS Comprehend, to discover topics, the NTM algorithm provides the fine-grained control and flexibility to uncover topics from long-form text.

Understanding how the Neural Topic Model works

The **Neural Topic Model (NTM)**, as we described previously, is a generative document model that produces multiple representations of a document. It generates two outputs:

- The topic mixture for a document
- A list of keywords that explain a topic, for all the topics across an entire corpus

NTM is based on the **Variational Autoencoder** architecture. The following illustration shows how NTM works:

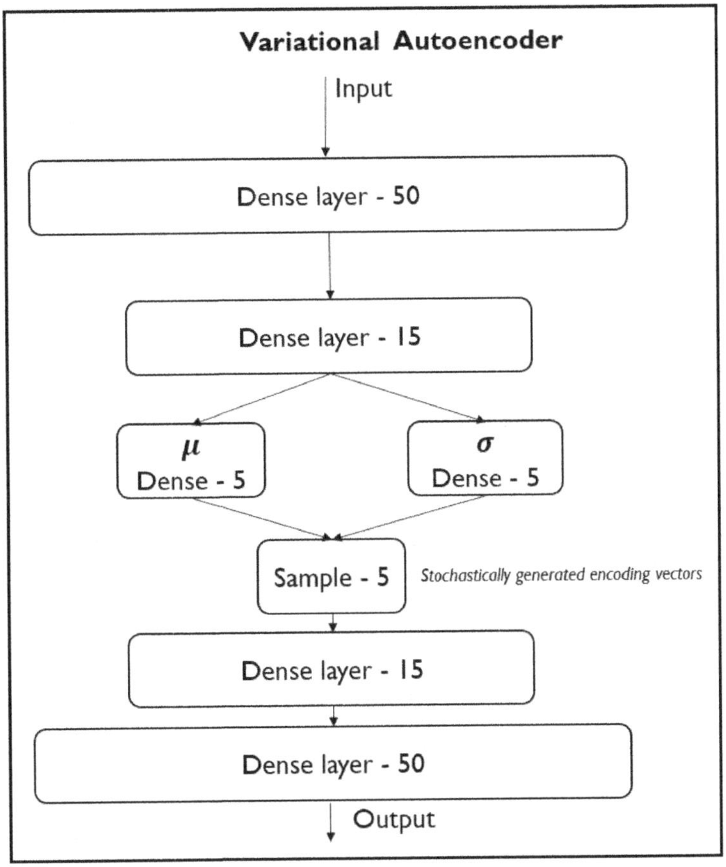

Let's explain this diagram, bit by bit:

- There are two components—an encoder and a decoder. In the encoder, we have a **Multiple Layer Perceptron** (**MLP**) network that takes a bag-of-words representation of documents and creates two vectors, a vector of means μ and a vector of standard deviation σ. Intuitively, the mean vector controls where encoding the input should be centered, while the standard deviation controls the area around the center. Because the sample that was generated from this area is going to vary each time it's generated, the decoder will learn to reconstruct different latent encodings of the input.

> MLP is a class of feedforward **artificial neuron networks** (**ANNs**). It consists of at least three layers of nodes: input, output, and a hidden layer. Except for the input node, each node is a neuron that uses a nonlinear activation function.

- The second component is a decoder, which reconstructs a document by independently generating words. The output layer of the network is a Softmax layer that defines the probability of each word by topic by reconstructing the topic words matrix. Each column in the matrix represents a topic, while each row represents a word. The matrix values, for a given column, represent the probability of the distribution of words for the topic.

> The Softmax decoder uses multinomial logistic regression, where we account for the conditional probability of different topics. The transformation is, effectively, a normalized exponential function that's used to highlight the largest values and suppress values that are significantly below the max value.

NTM is optimized by reducing reconstruction errors and KL divergence, as well as the learning weights and biases of the network. Therefore, NTM is a flexible neural network model for topic mining and producing interpretable topics. It is now time to look at training NTM in SageMaker.

Training NTM in SageMaker

In this section, we will train NTM on Enron emails to produce topics. These emails were exchanged between Enron, an American energy company that ceased its operations in 2007 due to financial losses, and other parties that did business with the company.

The dataset contains 39,861 emails and 28,101 unique words. We will work with a subset of these emails – 3,986 emails and 17,524 unique words. Additionally, we will create a text file, `vocab.txt`, so that the NTM model can report the word distribution of a topic.

Before we get started, make sure that both `docword.enron.txt.gz` and `vocab.enron.txt` have been uploaded to a folder called `data` on the local SageMaker compute instance. Follow these steps:

1. Create a bag-of-words representation of emails, as follows:

```
pvt_emails = pd.pivot_table(df_emails, values='count',
index='email_ID', columns=['word_ID'], fill_value=0)
```

   In the preceding code, we used the `pivot_table()` function in the pandas library to pivot emails so that email IDs are indexes and word IDs are columns. The values in the pivot table represent word counts. The pivot table contains 3,986 email IDs and 17,524 word IDs.

2. Now, let's multiply the word counts by the **Inverse Document Frequency (IDF)** factor. Our assumption is that words that occur frequently in an email and less frequently in other emails are important in discovering topics, while words that occur frequently in all the emails may not be important for discovering topics.

   IDF is calculated as follows:

```
dict_IDF = {name: np.log(float(no_emails) /
(1+len(bag_of_words[bag_of_words[name] > 0]))) for name in
bag_of_words.columns}
```

   IDF is given by $log(\frac{N}{1+df_i})$, where N is the number of emails in the dataset and df_i is the number of documents containing the word *i*.

   At the end of this step, a new DataFrame representing the pivoted emails with tf-idf values is created.

3. Now, we will create a compressed sparse row matrix from the bag of words representation of emails, as follows:

```
sparse_emails = csr_matrix(pvt_emails, dtype=np.float32)
```

In the preceding code, we used the `csr_matrix()` function from the `scipy.sparse` module to produce an efficient representation of the emails matrix. With the compressed sparse row matrix, you are able to run operations on only non-zero values, in addition to using less RAM for computation. The compressed sparse row matrix uses the row pointer to point to the row number and the column index to identify the column in the row, as well as the values for the given row pointer and column index.

4. Split the dataset into training, validation, and test sets as follows:

```
vol_train = int(0.8 * sparse_emails.shape[0])

# split train and test
train_data = sparse_emails[:vol_train, :]
test_data = sparse_emails[vol_train:, :]

vol_test = test_data.shape[0]
val_data = test_data[:vol_test//2, :]
test_data = test_data[vol_test//2:, :]
```

We use 80% of the emails for training, 10% for validation, and the remaining 10% for testing.

5. Convert the emails from a compressed sparse row matrix into RecordIO wrapped Protobuf format, as follows:

```
data_bytes = io.BytesIO()
smamzc.write_spmatrix_to_sparse_tensor(array=sprse_matrix[begin:fin
ish], file=data_bytes, labels=None)
data_bytes.seek(0)
```

Protobuf format, also known as **Protocol Buffers**, is a protocol from Google that's used to serialize or encode structured data. Although JSON, XML, and Protobuf can be used interchangeably, Protobuf is much more enhanced and supports more data types than other formats. RecordIO is a file format that stores serialized data on disk. Its purpose is to store data as a sequence of records for faster reading. Under the hood, RecordIO uses Protobuf to serialize structured data.

For distributed training, we take a training dataset and divide it into portions for distributed training. Please see the source code attached to this chapter for additional details. The `write_spmatrix_to_sparse_tensor()` function from `sagemaker.amazon.common` is used to convert each of these portions from the sparse row matrix format into the sparse tensor format. The function takes a sparse row matrix as input, along with a binary stream that RecordIO records will be written to. We then reset the stream position to the beginning of the stream by calling the `seek()` method—this is essential for reading data from the beginning of the file.

6. Upload the train and validation datasets to an S3 bucket, as follows:

```
 file_name = os.path.join(prefix, fname_template.format(i))
boto3.resource('s3').Bucket(bucket).Object(file_name).upload_fileob
j(data_bytes)
```

7. We provide the filename to the binary stream and specify the name of the S3 bucket, which is where the datasets will be stored for training. We call the `upload_fileobj()` method of the S3 object to upload the binary data to a designated location.
8. Now, we initialize SageMaker's `Estimator` object to prepare for training, as follows:

```
ntm_estmtr = sagemaker.estimator.Estimator(container,
 role,
 train_instance_count=2,
 train_instance_type='ml.c4.xlarge',
 output_path=output_path,
 sagemaker_session=sess)
```

9. The estimator object, `ntm_estmtr`, is created by passing the Docker registry path of the NTM image, the SageMaker execution role, the number and type of training instances, and the location of the output. Since the number of compute instances we are launching is two, we will be conducting distributed training. In distribution training, data is partitioned and training is conducted in parallel on several chunks of data.
10. Now, let's define the hyperparameters of the NTM algorithm, as follows:

```
num_topics = 3
vocab_size = 17524 # from shape from pivoted emails DataFrame
ntm_estmtr.set_hyperparameters(num_topics=num_topics,
 feature_dim=vocab_size,
 mini_batch_size=30,
 epochs=150,
```

```
num_patience_epochs=5,
tolerance=.001)
```

Let's take a look at the hyperparameters we specified in the preceding code:

- `feature_dim`: This represents the size of the feature vector. It is set to the vocabulary size, which is 17,524 words.
- `num_topics`: This represents the number of topics to extract. We chose three topics here, but this can be adjusted based on the model's performance on the test set.
- `mini_batch_size`: This represents the number of training examples to process before updating the weights. We specify 30 training examples here.
- `epochs`: This represents the number of backward and forward passes that are made.
- `num_patience_epochs`: This represents the maximum number of bad epochs (epochs where the loss does not improve) that are executed before stopping.
- `optimizer`: This represents the algorithm that's used to optimize network weights. We are using the Adadelta optimization algorithm. The Adaptive Delta gradient is an enhanced version of **Adagrad** (**Adaptive Gradient**), where the learning rate decreases based on a rolling window of gradient updates versus all past gradient updates.
- `tolerance`: This represents the threshold for change in the loss function – the training stops early if the change in the loss within the last designated number of patience epochs falls below this threshold.

11. Upload the text file containing the vocabulary or words of the dataset to the auxiliary path/channel. This is the channel that's used to provide additional information to SageMaker algorithms during training.
12. Fit the NTM algorithm to the training and validation sets, as follows:

```
ntm_estmtr.fit({'train': s3_train, 'validation': s3_val,
'auxiliary': s3_aux})
```

13. For training, we call the `fit()` method of the `ntm_estmtr` object by passing initialized `S3_input` objects from the `sagemaker.session` module. The `s3_train`, `s3_val`, and `s3_aux` objects provide the location of the train, validation, and auxiliary datasets, as well as their file format and distribution type.

Now, let's walk through the results from distributed training:

- Review the training output from the first ML compute instance, as follows:

```
# Finished training epoch 48 on 2126 examples from 71 batches, each of size 30.
```

Remember that there's a total of 3,188 training examples. Because we launched two compute instances for training, on the first instance, we trained on 2,126 examples.

- Review the results from the second training instance, as follows:

```
# Finished training epoch 23 on 1062 examples from 36 batches, each of size 30.
```

On the second compute instance, we trained on the remaining 1,062 examples.

- We will report the model's performance on the validation dataset next. For the metrics of the training dataset, please refer to the source code attached to this chapter.

Now, let's walk through the validation results of the trained model. The model is evaluated against 390 data points that are part of the validation dataset. Specifically, we will look at the following metrics:

- **Word Embedding Topic Coherence Metric** (**WETC**): This measures the semantic similarity of the top words in each topic. A good quality model will have top words that are located close to each other in a lower-dimensional space. To locate words in a lower-dimensional space, pre-trained word embeddings from GloVe (Global Vectors) are used.

- **Topic Uniqueness** (**TU**): This measures the uniqueness of the topics that are generated. The measure is inversely proportional to the number of times a word appears across all the topics. For example, if a word appears in only one topic, then the uniqueness of the topic is high (that is, 1). However, if a word appears across, say, five topics, then the uniqueness measure is .2 (1 divided by 5). To calculate the topic uniqueness across all the topics, we average the TU measures across all topics.
- Perplexity (logppx) is a statistical measure of how well a probability model predicts a sample (validation dataset). After training, the perplexity of the trained model is computed on the validation dataset (performance of the trained model on the validation dataset). The lower the perplexity, the better, since this maximizes the accuracy of the validation dataset.
- Total Loss (total) is a combination of the Kullback-Leibler Divergence loss and Reconstruction loss.

Remember that the Neural Topic Model optimizes across several epochs by minimizing loss in the following ways:

- **Kullback-Leibler Divergence loss** (**kld**): Builds a stochastic representation of emails (topic embeddings) that involve relative entropy, a measure of how one probability distribution is different from a second, that is, a proxy probability distribution.
- **Reconstruction loss** (**recons**): Reconstructs original emails from topic embeddings.

The following screenshot shows the validation results and lists all the loss types that were defined:

```
[09/02/2019 00:16:47 INFO 140663462225728] Finished scoring on 390 examples from 13 batches, each of size 30.
[09/02/2019 00:16:47 INFO 140663462225728] Metrics for Inference:
[09/02/2019 00:16:47 INFO 140663462225728] Loss (name: value) total: 8.47499898275
[09/02/2019 00:16:47 INFO 140663462225728] Loss (name: value) kld: 0.189580901464
[09/02/2019 00:16:47 INFO 140663462225728] Loss (name: value) recons: 8.28541795779
[09/02/2019 00:16:47 INFO 140663462225728] Loss (name: value) logppx: 8.47499898275
[09/02/2019 00:16:47 INFO 140663462225728] #quality_metric: host=algo-1, epoch=48, validation total_loss <loss>=8.4749989827
5
[09/02/2019 00:16:47 INFO 140663462225728] Loss of server-side model: 8.47499898275
[09/02/2019 00:16:47 INFO 140663462225728] Best model based on early stopping at epoch 42. Best loss: 8.46607227815
[09/02/2019 00:16:47 INFO 140663462225728] Topics from epoch:final (num topics:3) [wetc 0.26, tu 0.73]:
[09/02/2019 00:16:47 INFO 140663462225728] [0.26, 0.60] resource pending request create acceptance admin local type permanen
t nahoutrdhoustonpwrcommonelectric nahoutrdhoustonpwrcommonpower2region approval kobra click application date directory read
risk tail
[09/02/2019 00:16:47 INFO 140663462225728] [0.27, 1.00] andor instruction notification reserves buy responsible sources proh
ibited order securities downgraded based intelligence strong corp web solicitation privacy clicking coverage
[09/02/2019 00:16:47 INFO 140663462225728] [0.26, 0.60] request resource pending create approval type application date tail
 directory acceptance admin flip permanent counterparty head click swap kobra risk
```

- The **total** Loss is **8.47**, where 0.19 is defined as the **kld** Loss and **8.28** is defined as the **recons** loss.
- From the preceding screenshot, we can see that, across the three topics, **Word Embedding Topic Coherence** (**WETC**) is **.26**, **Topic Uniqueness** (**TU**) is **0.73**, and **Preplexity** (**logppx**) is **8.47** (same as the **total** Loss).
- The three topics and the words that define each of them are highlighted in the by rectangular boxes.

Now, it's time to deploy the trained NTM model as an endpoint.

Deploying the trained NTM model and running the inference

In this section, we will deploy the NTM model, run the inference, and interpret the results. Let's get started:

1. First, we deploy the trained NTM model as an endpoint, as follows:

```
ntm_predctr = ntm_estmtr.deploy(initial_instance_count=1,
instance_type='ml.m4.xlarge')
```

In the preceding code, we call the `deploy()` method of the SageMaker Estimator object, `ntm_estmtr`, to create an endpoint. We pass the number and type of instances required to deploy the model. The NTM Docker image is used to create the endpoint. SageMaker takes a few minutes to deploy the model. The following screenshot shows the endpoint that was provisioned:

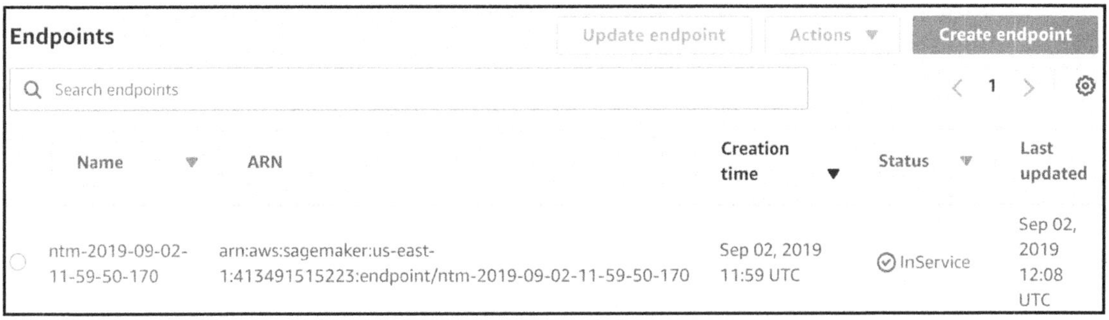

You can see the endpoint you've created by navigating to the SageMaker service, going to the left navigation pane, looking under the **Inference** section, and clicking on **Endpoints**.

2. Designate the request and response content types of test data, as follows:

```
ntm_predctr.content_type = 'text/csv'
ntm_predctr.serializer = csv_serializer
ntm_predctr.deserializer = json_deserializer
```

In the preceding code, the `deploy()` method of `ntm_estmtr` returns a `RealTimePredictor` object (from the `sagemaker.predictor` module). We assign the input content type of the test data and deserializer (the content type of the response) to `ntm_predctr`, the `RealTimePredictor` object we created.

3. Now, we prepare the test dataset for inference, as follows:

```
test_data = np.array(test_data.todense())
```

In the preceding code, we convert the test data format from a compressed sparse row matrix into a dense array using the numpy Python library.

4. Then, we invoke the `predict()` method of `ntm_predctr` to run the inference, as follows:

```
results = ntm_predctr.predict(test_data[1:6])
topic_wts_res = np.array([prediction['topic_weights'] for
prediction in results['predictions']])
```

In the preceding code, we passed the first five emails from the test dataset for inference. Then, we navigated through the prediction results to create a multi-dimensional array of topic weights, where rows represent emails and columns represent topics.

5. Now, we interpret the results, as follows:

```
df_tpcwts=pd.DataFrame(topic_wts_res.T)
```

In the preceding code, we transpose `topic_wts_res`, a multi-dimensional array, to create a dataframe, `df_tpcwts`, so that each row represents a topic. We then plot the topics, as follows:

```
df_tpcwts.plot(kind='bar', figsize=(16,4), fontsize=fnt_sz)
plt.ylabel('Topic % Across Emails', fontsize=fnt_sz)
plt.xlabel('Topic Number', fontsize=fnt_sz)
```

On the x-axis, we plot the topic numbers, and on the y-axis, we plot the percentage of emails represented by each topic, as follows:

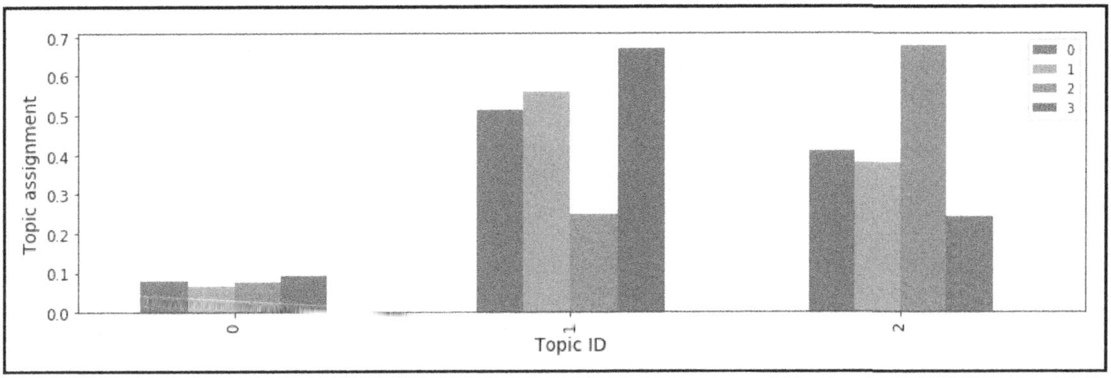

It is evident from the preceding graph that Topic 0 represents less than 10% of all five emails. However, Topics 1 and 2 are dominant to varying degrees in the emails—around 70% of the 4th email is represented by Topic 1, while around 60% of the 5th email is represented by Topic 2.

Now, let's look at the word cloud for each topic. It is important to understand the word mixture by each topic so that we know the words that predominantly describe a particular topic. Let's get started:

1. Download the trained model, as follows:

```
boto3.resource('s3').Bucket(bucket).download_file(model_path,
'downloaded_model.tar.gz')
```

   In the preceding code, we downloaded a trained NTM model from the path specified by the `model_path` variable (the location was specified when at the time of creating the Estimator, `ntm_estmtr`).

2. Now, we obtain the topic-word matrix from the trained model, as follows:

```
model_dict = mx.ndarray.load('params')
# Retrieve word distribution for each of the latent topics
W = model_dict['arg:projection_weight']
```

In the preceding code, we extracted the NTM model, `downloaded_model.tar.gz`, to load the learned parameters, `params`. Remember that the size of the output layer of the model is the same as that of the number of words (vocabulary) in the dataset. We then create a multi-dimensional mxnet array, *W*, to load word weights by topic. The shape of W is 17,524 x 3, where 17,524 rows represent words and 3 columns represent topics.

3. For each topic, run the softmax function on the word weights, as follows:

```
pvals = mx.nd.softmax(mx.nd.array(W[:, ind])).asnumpy()
```

In the preceding code, we run the softmax function on the word weights for each topic to bring their values to between 0 and 1. The sum of probabilities of words for each topic should add up to 1. Remember that the softmax layer, which is the output layer of the NTM network, highlights the largest values and mutes the values away from the max value.

4. Plot the word cloud by topic, as follows:

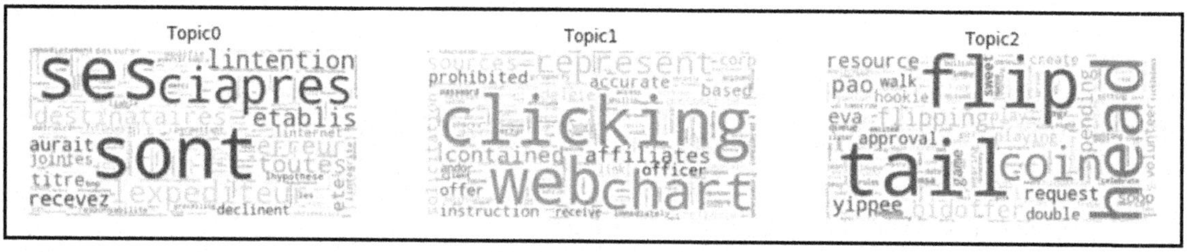

As we can see, **Topic0** is defined predominantly by the words *resource* and *pending*, while **Topic1** is primarily defined by the words *instruction, andor,* and *notification*.

Based on the top-ranking words in each of the topics, we can determine the topic that's being discussed in the emails:

- **Topic0 (access to Enron IT apps)**: Resource pending request create acceptance admin local type permanent nahoutrdhoustonpwrcommonelectric nahoutrdhoustonpwrcommonpower2region approval kobra click application date directory read risk tail.
- **Topic1 (energy trading)**: Andor instruction notification reserves buy responsible sources prohibited order securities downgraded based intelligence strong corp web solicitation privacy clicking coverage.

- **Topic2 (includes a combination of access to IT apps and energy trading)**: Request resource pending create approval type application date tail directory acceptance admin flip permanent counterparty head click swap kobra risk.

In this section, we have learned how to interpret results from topic modeling. Now, let's summarize all of the concepts we've learned about in this chapter.

Summary

In this chapter, we've reviewed topic modeling techniques, including linear and non-linear learning methods. We explained how the NTM from SageMaker works by discussing its architecture and inner workings. We also looked at distributed training of the NTM model, where the dataset is divided into chunks for parallel training. Finally, we deployed a trained NTM model as an endpoint and ran the inference, interpreting topics from Enron emails. It is essential to synthesize information and themes from large volumes of unstructured data for any data scientist. NTM from SageMaker provides a flexible approach to doing this.

In the next chapter, we will cover the classification of images using SageMaker.

Further reading

For references to topic modeling techniques—LDA, then please go to `http://blog.echen.me/2011/08/22/introduction-to-latent-dirichlet-allocation/`.

For an intuitive explanation of VAE, check out the following links:

- `https://jaan.io/what-is-variational-autoencoder-vae-tutorial/`
- `https://towardsdatascience.com/intuitively-understanding-variational-autoencoders-1bfe67eb5daf`

For references on neural variational inference for text processing, please go to `https://arxiv.org/pdf/1511.06038.pdf`.

10
Classifying Images Using Amazon SageMaker

Image classification has been one of the leading research fields in the last five years. This is not surprising because being able to successfully classify images solves many business problems across a variety of industries. For example, the entire autonomous vehicle industry is dependent on the accuracy of these image classification and object detection models.

In this chapter, we will look at how Amazon SageMaker drastically simplifies the image classification problem. Aside from gathering a rich set of images for training, we will look at how to specify hyperparameters (parameters internal to the algorithm), train Docker images, and use infrastructure specifications for training.

In this chapter, we will cover the following topics:

- Walking through convolutional neural and residual networks
- Classifying images through transfer learning
- Performing inferences on images through Batch Transform

Technical requirements

Please use the following link to refer to the source code for this chapter :`https://github.com/PacktPublishing/Hands-On-Artificial-Intelligence-on-Amazon-Web-Services`.

Walking through convolutional neural and residual networks

The SageMaker image classification algorithm is an implementation of **residual networks** (**ResNets**). Before we delve into the details of the algorithm, let's briefly understand **convolutional neural networks** (**CNN**) and ResNet and how they learn patterns from images.

Like any other neural network, CNNs are made up of input, hidden, and output layers. These networks have learnable parameters called weights and biases. These weights and biases can be adjusted through an appropriate optimizer, such as **Stochastic Gradient Descent** (**SGD**), with backpropagation. However, the difference between any feedforward artificial neural network and CNNs is that the hidden layers in CNNs are convolutional layers. Each convolutional layer consists of one or more filters. The job of these filters is to recognize patterns in input images.

These filters can have varying shapes, ranging from 1 x 1 to 3 x 3 and so on, and are initialized with random weights. As the input image passes through the convolutional layer, each filter will slide over every 3 x 3 block of pixels (in the case of a 3 x 3 filter) until the entire image is covered. This sliding is referred to as convolving. During the process of convolving, a dot product is applied to the filter weights and pixel values in the 3 x 3 block, thus learning about the image's features. The initial layers of the CNN learn basic geometric shapes, such as edges and circles, while later layers learn about more sophisticated objects, such as eyes, ears, feathers, beaks, cats, and dogs.

With deeper convolutional neural networks, as we stack more layers to learn complex features, vanishing gradient problems arise. In other words, during the training process, some neurons die (do not activate), causing a vanishing gradient. This happens when an activation function receives input with varying distributions (for example, if you're passing black and white images of cats as opposed to colored ones through the network, the input raw pixels belong to a different distribution, causing a vanishing gradient problem). If we restrict neuron output to the area to around zero, we can ensure that each layer will pass a substantive gradient back to the previous layers.

To solve the challenges that CNNs bring with them, deep residual learning combines what has been learned from previous layers with what has been learned from shallower models:

$$Residual\ Mapping = F(x) + x$$

Here, $F(x)$ is a convolutional layer or shallower model and x is the previous layer.

Residual networks, while addressing the challenges of CNNs, are an optimal approach to use when classifying images. In the next section, we will look at transfer learning as an approach to incrementally training an already-trained image classification model.

Classifying images through transfer learning in Amazon SageMaker

One of the key challenges in classifying images is the availability of large training datasets. For example, to create Amazon Go-type experiences, the e-commerce retailer may have trained their machine learning algorithms on large volumes of images. When we don't have images covering all types of real-world scenarios – scenarios ranging from time of the day (brightness), ambience around the target item, and item angle – we're unable to train image classification algorithms that are able to perform well in real-life environments. Furthermore, it takes a lot of effort to build a convolutional neural network architecture that is optimal for the dataset at hand. These considerations range from the number of convolutional layers to the batch size, to the optimizer, and to dropout rates. It takes multiple trial-and-error experiments to arrive at an optimal model iteration.

Because image classification requires a large number of images for training convolutional networks, an alternative approach can be used to classify images when the size of the training dataset is small. Transfer learning allows you to apply the knowledge of an already trained model to a different but related problem. We can reuse the weights of a pre-trained deep learning model that's been trained on millions of images and fine-tune the network with a new/custom dataset that's unique to our business case. Through transfer learning, low-level geometric features, such as edges, can already be recognized by a pre-trained ResNet-18 (18 layer network). However, for mid- to high-level feature learning, the top **fully connected** (FC) layer is reinitialized with random weights. Then, the whole network is fine-tuned with the new data—the random weights are adjusted by passing training data through the network and using an optimization technique, for example, stochastic gradient descent with backpropagation.

In this chapter, we'll employ SageMaker's image classification algorithm in transfer learning mode to classify some bakery and fast food items. We will use the pre-trained ResNet-18 that's provided by Amazon SageMaker. The image classification algorithm implements ResNets to categorize images. We can either train ResNets from scratch or use pre-trained networks. Since we have a small image dataset to train, we'll use an 18-layer pre-trained ResNet provided by Amazon SageMaker. We can also experiment with ResNet50, a 50-layer residual network, to determine which network yields a higher performance. Usually, deeper networks perform better than shallow networks since they are able to represent images better. However, given the type and complexity of the input images, the results can vary.

Our new dataset contains around 302 images with five categories (Hot Dog, Berry Donut, Glazed Twist, Muffin, and Peanut Butter Cookie). Each of these items contains 40 to 90 images, covering the item from varying angles, as well as brightness, contrast, and size.

The image classifier learns about the image's low-level features from a pre-trained ResNet and the high-level features by training the same ResNet-18 with a new dataset. The following is an illustration of how the features—low, mid, and high-level—of a Berry Donut are learned by SageMaker's image classification algorithm:

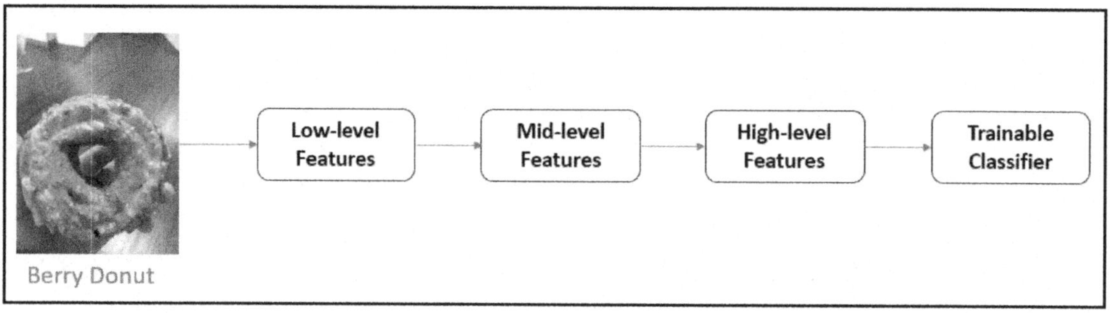

So far, we've reviewed what transfer learning is and when it is appropriate. We've also briefly described the image dataset that we're going to feed to the image classification algorithm in SageMaker. Let's get the images dataset prepared for training.

Creating input for image classification

Amazon SageMaker's image classification algorithm accepts images in file mode via two content types, namely:

- RecordIO (application/`x-recordio`)
- Image (image/`.png`, image/`.jpeg`, and application/`x-image`)

In this chapter, we will use the RecordIO format. **RecordIO** is a binary format for representing images efficiently and storing them in a compact format. Training and validation images are available in a zipped format as part of the source code associated with this chapter.

In order to create RecordIO files for our training and validation datasets, we will do the following:

- Extract `.zip` files, both training and validation (via the `extract_zipfile` function)
- Create list files for training and validation (via the `create_listfile` function)
- Create Record IO files for training and validation (via the `create_recordio` function)

For definitions of these functions, please refer to the accompanying source code folder:

```
# Extract training and validation zipped folders to merch_data/<train/val>

extract_zipfile(bucket, train_key, rel_train_path)
extract_zipfile(bucket, val_key, rel_val_path)

# Create List files (./merch_data)
create_listfile(rel_train_path, listfile_train_prefix) #data path, prefix
path
create_listfile(rel_val_path, listfile_val_prefix)

# # Create RecordIO file
# data path --> prefix path (location of list file)
# mxnet's im2rec.py uses ./merch_data folder to locate .lst files for train
and val
# mxnet's im2rec.py uses ./merch_data/<train/val> as data path
# list files are used to create recordio files

create_recordio(rel_train_path, listfile_train_prefix)
create_recordio(rel_val_path, listfile_val_prefix)
```

To create a RecordIO format for training and validation datasets, we need to create a list file that outlines the image index, followed by image classification (note that we have five categories of images) and the location of the image itself. We need to define these attributes for each of the images in the training and validation datasets. To create a list file for images, we will use the **im2rec** (**image to Recordio**) module of MXNet, an open-source deep-learning library for training and deploying deep learning models.

The following code snippet illustrates how to create a list file using the `im2rec` module. In order to create a list file, `im2rec` requires the location of the images:

```
# Create List file for all images present in a directory

def create_listfile(data_path, prefix_path):
    """
    input: location of data -- path and prefix
    """

    # Obtain the path of im2rec.py on the current ec2 instance
    im2rec_path = mx.test_utils.get_im2rec_path()

    with open(os.devnull, 'wb') as devnull:
        subprocess.check_call(['python', im2rec_path, '--list', '--
recursive', prefix_path, data_path], stdout=devnull)
```

The `create_listfile()` function produces the following output. The following is an excerpt of a sample list file:

```
292	4.000000	Peanut_Butter_Cookie/IMG_20180713_122625.jpg
160	2.000000	Hot_Dog_1/IMG_20180711_180650328.jpg
244	4.000000	Peanut_Butter_Cookie/IMG_20180711_194713371.jpg
132	2.000000	Hot_Dog_1/IMG_20180711_180400669_HDR.jpg
276	4.000000	Peanut_Butter_Cookie/IMG_20180711_194816799.jpg
222	3.000000	Muffin/UNADJUSTEDNONRAW_thumb_bbe.jpg
47	0.000000	Berry_Donut/IMG_20180711_181553159.jpg
78	0.000000	Berry_Donut/UNADJUSTEDNONRAW_thumb_a7a.jpg
137	2.000000	Hot_Dog_1/IMG_20180711_180423874.jpg
142	2.000000	Hot_Dog_1/IMG_20180711_180446447.jpg
220	3.000000	Muffin/UNADJUSTEDNONRAW_thumb_bbb.jpg
143	2.000000	Hot_Dog_1/IMG_20180711_180449768.jpg
21	0.000000	Berry_Donut/IMG_20180711_181514423.jpg
277	4.000000	Peanut_Butter_Cookie/IMG_20180711_194817776.jpg
69	0.000000	Berry_Donut/UNADJUSTEDNONRAW_thumb_a71.jpg
52	0.000000	Berry_Donut/IMG_20180711_181601582.jpg
155	2.000000	Hot_Dog_1/IMG_20180711_180624381.jpg
133	2.000000	Hot_Dog_1/IMG_20180711_180404276_HDR.jpg
299	4.000000	Peanut_Butter_Cookie/MVIMG_20180713_122610.jpg
33	0.000000	Berry_Donut/IMG_20180711_181530248.jpg
46	0.000000	Berry_Donut/IMG_20180711_181551527.jpg
97	1.000000	Glazed_Twist/IMG_20180711_193453363.jpg
32	0.000000	Berry_Donut/IMG_20180711_181529339.jpg
300	4.000000	Peanut_Butter_Cookie/MVIMG_20180713_122614.jpg
240	4.000000	Peanut_Butter_Cookie/IMG_20180711_194708448.jpg
```

From the list file we created, we produce a compressed representation of images via the RecordIO format—again, using the im2rec module from MXNet.

We will now upload the aforementioned training and validation datasets (`.rec` files) to an S3 bucket. Additionally, we will upload test images, separately from the training and validation images, to a test folder. Please refer to the accompanying source code folder. The following screenshot shows the S3 bucket, along with the relevant datasets:

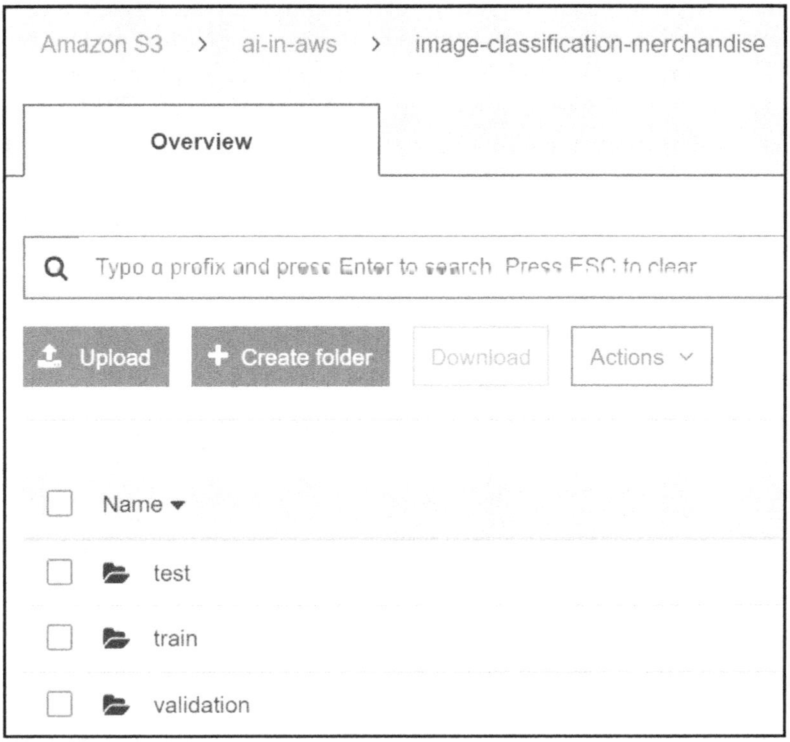

Now that we have all the datasets for training and inference, we are ready to define the parameters of the image classification algorithm.

Defining hyperparameters for image classification

There are two kinds of parameter that we need to specify before fitting the model to the training and validation datasets:

- Parameters for the training job
- Hyperparameters that are specific to the algorithm

The parameters for the training job deal with the input and output configuration, including the type of infrastructure to provision.

To train the job configuration, we need to do the following:

1. First, we need to define the image classification Docker image and training input mode (file versus pipe mode. Pipe mode is a recent addition to the SageMaker toolkit, where input data is fed on the fly to the algorithm's container with no need to download it before training).
2. Next, we define the location of the training output (`S3OutputPath`), along with the number and type of EC2 instances, to provision and the hyperparameters.
3. After that, we specify the *train* and *validation* channels, which are going to be the locations of the training and validation data. As for distribution training, the algorithm currently only supports `fullyreplicated` mode, where data is copied onto each machine.

The following hyperparameters are specific to the algorithm:

- `num_layers`: The number of layers for the network. In this example, we will use the default 18 layers.
- `image_shape`: Image dimensions (*width x height*).
- `num_training_samples`: This is the total number of training data points. In our case, this is set to `302`.
- `num_classes`: This is the number of categories. For our dataset, this is 5. We will classify five pieces of merchandise.
- `mini_batch_size`: The number of training samples that are used for each mini-batch. In a single machine multi-GPU setting, each GPU handles `mini_batch_size`/num of GPU samples. In the case of distributed training, where multiple machines are involved, the actual batch size is the number of `machines` * `mini_batch_size`.
- `epochs`: The number of iterations to go through to train the classification algorithm.
- `learning_rate`: This defines how big the steps should be when back-propagating to reduce loss. In the case of transfer learning, we will take smaller steps so that we can incrementally train the pre-trained network.

In the following code, we've defined the values of each of the hyperparameters:

```
# The algorithm supports multiple network depth (number of layers). They
are 18, 34, 50, 101, 152 and 200
# For this training, we will use 18 layers

num_layers = 18
image_shape = "3,224,224" # Number of channels for color image, Number of
rows, and columns (blue, green and red)
num_training_samples = 302 # number of training samples in the training set
num_classes = 5 # specify the number of output classes
mini_batch_size = 60 # batch size for training
epochs = 4  # number of epochs
learning_rate = 0.01 #learning rate
top_k=2
# Since we are using transfer learning, we set use_pretrained_model to 1 so
that weights can be initialized with pre-trained weights
use_pretrained_model = 1
```

It is now time for training: we will provide the *training parameters* that we defined as input to the `create_training_job` method of SageMaker. The SageMaker service is invoked using `boto3`, an Amazon Web Services SDK for Python. Once the training job has been created, we can check its status.

Use the following code to create a training job in SageMaker:

```
# create the Amazon SageMaker training job
sagemaker = boto3.client(service_name='sagemaker')
sagemaker.create_training_job(**training_params)

# confirm that the training job has started
status =
sagemaker.describe_training_job(TrainingJobName=job_name)['TrainingJobStatu
s']
print('Training job current status: {}'.format(status))

Output:
Training job current status: InProgress
Training job ended with status: Completed
```

We will now plot the results to evaluate the training and validation accuracy of ResNet-18. We want to ensure that we've not overfitted the network—a scenario where validation accuracy decreases as training accuracy increases. Let's have a look at the following graph:

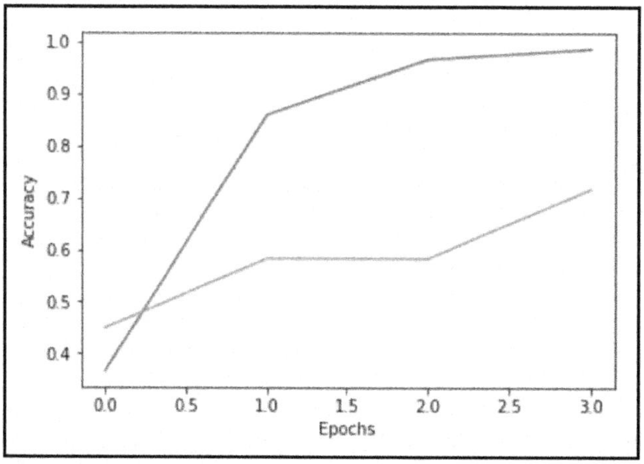

The results from training are available in the CloudWatch logs. The preceding representation is a visual of how the accuracy of the training and validation sets varies during the training period. The following code explains the blue and orange lines in the preceding graph:

```
Training: Blue Line -- trn_acc[0.366667, 0.86, 0.966667, 0.986667]

Validation: Orange Line -- val_acc[0.45, 0.583333, 0.583333, 0.716667]
```

As we can see, the trained ResNet model has picked up enough patterns from the fast-food and bakery images. We deployed the trained model for inference.

Performing inference through Batch Transform

In this section, we will classify (in batch mode) a few images that form part of the test dataset. Since we want to classify more than one image at a time, we will create a Batch Transform job. Please refer to `Chapter 8`, *Creating Machine Learning Inference Pipelines*, to learn about when and where Batch Transform jobs are used and how they work.

Before we create a Batch Transform job, we need to provision the trained model.

In the following code snippet, we are going to do the following:

1. We will create a trained model by calling the `create_model()` function of the SageMaker service (`boto3`, the AWS SDK for Python, is used to provision a low-level interface to the SageMaker service).
2. We will pass a Docker image of the image classification algorithm and the path to the trained model to this function:

```
info = sage.describe_training_job(TrainingJobName=job_name)
# Get S3 location of the model artifacts
model_data = info['ModelArtifacts']['S3ModelArtifacts']
print(model_data)
# Get the docker image of image classification algorithm
hosting_image = get_image_uri(boto3.Session().region_name, 'image-
classification')
primary_container = {
    'Image': hosting_image,
    'ModelDataUrl': model_data,
}
# Create model
create_model_response = sage.create_model(
    ModelName = model_name,
    ExecutionRoleArn = role,
    PrimaryContainer = primary_container)
print(create_model_response['ModelArn'])
```

3. Now that the trained model has been provisioned, we will need to create a Batch Transform job.

We will specify the transform input, output, and resources to configure a Batch Transform job. The following are the definitions:

- Transform input defines the location and format of images.
- Transform output defines the location of the results of the inference.
- Transform resources define the number and type of instances to provision.

In the following code snippet, we call the `create_transform_job` function of the SageMaker service by passing job specifications as part of the `request` JSON file:

```
sagemaker = boto3.client('sagemaker')
sagemaker.create_transform_job(**request)

print("Created Transform job with name: ", batch_job_name)

while(True):
    response =
sagemaker.describe_transform_job(TransformJobName=batch_job_name)
    status = response['TransformJobStatus']
    if status == 'Completed':
        print("Transform job ended with status: " + status)
        break
    if status == 'Failed':
        message = response['FailureReason']
        print('Transform failed with the following error:
{}'.format(message))
        raise Exception('Transform job failed')
    time.sleep(30)
```

4. In the previous code, we used the `describe_transform_job()` function of the SageMaker service to obtain the status of the Batch Transform job. The preceding code will return the following message:

```
Created Transform job with name: merch-classification-
model-2019-03-13-11-59-13
Transform job ended with status: Completed
```

It is now time to review the results. Let's navigate to the Batch Transform output and test dataset folders on the S3 bucket to review the results. For each of the images in the test dataset, we will print their highest classification probability, that is, what the trained model classifies an input image as:

1. The first image in the test dataset is a Hot Dog, as shown in the following screenshot. The trained model identifies the Hot Dog with 92% probability.

The following is the result of the prediction, that is, label: `Hot_Dog_1`, probability: `0.92`:

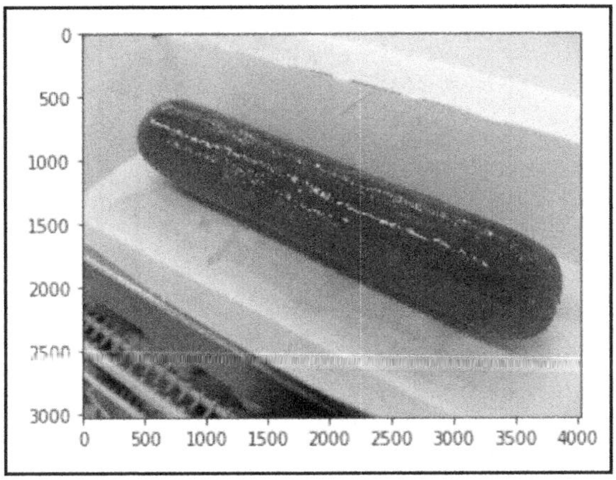

2. The second image is of a Berry Donut, as shown in the following screenshot. The trained model identifies the following screenshot as a Berry Donut with 99% probability:

3. The third image is a Muffin, as shown in the following screenshot. The trained model identifies the following screenshot as a Muffin with 66% probability:

4. In the case of the fourth image, however, the trained model does not correctly identify the image. While the real image is a Peanut Butter Cookie, the model misidentifies it as a Muffin. One interesting thing to note here is that the Cookie looks like a Muffin:

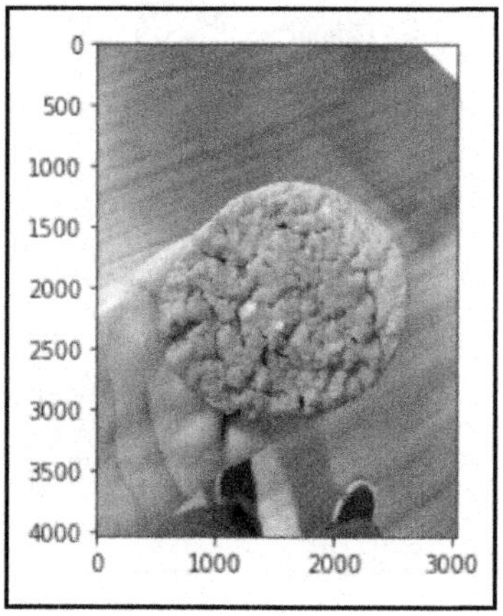

As we can see, out of the four images three were classified correctly. To improve the accuracy of the model, we can consider hyperparameter tuning and collecting large volumes of fast-food and bakery images. Transfer learning, therefore, is employed to incrementally train pre-trained image classification models with use-case-specific images.

Summary

In this chapter, we've gone through an overview of convolutional neural and residual networks. In addition, we've illustrated how SageMaker's image classification algorithm can be used to identify fast-food and bakery images. Specifically, we've reviewed training an image classification algorithm, including provisioning its infrastructure; creating a compressed image format (RecordIO) for training and validation datasets, and supplying formatted datasets for model fitting. For inference, we've employed the Batch Transform feature of SageMaker to classify multiple images in one go.

Most importantly, we've learned how to apply transfer learning to image classification. This technique becomes very powerful in instances where you do not have large amounts of training data.

In the next chapter, you'll learn how to forecast retail sales using the DeepAR algorithm from SageMaker—another use case where deep learning can be used to solve real business challenges.

Further reading

- **MXNet estimator in SageMaker**: `https://medium.com/devseed/use-label-maker-and-amazon-sagemaker-to-automatically-map-buildings-in-vietnam-a63090fb399f`
- **Vanishing Gradient**: `https://towardsdatascience.com/intuit-and-implement-batch-normalization-c05480333c5b`
- **AWS SageMaker Labs**: `https://github.com/awslabs/amazon-sagemaker-examples`

11

Sales Forecasting with Deep Learning and Auto Regression

Demand forecasting is key to many industries such as airlines, retail, telecommunications, and healthcare. Inaccurate and imprecise demand forecasting leads to missed sales and customers, significantly impacting an organization's bottom line. One of the key challenges facing retailers is effectively managing inventory based on multiple internal and external factors. Inventory management is a complex business problem to solve—the demand for a product changes by location, weather, promotions, holidays, day of the week, special events, and other external factors, such as store demographics, consumer confidence, and unemployment.

In this chapter, we will look at how traditional techniques of time series forecasting such as ARIMA and exponential smoothing are different from neural network-based techniques. We will also look at how DeepAR works, discussing its model architecture.

Following are the topics that will be covered in this chapter:

- Understanding traditional time series forecasting
- Understanding how the DeepAR model works
- Understanding model sales through DeepAR
- Predicting and evaluating sales

Technical requirements

For the following sections, we will employ the `retail` dataset containing sales of around 45 stores to illustrate how DeepAR predicts future sales given multiple factors such as holidays, promotions, and macro-economic indicators (unemployment).

In the `folder` associated with this chapter, you will find three CSV files:

- **Features dataset**: This contains the data of regional activity related to the store.
- **Sales dataset**: This contains historical sales data covering three years, from 2010 to 2012. It covers sales for 143 weeks.
- **Store dataset:** This contains anonymized information about the 45 stores, including the type and size of the store.

Please refer to the following link of GitHub for the source code of this chapter:

`https://github.com/PacktPublishing/Hands-On-Artificial-Intelligence-on-Amazon-Web-Services`

It is now time to understand traditional time series forecasting techniques.

Understanding traditional time series forecasting

Let's begin by looking at traditional time series forecasting techniques, specifically ARIMA and exponential smoothing to model demand in simple use cases. We will look at how ARIMA estimates sales using historical sales and forecast errors. Also, we'll review how exponential smoothing accounts for irregularities in historical sales and captures trends and seasonality to forecast sales.

Auto-Regressive Integrated Moving Average (ARIMA)

ARIMA is a time series analytical technique used to capture different temporal structures in univariate data. To model the time series data, differencing is applied across the series to make the data stationary. Differencing is the technique of subtracting the previous data point from the current one for every data point excluding the first one. The technique makes the mean and variance of the probability distribution of the time series constant over time, making future values of the series much more predictable. A specific number of lagged forecasts and forecast errors are used to model time series. This number is iteratively adjusted until the residuals are uncorrelated with the target (sales forecast) or all of the signals in the data have been picked up.

Let's unpack ARIMA to look at the underlying components—autoregressive, integrated, and moving average:

- **The number of autoregressive terms**: These establish a relationship between a specific number of historical data points and the current one that is, it uses historical demand to estimate the current demand.
- **The number of non-seasonal differences**: These make temporal or time series data stationary by differencing. We're assuming that future demand will look like historical demand if the difference in demand during the last few time steps is very small.
- **The number of moving-average terms (lagged forecast errors)**: These account for forecast error—actual versus forecasted demand—or a specific number of historical data points.

Let's look at the ARIMA equation, both in words and mathematical form:

Demand forecast = constant term + autoregressive terms + moving average terms

$$\hat{y} = \mu + \emptyset_1 y_(t-1) + \cdots + \emptyset_p y_(t-p) - \theta_1 e_(t-1) \ldots - \theta_q e_(t-q)$$

Here is a visual representation of how ARIMA works:

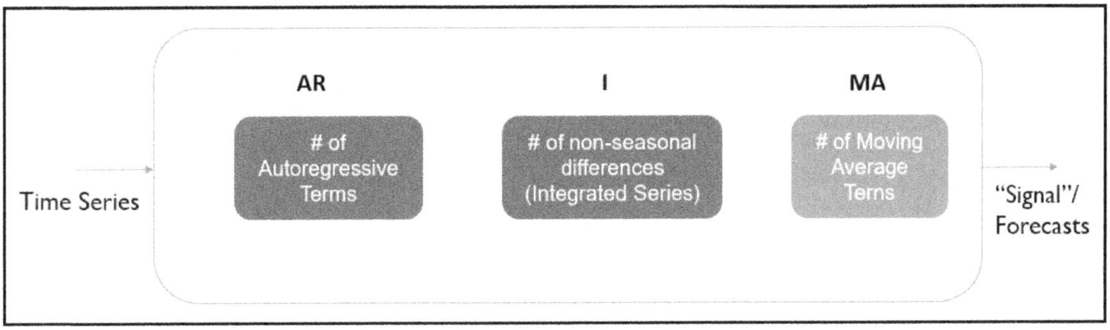

In the ARIMA model, the AR terms are positive, while the MA terms are negative; in other words, the autoregressive terms have a positive impact on demand while the moving-average of lagged errors has a negative impact.

Exponential smoothing

The other alternative to ARIMA is the exponential smoothing technique, which is also a time series forecasting method for univariate data, where random noise is neglected, revealing the underlying time structure. Although it is like ARIMA in that demand forecast is a weighted sum of past observations, the method of applying weights to lagged observations is different—instead of providing equal weights to past observations, the model employs exponentially decreasing weights for lags. In other words, the most recent observations are more relevant than historical ones. Exponential smoothing is used to make short-term forecasts, where we assume that future patterns and trends will look like current patterns and trends.

Following are the three types of exponential smoothing methods:

- **Single exponential smoothing**: As the name indicates, the technique does not account for seasonality or trend. It requires a single parameter, alpha (α), to control the level of smoothing. Low alpha means there are no irregularities in the data, implying that the latest observations are given lower weight.
- **Double exponential smoothing**: This technique, on the other hand, supports trends in univariate series. In addition to controlling how important recent observations are relative to historical ones, an additional factor is used to control the influence of trend on demand forecasts. The trend can be either multiplicative or additive and is controlled using a smoothing factor, β.
- **Triple exponential smoothing**: This one adds support for seasonality. Another new parameter, gamma (γ), is used to control the influence of the seasonal component on demand forecasts.

The following diagram illustrates the difference between the different types of exponential smoothing:

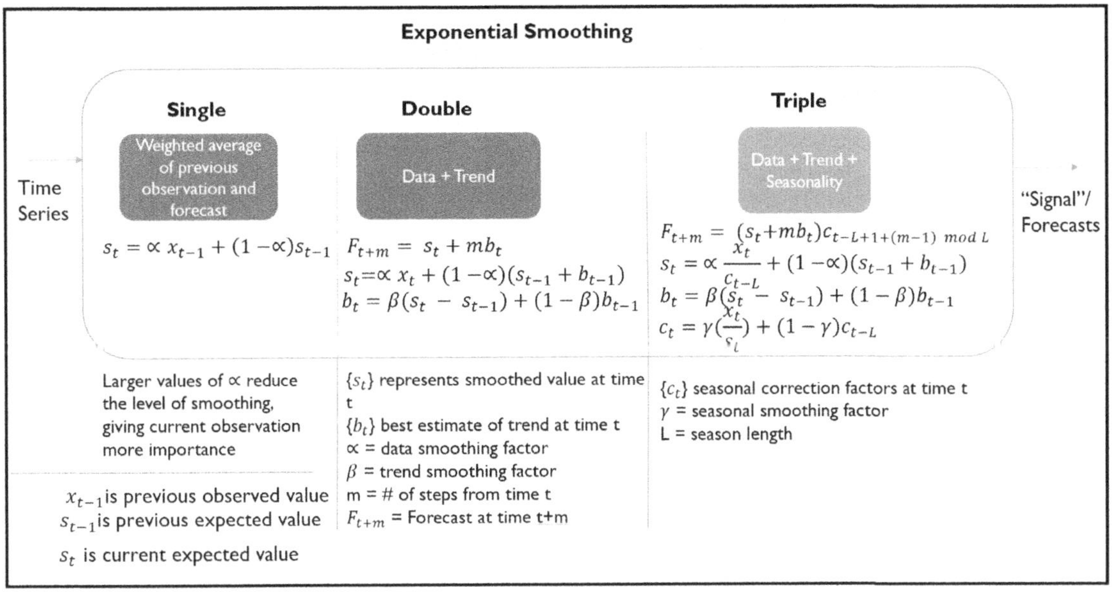

In the preceding diagram, we can see the following:

- Single exponential smoothing that forecasts demand at time, *t*, is based on estimated demand and forecast error (actual—estimated demand) at time, *t-1*.
- In the case of double exponential smoothing, demand is forecasted by capturing both trend and historical data. We use two smoothing factors here, data and trend (here's a visual on how double exponential smoothing captures trends):

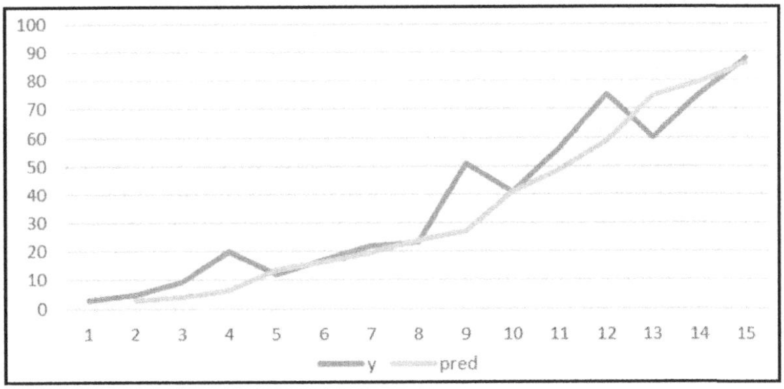

- For triple exponential smoothing, we also account for seasonality through a third smoothing factor called a seasonal smoothing factor. See the following diagram, which captures seasonal peaks and troughs, along with trend:

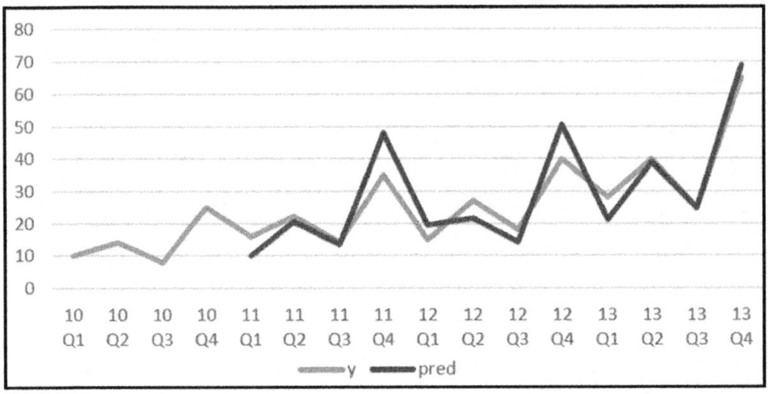

The problem with this approach is that it views past sales as indicative of future sales. Besides, they are all forecasting techniques for univariate time series. As detailed earlier, there could be other factors that impact current and future sales, such as weather, promotions, day of the week, holidays, and special events.

Let's look at how the DeepAR model from SageMaker can be leveraged to model multi-variate time series, defining a non-linear relationship between an output variable (demand) and input variables (includes historical sales, promotions, weather, and time of the day.)

How the DeepAR model works

The DeepAR algorithm offered by Sagemaker is a generalized deep learning model that learns about demand across several related time series. Unlike traditional forecasting methods, in which an individual time series is modeled, DeepAR models thousands or millions of related time series.

Examples include forecasting load for servers in a data center, or forecasting demand for all products that a retailer offers, and energy consumption of individual households. The unique thing about this approach is that a substantial amount of data on past behavior of similar or related time series can be leveraged for forecasting an individual time series. This approach addresses over-fitting issues and time—and labor-intensive manual feature engineering and model selection steps required by traditional techniques.

DeepAR is a forecasting method based on autoregressive neural networks and it learns about a global model from historical data of all-time series in the data set. DeepAR employs **Long Short-Term Memory (LSTM)**, a type of **Recurrent Neural Network (RNN)**, to model time series. The main idea of RNNs is to capture sequential information. Unlike normal neural networks, the inputs (and outputs) are dependent on each other. RNNs hence have a memory that captures information about what has been estimated so far. The following is a diagram of an unfolded RNN—to remember what has been learned so far, at each step, the hidden state is computed, not only based on the current input, but also the previous hidden state:

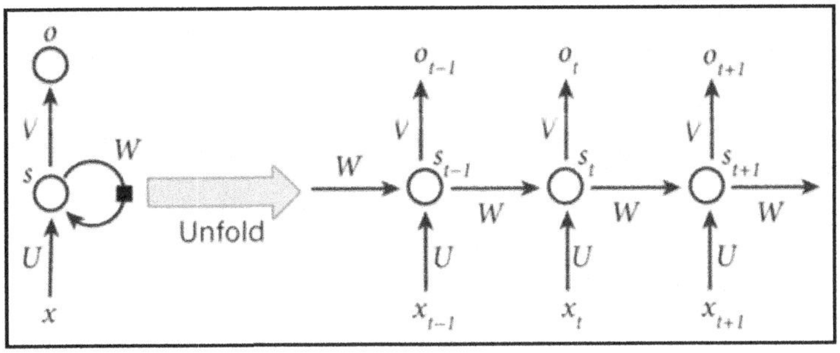

A recurrent neural network and illustration of sequential learning as the time steps are unfolded. Source: Nature; Image Credits `WildML.`

Let's explain in more detail:

- x is input at a time, *t*.
- S_t is the hidden state at time, *t*. This state is computed based on previous hidden state and current input, and in $S_t = f(Ux_t + Ws_{t-1})$, function, *f*, is an activation function.
- O_t is output at time, *t*, and $O_t = f(Vs_t)$. The activation function, *f*, can vary depending on the use case. For example, the softmax activation function is used when we need to predict which of the classes the input belongs to—in other words, whether the image being detected is a cat or a dog or a giraffe.
- The network weights, *U*, *V*, and *W*, remain the same across all of the time steps.

RNNs have interesting applications in different fields, such as the following:

- **Natural language processing**: From generating image captions to generating text to machine translations, RNNs can act as generative models.
- **Autonomous cars**: They are used to conduct dynamic facial analysis.
- **Time series**: RNNs are used in econometrics (finance and trend monitoring) and for demand forecasting.

However, general RNNs fail to learn long-term dependencies due to the gap between recent and older data. LSTMs, on the other hand, can solve this challenge: the inner cells of LSTMs can carry information unchanged through special structures called **gates**—input, forget, and output. Through these cells, LSTMs can control the information to be retained or erased.

Let's now look at the model architecture of DeepAR, an LSTM network.

Model architecture

The DeepAR algorithm employs the LSTM network and probability models to identify non-linear structures in time series data and provide probabilistic estimates of forecasts.

The model is autoregressive in that it consumes observations from the last time step as input. It is also recurrent since it uses the previous output of the network as input at the next time step. During the training phase, the hidden or the encoded state of the network, at each time step, is computed based on current covariates, previous observation, and previous network output. The hidden state is then used to compute parameters for a probability model that characterizes the behavior of time series (product demand, for example).

In other words, we assume the demand to be a random variable following a specific probability distribution. Once we have the probability model that can be defined through a set of parameters (say, mean and variance), it can be used to estimate forecasts. DeepAR uses the Adam optimizer, a stochastic gradient descent algorithm, to optimize the maximum log likelihood of training data, given Gaussian model parameters. Using this approach, we can derive (optimize) both probability model parameters and LSTM parameters to accurately estimate forecasts.

The following diagram demonstrates how the DeepAR algorithm works:

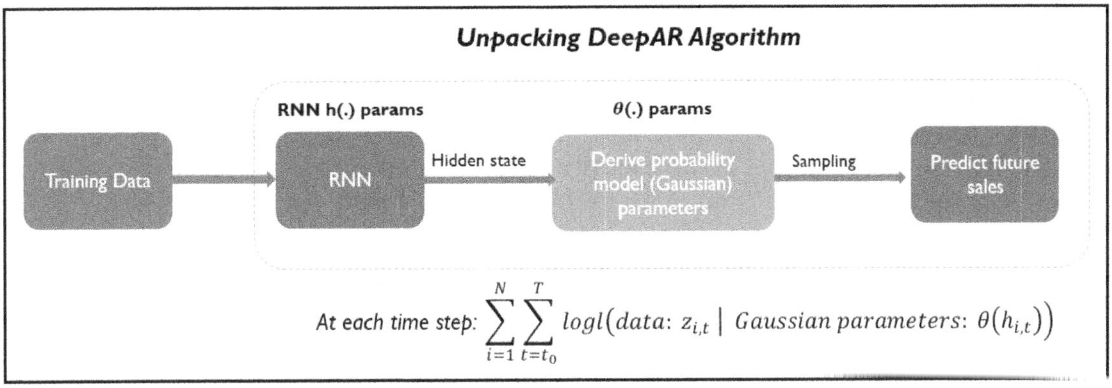

As shown in the preceding diagram, **Maximum Likelihood Estimation** (**MLE**) is used to estimate two sets of parameters, given all of the time series in the input dataset:

- **Parameters of RNN**: These parameters or the hidden state of the RNN network are used to compute Gaussian parameters.
- **Parameters of the Gaussian model**: The Gaussian parameters are used to provide probabilistic estimates of forecasts.

MLE is computed by leveraging data across all time series, i, where i goes from 1 to N—that is, there could be N different products the demand of which you're trying to estimate. T represents the length of the time series.

For more information on MLE, refer to this `article`.

Arriving at optimal network weights

The time series or observations are fed to DeepAR as part of the training. At each time step, current covariates, previous observations, and previous network output are used. The model uses **Back Propagation Through Time** (**BPTT**) to compute gradient descent after each iteration. In particular, the Adam optimizer is used to conduct BPTT. Through the stochastic gradient descent algorithm, Adam, we arrive at optimal network weights via back propagation.

At each time step, t, the inputs to the network are covariates, $x_{i,t}$; the target at the previous time step, $z_{i,t-1}$; as well as the previous network output, $h_{i,t-1}$. The network output, $h(h_{t-1}, z_{i,t-1}, x_{i,t}, \Theta)$, is then used to compute Gaussian parameters that maximize the probability of observing the input dataset.

The following visual illustrates sequence-to-sequence learning, where the encoder encapsulates demand patterns in the historical time series and sends the same ($h_{i,t0-1}$) as input to the decoder. The function of the decoder is to predict demand, taking into consideration the input from encoder:

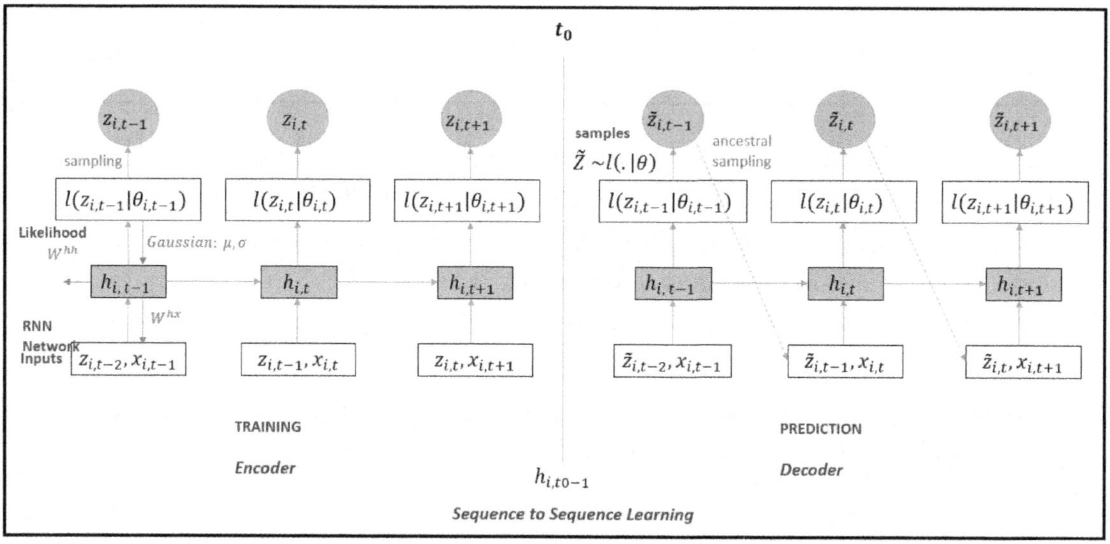

Source: Probabilistic Forecasting with Autoregressive Recurrent Networks (`link`)

For prediction, the history of the time series, $z_{i,t}$, is fed in for $t < t_0$, and, then, in the prediction range for $t >= t_0$, a sample $\hat{Z}_{i,t}$ is drawn and fed back for the next point until the end of the prediction range, $t = t_0 + T$.

DeepAR produces accurate forecast distributions learned from historical behavior of all of the time series jointly. Also, probabilistic forecasts provide optimal decisions under uncertainty versus point estimates.

Understanding model sales through DeepAR

As noted in the introduction to this chapter, managing inventory for retailers is a complex activity to handle. Holidays, special events, and markdowns can have a significant impact on how a store performs and, in turn, how a department within a store performs.

The Kaggle `dataset` contains historical sales for 45 stores, with each store belonging to a specific type (location and performance) and size. The retailer runs several promotional markdowns throughout the year. These markdowns precede holidays, such as SuperBowl, Labor Day, Thanksgiving, and Christmas.

Brief description of thc dataset

Let's briefly consider the dataset that we are about to model:

- **Features data:** This is data of regional activity related to the store:
    - **Store**: Numeric store ID for each store.
    - **Date**: Important dates for store.
    - **Fuel price**: Current fuel prices.
    - **Markdowns**: The discount you take on merchandise in your retail store from the original marked sale price.
    - **CPI (Consumer Price Index)**: A measure that examines the weighted average of prices of a basket of consumer goods and services, such as transportation, food, and medical care.
    - **Unemployment**: Current unemployment rate.
    - **IsHoliday**: Whether it's a holiday or not, on a particular date.
- **Sales data**: This is historical sales data covering three years, from 2010 to 2012. It covers sales for 143 weeks:
    - **Store**: Numeric store ID for each store.
    - **Dept**: Numeric department ID for each department of the store.
    - **Date**: Important dates for the store.
    - **Weekly sales**: Weekly sales to measure the sales performance of each store.
    - **IsHoliday**: Is it a holiday or not on a particular date.

- **Store data:** This is anonymized information about the 45 stores, including the type and size of the store:
    - **Store**: Numeric store ID for each store.
    - **Type**: The type of store.
    - **Size**: The size of the store.
- **Model Input and Output:** Now let's look at the input and output formats including the hyperparameters of the SageMaker DeepAR algorithm.

The algorithm has two input channels and it takes training and test JSONs as input through two channels. The training JSON contains only 134 weeks of sales, while the test JSON contains sales from all 143 weeks.

The following is the structure of the training JSON:

```
Training JSON
{
Start: The starting date of weekly sales
Target: Weekly sales
Cat: Category or Department used to group sales
Dynamic_feat: Dynamic features used to explain variation in sales.
Beyond holidays, these features can include price, promotion and
other covariates.
}
{"start":"2010-01-01 00:00:00","target":[19145.49, 17743.27,
14700.85, 20092.86, 17884.43, 19269.09, 22988.12, 17679.72,
16876.61, 14539.77, 16026.23, 14249.85, 15474.07, 22464.57,
19075.56, 20999.38, 18139.89, 13496.23, 15361.65, 16164.48,
15039.44, 14077.75, 16733.58, 16552.23, 17393.2, 16608.36,
21183.71, 16089.01, 18076.54, 19378.51, 15001.62, 14691.15,
19127.39, 17968.37, 20380.96, 29874.28, 19240.27, 17462.27,
17327.15, 16313.51, 20978.94, 28561.95, 19232.34, 20396.46,
21052.61, 30278.47, 47913.44, 17054.1, 15355.95, 15704.19,
15193.36, 14040.86, 13720.49, 17758.99, 24013.25, 24157.54,
22574.19, 12911.72, 20266.06, 18102.13, 21749.04, 22252.73,
21672.82, 15231.31, 16781.35, 14919.64, 15948.11, 17263.32,
16859.26, 13326.75, 17929.47, 15888.17, 13827.35, 16180.46,
22720.76, 15347.18, 15089.43, 14016.56, 17147.61, 14301.9,
16951.62, 16623.8, 19349.35, 24535.59, 18402.46, 19320.64,
20048.28, 14622.65, 19402.27, 19657.79, 18587.11, 20878.24,
19686.7, 23664.29, 20825.85, 27059.08, 15693.12, 29177.6, 45362.67,
20011.27, 13499.62, 15187.32, 16988.52, 14707.59, 20127.86,
23249.25, 20804.15, 19921.62, 16096.04, 18055.34, 17727.24,
16478.45, 16117.33, 15082.89, 15050.07, 17302.59, 20399.83,
17484.31, 14056.35, 16979.18, 17279.4, 14494.48, 14661.37,
13979.33, 13476.7, 18898.57, 13740.2, 15684.97, 15266.29, 16321.69,
15728.07, 17429.51, 17514.05, 20629.24],
```

```
"cat":[15], "dynamic_feat":[[0, 0, 0, 0, 0, 0, 0, 0, 0, 0, 0, 0, 0,
0, 0, 0, 0, 0, 0, 0, 0, 0, 0, 0, 0, 0, 0, 0, 0, 0, 0, 0, 0, 0, 1,
0, 0, 0, 0, 0, 0, 1, 1, 0, 0, 0, 0, 1, 0, 0, 0, 0, 0, 0, 0, 0, 0,
0, 0, 0, 0, 0, 0, 0, 0, 0, 0, 0, 0, 0, 0, 0, 0, 0, 0, 0, 0, 0, 0,
0, 0, 0, 1, 0, 0, 0, 0, 0, 0, 0, 0, 1, 0, 0, 0, 1, 0, 0, 0, 1, 0,
0, 0, 0, 0, 0, 0, 0, 0, 0, 0, 0, 0, 0, 0, 0, 0, 0, 0, 0, 0, 0, 0,
0, 0, 1, 0, 0, 0, 0, 0, 0, 0, 0, 0, 0, 0, 1, 0, 0, 0, 0, 0]]}
```

In the preceding structure, we can see the following:

- `start`: Is the start date of weekly sales.
- `target`: Is for sorted weekly sales.
- `cat`: Is the category to group time series.
- `Dynamic_feat`: Includes the dynamic features to account for factors impacting sales such as holidays.

The test JSON also has the same format as that of the training JSON. Let's have a look at the following code:

```
Test JSON
{"start":"2010-01-01 00:00:00","target":[19145.49, 17743.27,
14700.85, 20092.86, 17884.43, 19269.09, 22988.12, 17679.72,
16876.61, 14539.77, 16026.23, 14249.85, 15474.07, 22464.57,
19075.56, 20999.38, 18139.89, 13496.23, 15361.65, 16164.48,
15039.44, 14077.75, 16733.58, 16552.23, 17393.2, 16608.36,
21183.71, 16089.01, 18076.54, 19378.51, 15001.62, 14691.15,
19127.39, 17968.37, 20380.96, 29874.28, 19240.27, 17462.27,
17327.15, 16313.51, 20978.94, 28561.95, 19232.34, 20396.46,
21052.61, 30278.47, 47913.44, 17054.1, 15355.95, 15704.19,
15193.36, 14040.86, 13720.49, 17758.99, 24013.25, 24157.54,
22574.19, 12911.72, 20266.06, 18102.13, 21749.04, 22252.73,
21672.82, 15231.31, 16781.35, 14919.64, 15948.11, 17263.32,
16859.26, 13326.75, 17929.47, 15888.17, 13827.35, 16180.46,
22720.76, 15347.18, 15089.43, 14016.56, 17147.61, 14301.9,
16951.62, 16623.8, 19349.35, 24535.59, 18402.46, 19320.64,
20048.28, 14622.65, 19402.27, 19657.79, 18587.11, 20878.24,
19686.7, 23664.29, 20825.85, 27059.08, 15693.12, 29177.6, 45362.67,
20011.27, 13499.62, 15187.32, 16988.52, 14707.59, 20127.86,
23249.25, 20804.15, 19921.62, 16096.04, 18055.34, 17727.24,
16478.45, 16117.33, 15082.89, 15050.07, 17302.59, 20399.83,
17484.31, 14056.35, 16979.18, 17279.4, 14494.48, 14661.37,
13979.33, 13476.7, 18898.57, 13740.2, 15684.97, 15266.29, 16321.69,
15728.07, 17429.51, 17514.05, 20629.24, 17730.73, 18966.48,
20781.46, 22979.73, 16402.34, 20037.44, 18535.65, 16809.01,
19275.43], "cat":[15], "dynamic_feat":[[0, 0, 0, 0, 0, 0, 0, 0, 0,
0, 0, 0, 0, 0, 0, 0, 0, 0, 0, 0, 0, 0, 0, 0, 0, 0, 0, 0, 0, 0, 0,
```

```
0, 0, 0, 1, 0, 0, 0, 0, 0, 0, 1, 1, 0, 0, 0, 0, 1, 0, 0, 0, 0, 0,
0, 0, 0, 0, 0, 0, 0, 0, 0, 0, 0, 0, 0, 0, 0, 0, 0, 0, 0, 0, 0, 0,
0, 0, 0, 0, 0, 0, 0, 1, 0, 0, 0, 0, 0, 0, 0, 0, 1, 0, 0, 0, 1, 0,
0, 0, 1, 0, 0, 0, 0, 0, 0, 0, 0, 0, 0, 0, 0, 0, 0, 0, 0, 0, 0, 0,
0, 0, 0, 0, 0, 0, 1, 0, 0, 0, 0, 0, 0, 0, 0, 0, 0, 0, 1, 0, 0, 0,
0, 0]]
```

DeepAR supports a range of hyperparameters. Following, is a list of some of the key hyperparameters. For a detailed list, check out Amazon documentation `here`:

- **Time frequency**: Indicates whether the time series is hourly, weekly, monthly, or yearly.
- **Context length**: How many time steps in the past the algorithm should look at for training.
- **Prediction length**: The number of data points to predict.
- **Number of cells**: The number of neurons to use in each of the hidden layers.
- **Number of layers**: The number of hidden layers.
- **Likelihood function**: We will choose the Gaussian model since weekly sales are real values.
- **epochs**: The maximum number of passes over the training data.
- **Mini batch size**: The size of the mini-batches used during training.
- **Learning rate**: The pace at which the loss is optimized.
- **Dropout rate**: For each epoch, the percentage of hidden neurons that are not updated.
- **Early stopping patience**: The training stops after a designated number of unsuccessful epochs, those in which the loss doesn't improve.
- **Inference**: For a given department, we sent 134 weeks of historical sales, along with the department category and holiday flag across all of the weeks.

Following, is a sample JSON output from the model endpoint. Because DeepAR produces probabilistic forecasts, the output contains several sales samples from the Gaussian distribution. Mean and quantiles (50% and 90%) of these samples are also reported, as shown in the following:

```
{
    "predictions": [
        {
            "quantiles": {
                "0.9": [...],
                "0.5": [...]
            },
            "samples": [...],
```

```
            "mean": [...]
        }
    ]
}
```

We have just reviewed sample input and output of the DeepAR algorithm for items with historical weekly sales.

DeepAR also offers unique capabilities that account for complexities in real-world time series problems. For new items or products, the length of time series is going to be shorter than that of regular items that have full sales history. DeepAR captures the distance to the first observation for new items or products. Because the algorithm learns item demand across multiple time series, it can estimate demand even for newly introduced items—the length of weekly sales across all time series need not remain the same. Additionally, the algorithm can also handle missing values, with missing values replaced with "Nan".

The following screenshot is a visual representation of the variety of inputs and output of DeepAR:

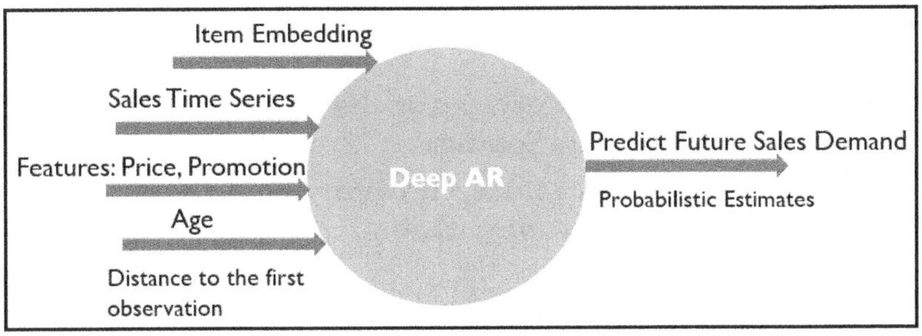

As shown in the preceding, the probabilistic forecasts of weekly sales can be produced by modeling historical weekly sales (**Sales Time Series**) across all new (**Age**) and regular items, along with taking into input item category **(Item Embedding)** and other features (**Price** and **Promotion**).

Exploratory data analysis

Although there are 45 stores, we will select one store, store number 20, to analyze performance across different departments across three years. The main idea here is that, using DeepAR, we can learn the sales of items across different departments.

In SageMaker, through Lifecycle **Configurations**, we can custom install Python packages before notebook instances are started. This eliminates the need to manually track packages required before the notebooks are executed.

For exploring the retail sales data, we will need the latest version, 0.9.0, of `seaborn` installed.

In SageMaker, under **Notebook**, click on **Lifecycle Configurations**:

1. Under **Start notebook**, enter the command to upgrade the `seaborn` Python package, as shown:

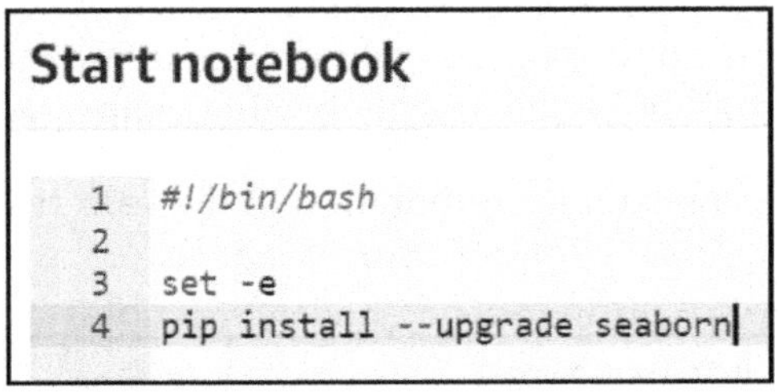

2. Edit the notebook settings by clicking on the notebook instance, selecting **Actions**, and picking **Update Settings**.
3. Under the **Update Settings a Lifecycle configuration** section, select the name of the newly created Lifecycle **configuration**.

This option enables SageMaker to manage all Python pre-requisites before the notebook instances are made available, as shown:

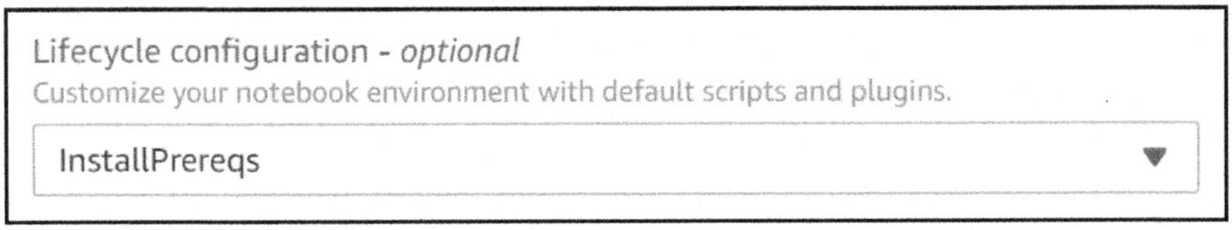

Let's merge the data across the sales, store, and features CSV files:

1. We will import the key Python libraries, as shown in the following:

```
import numpy #library to compute linear algebraic equations
import pandas as pd
import matplotlib.pyplot as plt
import seaborn as sns
```

2. Let's read the `.csv` files into Python DataFrames, as shown:

```
features = pd.read_csv('Features data set.csv')
sales = pd.read_csv('sales data-set.csv')
stores = pd.read_csv('stores data-set.csv')
```

3. Let's look at the shape of each of the DataFrames created, as in the following:

```
features.shape #There are 8,190 store, date and holiday
combinations
sales.shape #There are 421,570 sales transactions
stores.shape #There are 45 stores in question
```

4. Now, merge the `features` DataFrame with `sales` and `stores` to create one DataFrame containing all of the required information, as shown:

```
merged_df = features.merge(sales, on=['Store', 'Date',
'IsHoliday']).merge(stores, on=['Store'])
merged_df.head()
```

5. Convert `IsHoliday` into numerical form and convert the `Date` field into the `pandas` date format, as in the following:

```
merged_df = features.merge(sales, on=['Store', 'Date',
'IsHoliday']).merge(stores, on=['Store'])
merged_df.head()
```

6. Write merged dataset to `.csv` with the help of the following code:

```
merged_df.to_csv('retailsales.csv')
```

7. Now, let's look at the distribution of each of the key factors (`Temperature`, `Fuel_Price`, `Unemployment`, and `CPI`) that may impact sales, as shown:

```
#Create a figure and a set of subplots
f, ax = plt.subplots(4, figsize=(15, 15)) #f=figure; ax=axes
sns.distplot(merged_df.Temperature, ax=ax[0])
sns.distplot(merged_df.Fuel_Price, ax=ax[1])
sns.distplot(merged_df.Unemployment, ax=ax[2])
sns.distplot(merged_df.CPI, ax=ax[3])
```

We use the `seaborn` Python library to plot the distribution of `Temperature`, `Fuel_Price`, `Unemployment`, and `CPI` in the dataset. Let's have a look at the following output:

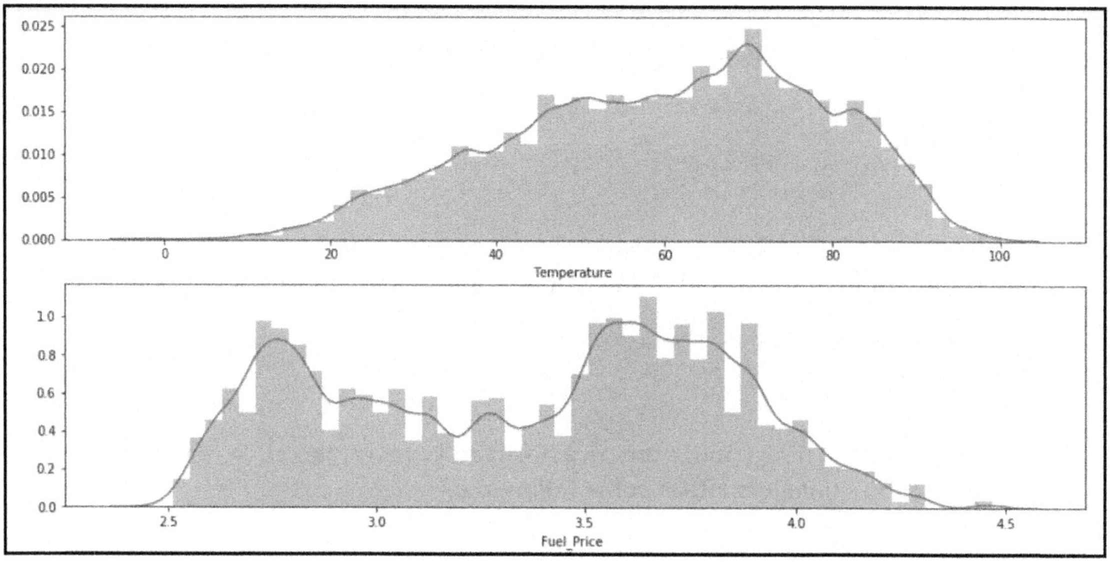

As can be seen from the preceding distributions, the temperature is mostly between 60 to 80 degrees when the sales happened. Also, fuel prices were around $2.75 and $3.75 during the majority of the sales activity:

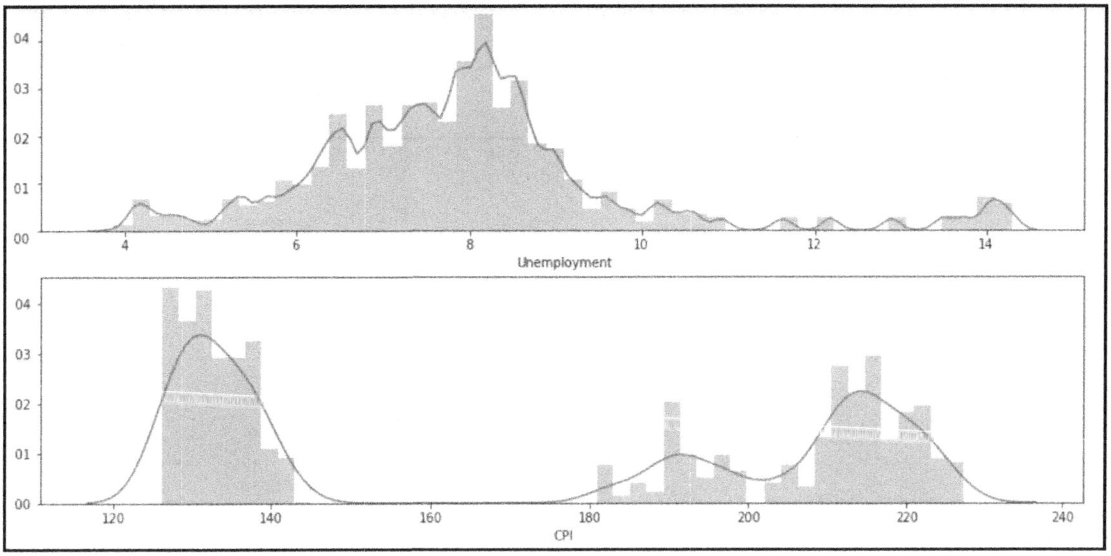

From the preceding visual, unemployment rate was between 6% and 9% during the majority of the sales activity. As for CPI, sales activity occurred during both low and high CPI levels.

Now that we have looked at the distribution of each of the key features, let's see how they are correlated to weekly sales:

1. First, let's look at the scatter plot between sales (target) and each of the explanatory variables— `Holidays`, `Temperature`, `CPI`, `Unemployment`, and `Store Type`:

```
f, ax = plt.subplots(6, figsize=(20,20))
sns.scatterplot(x="Fuel_Price", y="Weekly_Sales", data=merged_df,
ax=ax[0])
sns.scatterplot(x="Temperature", y="Weekly_Sales", data=merged_df,
ax=ax[1])
```

In the preceding code, we've plotted a scatterplot between sales and fuel price and sales and temperature. Let's analyze how fuel price and temperature are related to sales:

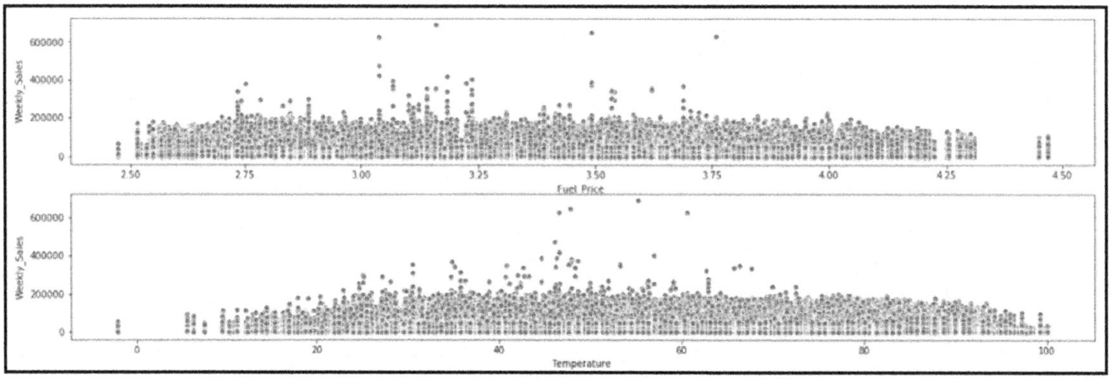

2. It is evident from the preceding visual that the fuel price between $3.25 and $3.75 is generating higher weekly sales. Also, a temperature between 50 and 65 degrees is generating higher weekly sales.

Let's now plot holiday or not and CPI against sales, as shown in the following code:

```
sns.scatterplot(x="IsHoliday", y="Weekly_Sales", data=merged_df,
ax=ax[2])
sns.scatterplot(x="CPI", y="Weekly_Sales", data=merged_df,
ax=ax[3])
```

Let's look at how sales vary with a holiday or not and CPI in the following screenshot:

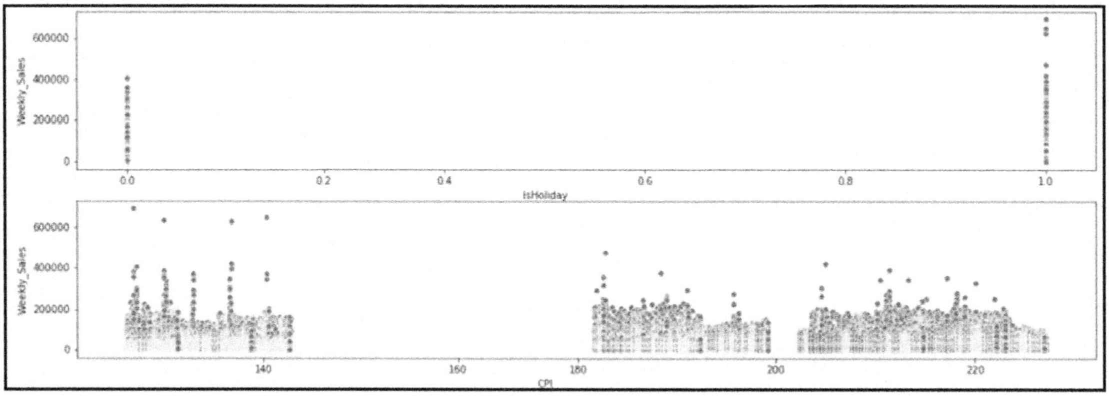

3. It seems that holiday sales are higher than non-holiday sales. Also, there appears to be no material impact of CPI on weekly sales.

   Let's now plot `Unemployment` and `Store Type` against sales, as shown in the following code:

```
sns.scatterplot(x="Unemployment", y="Weekly_Sales", data=merged_df,
ax=ax[4])
sns.scatterplot(x="Type", y="Weekly_Sales", data=merged_df,
ax=ax[5])
```

   Let's see how sales vary with unemployment and store type in the following screenshot:

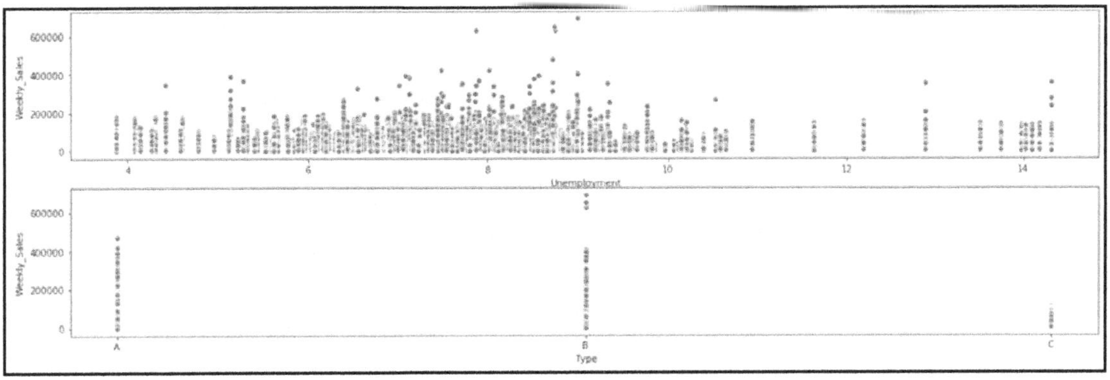

   From the preceding visual, weekly sales appear to be higher when unemployment rate is lower (7 to 8.5) and B type stores seem to have higher weekly sales.

4. Second, let's look at a heatmap across all of the features to identify what features impact sales. Let's draw a heatmap to see correlations between sales and several sales predictors all in one go.

The following screenshot is a heatmap of numerical attributes in the dataset—we drop store and department from the dataset since they are categorical variables:

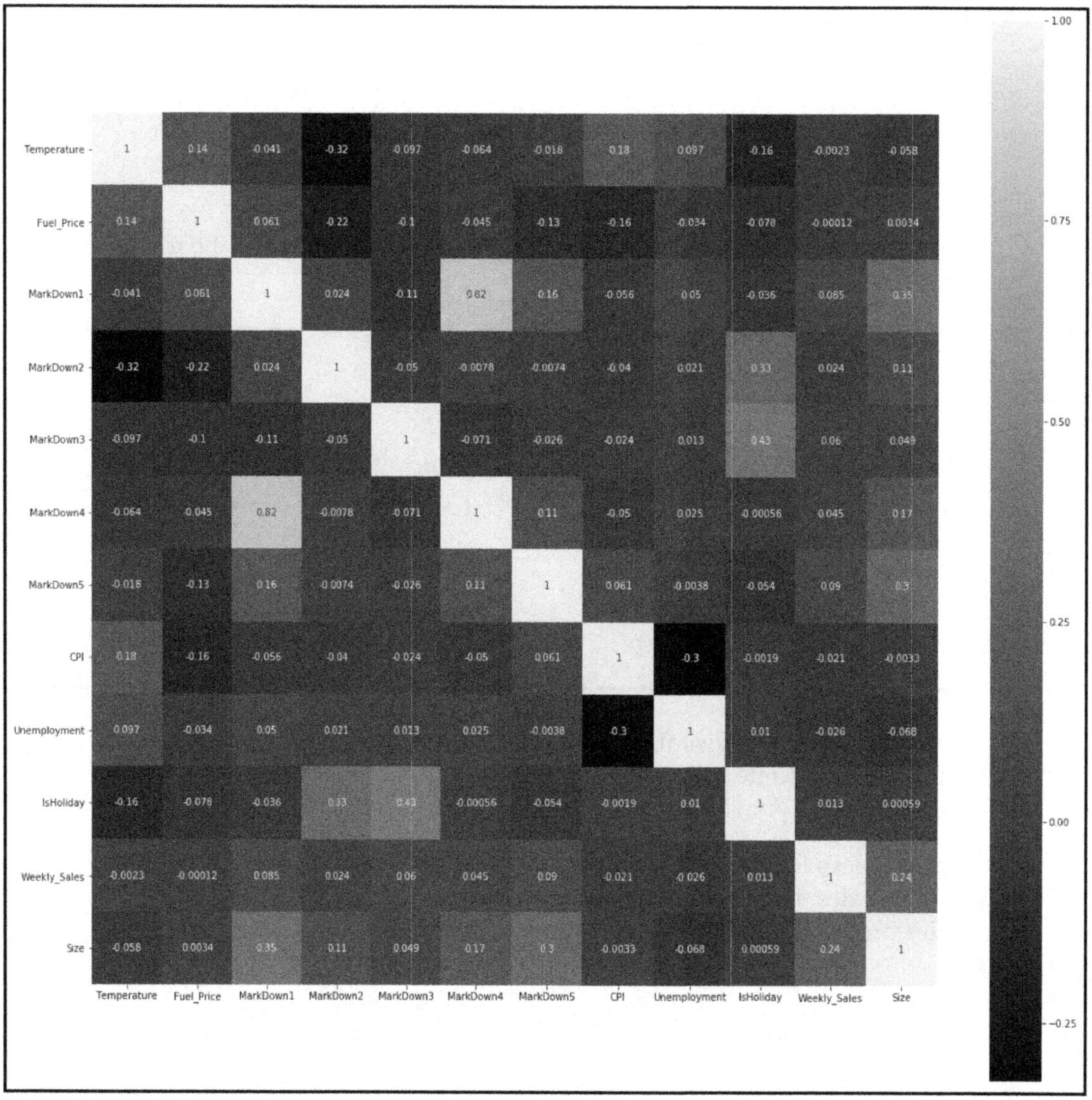

From the scatter plot and heat map, the following is apparent:

- Markdowns are happening during holidays.
- Sales are higher during holidays.

- Type B stores generate higher sales.
- Lower fuel prices (between $3 and $3.75) generate higher sales.
- The ideal temperature (between 50 and 65 degrees) generates higher sales.

For our further modeling, we will pick the best performing store, store 20, to model sales across different departments and years. For each of the time steps in the time series, we will also pass whether a particular day was observed as a holiday or not.

Data pre-processing

Let's begin with preparing the dataset for modeling:

- Create a module named `retailsales.py` to create JSON files that DeepAR can consume for training and validation.
- Create a module named `salesinference.py` to build inference data and retrieve and plot predictions.

For details on the modules, please refer to the source code associated with this chapter.

To modularize the code to test DeepAR, we will package the two modules, `retailsales` and `salesinference`. To package the modules, we will create the `__init__.py` file to import the modules. We will then create `setup.py`, detailing the pre-requisite packages to be installed.

Following, is the folder structure of the DeepAR project:

```
DeepAR project structure.
Project Organization
------------
    ├── notebooks/          <- All notebooks are residing here.
    ├── data/               <- Input data is residing here
    ├── deepar/             <- Python package with source code of this
project.
      ├──retailsales.py     <- Creating training and testing datasets
for DeepAR.
      ├──salesinference.py  <- Preparing data for predictions, obtaining
and plotting predictions from DeepAR
    ├── README.md           <- The top-level README for developers using
this project.
    ├── setup.py            <- Defines pre-requisite packages to install
and distribute package.
```

Let's take a look at the following steps:

1. In `setup.py`, we will define pre-requisite packages to be installed:

```
import os
from setuptools import setup, find_packages

def read(fname):
    return open(os.path.join(os.path.dirname(__file__),
fname)).read()

setup(
    name="deepar",
    description="DeepAR project structure.",
    author="<your-name>",
    packages=find_packages(exclude=['data', 'figures', 'output',
'notebooks']),\
    long_description=read('README.md'),
)
```

2. In `_init_.py`, we will import the modules, `retailsales` and `salesinference`, defined earlier:

```
from . import retailsales
from . import salesinference
```

3. We will now install the package for the modules to be available while training DeepAR:

```
#Navidate to deep-ar directory to install the deepar package
containing commonly used functions
path = ".."
os.chdir(path)

#install predefined functions
!pip install .

#Navigate to the parent directory to train the DeepAR model
# org_path = ".."
# os.chdir(org_path)
```

We are now ready with all of the packages required to pre-process weekly sales data. Pre-processing included not only converting categorical data into numerical, but also creating training and testing data in JSON formats required by the DeepAR algorithm.

Training DeepAR

In this section, we will fit DeepAR to the weekly sales. Let's start by preparing training and test datasets in JSON format.

Let's have a look at the following code, which demonstrates the creation of `json` lines:

```
import deepar as da

train_key      = 'deepar_sales_training.json'
test_key       = 'deepar_sales_test.json'
#Prediction and context length for training the DeepAR model
prediction_length = 9

salesfn = 'data/store20_sales.csv'
salesdf = da.retailsales.prepareSalesData(salesfn)
testSet = da.retailsales.getTestSales(salesdf, test_key)
trainingSet = da.retailsales.getTrainSales(salesdf, train_key,
prediction_length)
```

In the preceding code block, we have created JSON lines for training and testing the datasets:

- The `prepareSalesData()` function is used to select departments with sales across all of the 143 weeks. This step is to ensure that there were no missing values in the data. Although DeepAR can handle missing values, we've tried to make the problem less complex by only considering departments that have sales in almost all weeks.
- We use department numbers to group or categorize the time series for the DeepAR algorithm. This grouping will be used by DeepAR to make demand predictions by department.
- The `getTestSales()` function is used to create JSON lines for the testing dataset.
- The `getTrainSales()` function, on the other hand, is used to create JSON lines for the training dataset, which is a subset of the testing dataset. For each of the departments, we will chop the last nine weekly sales determined by prediction length.

Now, we will look at uploading the `json` files to the S3 bucket, as shown in the following code:

```
bucket         = 'ai-in-aws'
prefix         = 'sagemaker/deepar-weekly-sales'
```

```
train_prefix    = '{}/{}'.format(prefix, 'train')
test_prefix     = '{}/{}'.format(prefix, 'test')
output_prefix   = '{}/{}'.format(prefix, 'output')

sagemaker_session = sagemaker.Session()

train_path = sagemaker_session.upload_data(train_key, bucket=bucket,
key_prefix=train_prefix)
test_path = sagemaker_session.upload_data(test_key, bucket=bucket,
key_prefix=test_prefix)
```

In the preceding code, the newly created `json` files are uploaded to the designated S3 bucket via the `upload_data()` function from the Sagemaker session object (Sagemaker Python SDK).

We will be obtaining the URI of the DeepAR Docker image with the help of the following code:

```
role = get_execution_role()
output_path = r's3://{0}/{1}'.format(bucket, output_prefix)

container = get_image_uri(boto3.Session().region_name, 'forecasting-
deepar')

deepAR = sagemaker.estimator.Estimator(container,
                                       role,
                                       train_instance_count=1,
                                       train_instance_type='ml.c4.xlarge',
                                       output_path=output_path,
                                       sagemaker_session=sagemaker_session)
```

In the preceding code block, we can see the following:

- The `get_image_uri()` function from the SageMaker estimator object is used to obtain `uri` of the DeepAR Docker image.
- Once `uri` is obtained, the DeepAR estimator is created.
- The constructor parameters include the Docker image `uri`, execution role, training instance type and count, and `outpath` path to save the trained algorithm and SageMaker session.

Hyperparameters are used to configure the learning or training process. Let's have a look at `hyperparameters` used in the following code:

```
hyperparameters = {
    "time_freq": 'W',
    "context_length": prediction_length,
```

```
        "prediction_length": prediction_length,
        "num_cells": "40",
        "num_layers": "2",
        "likelihood": "gaussian",
        "epochs": "300",
        "mini_batch_size": "32",
        "learning_rate": "0.00001",
        "dropout_rate": "0.05",
        "early_stopping_patience": "10"
}
deepAR.set_hyperparameters(**hyperparameters)
```

In the preceding code, we came across the following hyperparameters:

- `learning_rate`: Defines how fast the weights are updated during training.
- `dropout_rate`: To avoid overfitting, for each iteration, a random subset of hidden neurons are not updated.
- `num_cells`: Defines the number of cells to use in each of the hidden layers.
- `num_layers`: Defines the number of hidden layers in the RNN.
- `time_freq`: Defines the frequency of time series.
- `epochs`: Defines the maximum number of passes over the training data.
- `context_length`: Defines look back period—how many data points are we going to look at before predicting.
- `prediction_length`: Defines the number of data points to predict.
- `mini_batch_size`: Defines how often weights are updated—that is, weights are updated after processing the designated number of data points.

In the following code, we fit `deepAR` to the training dataset:

```
data_channels = {"train": train_path, "test": test_path}\
deepAR.fit(inputs=data_channels)
```

In the preceding code, we can see the following:

- We passed the location of the training and testing JSONs on the S3 bucket.
- The testing dataset is used to evaluate the performance of the model.
- For training, we called the `fit()` function on the DeepAR estimator.

Following is the output from training DeepAR:

```
#test_score (algo-1, RMSE): 7307.12501604
#test_score (algo-1, mean_wQuantileLoss): 0.198078
#test_score (algo-1, wQuantileLoss[0.1]): 0.172473
```

```
#test_score (algo-1, wQuantileLoss[0.2]): 0.236177
#test_score (algo-1, wQuantileLoss[0.3]): 0.236742
#test_score (algo-1, wQuantileLoss[0.4]): 0.190065
#test_score (algo-1, wQuantileLoss[0.5]): 0.1485
#test_score (algo-1, wQuantileLoss[0.6]): 0.178847
#test_score (algo-1, wQuantileLoss[0.7]): 0.223082
#test_score (algo-1, wQuantileLoss[0.8]): 0.226312
#test_score (algo-1, wQuantileLoss[0.9]): 0.170508
```

As it is seen in the preceding output, the **Root Mean Squared Error** (**RMSE**) is used as a metric to pick the best performing model.

We have successfully trained the DeepAR model on our training dataset, which had 134 weekly sales. To fit training data to the model, we have defined the location of training and testing JSONs on the S3 bucket. Also, we've defined hyperparameters to control the learning or fitting process. The best performing model (based on the lowest RMSE—in that predicted sales are close as possible to actual sales) is then persisted.

Predicting and evaluating sales

In this section, the trained model will be deployed, so that we can predict weekly sales for the next nine weeks for a given department.

Let's have a look at the following code :

```
deepAR_predictor = deepAR.deploy(initial_instance_count=1,
instance_type='ml.m4.xlarge')
```

In the preceding code, the `deploy` function of the `deepAR` estimator is used to host the model as an endpoint. The number and type of hosting instances should be specified through the following parameters :

- `initial_instance_count`
- `instance_type`

To assess the model performance, we use department number 90, as shown in the following code:

```
#Predict last 9 weeks of a department and compare to ground truth

deepAR_predictor.content_type = 'application/json'
dept = 90

prediction_data = da.salesinference.buildInferenceData(dept, trainingSet,
```

```
testSet)
#print(prediction_data)
result = deepAR_predictor.predict(prediction_data)

y_mean, y_q1, y_q2, y_sample = da.salesinference.getInferenceSeries(result)
print("Predicted Sales: ", y_mean)
print("Actual Sales: ", list(testSet[dept]['Weekly_Sales'][134:]))

da.salesinference.plotResults(prediction_length, result, truth=True,
truth_data=testSet[dept]['Weekly_Sales'][134:], truth_label='truth')
```

In the preceding code, we can see the following:

- The `buildInferencedata()` function is used to prepare the time series data in JSON format. We build inference data, by a given department, listing holidays across the entire 143 weeks, weekly sales for 134 weeks, and corresponding item category. The goal here is to estimate sales in the last nine weeks, where `9` is the prediction length.

  Following is a JSON sample produced by the `buildInferenceData` function:


```
{"start":"2010-01-01 00:00:00","target":[15025.97, 10772.45, 11356.31, 16040.95, 13569.0, 13415.4, 16416.73, 11083.99, 9973.39, 9670.09,
10121.81, 10427.95, 8803.85, 17597.83, 13785.2, 14090.44, 9983.96, 8612.86, 8993.17, 11924.96, 10041.76, 10423.52, 9124.67, 12518.18,
11128.51, 13094.94, 15675.2, 11000.72, 13431.07, 11374.58, 8047.1, 10920.96, 15012.27, 12924.54, 15722.33, 27248.61, 13489.89, 12789.37,
12348.41, 11995.02, 15988.2, 35945.64, 16298.3, 12608.21, 14094.12, 29305.11, 37299.44, 14146.24, 12292.46, 11324.01, 9045.87, 9715.5,
11031.41, 14970.66, 15591.17, 20828.8, 14595.13, 8733.83, 13735.67, 11582.0, 18335.13, 14878.61, 14029.94, 10153.5, 11042.37, 9968.82,
12899.81, 11271.97, 11157.23, 8137.44, 12275.77, 10813.85, 10520.0, 12974.75, 16322.45, 11150.08, 14264.86, 13242.16, 13138.48, 13553.09,
15027.93, 11899.11, 16522.82, 18795.93, 15673.45, 14552.02, 16145.57, 8211.46, 13219.43, 12745.28, 11699.95, 20003.98, 13843.93, 13679.46,
14767.06, 30115.45, 14543.76, 24536.38, 37090.11, 21357.65, 10988.52, 11211.32, 10995.8, 10113.03, 15330.99, 19201.65, 18816.67, 15997.24,
15330.88, 14392.26, 13146.1, 12705.97, 11186.05, 10373.36, 9862.26, 9921.92, 15120.47, 9686.48, 9398.01, 12759.27, 12595.63, 12345.64,
11072.47, 10768.21, 9830.74, 14332.92, 12159.36, 12175.34, 13344.99, 12572.01, 13162.14, 13521.27, 12618.7, 18051.37], "cat":[18],
"dynamic_feat":[[0, 0, 0, 0, 0, 0, 0, 0, 0, 0, 0, 0, 0, 0, 0, 0, 0, 0, 0, 0, 0, 0, 0, 0, 0, 0, 0, 0, 0, 0, 0, 0, 0, 0, 0, 0, 1, 0, 0, 0, 0, 0, 0,
1, 1, 0, 0, 0, 0, 1, 0, 0, 0, 0, 0, 0, 0, 0, 0, 0, 0, 0, 0, 0, 0, 0, 0, 0, 0, 0, 0, 0, 0, 0, 0, 0, 0, 0, 0, 0, 0, 0, 0, 0, 0, 0, 1, 0, 0, 0, 0, 0,
0, 0, 0, 1, 0, 0, 0, 1, 0, 0, 0, 1, 0, 0, 0, 0, 0, 0, 0, 0, 0, 0, 0, 0, 0, 0, 0, 0, 0, 0, 0, 0, 0, 0, 0, 0, 0, 0, 0, 1, 0, 0, 0, 0, 0, 0, 0, 0]]}
```


- The SageMaker predictor object is used for inference.
- The `getInferenceSeries()` function is used to parse the JSON results from the DeepAR algorithm to identify mean sales, sales in the 10 percentile, and sales in the 90 percentile. Note that, using Gaussian distribution, DeepAR generates 100 samples of weekly sales for the next nine weeks. Therefore, sales in 10 percentile and 90 percentile indicate the lower and upper bounds of weekly sales during the prediction period.
- The results returned from the endpoint are then plotted against actual sales via the `plotResults()` function. For each of the nine weeks, we will look at mean sales, ground truth sales, sample sales, 10 percentile sales, and 90 percentile sales.

As shown in the following, the mean estimated sales are close to the actual sales, indicating that the DeepAR algorithm has adequately picked up sales demand across different departments. Change the department number to evaluate model performance across all departments. The probabilistic sales estimates hence enable us to estimate demand more accurately than point estimates. Here is the output of the preceding code:

```
Predicted Sales:  [92707.65625, 101316.90625, 86202.3984375, 87715.5625,
95967.359375, 101363.71875, 106354.90625, 94017.921875, 103476.71875]

Actual Sales:  [100422.86, 94987.08, 90889.75, 115695.71, 100372.02,
96616.19, 93460.57, 99398.64, 105059.88]
```

In the following graph, we can see the following:

- The blue line indicates mean sales from the prediction of nine weeks in the future.
- The purple line, on the other hand, reflects ground truth.
- The two lines are close enough, indicating that the model has done a decent job capturing patterns in sales, given holidays and historical weekly sales:

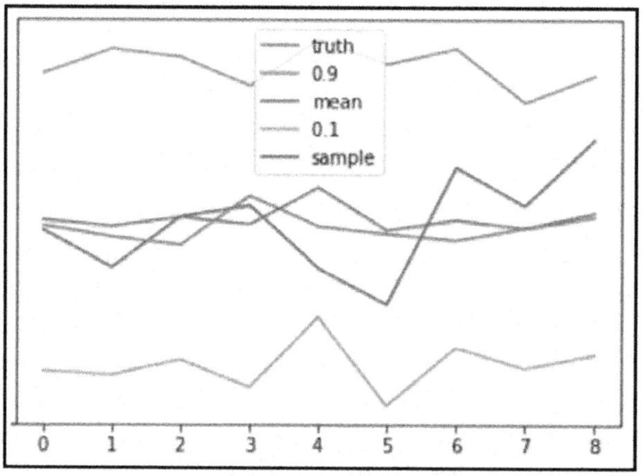

We have only looked at store 20 sales. However, you can train on all store sales by including the store number in the category list—for each time series in the train and test sets, include the following code:

```
"cat": [department number, store number]
```

With a large number of time series across different products and stores, we would have been able to achieve better performance.

Summary

In this chapter, we briefly looked at univariate time series forecasting techniques, such as ARIMA and exponential smoothing. However, as demand varies by multiple variables, it becomes important to model multi-variate series. DeepAR enables modeling of multi-variate series, along with providing probabilistic forecasting. While point estimates may work in some situations, probabilistic estimates provide better data for improved decision making. The algorithm works by generating a global model that is trained across a large number of time series. Each item or product across several stores and departments will have its own weekly sales. The trained model accounts for newly introduced items, missing sales per item, and multiple predictors that explain sales. With the LSTM network and Gaussian likelihood, DeepAR in SageMaker provides a flexible approach to demand forecasting. Additionally, we walked through model training, selection, hosting, and inference in SageMaker through the SageMaker Python SDK.

Now, that we've experienced SageMaker's capabilities to solve demand forecasting at scale, in the next chapter, we will walk through model monitoring and governance and will learn about why models degrade in production.

Further reading

Overview of a variety of univariate time series forecasting methods:

- `https://machinelearningmastery.com/exponential-smoothing-for-time-series-forecasting-in-Python/`
- `https://towardsdatascience.com/unboxing-arima-models-1dc09d2746f8`

Details on how the DeepAR algorithm works:

- `https://docs.aws.amazon.com/sagemaker/latest/dg/deepar_how-it-works.html`

Details on DeepAR inference formats:

- `https://docs.aws.amazon.com/sagemaker/latest/dg/deepar-in-formats.html`

4
Section 4: Machine Learning Model Monitoring and Governance

In this section, we will focus on understanding the guardrails that are essential once the models are put into production. Specifically, we will understand what model degradation is and how to respond to it in order to have an optimal positive impact on business decisions. You will also review AWS AI frameworks and AI infrastructure to get a sense of the endless possibilities AWS offers in terms of building AI solutions at scale.

This section comprises the following chapters:

- `Chapter 12`, *Model Accuracy Degradation and Feedback Loops*
- `Chapter 13`, *What Is Next?*

12
Model Accuracy Degradation and Feedback Loops

In this chapter, we will learn about the concept of model performance deterioration using an example of ad-click conversion. Our goal is to identify ad-clicks that result in mobile app downloads. In this case, the ads are for marketing mobile apps.

To address the deterioration of model performance, we will learn about **feedback loops**, pipelines in which we retrain models as new data becomes available and assess model performance. Consequently, trained models are constantly kept up to date with the changing patterns in input or training data. The feedback loop is very important when it comes to making sound business decisions based on model output. If a trained model does not adequately capture patterns in dynamic data, it is likely to produce sub-optimal results.

We will cover the following topics in this chapter:

- Monitoring models for degraded performance
- Developing a use case for evolving training data—ad-click conversion
- Creating a machine learning feedback loop

Technical requirements

This book's GitHub repository, which contains the source code for this chapter, can be found at `https://github.com/PacktPublishing/Hands-On-Artificial-Intelligence-on-Amazon-Web-Services`.

Monitoring models for degraded performance

In real-world scenarios, the performance of deployed machine learning models degrades over time. To explain this in the case of fraud detection, the models may not capture evolving fraudulent behaviors. Because fraudsters adapt their methods and processes over time to game systems, it is important to retrain fraud detection engines on the latest and greatest data (reflecting anomalous behavior) available. Take a look at the following diagram:

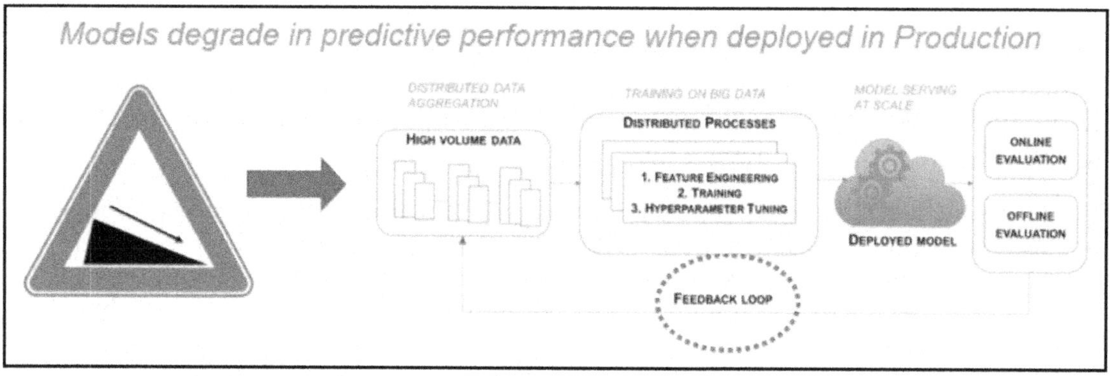

The preceding diagram shows how models degrade in terms of predictive performance when they are deployed in production. As another example, in the case of recommender systems, customer preferences keep changing based on a number of contextual and environmental factors. Therefore, it becomes important for personalization engines to capture such preferences and present the most relevant suggestions to customers.

Developing a use case for evolving training data – ad-click conversion

Fraud risk is prevalent in almost every industry, for example, airlines, retail, financial services, and so on. The risk is especially high in online advertising. For companies investing in digital marketing, it is important to contain costs from fraudulent clicks on ads. Online advertising can become cost-prohibitive if fraudulent behavior is rampant across online ad channels. In this chapter, we will look at ad-click data for mobile apps and predict which clicks will likely yield app downloads. The outcome of this prediction exercise will allow mobile app developers to efficiently allocate online marketing dollars.

Ad-click behavior is very dynamic. This behavior changes across time, location, and ad channels. A fraudster can develop software to automate clicking on mobile app ads and conceal the identity of clicks—clicks can be generated from multiple IP addresses, devices, operating systems, and channels. To catch this dynamic behavior, it is important to retrain classification models to cover new and emerging patterns. Implementing a feedback loop becomes critical if we wish to accurately determine which clicks will result in app downloads. For instance, clicks on ads for the Helix Jump app may not result in app downloads if these clicks are generated during the eleventh hour, are from the same IP address, and are a few minutes apart. However, if these clicks are produced during business hours, are from different IP addresses, and are spread across the day, then they will result in app downloads.

The following diagram describes ad-click behavior, along with a binary outcome—whether the mobile app is downloaded or not:

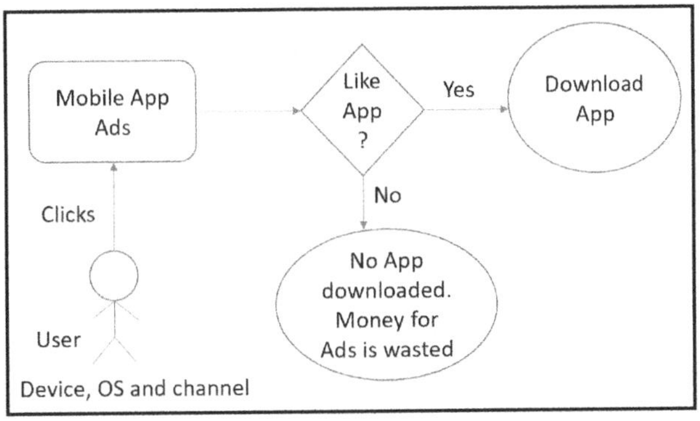

Depending on how the ad is clicked by the user—whether a device, operating system, or a channel is used, when it is clicked, and for what app—the click may or may not convert into a mobile app download. We will use this dynamic click behavior to illustrate the importance of a feedback loop in machine learning.

Creating a machine learning feedback loop

In this section, we will demonstrate how retraining a classification model as new data becomes available will enhance model performance; that is, it will predict which ad-clicks will result in mobile app downloads.

We have created a synthetic/artificial dataset simulating 2.4 million clicks across four days (Monday through Thursday; July 2 to July 5 of 2018). The dataset can be found here: `https://github.com/PacktPublishing/Hands-On-Artificial-Intelligence-on-Amazon-Web-Services/tree/master/Ch12_ModelPerformanceDegradation/Data`

The dataset contains the following elements:

- `ip`: the IP address of the click
- `app`: The type of mobile app
- `device`: The type of device the click is coming from (for example, iPhone 6 plus, iPhone 7)
- `os`: The type of operating system the click is coming from
- `channel`: The type of channel the click is coming from
- `click_time`: The timestamp of the click (UTC)
- `is_downloaded`: The target that is to be predicted, indicating the app was downloaded

Having access to the latest and greatest data is a challenge. Data lake and data warehouse environments typically lag by a day (24 hours). When predicting whether clicks that occurred toward the end of the day on Thursday will result in app downloads, it is important to have current data up to and including Thursday, excluding the clicks that we are scoring, for model training.

To understand the significance of a feedback loop, we will train a tree-based model (XGBoost) to predict the probability of an ad-click (related to an app) that results in the app being download. We will run three different experiments:

- **Experiment 1**: Train on the click data for Monday and predict/score a portion of the clicks from Thursday (clicks from a later part of the day).
- **Experiment 2**: Let's assume that we have more data available in the data lake environment to retrain the classification model. We will train on the click data for Monday, Tuesday, and Wednesday and predict/score a portion of the clicks from Thursday.
- **Experiment 3**: Similarly, we will train on click data for Monday, Tuesday, Wednesday and part of Thursday and predict/score a portion of the clicks from Thursday.

With each iteration or experiment, you will see the following:

- The classification model's performance measured by **area under curve** (**AUC**) increases. AUC is measured by plotting the true positive rate against the false positive rate.
- That a random classifier has an AUC of 0.5.
- For an optimal model, the AUC should be closer to 1.
- In other words, the true positive rate (the proportion of the app downloads that you've correctly identified) should be higher than the false positive rate (the proportion of clicks that did not result in any app downloads but has been identified as yielding app downloads).

Now we need to load and explore the data to determine the best indicators for predicting app downloads.

Exploring data

Amazon SageMaker offers built-in tools and capabilities for creating machine learning pipelines that incorporate feedback loops. Since machine learning pipelines were covered in `Chapter 8`, *Creating Machine Learning Inference Pipelines*, here, we will focus on the significance of incorporating a feedback loop. Let's begin:

1. Install the relevant Python packages and set the locations for the training, validation, and model outputs on the S3 bucket, as follows:

```
!pip install pyarrow
!pip install joblib
!pip install xgboost
#Read the dataset from S3 bucket
s3_bucket = 'ai-in-aws'
s3_prefix = 'Click-Fraud'

s3_train_prefix = os.path.join(s3_prefix, 'train')
s3_val_prefix = os.path.join(s3_prefix, 'val')
s3_output_prefix = os.path.join(s3_prefix, 'output')

s3_train_fn = 'train_sample.csv.zip'
```

2. Read the prepared synthetic dataset from the local SageMaker instance, as shown in the following code:

```
file_name = 'ad_track_day'
fn_ext = '.csv'
num_days = 4
dict_of_ad_trk_df = {}

for i in range(1, num_days+1):
dict_of_ad_trk_df[file_name+str(i)] =
pd.read_csv(file_name+str(i)+fn_ext)
```

3. We will now explore the data so that we can prepare features that indicate the following:
    - **Where** the ad-clicks are coming from, that is, `ip`, `device`, and `os`
    - **When** they come, that is, `day` and `hr`
    - **How** they come, that is, `channel`
    - A combination of where, when, and how
4. Create chunks of data for each of the experiments. We will use the `pandas` library to aggregate ad-clicks by days in the experiment, as shown in the following code:

```
df_ckFraud_exp1 = pd.concat([dict_of_ad_trk_df[key] for key in
["ad_track_day1"]], ignore_index=True)

df_ckFraud_exp2 = pd.concat([dict_of_ad_trk_df[key] for key in
["ad_track_day1", "ad_track_day2", "ad_track_day3"]],
ignore_index=True)

df_ckFraud_exp3 = pd.concat([dict_of_ad_trk_df[key] for key in
["ad_track_day1", "ad_track_day2", "ad_track_day3",
"ad_track_day4"]], ignore_index=True)
```

Let's understand whether the most frequently occurring factors, such as the type of app, device, channel, operating system, and IP address the click is originating from, result in app downloads.

Popular apps, which are defined by the number of relevant ad-clicks, are not the same when an app is not downloaded as opposed to when it is downloaded. In other words, although certain mobile app ads are frequently clicked, they are not necessarily those that are downloaded.

Top Apps for Monday: Let's plot the distribution of the number of ad-clicks by app when apps are downloaded as opposed to when they aren't, as shown in the following code:

```
%matplotlib inline
plot_clickcnt_ftr(df_ckFraud_exp1, 'app', '1')
```

For the definition of the `plot_clickcnt_ftr()` function from this code, please refer to the associated source code for this chapter. The first bar chart shows when apps are not downloaded, while the second one reflects when apps are downloaded:

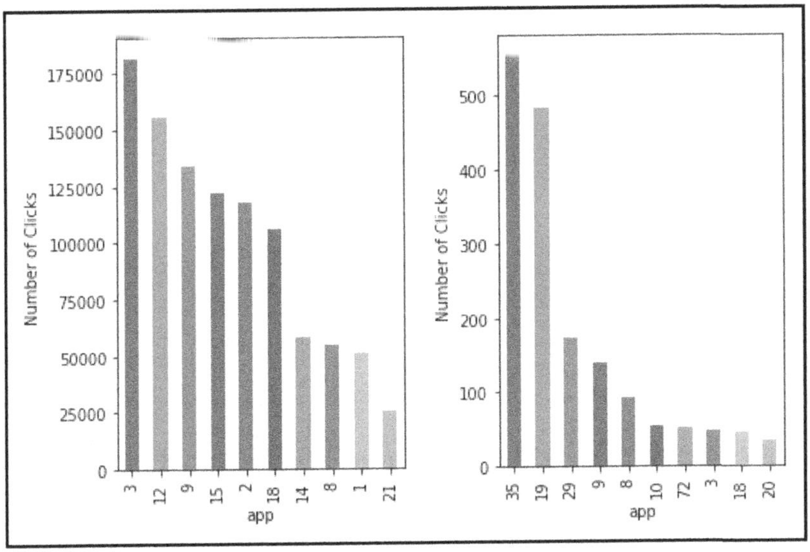

As we saw previously, apps 12, 3, 9, and 15 are the top 4 apps in terms of apps that aren't downloaded. On the other hand, apps 19, 34, 29, and 9 are popular apps when ad-clicks result in app downloads.

Top Devices for Monday: Now let's plot the distribution of the number of ad-clicks by device when apps are downloaded as opposed to when they aren't, as shown in the following code:

```
%matplotlib inline
plot_clickcnt_ftr(df_ckFraud_exp1, 'device', '1')
```

The same theme holds true; popular devices when clicks do not result in app downloads are different from those when clicks result in app downloads, as shown in the following output:

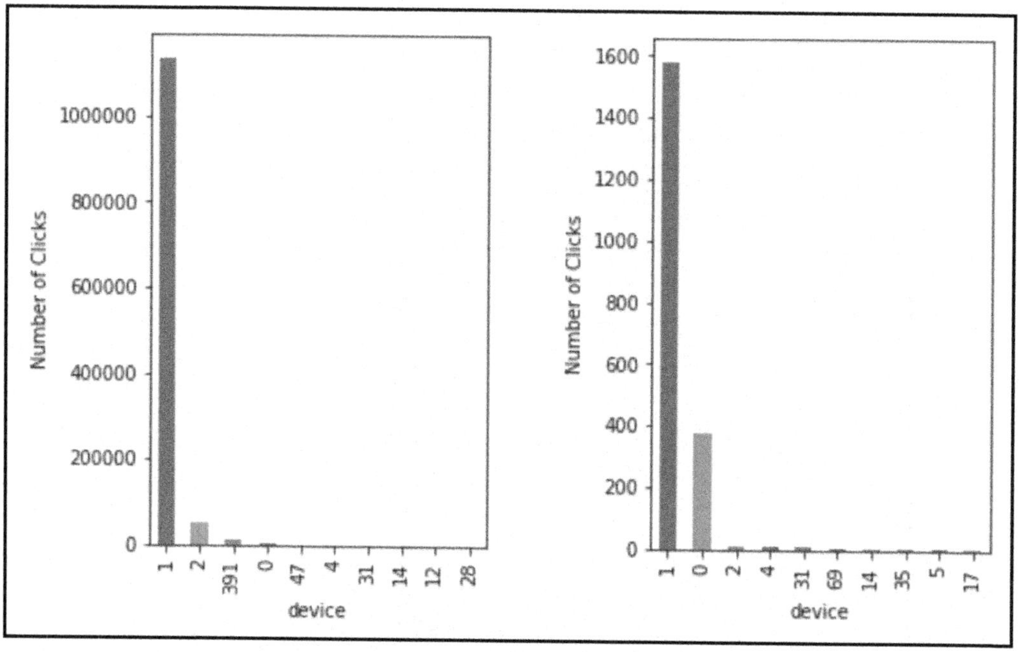

Even in terms of the operating system and the channel, the same theme is sustained. Therefore, it seems reasonable to note that ad-clicks coming from certain devices, operating systems, and channels for certain apps are indicative of app downloads. It may also be possible that clicks originating from a popular channel, operating system, or device for popular apps may have a higher incidence of being converted into app downloads. Popular is synonymous with a high volume of clicks.

Creating features

Now that we have explored the data, it is time to create some features. Let's begin by looking at categorical variables in the data.

The unique IDs of each of the category columns, namely app, device, os, and channel, are not useful in and of themselves. For a tree-based model, for example, a lower app ID is not better than a higher app ID or vice versa in terms of predicting app downloads. Therefore, we will calculate the frequency of each of these categorical variables, as shown in the following code:

```
def encode_cat_ftrs(df_ckFraud):
cat_ftrs = ['app','device','os','channel']

for c in cat_ftrs:
df_ckFraud[c+'_freq'] = df_ckFraud[c].map(df_ckFraud.groupby(c).size() /
df_ckFraud.shape[0])
return df_ckFraud
```

1. First, we create a list of categorical variables called cat_ftrs. We do this for each of the categorical variables.
2. We calculate the frequency by dividing the number of clicks originating from the variable by the total number of clicks in the dataset.

   For each of these experiments, we call the encode_cat_ftrs() function to create frequency-related features for all the categorical variables, as follows:

   ```
   df_ckFraud_exp1 = encode_cat_ftrs(df_ckFraud_exp1)
   df_ckFraud_exp2 = encode_cat_ftrs(df_ckFraud_exp2)
   df_ckFraud_exp3 = encode_cat_ftrs(df_ckFraud_exp3)
   ```

3. Now let's look at time-related features. From the click_time column, we'll create a variety of time-related features, that is, day, hour, minute, and second. These features may help uncover click patterns given the day of the week and hour of the day.

   From the datetime column, we extract day, hour, minute, and second, as shown in the following code:

   ```
   def create_date_ftrs(df_ckFraud, col_name):
   """
   create day, hour, minute, second features
   """
   df_ckFraud = df_ckFraud.copy()

   df_ckFraud['day'] = df_ckFraud[col_name].dt.day.astype('uint8') ##
   dt is accessor object for date like properties
   df_ckFraud['hour'] = df_ckFraud[col_name].dt.hour.astype('uint8')
   df_ckFraud['minute'] =
   df_ckFraud[col_name].dt.minute.astype('uint8')
   df_ckFraud['second'] =
   ```

```
    df_ckFraud[col_name].dt.second.astype('uint8')

    return df_ckFraud
```

4. We use the `dt` accessor object of the datetime column to obtain time-related features. As with calling `encode_cat_ftrs` on each of the datasets related to the experiments, we will call `create_date_ftrs` on each of them.
5. Finally, let's create features that reflect `when` and `where` the clicks are coming from. Therefore, we will count clicks via the following:
    - IP Address, Day, and Hour
    - IP Address, Channel, and Hour
    - IP Address, Operating System, and Hour
    - IP Address, App, and Hour
    - IP Address, Device, and Hour

For information on the function used to count clicks by each of the combinations, `count_clicks`, please refer to the source code associated with this chapter. `count_clicks` is called on each of the datasets pertaining to the experiments.

Now let's take a look at the prepared dataset after feature engineering:

app	device	os	channel	is_downloaded	day	hour	minute	second	clicks_by_ip_day_hr	clicks_by_ip_hr_chnl	clicks_by_ip_hr_os
2	1	18	51	0	4	0	10	27	58	19	3
3	2	13	84	0	4	0	10	27	32	2	11
3	1	13	110	0	4	0	10	27	3	2	3
1	1	22	42	0	4	0	10	27	56	9	3
11	1	19	45	0	4	0	10	27	59	4	59

As you can see, we have all the engineered features:

clicks_by_ip_hr_app	clicks_by_ip_hr_device	app_freq	device_freq	os_freq	channel_freq
24	94	0.091979	0.947446	0.047518	0.020742
7	12	0.169171	0.039588	0.221243	0.058326
2	3	0.169171	0.947446	0.221243	0.025615
7	139	0.046613	0.947446	0.038723	0.029306
5	80	0.014798	0.947446	0.247792	0.007015

In the preceding screenshot, we have:

- `day`, `hour`, `minute`, and `second` for each ad-click
- `app`, `device`, operating system (`os`), and channel frequency
- Number of clicks by when (`time`), where (`os`, `device`, and `ip` address), and how (`channel`)

6. Now let's see how all of these features are related to each other. We will use a correlation matrix to view the relationship among all the attributes, as shown in the following code:

```
# Correlation
df_ckFraud_exp1.corr()
```

The following is part of the correlation matrix generated by the `corr` function of the `pandas` DataFrame:

	app	device	os	channel	is_downloaded	day	hour	minute	second	clicks_by_ip_day_hr
app	1.000000	0.158022	0.141765	-0.030068	0.058519	.014786	-0.014782	0.010294	-0.001414	-0.008291
device	0.158022	1.000000	0.851941	-0.077587	0.007776	0.006948	-0.006943	0.001043	-0.000758	-0.006281
os	0.141765	0.851941	1.000000	-0.056749	-0.001451	0.008148	-0.008140	-0.000644	-0.001469	-0.002912
channel	-0.030068	-0.077587	-0.056749	1.000000	-0.016482	0.053915	-0.053976	0.019662	-0.003592	-0.018300
is_downloaded	0.058519	0.007776	-0.001451	-0.016482	1.000000	0.001237	-0.001237	0.003675	-0.000239	-0.007840
day	0.014786	0.006948	0.008148	0.053915	0.001237	1.000000	-0.999996	-0.087434	-0.006234	-0.116006
hour	-0.014782	-0.006943	-0.008140	-0.053976	-0.001237	-0.999996	1.000000	0.086775	0.006227	0.116030
minute	0.010294	0.001043	-0.000644	0.019662	0.003675	-0.087434	0.086775	1.000000	-0.067187	0.012484
second	-0.001414	-0.000758	-0.001469	-0.003592	-0.000239	-0.006234	0.006227	-0.067187	1.000000	-0.000716
clicks_by_ip_day_hr	-0.008291	-0.006281	-0.002912	-0.018300	-0.007840	-0.116006	0.116030	0.012484	-0.000716	1.000000
clicks_by_ip_hr_chnl	-0.043687	-0.004494	-0.001291	-0.076272	-0.010863	-0.115471	0.115493	0.018248	0.000794	0.652071
clicks_by_ip_hr_os	-0.025790	-0.027571	-0.038357	-0.030014	-0.010035	-0.093681	0.093705	0.013310	0.000698	0.706241
clicks_by_ip_hr_app	-0.058217	-0.011063	-0.007185	-0.022824	-0.009858	-0.102169	0.102188	0.017185	-0.000601	0.800414
clicks_by_ip_hr_device	-0.020919	-0.030611	-0.026420	-0.011767	-0.008612	-0.112401	0.112425	0.012277	-0.000316	0.947810
app_freq	-0.425326	-0.041630	-0.043836	0.049374	-0.062210	-0.[illegible]06360	0.006313	0.022707	-0.004619	0.025189
device_freq	-0.096505	-0.423654	-0.380922	0.085903	-0.042520	0[illegible]43364	-0.043379	-0.003262	-0.000812	-0.069033
os_freq	-0.044316	-0.104758	-0.184141	0.018447	-0.005146	0.009874	-0.009892	0.003801	-0.002031	0.005872
channel_freq	-0.068054	0.021604	0.000538	-0.331483	-0.038358	[illegible]100819	0.100861	-0.007235	-0.004171	0.009254

As we can see, the type of app, the proportion of clicks originating from the device and channel, and the proportion of clicks for an app are key indicators that are predictive of app downloads. Plotting a heatmap for each of the experiments also indicates that these observations are valid. Please refer to the source code associated with this chapter for more information.

Using Amazon's SageMaker XGBoost algorithm to classify ad-click data

To understand the significance of a feedback loop, we will train a tree-based model (XGBoost) to predict the probability that an ad-click results in an app download.

For all of these experiments, we have one test dataset. This contains ad-clicks, along with apps that were downloaded during the later part of the day on Thursday—the last 120,000 clicks from the day. Let's get started:

1. We will select 5% of the clicks from the third dataset, which contains clicks from Monday, Tuesday, Wednesday, and Thursday. The third dataset is sorted by time, so we pick the last 120,000 clicks that were generated on Thursday, as shown in the following code:

```
# Sort by hour, minute and second --> pick the last 5% of records
test_data = df_ckFraud_exp3.sort_values(['day', 'hour', 'minute',
'second'], ascending=False).head(n=120000)
```

2. We will also need to rearrange the datasets for all the experiments, so `is_downloaded`, our target variable, is the first column in the dataset. This format is required by the SageMaker XGBoost algorithm.
3. Now we need to rearrange the test dataset, as follows:

```
# Rearrange test data so that is_downloaded is the first column
test_data = pd.concat([test_data['is_downloaded'],
test_data.drop(['is_downloaded'], axis=1)], axis=1)
```

4. For each experiment, we will start by creating training and validation datasets.
5. We will split the current experiment data into training and validation sets, as shown in the following code:

```
train_data, validation_data =
np.split(current_experiment.sample(frac=1, random_state=4567),
[int(0.7 * len(current_experiment))])
```

6. We use NumPy's split function to do so. 70% of the data is allocated for training, while 30% is allocated for validation.

7. Once we have the training, validation, and test datasets, we upload them to S3. Please refer to the source code associated with this chapter for details.

It is time to prepare for model training. To train the XGBoost model, the following hyperparameters are defined (only a few are reported). For detailed information, please refer to the AWS docs (`https://docs.aws.amazon.com/sagemaker/latest/dg/xgboost_hyperparameters.html`):

- `max_depth`: The maximum number of levels between the tree's root and a leaf.
- `eta`: Learning rate.
- `gamma`: The node is only split when the resulting split gives a positive reduction in the loss function. Gamma specifies the minimum loss reduction required to make a split.
- `min_child_weight`: This is used to control tree complexity and the minimum sum of instance weight needed in a child. If this threshold is not met, then tree partitioning will stop.
- `subsample`: The fraction of observations to be randomly sampled for each tree.
- `colsample_bytree`: The fraction of columns to be randomly sampled for each tree.
- `scale_pos_weight`: The dataset is highly imbalanced, where we have a large number of clicks (> 90%) that did not result in app downloads. To account for this, the `scale_pos_weight` hyperparameter is used to give clicks that resulted in app downloads more weight. These clicks are heavily underrepresented in the dataset.
- `alpha`: A regularization parameter to prevent overfitting. Alpha is used to implement L1 regularization, where the sum of the weights of leaves is part of the regularization term (of the objective function).
- `lambda`: This is used to control L2 regularization, where the sum of the squares of weights is part of the regularization term.

8. Then, we define some of the hyperparameters of the XGBoost algorithm, as follows:

```
xgb.set_hyperparameters(max_depth=4,
 eta=0.3,
 gamma=0,
 min_child_weight=6,
```

```
colsample_bylevel = 0.8,
colsample_bytree = 0.8,
subsample=0.8,
silent=0,
scale_pos_weight=scale_pos_weight,
objective='binary:logistic',
num_round=100)
```

While most of the default values for the hyperparameters are accepted, some are explicitly defined here. For instance, `min_child_weight` is set to `6`, while the default value is `1`. This means that a leaf node should have a sizeable number of instances or data points before it can be split further. These values can be tuned for the data in question. **Hyperparameter optimization** (**HPO**), from SageMaker, can be used to automate the process of finding optimal values for hyperparameters.

9. We will now fit the XGBoost algorithm to the experiment data (training and validation), as shown in the following code:

```
xgb.fit({'train': s3_input_train, 'validation':
s3_input_validation})
```

The `fit()` function of the XGBoost estimator module (SageMaker Python SDK) is invoked for model training. The location of both the training and validation datasets is passed as an input for model training.

Once training concludes, the trained model will be persisted to the location specified (in the S3 bucket). We will need to repeat the same training steps for each of the experiments. In the end, we will have three trained models.

Evaluating model performance

In this section, we will evaluate the performance of the three trained models. Our hypothesis is that the first model, which was trained on clicks from Monday and Tuesday, is less predictive of app downloads on the later part of Thursday compared to the second and third models. Similarly, the performance of the second model, which was trained on clicks from Monday through Wednesday, should be less than that of the third model, which was trained on clicks from Monday through the majority of Thursday.

We will begin by analyzing the features that are deemed important for each of the models, as shown in the following code:

```
exp_lst = ['exp1', 'exp2', 'exp3']
for exp in exp_lst:
   model_file = os.path.join(sm_output_loc, exp, s3_output_fn)
    plot_ftr_imp(model_file)
```

The preceding code is explained as follows:

1. First, we retrieve the location of the trained model for each of the three experiments.
2. Then, we pass the location to the `plot_ftr_imp()` function to create a diagram showing feature importance. To plot feature importance, the function does the following:
    - Extracts the trained model from the `.tar` file
    - Loads the XGBoost model
    - Calls the `plot_importance()` function on the loaded model

   The following diagram shows feature importance for the three trained models, starting with the first model on the left:

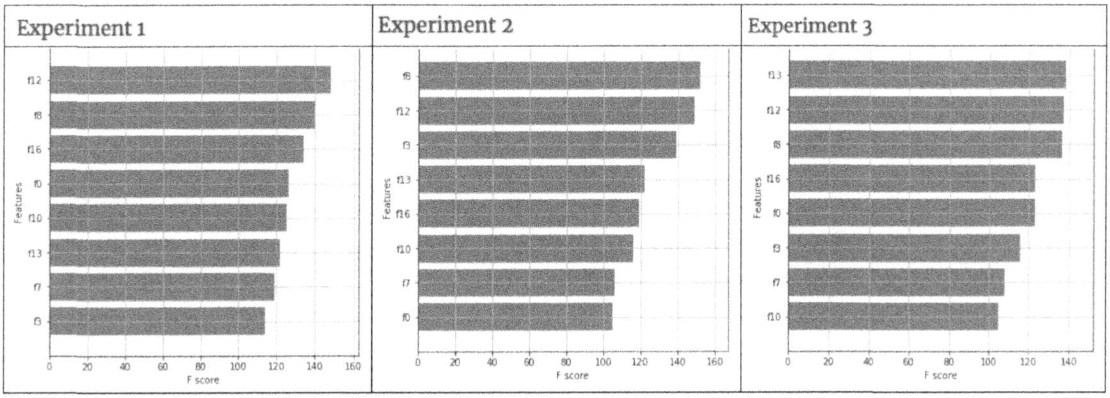

As we can see, most key predictors have maintained their importance as more data became available, while the order of importance changed. To see how the features look when mapped, take a look at the following diagram:

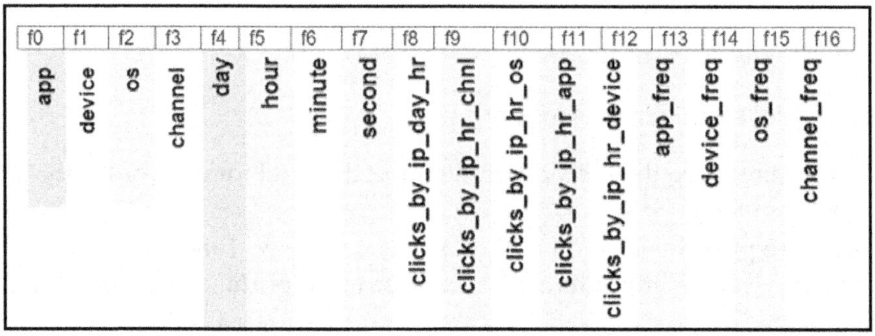

XGBoost numbers the features from the input dataset, where the first column is the target variable, while features are ordered from the second column onward.

3. Now we will evaluate performance across all three experiments. Let's deploy all three trained models as endpoints as shown in the following code:

```
model_loc = os.path.join(data_loc, s3_output_fn)
xgb_model = Model(model_data=model_loc, image=container, role=role)
xgb_model.deploy(initial_instance_count=1,
instance_type='ml.m4.xlarge')
```

In the preceding code, for each of the experiments, to deploy a trained model as an endpoint, we will do the following:

1. First, we will retrieve the trained model from the location (S3 bucket) where it is saved.
2. Then, we will create a SageMaker model by passing the trained model, a Docker image of the XGBoost algorithm, and SageMaker's execution role.
3. Finally, we will invoke the `deploy` method of the newly created XGBoost Model object. We pass in the number of EC2 instances to provision, along with the type of instance, to the deploy function.

The following screenshot shows the endpoints that were created after the trained models were deployed:

○	xgboost-2019-06-24-15-40-47-429	arn:aws:sagemaker:us-east-1:109099157774:endpoint/xgboost-2019-06-24-15-40-47-429	Jun 24, 2019 15:40 UTC	InService	Jun 24, 2019 15:49 UTC
○	xgboost-2019-06-24-15-31-29-918	arn:aws:sagemaker:us-east-1:109099157774:endpoint/xgboost-2019-06-24-15-31-29-918	Jun 24, 2019 15:31 UTC	InService	Jun 24, 2019 15:39 UTC
○	xgboost-2019-06-24-15-22-33-935	arn:aws:sagemaker:us-east-1:109099157774:endpoint/xgboost-2019-06-24-15-22-33-935	Jun 24, 2019 15:22 UTC	InService	Jun 24, 2019 15:30 UTC

4. To view the deployed models, navigate to SageMaker service and expand the **Inference** section. Under this section, click on **Endpoints** to view endpoint names, the creation time, the status, and the last updated time.

Now it is time to predict app downloads for the last 120,000 clicks on Thursday.

We will create a `RealTimePredictor` object for this, as shown in the following code:

```
xgb_predictor = sagemaker.predictor.RealTimePredictor(endpoint,
sagemaker_session=sess, serializer=csv_serializer,
deserializer=None, content_type='text/csv', accept=None)
```

The `RealTimePredictor` object is created by passing the name of the `endpoint`, the current `sagemaker` session, and the `content` type.

5. Collect the `predictions` for the test data, as follows:

```
predictions[exp_lst[ind]] =
xgb_predictor.predict(test_data.as_matrix()[:10000,
1:]).decode('utf-8')
```

6. As we can see, we invoke the predict method of `RealTimePredictor` (the SageMaker Python SDK) by passing the first 10,000 data clicks.

   We are now ready to compare the predicted results with the actual app downloads. We use the `confusion_matrix` module from the `sklearn` library to obtain the true positive rate and the false positive rate. We also use the `roc_auc_score` and `accuracy_score` modules from `sklearn` to compute the area under curve and accuracy, respectively.

The following is the output for each of the experiments:

```
For exp1 auc is 0.802, accuracy is 0.9864, and confusion matrix is [[19822   142]
 [   14    22]]
For exp2 auc is 0.8556, accuracy is 0.9864, and confusion matrix is [[19745   219]
 [   10    26]]
For exp3 auc is 0.8684, accuracy is 0.9864, and confusion matrix is [[19700   264]
 [    9    27]]
```

The following is the AUC, which shows the performance of all the experiments:

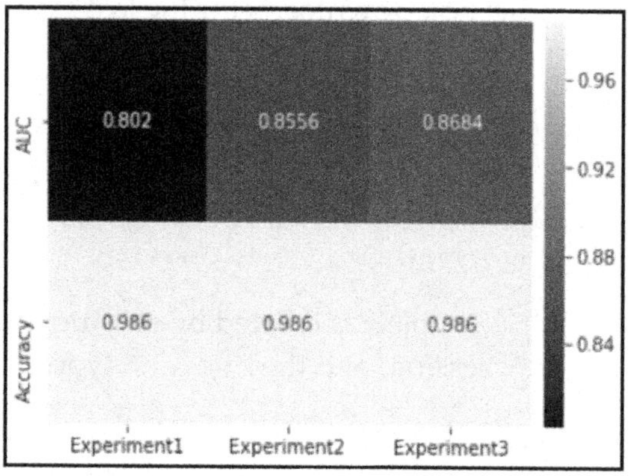

As we can see **Experiment2** performed better than **Experiment1**, while **Experiment3** performed the best since it had the highest **AUC**. In **Experiment3**, the true positive rate is higher than the false positive rate relative to **Experiment1** and **Experiment2**. Accuracy remained the same across all the experiments. Since AUC is independent of the underlying class distribution of the test dataset, it is an important and key metric when it comes to measuring the model's discriminative power. On the other hand, metrics such as accuracy, recall, and precision are likely to change as the test set changes.

Therefore, after the trained model is deployed in production, it is important to seek feedback while the model is in operation. As patterns in data change and as new data becomes available, it becomes important to retrain and tune models for optimal performance.

Summary

In this chapter, we have learned why it is important to monitor models for degraded performance. To illustrate this idea, we used a synthetic dataset that captures ad-click behavior for mobile app downloads. First, we explored the data to understand the relationship between app downloads and ad-clicks. Then, we created features by aggregating existing click attributes in multiple dimensions. Next, we created three different datasets on which to run three experiments to explain the idea of model performance deterioration as new data becomes available. Next, we fitted the XGBoost model for each of the experiments. Finally, we evaluated performance across all the experiments to conclude that the model with the best performance is the one that took into account the latest and greatest click behavior.

Consequently, implementing a feedback loop in a machine learning life cycle is critical to maintaining and enhancing model performance and adequately addressing business objectives, whether it is for fraud detection or capturing user preferences for recommendations.

In the next chapter, which is the final one, we'll summarize all the concepts we've learned about in this book and highlight some machine and deep learning services from Amazon Web Services that are worth exploring.

Further reading

Refer to the following link for more information on model accuracy degradation and feedback loops: `https://docs.aws.amazon.com/sagemaker/latest/dg/xgboost_hyperparameters.html`.

13
What Is Next?

In the preceding chapters, as the title of this book suggests, we took a hands-on approach to help you become better AI practitioners. Through the hands-on projects in this book, you developed the skills to embed AWS AI capabilities into applications and create custom AI capabilities using AWS ML platforms. More importantly, you developed the intuition to create well-designed, intelligence-enabled solutions that can help solve real-world problems. These projects not only taught you about a variety of AI technologies, they also showed you the various problem domains and business contexts where AI can be applied. As AI practitioners, it is important to see AI through the lens of business capabilities rather than just technologies.

In this chapter, we will cover the following topics:

- Summarizing the concepts we learned in Part I
- Summarizing the concepts we learned in Part II
- Summarizing the concepts we learned in Part III
- Summarizing the concepts we learned in Part IV
- What's next?

Summarizing the concepts we learned in Part I

In Part I, we introduced you to a plethora of AI offerings from AWS and grouped them into two categories:

- AI services
- ML platforms

Our recommendation to you is to first leverage AWS-managed AI services, such as Rekogntion, Translate, and Comprehend, in your solution development. Only when there is a need for custom AI capabilities should you then build them with AWS ML platforms such as SageMaker. This approach will improve your speed to market and the return on investment for your intelligent-enabled applications. We also explained that the true power of developing intelligent-enabled solutions on AWS is to combine AWS AI offerings with the rest of the AWS cloud computing ecosystem, including S3, DynamoDB, and EMR.

We also discussed architecture design for AI applications and how a well-designed architecture allows for rapid iteration and adaptability to market changes. We laid out an architecture design template for the hands-on projects in Part II and also showed you how the custom AI capabilities we built in Part III can easily integrate into this architecture. This architecture template can be adopted and modified for your next intelligent solution that's built on top of AWS AI services or your own custom AI capabilities.

Summarizing the concepts we learned in Part II

In Part II, we focused on embedding AI capabilities into applications by doing the following:

- We used many AWS-managed AI services to build several end-to-end intelligent-enabled solutions.
- We introduced to you the AWS SDK, boto3, to interact with cloud services and their infrastructure.
- We used the AWS Chalice framework to develop and deploy serverless applications to the API Gateway and AWS Lambda.
- We used HTML, CSS, and JavaScript to build user interfaces for these solutions.
- Along the way, we shared our tips and tricks for the development, testing, maintenance, and evolution of AI applications on AWS.

In `Chapter 3`, *Detecting and Translating Text with Amazon Rekognition and Translate,* we built a Pictorial Translator that not only detects text within an image but also translates it into any language (English, for our project). This application can be used by travelers to a foreign land or by the visually impaired who wish to interact with the real world.

In Chapter 4, *Performing Speech-to-Text and Vice Versa with Amazon Transcribe and Polly,* we built a modestly named Universal Translator that can enable verbal communication between people who are speaking different languages. This application can be used by travelers, students, and so on.

In Chapter 5, *Extracting Information from Text with Amazon Comprehend,* we built a Contact Organizer that helps automate the extraction of contact information from pictures of business cards. We introduced the human-in-the-loop concept to improve our end-to-end solution's accuracy. This type of application can help reduce manual works for many back-office tasks so that workers can focus on more creative tasks.

In Chapter 6, *Building a Voice Chatbot with Amazon Lex,* we built an intelligent assistant, Contact Assistant, that can search for contact information through a conversational interface. This intelligent assistant not only understands us through natural language, it also remembers the context of the conversation to make the interface even more fluid. These types of intelligent assistant interface improve many of our daily tasks, such as information searches, communication, reminders, and much more.

Summarizing the concepts we learned in Part III

In Part III, we focused on how SageMaker can be leveraged to train and deploy ML models, both built-in and custom, to solve business problems that cannot be readily solved using AWS AI services.

We started with Chapter 7, *Working with Amazon SageMaker,* where we learned how to process large datasets, conduct training, and optimize hyperparameters in SageMaker.

- Additionally, we looked at how SageMaker makes it seamless to run multiple experiments and deploy the best performing model for inference.
- We also illustrated how bringing your own model and container to SageMaker allows you to readily leverage capabilities such as model training, deployment, and inference at scale.

In Chapter 8, *Creating Machine Learning Inference Pipelines,* we learned how to conduct data preprocessing via Glue, a serverless ETL AWS service. A machine learning pipeline was built to reuse data preprocessing logic for both training and inference. We also learned how to use the ML pipeline for both real-time and batch predictions.

In `Chapter 9`, *Discovering Topics in Text Collection,* we reviewed various approaches—linear and non-linear – so that we could discover topics in text collection. Then, we delved into how topic modeling can be handled through the built-in NTM algorithm (variational autoencoder). The model training, deployment, and inference steps in SageMaker were explained through a sample dataset of *Enron Emails*.

In `Chapter 10`, *Sales Forecasting with Deep Learning and Auto Regression,* we looked at the difference between traditional time series forecasting methods, such as exponential smoothing and ARIMA, and more flexible and scalable methods, such as auto-regressive recurrent networks. We then looked at how the DeepAR algorithm in SageMaker can be used to model retail sales given a variety of factors, such as holidays, promotions, and unemployment.

In `Chapter 11`, *Classifying Images using Amazon SageMaker,* we reviewed convolutional neural networks and the purpose of residual networks. Then, we introduced the concept of incremental learning through transfer learning. We also explained how to classify bakery items through transfer learning, even with small image datasets.

Summarizing the concepts we learned in Part IV

In Part IV, that is, `Chapter 12`, *Model Accuracy Degradation and Feedback Loops,* we defined the concept of model performance deterioration through an ad-click conversion dataset. We walked through the idea of a feedback loop and why it becomes important in modeling dynamic ad-click behavior. Then, we demonstrated how model performance improves—through a feedback loop—in predicting whether an ad click results in app downloads.

What's next?

We've covered a lot of concepts and techniques in AI, but with this book we have only scratched the surface of this broad and deep field. Armed with the necessary AI skills and intuition, what's next for an AI practitioner? The following are some recommendations from us so that you can explore this growing field more comprehensively.

Artificial intelligence in the physical world

One way to grow as an AI practitioner is to broaden your experience with different applications of AI. One growing group of AI applications aims to combine AI capabilities with sensors and actuators in the physical world. Examples of such physical-world applications include home automation, smart factories, self-driving cars, and robots. The idea of building physical machinery, vehicles, and robots might be daunting to some AI practitioners. Luckily, AWS provides several products to make getting started with this group of AI applications easier.

AWS DeepLens

AWS DeepLens is a physical device that has a video camera and compute, storage, and internet connectivity packaged into a small device. Along with other AWS AI services and tools, DeepLens becomes a powerful platform when you want to get hands-on experience with deep learning applications. Take a look at the following screenshot showing AWS DeepLens:

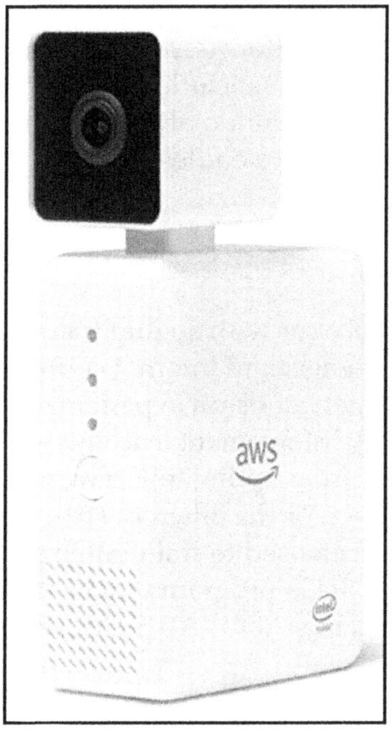

Let's talk about some of the remarkable features of DeepLens:

- DeepLens can capture images and videos in **high definition** (**HD**), and has enough onboard power to process HD videos in real-time.
- AI practitioners can quickly get started with projects on DeepLens with AWS AI services. For example, it integrates with Amazon Rekognition to analyze images and videos that have been taken by the camera.
- DeepLens is fully programmable using AWS Lambda to invoke a broad set of functionalities and actuators connected to the internet.
- DeepLens also supports custom ML models that are trained with Amazon SageMaker.
- AI practitioners can choose from a broad set of deep learning frameworks, including TensorFlow and Caffe, to train ML models and run them on DeepLens' onboard inference engine.
- These custom ML models can be deployed to DeepLens with just a few clicks or API calls.

By reading this book, you are already familiar with many of the tools that we just mentioned and have already developed many of the skills you need to get started with AWS DeepLens. With this powerful platform, AI practitioners can build a broad set of applications. A few example applications include home security, bird watching, traffic monitoring, delivery notification, home automation, and many more. Combined with other sensors and actuators, the possibilities are endless.

AWS DeepRacer

AWS DeepRacer is a 1/18th scale race car with an integrated camera, accelerometer, and gyroscope; it also has compute, storage, and internet connectivity onboard. DeepRacer is designed to help AI practitioners get hands-on experience with reinforcement learning through autonomous car racing. Reinforcement learning is a branch of ML that aims to create intelligent agents that learn from optimizing reward functions rather than learning from examples (supervised learning) or the inherent structure of the data (unsupervised learning). This AI technique has been used to train intelligent agents to run, drive, and play games. For example, Google's AlphaGo program that beat the top Go player in the world uses this ML technique. The following shows AWS DeepRacer:

DeepRacer brings the following AI capabilities into the real world:

- By using the camera and other on-board sensors, an AI practitioner can develop reinforcement models to control DeepRacer's throttle and steer it.
- DeepRacer comes with a 3D racing simulator for easy development and testing of its AI racing capabilities.
- Like DeepLens, DeepRacer also integrates with AWS AI services and the cloud infrastructure.
- You can use Amazon SageMaker to train reinforcement learning models and deploy them to your racer with ease.
- There is even a DeepRacer League to test out any AI racing capabilities you've developed for prizes and glory.

The applications that are built on top of this platform don't have to be limited to racing either. With a camera on wheels, there are many options available, such as home surveillance, pet training, and item delivery. We are willing to bet that a DeepDrone has been proposed at AWS at some point.

Internet of Things and AWS IoT Greengrass

For AI applications to function well in the physical world, there is a need for AI capabilities at the edge.

AWS IoT Greengrass lets connected devices seamlessly and securely interact with other devices and cloud applications. Greengrass brings many benefits to AI applications, including the following:

- It brings faster response times when you wish to act on local events and data without needing a trip to the cloud.
- It improves the cost efficiency of running IoT by reducing the bandwidth requirements for data transport between the edge and the cloud.
- It simplifies data security and privacy by processing and anonymizing sensitive information locally for applications in certain sectors such as healthcare.

AWS IoT Greengrass can also extend the power of AI capabilities to edge devices, thus creating an intelligent edge. The following architectural diagram shows how edge devices can run machine learning inferences locally and then connect to AWS IoT Core to send messages or inferences to the cloud for further analytics through Greengrass Core:

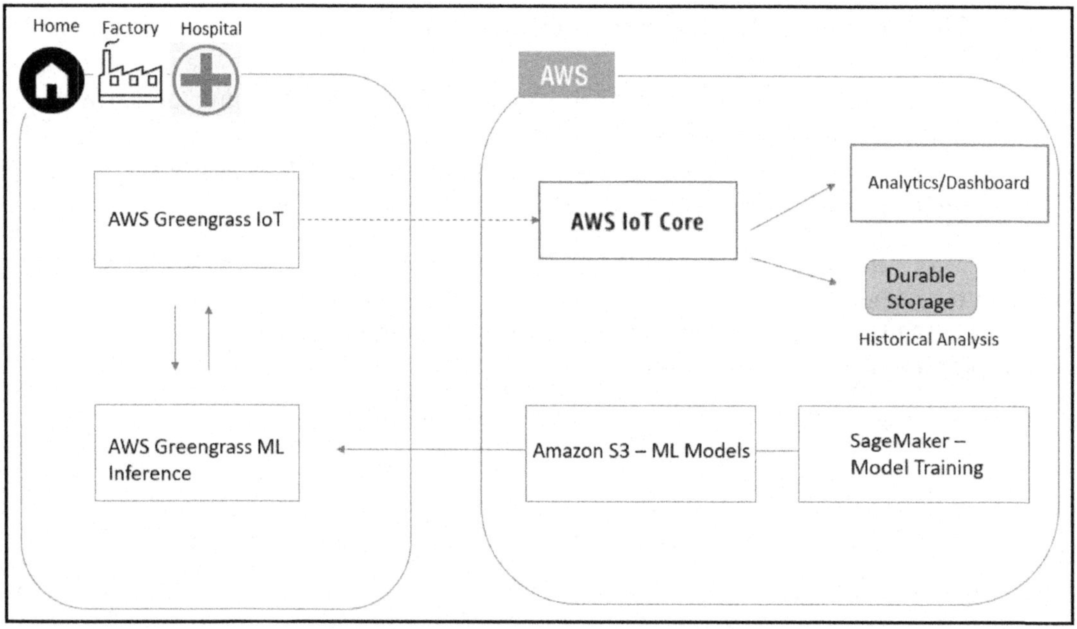

In this architecture, we can see the following:

- Models that are trained in Amazon SageMaker are persisted in the S3 bucket.
- Data that's generated at the edge is then scored by these trained models via local lambda functions.
- AWS Greengrass' core controls communication between the edge and the cloud, including security, messaging, and offline compute operations.
- AWS IoT Core, on the other hand, orchestrates a connection with other AWS services, that is, durable storage or analytics.

Several business problems can be solved by leveraging the edge intelligent architecture. With autonomous vehicles, there's a need for an intelligent edge to steer the car around the local environment without latency from the network. If you manufacture plants, by running ML inferences on the edge, you can predict the end of life of machinery locally and take instant actions to improve safety. With health care applications, sensitive medical information can be used locally to perform intelligent diagnoses with low latency and without putting the patient's privacy at risk in the cloud.

Artificial intelligence in your own field

Another way to grow as an AI practitioner is to delve more deeply into a particular field or business domain. A good approach is to apply AI to a field you have expertise in or have an interest in. You know better than anyone else which field to choose.

In that chosen field, you will find a particular set of business problems, and then develop the relevant AI skills that are needed to solve those problems. The problems in your field might require computer vision, natural language processing, speech recognition, knowledge reasoning, or a combination of these techniques. As an AI practitioner, you will then develop more specialized skills in those AI techniques.

In that chosen field, you might know about some existing problems you wish to solve or you might need to discover new problems to solve. Finding and defining those problems is the key to gaining a competitive advantage over other AI generalists. To start on this path, however, we recommend that you just get started with small hands-on projects related to the field. Just like the recommendation from this book, you should develop your intuition by doing hands-on work, even if it's just replicating an existing solution from your field. Over time, you will gradually build up better insights into how to solve related problems.

Summary

In this book, we have covered various AI fundamentals in AWS, highlighting AI application development, pre-defined AI APIs, model building, training, deployment, management, and experimentation through ML pipelines. We have suggested two ways that you can continue your journey as an AI practitioner on AWS, that is, either going broad or going deep. We hope that you've enjoyed reading (and working through) this book and that you are all set to solve challenging business problems through AWS Artificial Intelligence-related services.

Other Books You May Enjoy

If you enjoyed this book, you may be interested in these other books by Packt:

Machine Learning with AWS
Jeffrey Jackovich, Ruze Richards

ISBN: 9781789806199

- Get up and running with machine learning on the AWS platform
- Analyze unstructured text using AI and Amazon Comprehend
- Create a chatbot and interact with it using speech and text input
- Retrieve external data via your chatbot
- Develop a natural language interface
- Apply AI to images and videos with Amazon Rekognition

Mastering Machine Learning on AWS
Saket Mengle, Maximo Gurmendez

ISBN: 9781789349795

- Manage AI workflows by using AWS cloud to deploy services that feed smart data products
- Use SageMaker services to create recommendation models
- Scale model training and deployment using Apache Spark on EMR
- Understand how to cluster big data through EMR and seamlessly integrate it with SageMaker
- Build deep learning models on AWS using TensorFlow and deploy them as services
- Enhance your apps by combining Apache Spark and Amazon SageMaker

Leave a review - let other readers know what you think

Please share your thoughts on this book with others by leaving a review on the site that you bought it from. If you purchased the book from Amazon, please leave us an honest review on this book's Amazon page. This is vital so that other potential readers can see and use your unbiased opinion to make purchasing decisions, we can understand what our customers think about our products, and our authors can see your feedback on the title that they have worked with Packt to create. It will only take a few minutes of your time, but is valuable to other potential customers, our authors, and Packt. Thank you!

Index

A

E

F

G

H

I

J

L

M

N

O

P

R

S

T

U

V

W

Made in the USA
Columbia, SC
14 November 2020

24566569R00233